STRUGGLING FOR DEMOCRACY IN HONG KONG

MY STORY

Joseph Yu-Shek Cheng

First published in Australia by Aurora House
www.aurorahouse.com.au

This edition published 2023
Copyright © Joseph Yu-Shek Cheng 2023

Typesetting and e-book design: Prepress Plus | www.prepressplus.in
Cover Designer: Donika Mishineva | www.artofdonika.com

The right of Joseph Yu-Shek Cheng to be identified as Author of the Work has been asserted in accordance with the Copyright, Designs and Patents Act 1988.

ISBN number: 978-1-922697-62-2 (Paperback)

All rights reserved. No part of this publication may be reproduced, stored in a retrieval system, or transmitted, in any form or by any means without the prior written permission of the publisher, nor be otherwise circulated in any form of binding or cover other than that in which it is published and without a similar condition being imposed on the subsequent purchaser.

 A catalogue record for this book is available from the National Library of Australia

Distributed by:
Ingram Content: www.ingramcontent.com
Australia: phone +613 9765 4800 |
email lsiaustralia@ingramcontent.com
Milton Keynes UK: phone +44 (0)845 121 4567 |
email enquiries@ingramcontent.com
La Vergne, TN USA: phone +1 800 509 4156 |
email inquiry@lightningsource.com

*This book is dedicated to
my wife Grace,
our children
and
grandchildren*

Introduction

Born in 1949 and educated in the British colonial Hong Kong, the author tells of his rich life experiences in the period (1949–2020) that represents the significant economic and political developments of Hong Kong since the founding the People's Republic of China in 1949. He represents the first generation of residents who consider themselves Hongkongers and possess a sense of identity and pride regarding the territory.

He had a poor childhood since the age of seven owing to the business failure of his father who fled from China to Hong Kong in 1949. His academic results made him proud in his student years, and he never felt inferior to anyone. He was respected by his teachers and classmates alike. He began to take up part-time tutor jobs from Form 4 (Year 10) to his university years to support his family. Working hard for public examinations at the same time, extra-curricular activities to him were a luxury.

He had the opportunity to study overseas, first in New Zealand on a Commonwealth scholarship, and later in Australia for his post-graduate studies. It was in these two countries that he observed and appreciated Western democracies at play. After returning to Hong Kong to teach, he witnessed the Sino-British negotiations on Hong Kong's future sovereignty in the early 1980s.

To preserve his integrity, dignity and honesty, the author chose to establish himself as a respected political scientist and educator by profession, and a well-recognised international media commentator and critic on political developments in China and Hong Kong.

He participated actively in the promotion of subsequent democratic reforms in the territory, and was an important activist in the pro-democracy movement fighting for universal suffrage in a fairer electoral system in Hong Kong for decades. He became a target of a prolonged defamation campaign.

His memoirs, supported by vigorous analyses and research, tell of the struggles, attempts, successes and failures to bring forth Hong Kong's democratic reforms in the past decades.

Table of Contents

1	Early Childhood in Hong Kong's Difficult Years	1
2	My Formative Years at La Salle College	29
3	Student Life at the University of Hong Kong	55
4	Overseas Study, a New Life	81
5	My Academic Career Began	115
6	Hong Kong's Future Was Sealed Behind Closed Doors	145
7	The Intriguing 1980s – Political Participation as a Concerned Academic	175
8	The Crisis of the Tiananmen Incident 1989	213
9	At the Central Policy Unit, 1991–1992	239
10	Life of a Faculty Dean	255
11	Quiet Academic Life in the Midst of Change	275
12	Approaching 1997 – Political Transitions	301

13	Power for Democracy, Building a Mediating Platform for Electoral Candidates	339
14	Power for Democracy, Successes and Failures 2006–2019	373
15	I Joined the Civic Party	411
16	New School for Democracy: What Democracy Means	447
17	Alliance for True Democracy: the Fight for Universal Suffrage amidst Contradictions	473
18	Alliance for True Democracy: a Mission Impossible	501
19	Experiencing China's United Front – Best Friend or Worst Enemy	529
20	I Became a Major Target in a Hong Kong Version of Cultural-Revolution-Style Defamation Campaign	563
21	"Quiet" Retirement	589
22	The Emergence of Radical Politics and the Political Crisis, 2019–2020	613

Epilogue	645
Appendix I: District Council Election Results, 1999–2019	675

Chapter 1

Early Childhood in Hong Kong's Difficult Years

"It is advantageous to be the eldest in rich families, and the youngest in poor families." Hong Kong, a city of Mainland Chinese refugees, turned challenges into opportunities.

I was born on November 11, 1949, slightly more than a month after the formal establishment of the People's Republic of China. As a Hong Kong citizen and a pro-democracy activist, developments in China and its policy towards the territory naturally had an important impact on my life.

1949 and 1950 were difficult years for Hong Kong, especially with the huge influx of immigrants from Mainland China[1]. The initial flows came between 1945

---

1   In 1941, Hong Kong's population was merely 12,000. It then grew to 300,000 at the beginning of the twentieth century, and expanded rapidly to 1.64 million in 1941. Japan's invasion of Hong Kong led to the dispersal of the residents into Mainland China. But when World War II ended, Hong Kong's population quickly increased from 0.6 million to 1.55 million in 1945-46. It then continued to expand to 2.24 million in 1950, 3.17 million

1

and early 1947, as Hong Kong residents who had left for the Mainland in search of food during the Japanese Occupation from December 1941 to August 1945 returned. Then refugees from China started to come during the civil war years of 1947 to 1949; in fact, it was still relatively easy to come to Hong Kong from the Mainland until early 1951[2].

A considerable segment of the refugees was well-educated and had professional qualifications, though these were not recognised by the colonial government, which only accepted educational and professional qualifications acquired within the British Empire and later the British Commonwealth. A strange phenomenon was that many tutors at the medical school of the University of Hong Kong up till the 1970s were experienced doctors from prestigious hospitals in major cities in China who could not practise medicine in the territory, but their students soon became doctors who tended to do very well in the era of doctor shortage.

Among the refugees was a very small number of elite business leaders from Shanghai (more accurately,

---

in 1961, 4.05 million in 1971, 5.15 million in 1981 and 5.66 million at the end of 1987. See Government Information Services, *Hong Kong 1988*, Hong Kong: Government Printer, 1988, p. 302.

2   The British administration did not seem to have a clearly defined border policy in the 1940s. A simple chain link wire fence was built between 1950 and 1953 along the border with Mainland China. A stronger fence, made of concertina wire, was constructed slightly south of the original fence in 1962.

the Yangtze Delta) who arrived with capital, business expertise and networks, and in some cases even machinery[3]. Some of them formed the backbone of the textiles industry that emerged in the 1950s and it was largely based in Tsuen Wan in the New Territories. Another area of contribution from the Shanghainese tycoons was shipping industry. The father of C.H. Tung, the first Chief Executive of the Hong Kong Special Administrative Region (HKSAR) government, Tung Chao-yung (董浩雲) was a leading shipping magnate from Shanghai then. Sir Y.K. Pao's shipping empire developed later, and his son-in-law, Peter Woo Kwong-ching (吳光正), was one of the four leading candidates in the first Chief Executive election in 1997.

The conditions of the ordinary refugees were, as could be expected, difficult. Housing was in acute short supply; often thirty people and more squeezed in a small flat of six or seven hundred square feet. A considerable portion of the older buildings did not have sewage facilities, and the Urban Services Department employed a troop of women workers collecting night-soil well into the early 1970s. At the same time, temporary squatter huts built from tin sheets and wooden planks appeared on the rooftops and slopes of many of the territory's

---

3   The famous Shanghainese tycoons in the 1950s and 1960s included Tang Ping-yuan (唐炳源) in the textiles, Ting Hsiung-chao (丁熊照) in the plastics and toys industries, and Tung Chao-yung (董浩雲) in shipping; they were collectively known as the three "Ts" in the Hong Kong economy.

gentle hills. The environment was hazardous, but most endured. The big fire in Shek Kip Mei on Christmas day 1953 lasted for 6 hours, turned these huts into ashes, and made over 50,000 homeless. This led the government to start the first public housing programme, to build multi-storey standardised housing estates or blocks for resettlement.

Squatters often had to queue up to fill their water buckets from public taps and they had to carry them up the hill on both ends of a wooden pole. I could still remember vividly that the queues for filling up water buckets at public taps were particularly long during the drought in 1963. Soon after, the Hong Kong government purchased water from China's Pearl River by using water tankers, and later from the East River through the construction of pipelines.

Around the time of 1967 riots, China restricted their water supplies temporarily. With the limited water supply from Hong Kong's own reservoirs, water could only be available for four hours a day every four days. At our home, where water was available from taps once every four days, we had to store water in specially made clear plastic cylindrical bags or tanks, about two metres in height and 40 centimetres in diameter, for four days' use. Water supply from China resumed towards the end of the year.

Employment was another obvious challenge. Up till the late 1950s, it was not uncommon for unskilled workers to receive, instead of wages, only two meals a day, basic accommodation in the form of canvas-beds to be set up at night in the workplace, and small amounts of pocket money during the major traditional Chinese festivals including the Ching Ming Festival in spring, Dragon Boat Festival in summer, the Moon Festival in autumn, Winter Solstice in winter (sort of Thanksgiving Day) and of course the Chinese New Year. Wages for skilled labour began to rise in 1959, and wages in general started to increase around 1961 or so, reflecting the general demand for labour from the fast-developing manufacturing sector especially in textiles and plastics.

During the Korean War years, there was a lot of speculative activities in the local gold market, and to a considerably lesser extent, in the local currency market. So Hong Kong established or reinforced its reputation as a speculators' paradise then. In contemporary Chinese novels, there were many stories of people who had gone bankrupt. Refugees who had some money but had very limited means of starting a business or seeking employment were easily among those who lost their fortunes.

The Korean War, however, offered a good example of how Hong Kong turned challenges into opportunities. Due to the embargo imposed on China because of its role in the Korean War, the territory's function as an *entrepot* serving the Chinese hinterland could not be maintained, and to survive, the business community turned to labour-intensive industries for exports. They were successful and Hong Kong, together with Singapore, South Korea and Taiwan, became one of the "four little dragons of Asia". There were smuggling activities in bringing strategic materials, especially Western medicine, into China. Those involved in violating the embargo were seen to be patriotic by Beijing and were rewarded with political honours.

As a baby and a small child, I had a happy and prosperous time. I was conceived in Guangdong and born in Hong Kong; my father was among those who frequently moved between the Pearl River Delta and the British colony in the 1930s and 1940s. He was a small businessman, had no formal education, was probably quite entrepreneurial by the standards then, and was able to provide his family a very decent living standard. My mother entered the prestigious Belilios Public School; she was not even able to finish Form 1 (year 7) because of the Japanese Occupation. She had to follow her family to Macau for a while and was unable to continue her education afterwards. But by the standards of her times, she was considered educated. Both my parents did not talk of their family histories; I do not understand why and I know very little about them.

I studied at Pui Ching kindergarten, which was affiliated to Pui Ching Middle School at Waterloo Road,

Kowloon. To save money, I joined one semester later and had one and a half years of kindergarten education instead of two in 1954–1955. Pui Ching Middle School was a famous Chinese school, and quite a number of its graduates managed to further their studies in the U.S. Its Baptist affiliation probably helped, and it claimed to have an alumni organisation in North America.

In those days, to be able to study in a kindergarten certainly reflected my family's middle-class status; kindergarten education was beyond most small children in the 1950s. They were private and the fees were high, often amounting to one-tenth of a junior government clerk's salary. Since my parents lived in Causeway Bay then, I stayed with my grandparents on my mother's side at Ho Man Tin Street, a residential area for the newly rich. My maternal grandfather was a foreman and then a sub-contractor for the Hong Kong and China Gas Company Limited; he made his first "bucket of gold" there and then entered the construction industry. My maternal grandmother loved me and treated me very well, though my maternal grandfather probably did not like me; a probable reason was that my maternal grandparents did not get along. My aunt, Christine Pang, my mother's youngest sister, attended Primary 3 and 4 at Pui Ching Primary School in my kindergarten years and she took me to school and back home every day.

1995. At Grandparents' house, Homantin, Hong Kong.

My paternal grandparents stayed in our home village Yongmo (雍陌) near Shiqi (石岐) in Zhongshan County (中山, bordering Macau) all their lives. My grandfather passed away in the late 1950s and I never had the opportunity of meeting my grandparents. Since he was a landowner who inherited land bought by my great-grandfather with money earned working in a pineapple plantation in Hawaii, he and his family suffered much in the political campaigns in the first decade of the People's Republic of China. This was a rather typical story of Zhongshan, which produced quite a number of compradors as well as many migrant workers in the U.S. and Australia.

This could be traced back to Yung Wing (容閎), who came from Zhongshan County (then Xiangshang County 香山縣). Yung was perhaps the first Chinese Ph.D. from the U.S. (Yale University) and he played a key role in organising elite young students from China to study in the U.S. in the beginning of the twentieth century. He probably contributed to the links between his hometown and the U.S.

My grandfather's sufferings in his home village were often briefly told by my father, including having to kneel on glass chips. The story contributed to my anti-Communist values during my formative years. The anti-Communist newspapers that my family subscribed to (*Kung Sheung Daily News* 工商日報 and *Sing Tao Evening News* 星島晚報) apparently made a major impact. I still remember that I rejoiced at the victories of the Kuomintang regime in the military campaigns in the Taiwan Straits in the 1950s, as reported by these newspapers.

When I was admitted to the Gold and Silver Exchange Society Primary School in 1955–1956 in Caroline Hill near the Hong Kong Stadium, I returned home at the then Lee Garden Street (利園街) in Causeway Bay (now known as Lee Garden Road 利園山道). I remember little about these years as I was too small. But I still remember that my attendance of kindergarten offered me some exposure to musical instruments and involved me in class singing. Soon after I realised that I had no talents in music at all, but I do believe that such exposure is very important for young children.

After one year, my family moved to Hak Po Street in Kowloon, and I attended Primary 2 and 3 at Tak Ming Primary School (德明小學) just across the street. Entry was not easy, though the quality of curriculum was mediocre and school fees high; it was a reflection of the acute shortage of education opportunities then. Tak Ming was operated by Chan Shu-woon (陳樹桓), son of a Guangdong warlord, Chen Jitang (陳濟棠). It preached anti-Communist values as the entire teaching staff shared those values, and the school uniform for male students was modelled after that of the Kuomintang army. It was in this context that I followed news of the military encounters in the Taiwan Straits in the 1950s.

Tak Ming was a relatively expensive private school, and it offered a whole day programme for primary school students. It was a relatively rare practice for primary schools in the territory. Partly to earn more money, the school offered three additional two-hour sessions for students at 4–6 p.m., 6–8 p.m. and 8–10 p.m. Teachers often took up extra sessions to enhance their meagre incomes. One of my teachers was admitted to a government teacher-training programme. He and his wife (also a teacher in the same school) were very pleased because he could later join a school in the public sector offering a much better remuneration package.

The headmaster Chan Shu-woon ran for a seat in the Urban Council, and the teachers were mobilised to work for his election campaign. Political gossips emerged that he was later forced to leave Hong Kong because of his political activities. Schools in general had very limited space, and the vast majority of them had to use public playgrounds for physical education classes. In the poorer areas, there were often roof-top schools for students who could not afford to pay expensive school fees.

My luck turned for the better when my mother's friend suggested that I should apply for La Salle Primary School, a very prestigious Catholic primary school. My mother had to get up at about 4 a.m. on the day of enrolment and started queueing up at around 6 a.m. to secure an application form. The school provided teachers to help those who did not have the command of English to complete the forms. I passed the written entrance examination and an oral examination/interview conducted by the headmaster, Brother Henry Pang, who served in this capacity for many years and was fondly remembered by the students and parents.

I repeated Primary 3 and had to overcome the challenge of being taught in English in all subjects except Chinese. I failed dictation in the first week and was detained after class. In the Catechism class, I had to learn all the prayers, including The Apostles' Creed with its many hard words; basically I had to memorise the whole thing and write it out. I was determined to overcome the challenges, and I came out joint first in the first and second semester. I survived and became a top student in an elite school. La Salle Primary was a small school when I first entered; it started in Primary 3 and had only two classes for each of the four grades up to Primary 6. Brother Henry could recognise most of the students. He recognised me, and when the school expanded after securing the impressive building across La Salle Road, which was used as an army hospital, my brother Philip Yim Kwong was accepted by the headmaster into Primary 2 when I was promoted to Primary Four. Having a family member already in the school always helps even for now.

School life was happy; I did well in the examinations and was respected by my teachers when I reached Primary 5 and 6. There was a large sandy field for playing soccer at the primary school grounds. Falling down could cause painful cuts and even small scars on the knees. No one complained. Some students came from very wealthy families, and a few from poor families. But this did not affect the friendship among classmates. Looking back, I was very grateful and proud of my school.

In the Primary 4 year, classes were held in the big building with an impressive dome, which later was used exclusively for the secondary school. Meanwhile the old primary school building was torn down to construct a new and considerably bigger building. That year was especially fun, and an interesting hobby of mine was catching grasshoppers in the untidy lawns in the school campus. The experience of studying in such a big building with ample open space was rather awesome for Hong Kong primary school students. Facilities were quite backward by modern standards, but there were lots of fun without expensive sports shoes and sophisticated toys.

Some teachers imposed physical punishment, usually in the form of hitting the students' palms with long rulers. Slapping occasionally occurred. Parents never complained in those days; they tended to accept physical punishment. A few parents even told teachers to beat their kids if they did not behave. In most cases, students who were punished dared not report back to their parents. Later when I attended La Salle College, students engaged in fighting were sometimes caned by the headmaster. The usual form of punishment was standing outside the classroom though. However, students who were punished were not mocked by their classmates; to most, it was simply not an issue. This probably was a form of solidarity among classmates.

At La Salle Primary, we wore white short-sleeved shirts and white cotton shorts with a school badge attached to the shirt pocket as the summer uniform. This was common for boys. My family did not have a washing machine, and synthetic easy-clean materials were not yet common. I had two changes of uniforms per week, and the white shorts were often quite dirty. Washing clothes by hand in the traditional way was a difficult task for my mother, and she often complained and scolded me for being careless. I often felt a bit apologetic taking off my white cotton shorts for washing by my mother. But of course I did not change my playing habits. I later wondered if my fellow classmates had similar problems. I guessed so, but I never asked.

At Primary 6, I clearly emerged as the top student of the school. The curriculum concentrated on preparing students for the Joint Primary 6 Examination, known as the Secondary School Entrance Examination then. Though the students taking the examination might not be aware (they were normally between twelve and fourteen years old, and I was twelve and a half when I sat for the examination), it was a very important opportunity for upward social mobility.

Examination results would determine which secondary school you go to. Getting into a prestigious government school or a grant-in-aid school would ensure a decent secondary education with affordable school fees. Failure to get into the public or subsidised sector meant that one had to go to a private school, where the quality of education was often inferior and the school fees exorbitant, especially for working-class families. In my student days, the school fees for La Salle Primary were HK$12 per month, and for La Salle College they were HK$40 per month. Inflation was low in Hong

Kong in the 1950s and 1960s. Newspapers were sold at ten cents per copy for more than ten years, and the same amount of money could fetch you a bowl of rice congee or a piece of fried dough at street stalls during the same period of time.

For students already in prestigious grant-in-aid primary schools, they had a better chance of being admitted to their respectively affiliated secondary schools, like La Salle College in my case. For students in ordinary schools, outstanding results would normally lead them to the very top government schools like King's College and Queen's College. I had a friend about nine or ten years younger than me; he lived in Cheung Chau, an outlying island where schools were of ordinary standards. He did very well in the Secondary School Entrance Examination and went to Queen's College; he then entered the Medical School of the University of Hong Kong and became a doctor. His would be considered an enviable success story based on hard work, exploiting the chances to move up in social status offered by the education system, and these opportunities contributed to social and political stability under a colonial regime.

In the 1950s–1970s when only 1–2% of young people of the age cohort of 18–24 years old could enter local universities, graduation from a prestigious secondary school was a decent qualification that could easily guarantee a clerical position in the government or a major corporation. This would mean a stable and secure career with chances of considerable development; if the spouse also had a job, the family could soon acquire its own accommodation and enjoy solid middle-class status. This qualification would also allow its holders to join teacher-training or nurse-training programmes, promising career paths and respectable incomes.

In these decades, there was very little family-planning. I was the eldest of the family, and had a younger brother and two sisters. My mother received tubal ligation after her fourth child. My wife, Grace, was the youngest in the family with five elder brothers and sisters. We had only two children. There was a saying at that time that it was advantageous to be the eldest in rich families, and the youngest in poor families. The eldest son in a rich family was naturally in the best position to inherit his father's business and assets. The youngest in less endowed families had better educational opportunities as his or her older siblings had gone to work to improve the family income. There were numerous stories of the eldest daughter in a poor family having to work in factories after some years of schooling, while the youngest would even have an opportunity to study in overseas universities later as his or her elder siblings had gone to work.

My wife's eldest sister became a government school teacher after secondary school education and a teacher training college programme, and her eldest brother could only receive university education after teaching for a few years in order to save up for college education, while the rest could all afford to attend universities immediately after high school.

My mother was not able to stay at Belilios Public School. She married early and became a housewife. During her time, she could have easily joined a non-government hospital and received nurse training after two or more years at the Belilios (she didn't even have to graduate). A good friend of hers did exactly that and eventually became a top nurse at Kwong Wah Hospital in the 1960s. My mother was the eldest in the family and did not benefit from her father's improving fortunes. The brother immediately after her joined Taikoo Dockyard as a mechanic apprentice. This was very decent vocational training in the early 1950s. Her three younger brothers and sister all went overseas to British universities and became engineers and doctors. Her youngest sister also went to study in Britain.

My mother probably felt inferior and was frustrated. This feeling of inferiority was exacerbated when my father's small business failed and had to become dependent on his father-in-law, my mother's newly rich father. As a primary school student, I certainly could not understand her feelings; this understanding came much later. Yet I suffered from her frustration. Despite his occasional emotional outbursts, my father did not lay hands on his children, but my mother would use the rattan cane (藤條) fiercely.

There was a "collective responsibility system" in my family. When one of the children was considered naughty, all four of us were caned. I received most lashes because I was the eldest; my mother usually let my two sisters get away lightly because they were small girls. At that time, I found it difficult to understand why I was caned a few times a year even though I was a top student. I never bore any grudge against my mother nonetheless. I often expressed my love and sympathy to her when I was in secondary school on occasions when she was not treated well by my father. I later discovered that physical punishment of children by their parents was quite common among poor families in Hong Kong in my childhood era. Family relations did not seem to have been adversely affected then and afterwards.

Brother Henry told my father in one of their rare meetings in the late 1950s that he had to send me to university. My father was impressed. He had never thought of his son going to university before. His enthusiasm led him to employ private tutors for me and my younger brother when I was in Primary 5 and 6. They were not very helpful, but the lady tutor I had in the summer holidays after Primary 5 helped me a lot to improve my English vocabulary.

The entire Primary 6 was actually devoted to preparations for the Secondary School Entrance Examination concentrating on Mathematics, English and Chinese. I was quick in calculations and the application of formulae, and I really excelled. My teachers were very impressed. But this did not mean I had talents for mathematics, as I later discovered in senior high school. My command of the Chinese language was truly outstanding for my age.

Free air broadcast television was not available in Hong Kong until 1967, when I was in Form 5. My family did not have a television until after my graduation from university. The simple reason was that my younger brother and sisters had to concentrate on their public examinations at different levels. Radio programmes were the principal entertainment available, and I read a lot of Chinese novels from Primary 3 or 4 onwards. My wife was "luckier" as her family bought their first television set in the early summer of 1967, right when she was taking the important public examinations (the Hong Kong School Certificate Examinations) for proceeding to matriculation. She could still remember how she resisted the temptation to watch the novelty television programmes by hiding herself in the patio while the rest of the family were watching.

I read any novels that I could lay my hands on. The swordsmen novels by Jin Yong (金庸) were my favourites; I had read almost all his novels twice or three times. In those years, there were small street stalls renting these novels; they demanded the borrowers' report cards as collateral. After the semester examinations in my secondary school years, I would rent one series of novels by Jin Yong, usually in two to three dozen thin volumes, and I, my brother and sisters would go through them for two or three days. *The Sing Tao Evening News* (星島晚報) had one whole page of seven or eight columns of novels by famous writers of the times, and I went through them all every evening.

I was not at all selective in my reading. I did not have much to do, so I read the more macho banditry stories by Taiwan novelists like Sima Zhongyuan (司馬中原) and Chu Hsi-ning (朱西甯), as well as the romance novels by Chiung Yao (瓊瑤) and Kuo Liang-hui (郭良蕙). I was attracted to the classics like *The Water Margin* (水滸傳), *The Romance of the Three Kingdoms* (三國演義) and *Liaozhai Zhiyi* (聊齋誌異). These readings helped me to do very well in the subject of Chinese at the Primary 6 level, and in Chinese literature and Chinese history throughout my secondary school years.

My English was just above average. I had a poor start. At Primary 2 at Tak Ming Primary School, students were taught the alphabets with a word attached to each of them, from apple, ball to zebra. The lady English teacher held a beautiful picture book for all to see. Students did not have textbooks, but we started to write the alphabets in the form of copybooks. At Primary 3, we used the common textbook, which began with "a man, a pan, a man and a pan, a pan and a man".

At La Salle Primary School, I was able to catch up. The Secondary School Entrance Examination suited me well with its distinct emphasis on vocabulary and, to a lesser extent, comprehension. Students had to memorise opposites and similes to answer multiple-choice questions. I had very good memory and worked hard, so I was able to do well in examinations. Somehow I did not read any English novels at all in my primary school days, probably because of lack of access.

Finally, my teachers in La Salle Primary School certainly deserve a word of praise. They all seemed competent and professional, and all worked hard. There was one lady teacher from Singapore who taught us English and penmanship. She frequently slapped us and pinched our ears, and was a terror to the young boys.

In contrast, there was William Chan who was my class master at Primary 5C. He often took his students for picnics during the holidays, and he offered extra lessons to his class students at his home (he lived with his parents) in the mornings when Primary 1, 3 and 5 students attended class in the afternoons. He taught us how to observe and tell the differences between evergreen and deciduous trees, as well as the names of trees we came across in the streets; Hong Kong students then were very ignorant regarding these matters.

Chan actually told us how to make gunpowder. This was an interesting episode in Primary 6 that had made an impact in my primary school life that I would not forget. At that time, most pupils concentrated on doing exercises and drills in languages and arithmetic for the public Secondary School Entrance Examinations, as good results would lead them to prestigious secondary schools, and a very important door to a solid career.

We were told that the materials required for gunpowder were charcoal, Sulphur and Saltpetre. Out of curiosity, my best friend Peter and I wanted to do the experiment. We got carbon by scratching soot from the bottom of an old cooking wok (pan) at home. (In those days, most kitchens in Hong Kong in the 1960s were using chopped woods for cooking, and hence a layer of soot would accumulate at the bottom of cooking utensils such as iron woks.) A classmate of ours helped to buy Sulphur and Saltpetre from the shops specialising in industrial chemicals and raw materials in Kowloon's Shanghai Street. One afternoon after school, we tried it in the open sandy grounds behind the school. The experiment failed. We found out later that what our classmate bought was not Saltpetre. It almost ended in great trouble for us. It was a lesson learned.

My father lost his business in the mid-1950s. My maternal grandfather became quite rich though, and he provided money for my father and his eldest son to start a textile and apparel factory. It was well endowed by contemporary standards, with the factory premises owned by my grandfather and modern machinery imported from Britain. It followed the tide of industrialisation in the territory that engaged in labour-intensive industries for export to the developed countries, especially the U.K. It was then that the "Made in Hong Kong" label on garments started to become a symbol of high-quality product. The factory did quite well. My grandfather believed that my father had business experiences and my eldest uncle had a respectable mechanic background, and between them, they should be able to run a factory.

The factory was able to make money in the initial years. With the benefit of hindsight, it was not too difficult. Our family was able to enjoy decent living standards with my father working as a manager in a factory. While my father was co-managing the apparel factory, a fatal accident occurred. A woman labourer had washed her hair and neglected to tie it up. Her hair was then entangled in a spinning machinery, which led to her death. My father was taken to court, and was fined for negligence in industrial safety because the machinery had not been properly covered to prevent the accident. It was probably quite common in those years, when factories emphasised efficiency and neglected safety, and inspectors from the Labour Department could be bribed. My father got off lightly. He could have been jailed, though this was common negligence in those days.

The good time did not last very long. My father quarrelled with my uncle and then my grandfather. He had to leave the factory; in compensation, my grandfather waived the earlier loan to my father for purchasing the flat. We left the old flat at Hak Po Street in 1962, which was to be demolished by the owner to build a new, much taller building. The tenants received some compensation either by negotiations or by court ruling when negotiations failed. Our family tried to apply for public housing, but we did not succeed because our family of six lived in a relatively spacious old flat. The tearing down of old buildings and constructing new ones was a sign of Hong Kong's development in the 1960s to the 1980s.

My father managed to buy a relatively "new" flat not long afterwards with the compensation money and the loan from my grandfather. My mother still lives in this old flat at the time of writing. The building was considered the latest style of a "Chinese house (唐樓)" mixing Chinese and Western architectural styles commonly found in Southern China. It was a concrete building, rather than a brick one, seven storeys high, with clean rounded corners on the exterior. To maximise the size, the building extended over the pavement below it, and the over-hanging "balconies" were enclosed by metal frame glass windows.

Our flat was on the sixth floor, but there were no lifts, so we had to walk up six flights of stairs to reach home. Since we were all young, six flights of stairs did not matter much to us. The most important improvement was the flush toilet facilities; the previous flat in which we lived had to depend on night soil collection. The flat had an area of about seven hundred square feet, and was partitioned into four rooms by wooden board panels that were opened at the top. We could hear each other as we spoke.

As the demand for housing was high, many such buildings had been demolished and rebuilt as high-rise residential or commercial buildings, that is, when property developers managed to persuade most owners to sell. In 2000's, there were a few offers from real estate developers wanting to demolish our building for reconstruction. The offer price was HK$5,000 per square foot, while the market price for new properties in the same district was around HK$10,000. A number of owners refused to sell, since the offer price was not enough to cover the cost of buying an equivalent property in the neighbourhood of high land prices. As property prices continued to rise quickly, a few owners that my mother knew were waiting for better prices to sell.

On the other hand, one such old "Chinese house" in Kowloon was reported in 2010 to have suddenly collapsed resulting in a few deaths. Although it was a rare event, it served as a warning. With the facilitation of the government, our building was subsequently refurbished to extend the building's life.

My father lost his job and the family encountered serious financial difficulties. My father was quite an arrogant man. Deep down, he did not respect my grandfather and he thought my uncle was not bright. He probably resented the fact that he had to rely on his wife's family. I was almost fourteen years old when the crisis hit the family. My teenage pragmatism was that my father should forget his pride and respectfully worked for my grandfather to provide for the family. If he were so proud, he should have tried harder to find a job. He did neither, and the family suffered.

The family suffered not only because of the financial difficulties but also because of my father's emotional problems. He was frustrated that he could not find respectable employment since he had no formal qualifications, and he was already slightly over fifty years old then. It was difficult to demonstrate the value of his experiences as a small businessman. He felt too proud to take up what was to him low-level jobs, such as a hawker, a security guard, etc. His loss of pride made him angry, and he turned on his wife and children, making life difficult for us. The home was a happier place when he was not around.

My parents started to sub-let the two bigger rooms to tenants for about one hundred dollars each per month, which generated some basic income for the family, so there were three families in the 700 square feet flat. Since there were no walls, just partitions, and one toilet/bath had to be shared among three families, it was not easy to maintain privacy. My parents took great care in choosing our tenants. Fortunately, we got on rather well with our tenants, and we maintained contact even after they moved out.

My mother had other types of difficulties. The principal source of family income was the rent from sub-letting, which was not enough. My grandmother was most sympathetic. She did not have access to her husband's money, but she helped us with her own limited pocket money. She also asked her two engineer sons to help us as they enjoyed good salaries. This financial dependence humiliated my mother and the whole family in the eyes of my grandfather's family. The humiliation was worse than poverty, and it hurt me as a teenager. We still attended my grandfather's family functions like weddings, birthday parties, Chinese New Year and traditional festivals, etc. My father refused to go to these functions. Getting respectable clothes was a problem, and we often felt embarrassed and humiliated among rich relatives in their large villas.

My grandmother was very nice to me. She occasionally gave me ten dollars for pocket money. This was a very attractive sum when an ice-cream cost 30 cents, a bowl of wanton noodle soup in a shop cost 50 cents, and a seat for a new movie in a cinema cost $1.20 to $3.50. In those days, two kids could share one seat in the cinema, and my brother and I went to see some of the famous Hollywood movies like *The Longest Day*, *Lawrence of Arabia*. Watching the big screens from the front rows cost less even though it was slightly difficult for the neck. Going to movies was a big treat nonetheless.

Chapter 2

My Formative Years at La Salle College

"I was respected at school and in my family because I did well in school and was recognised as the hope of the family... I often mentioned respect because I cared, then and for the rest of my life."

My years at La Salle College were happy and fruitful. I earned the respect of my teachers very early; I was undisputedly the very top student of my cohort (six classes of over forty students each). This status was eroded somewhat at the end of Form 4 and afterwards because I did not do so well in Mathematics and Physics. I came seventh in the Joint Primary 6 Examination in 1962 and secured a Grantham Scholarship for five years, so I was a scholarship boy. I worked hard and managed to concentrate well. I could sit up every evening and work for three or four hours non-stop. This concentration is rare among teenagers nowadays.

I was respected in school not only because of my academic achievements but also because of my maturity. Despite some difficult times imposed by my father, I was respected in my family too because I did well in school and was recognised as the hope of the family. Above all, since the end of Form 2, I began earning money by giving private tuition. My mother's third brother migrated to Australia, so his financial support terminated soon after. Her fifth brother gave us HK$50 a month, which was inadequate to cover the family's expenses shortfall. I started giving tuition to a classmate who had to repeat in Form 1, and I received HK$40 a month for an hour of private tuition five days a week at his home, monitored by his mother.

With that money, and some other incomes in the summer holidays after Form 2, I was responsible for the acquisition of textbooks for all the four siblings in the family. My mother could not find the extra money as we basically spent all our incomes at the end of every month. I was promoted to Form 3 and my brother Philip to Form 1; we are twenty-seven months apart. My other sister, Christina, came a bit more than two years after Philip, and the youngest sister, Winnie, arrived at roughly the same interval afterwards. Textbooks for Form 3 students were expensive because we had to buy the science textbooks, and textbooks for Form 1 were also costly because it was the beginning of the secondary school stage.

To save money, I went to the used book stalls in Nelson Street in Mongkok district, not far from where we lived. Second-hand textbook stalls emerged during the summer holidays in the 1960s and 1970s to serve those who could not afford new books. There was a lot of cheating, as the purchasers often did not have the knowledge of the prices of new books. As a fourteen-and-a-half-year-old teenager, I suspected that I might have been cheated too. I simply assumed the responsibility automatically without anyone actually asking me, by just filling in the gap that the family needed. I was a bit disappointed when my brother Philip complained that he did not get new textbooks; I knew that he could not comprehend the family's financial difficulties. Many years later, some community organisations offered non-profit making services in the sales of old textbooks; I remembered my own experiences and considered these services a real contribution.

When I was in Form 4, Brother Herman, the class master of Form 3A who taught me the year before, offered me a part-time teaching job in his evening school. He was given the responsibility of running an evening school for La Salle College roughly from 4–8 p.m. The impressive school building and the name of La Salle were attractive enough, though no elite students would opt for an evening school. It was a bold attempt to offer help to the poor or less qualified students.

It could hardly be imagined that a sixteen-year-old teenager was asked to teach Mathematics at the Form 1 level. I was most grateful for the trust and responsibility. The job paid me over HK$200 a month; a government clerk received a starting pay of HK$370 or so a month. The subject taught was simple enough, but the maturity to face the class and teaching in English were demanding. Sometimes my classmates watched me teach from outside the classroom and it could be embarrassing.

I did not teach when I was in Form 5 as I had to concentrate on the public examination, the then English School Certificate Examinations. I resumed teaching in the Chan Sui Ki (La Salle) Evening College when I was in Form 6 and Form 7. I offered a lot of private tuition, which by then provided me with a decent income; I managed to earn HK$600 to HK$700 a month. I bought a new refrigerator and a new washing machine for my mother; I could occasionally give a little money to my brother and sisters to buy new clothes. Our family eventually gave up the sub-letting and had the flat to ourselves when I was in the final year in university. My family's financial situation stabilised from a deep financial crisis when I was in Form 1 (year 7) to the year when I was in Form 6 (year 13).

I was grateful for the friendship among classmates at La Salle College. We did not pay attention to each other's clothes and shoes and where we went for holidays in the summer. If my classmates were observant, they could easily tell that my uniforms were cheap stuff, that I wore the same school blazer for more than two years, and that during holidays I did not have expensive clothes when we met outside school. Fortunately, I could be very proud of my academic achievements and earned respect from my teachers, fellow classmates and students, and I did not feel inferior at all. I often mentioned respect because I cared then, and for the rest of my life.

La Salle College offered its students a liberal education in the sense that it accepted diversity of values, tolerated a lax in discipline, and did not push the students hard to do well in public examinations. Brother Casimir was the principal of the college in the latter half of the 1960s. He was very particular about students being late for school. He often attempted to personally catch the students coming late, but those who managed to escape his notice arrived at the classrooms and were accepted by their teachers who never thought of reporting the students to the principal.

Our winter uniform was a black blazer, and naturally the school rule demanded that a college badge be attached to the blazer's upper pocket. The general expectation was that the badge should be firmly sewn onto the blazer. However, as teenagers, some boys did not want to walk in the streets in the school uniform, and some poor students would like to use the blazer for normal daily use as they might not have other decent jackets, so there were all sorts of innovative ways of attaching the badges to the blazers with the intention of removing them with ease. This was tolerated by the teachers who did not make the efforts to ensure that badges were securely sewn onto the blazers. In general, our teachers were not keen to enforce discipline, and La Salle students were able to enjoy school life more.

Teenage rebellion was common among students, and perhaps more so in La Salle. For Form 6 and Form 7 students, those in the arts stream were allowed a choice of subjects. I did not take geography; during geography lessons, I was supposed to study in the library. Classes were usually double sessions and that meant one hour and twenty minutes. With this opportunity, it was common practice for these students to leave the school campus, and even went to dim-sum houses in Kowloon City. The whole idea was to demonstrate a certain privilege and readiness to break the rules. One of my best friends, Terence Yau, frequently did that with me. In Form 6, we were both class prefects and I was the head prefect of the College; if we were caught, it could be rather embarrassing. This probably could not be imagined in other prestigious secondary schools.

Since there was no particular emphasis on academic achievements, students' peer heroes were often outstanding soccer players, top athletes, and pop music band singers and musicians. In my years, Ip Sheung-wah was captain of the College soccer team, and the team won many championships; Ip was definitely the best-known student in La Salle College then. Another popular hero was Philip Chan, a pop band lead singer; he too was the envy of fellow students, especially when it was generally believed that many young girls adored band singers.

Students felt proud to be chosen to the school sports teams, with white singlets and red short pants as the common uniform. The red short pants with the College label sewn onto them were status symbols. I did not qualify as I was not very athletic, did not have the talents, was discouraged by my parents (to concentrate on my studies), and later had to earn money through giving private tuition. In most secondary schools, many parents asked their children to withdraw from the school sports teams from Form 4 onwards to concentrate on the coming public examinations. Such cases seemed very rare in La Salle College.

The grading system for sports competition in dividing secondary school students into A, B, and C grades was not very fair, as it simply depended on their heights. Those above five feet six were categorised as A Graders; those between five feet four and five feet six as B Graders; and those below five feet four as C Graders. Hence, in order to stay in a lower grade for competitive advantage, physical education teachers asked students to breathe out while they were being measured. I was quite tall for my age, and I joined A Grade when I was in Form 1; how could I compete with Form 6 and form 7 students? On the other hand, I witnessed Form 4 classmates who still remained in C Grade and won medals.

La Salle College had a student philharmonic orchestra, a symbol of prestige among secondary schools in those years. It did not interest me because I was quite aware that I had no talents in the fine arts, and I also knew my family could not afford it. I wanted to be a Boys Scout though; I would certainly enjoy camping and securing all those badges of honour. Yet again, I knew I could not afford it. I managed to keep myself occupied though. I read a lot, mainly in Chinese, and I went through my textbooks thoroughly. Fortunately, I did not suffer much from a sense of deprivation. I enjoyed the soccer games after school in the early stage of my secondary school years; later I had to spend the leisure time doing teaching and private tuition.

The differences between the rich and poor families began to show when we reached Form 4. A few students who came from rich families were already making arrangements to study abroad. There were two types. One type were top students whose parents were rich and educated; they planned to send them to the expensive public schools in Britain to prepare them for Cambridge and Oxford later. The other type were students who did not do well academically and simply wanted to avoid taking the English School Certificate Examinations. My family did not understand these options at all; we all realised that studying abroad was an opportunity available only to the rich, and we needed not bother.

The next batch of students who went abroad left after Form 6. They usually came from well-to-do families. Irrespective of their academic performance, they often would like to study in the U.S., and seek admission to the prestigious universities there if they were top students. Due to the four-year university system in the U.S., they could avoid Form 7 in Hong Kong and save one year.

The final batch departed after Form 7. They had worked hard for the Matriculation Examinations and had intended to stay in the territory if they could get into the University of Hong Kong. This batch often came from middle-class families. In those years, I knew from personal experience that some Hong Kong students arrived at the U.S. with only one or two hundred U.S. dollars in their pockets, and they had to start looking for part-time jobs immediately. Their families only offered them one-way air tickets and paid for their university tuition for the first semester. They had to be on their own afterwards. But at least their families understood the options available. The poor and less educated families could not even consider such options.

The 1967 riots took place when the leftists in Hong Kong challenged the British colonial rule around the time of the Cultural Revolution. It was when we had to sit for the public English School Certificate Examinations then. Every day, I listened attentively to the radio news programmes to make sure that we followed closely the re-arrangements for some examinations. Some examination sessions were indeed cancelled. My wife's school was situated right above Queen's Road East in North Point where the protests occurred. Even though the school was right on top of the hill, she could still hear the shouts from protesters and smell the irritating tear gas used by the police during an examination session.

The riots prompted some families who could afford it to send their children to study abroad. During that academic year, the University of Hong Kong allowed some late registrations till the end of October when the academic year had already started, because some students who had paid the tuition fees failed to show up as they had decided to go abroad. These decisions changed the lives of some people. For ordinary families, the serious challenge was to survive the economic downturn and hold onto their jobs. I followed the newspapers quite closely but did not have strong political positions.

Basically I strongly opposed violence and could not support the riots that severely disrupted the economy and people's daily life, especially transport disruptions, as well as the use of bombs and explosives. But I also had certain anti-colonial feelings and resented the privileged position of the Western expatriates. I was aware that ordinary Hong Kong people were all the time inferior in front of the British colonialists.

I also encountered the other side of the story. I had two distant cousins from my father's village who were working in The Hong Kong and China Gas Company Ltd. They were active members of a trade union loyal to Beijing and took part in the occupation of the gas plant.

When the British administration later realised that the local rioters did not have the support of the Chinese authorities in Beijing, it immediately implemented a crackdown. The police re-occupied the gas plant, and the workers who stayed behind and resisted were badly beaten, including my two cousins. One of them had to return to his home village for medical treatment for several months; he subsequently lost his job too. He occasionally took my brothers and me out to play, and I felt very sorry for him.

When I was in Form 6, I had a political exchange with a Portuguese classmate. I commented that Hong Kong should not be a colony forever; he replied that I should go back to Communist China. And I said, Hong Kong belongs to China, it is Chinese land. La Salle had some English and Portuguese students who took French instead of Chinese. There was no tension between the Chinese students and the European students, but the two groups did not mix closely. The Western students tended to stay as a group on their own.

While the 1967 riots had an impact on my rich classmates on further studies, I made a decision in the first few weeks of my Form 5 year. I won the Science Prize at the end of Form 4, which meant I got the highest marks in physics, chemistry and biology as a whole. I did very well in the latter two subjects, so I had the common ambition of seeking admission to the medical school of the University of Hong Kong too.

But I came to understand that I had to do a lot of part-time jobs to support my family, and I did not have the time and concentration to study medicine, so I asked to move from Form 5A to Form 5C; the move would give me the option of doing arts in Form 6. I made the decision on my own, my parents were in no position to advise me, and there was no one to guide me in my career planning.

I did very well in the English School Certificate Examinations. I received a government scholarship for my matriculation course. Again, I had the academic results qualifying me to do Form 6 in Queen's College, which would give me a better chance of entering the medical school of the University of Hong Kong through its vigorous preparation for public examinations. I struggled for a week or so, and I decided to move to the arts stream in Form 6. It was quite a surprise for my teachers and classmates as I had one of the best results among my classmates in the science subjects.

La Salle College did not do very well in the Matriculation Examinations in my years. The top government secondary schools like King's College and Queen's College were the best. Queen's College students especially often achieved outstanding results, which gave them a very good chance to be admitted to the medical school of the University of Hong Kong. This was commonly perceived as the most reliable route of upward social mobility. Purely in terms of academic performance, St. Paul's Co-educational College was consistently the best. Most of its graduates went on to prestigious universities in the U.S. though, and did not seem to be too interested in entering the University of Hong Kong. In my high school years, Diocesan Girls' School appeared to offer the most progressive modes of teaching like holding tutorials.

Our teachers at La Salle College did not engage us in preparing meticulously for the public examinations, nor were they very enlightening or effective in their teaching methods. Students were very much left on their own. I chose four subjects: English Literature, History, Chinese Literature and Chinese History. I received distinctions for the latter two subjects in the English School Certificate Examinations, and I had no trouble with them. I did not do History and English Literature in Form 4 and 5, as I was in the Science stream. History gave me no problem, and I enjoyed the subject very much; one of the three papers was on modern Chinese history, and I had adequate confidence. English Literature gave me some trouble; *King Lear* was the first Shakespearean play that I read, and is the only one till now.

I was very confident that I could manage to get into the University of Hong Kong, and this confidence allowed me to do a lot a part-time teaching and holding private tuition classes at home. I even used the school lunch hour (one hour twenty-five minutes) to have a quick lunch and gave private tuition. I was given the nickname of the "iron man of Asia" because I worked for about sixty-five hours a week at the minimum. I was young and energetic then.

I had to earn money because I was poor, which was well-known to my classmates. Yet occasionally one or two of them came to me to borrow money, usually when they had lost their money in gambling. I did not turn them down because I had the money. This was quite paradoxical though. The debts were seldom repaid.

I did not have any extra-curricular activities, though I was elected head-prefect when I was in Form 6. Classmates planning to study abroad were eager to strengthen their curriculum vitae demonstrating their leadership or at least active participation in various student activities. Hence, I had no difficulty finding volunteers to help. But I felt a sense of detachment because I was very much a part-time student. I skipped classes often, pretending to be sick, and I wrote my own sick leave letters on behalf of my father since he did not know English. On one occasion in Form 7, our class had a soccer match with the other Form 7 Science class. Our class team won and the entire class was enjoying the victory and solidarity. I did not join the game and did not even go to support it; I wanted to use the two or three extra hours to study and I did not want to get my clothes dirty, as I had to work as a part-time teacher immediately after school.

Social stratification emerged after the English School Certificate Examinations, though the rich and the poor students were not at all socially segregated at La Salle College, and we were definitely equal in the after-school soccer games. For every form in La Salle College in those years, there were six classes with over forty students in each class. At the Form 6 level, there were three classes, the arts stream class; the science/engineering stream class doing Pure Mathematics, Applied Mathematics, Physics and Chemistry; and the medicine stream class doing Physics, Chemistry and Biology, with an initial class size of around thirty to thirty-five students. Less than half of the students went on to do matriculation in an elite school like the La Salle College. For the territory as a whole, the statistical ratio was about one third, but this proportion included the intakes of profit-seeking private schools.

These private schools charged very high school fees. The costs were high as the schools in the public and subsidised sectors received substantial financial support from the government. Furthermore, they had to make a profit too. Their teachers tended to specialise in drilling students for the public examinations. They admitted students who wanted to repeat Form 5 or Form 7, as they often had few other options. The serious disadvantage of these schools was that they offered no extra-curricular activities, and little interaction existed among students.

At that time, only 1–2% of the young people in the age cohort of 18–24 years old managed to enter the two public universities; going abroad was often the option of the rich. There were private colleges like the Baptist College and the Shue Yan College, but their qualifications were not formally recognised by the government then, though both had famous journalism departments producing a high proportion of the territory's journalists.

My classmates who did not do well in the English School Certificate Examinations and did not come from rich families joined the labour force. Finding a job was not difficult then. When I was in Form 6, a classmate went to work in a restaurant in Tsim Sha Tsui, and another became a transport worker in a dairy farm. We met while they were working, and we were embarrassed as we realised our social differences. There were those who joined the major banks as bank clerks; they had fairly good chances of career advancement, and perhaps eventually might become branch managers. Four or five of them were admitted into the Northcote College of Education, which offered a two-year training programme with provision of dormitory and no school fees; as teachers in Hong Kong, they subsequently enjoyed reasonable salaries and a steady career path. A Form 5 graduate could become a police inspector then, and political officers were paid very well in the 1970s and afterwards since the establishment of the

Independent Commission against Corruption (ICAC) in 1974 to seriously combat corruption. Given seniority, they also received respectable accommodation. One had to be physically fit and have very good eyesight, and wearing glasses would not be qualified.

The job openings for Form 7 graduates were considerably wider even though they were not admitted into the public universities. One could join the civil service as executive officers, housing assistants, police inspectors, inspectors in various disciplinary forces, etc. As officers in the civil service, they had well-defined career paths and especially for those in the disciplinary forces. One could secure executive trainee positions in some major corporations, banks, etc., and executive positions in small and medium-sized firms. One could teach in private schools, though the careers were uncertain. One could start work, save some money, then go abroad to study; this mainly required determination.

When I was in Form 6, the government started a grants system, offering limited subsidy to students in need. I applied and was given forty dollars a month, a very small sum; the main reason was that our family owned the flat in which we lived. A classmate of mine, whose father owned a factory, went to apply also; apparently he could produce the documents showing that his father earned a very low salary. He received about eighty dollars a month. He boasted about it, and that was why I knew. I felt a bit angry, but never thought of reporting the case to the authorities. I also considered the government bureaucracy insensitive, that it did not enforce a checking system, and was unfair. This probably led me to become a critic when I finished my postgraduate studies.

A small highlight in my matriculation years was that I won the first prize in an essay competition in the senior students group held by *Kung Sheung Daily News* at the end of 1967. The senior students group was open to matriculation students and university students, and I, as a relatively new Form 6 student, came ahead of two students from the Chinese University of Hong Kong majoring in economics and business studies. I had no economics background, and my understanding of the topic "The Future of Hong Kong Industries" came from my reading of newspapers. My photo appeared in the newspaper, and the title of the news story was "Secondary School Student Outperformed University Students". I was quite proud of this because I had no extra-curricular activities to speak of. Moreover, La Salle students were never recognised for their good command of Chinese; they were perceived as "kids following Western/barbarian learning (番書仔)". This probably marked the beginning of my writing for the media.

The prize was HK$400 in gift coupons from a posh department store in Tsim Sha Tsui. I bought a pair of high-quality leather shoes for my brother and me. I also bought a nice woollen sweater for myself too. The

1967. Won the Chinese Essay Competition for the "Senior students group" at the Hong Kong Festival in Form 6. Kung Sheung Daily News: "Secondary school student outperformed university student."

rest of the money I spent in installments, buying cans of Campbell soup and Danish ham for the family as occasional treats. My brother and sisters loved Campbell soup, and so did I.

Talking about food, my mother was a very good cook. Despite our family's meagre income, her food was delicious. I did not notice this when I was young because I was used to it, and of course enjoyed it. Our family was very fortunate in this regard. One of my best friends, Peter Yeung, also appreciated my mother's cooking, and he complained about his home food. My father enjoyed good food, especially good soup, so when he had money, he would buy some good food and asked my mother to cook it. Before his unemployment, he would bring us to have dim-sums from time to time, but he very seldom took us to dinners in restaurants. When I first earned money in Form 4 as a part-time teacher, I invited my family (except my father, as we dared not involve him) to a famous, small restaurant near our home. The five of us had altogether twenty bowls of rice. We just enjoyed the idea of going out for a meal very much.

My parents were both very old fashioned in terms of sports and other student activities for children, so I did not know how to swim, how to ride a bicycle, how to dance, and so on. As the eldest in the family, I had no one to turn to for guidance. I could not help my younger brother and sisters either.

My younger brother, Philip, wanted to study medicine. His English School Certificate Examinations results secured him a place in Form 6 in the medicine/biology stream at La Salle College, but he failed to get into the University of Hong Kong in 1971. He repeated Form 7 at La Salle College, but failed to secure a university place again. He told me that repeating was an embarrassment and he felt uneasy in a class in which his classmates came from a junior class a year ago. Then he became a teacher in a private secondary school. Later he went to Sydney in Australia, completed a course in computer programming, and became a computer programmer for a while. He saved up enough money to finish university, majored in business studies, and landed in a job at a multinational oil corporation in Australia.

The acute shortage of university places in the 1960s to the 1980s generated a lot of disappointment and frustration, but the employment situation remained favourable, and there were many opportunities. Young people managed to adjust. Adequate upward social mobility opportunities were essential to the maintenance of social stability and the legitimacy of the British colonial administration, and the latter had a good understanding of this. It also helped to ensure that education would provide the major channel of upward social mobility. Hong Kong was quite corrupt before the establishment of the ICAC in 1974. In the eyes of ordinary people, the police were quite corrupt, but those who better understood the workings of the government said that the Public Works Department was more so. When I was in Tak Ming Primary School, one evening (probably in 1957) the police came to search our flat in Hak Po Street with a proper warrant. Three or four policemen examined the belongings of the family for half an hour or so, even my pencil box. Then they left. My parents figured that there was a narcotics den one floor below ours. The police probably pretended to search our flat by mistake or on the pretence of faulty intelligence and thus gave ample warning to the drug dealers downstairs.

I lived in the Mongkok district from 1956 till early 1973 when I left for New Zealand for further study. I often went to the street stalls near home for late night suppers as I stayed late into the early mornings to study. When I was in the final years of secondary school and in my university years, I had the money to take my younger brother and sisters to these street stalls two or three times a month, visiting two or three of them each time, including, for example, a roast goose rice noodles stall, a congee and fried dough stall and sometimes a dessert stall. These were probably the moments we were closest together. We were young and could always take some extra food at night. Our observations of corruption in progress were that we often saw police jeeps passing by these street stalls collecting food without payment for the policemen's late-night suppers.

These street stalls worked till early mornings, closing at around 3 a.m. in the morning. Then around 4:30 a.m. in the morning some dim-sum restaurants would begin their services for people who started the day early like taxi drivers, minivan drivers, street hawkers and the like around Shantung Street north of Nathan Road. In the early mornings, one often found night club hostesses eating fish balls and seafood with their clients in the more expensive street stalls; sighting them was quite an attraction for a teenage boy. Subsequently, the hawker street in Mongkok (and in Yaumatei's Temple Street, Stanley, Shamshuipo, etc.) have become an iconic symbol for Hong Kong tourists.

Movies were made in the 1980s and 1990s on the police station sergeants (華探長) making huge fortunes in the previous two decades or so. One of them who fled Hong Kong upon the establishment of the ICAC was said to have accumulated a fortune of HK$400 million. Corruption in Hong Kong in those decades was more serious at the grassroots level than at the very top. These Cantonese-speaking junior officers controlled prostitution, gambling and narcotics at the street level and were able to collect substantial bribes. Sometimes they might even run these operations directly through their associates. Their expatriate superiors did not have the local language and the grassroots contacts. They received bribes through the control of the promotions and assignments. They were probably unaware of how much their subordinates were making.

In contrast, the senior expatriate officials of the British colonial government were relatively clean. Some of them might have received very expensive gifts from local businessmen. In Japan and perhaps South Korea, corruption was more serious at the top level in the context of close collusion between the ruling parties and major business groups and between leading politicians and very rich businessmen. Policemen at the grassroots level, on the other hand, were generally clean. In the Philippines, for example, and many Third World countries, corruption was rampant at all levels.

Despite the prevalent corruption in the territory in those decades, public examinations and recruitment into the elite government schools system were basically free of corruption and were perceived as fair by the public. The other elite grant-in-aid or subsidised schools were mainly run by church organisations, and Hong Kong people trusted that they were clean. This was significant in providing opportunities for upward social mobility, which played a major role in maintaining social stability and the legitimacy of the colonial regime. Similarly in Mainland China, in the context of spreading common corruption in the era of reforms and opening to the external world, the public examination system governing entrance to universities has been perceived as relatively clean by the general public.

I became a Catholic when I studied at La Salle Primary School. The school principal, Brother Henry, persuaded the new students to be baptised, and it was difficult to refuse. My parents accepted this, which was a bit surprising to me then and when I thought about it in later years. My parents claimed to be Buddhists in the general sense, and they were rather superstitious and worshipped the traditional gods and goddesses. I often wondered why they accepted that their eldest son should reject ancestral worship in becoming a Catholic. I guessed that they were very pragmatic and happy that I was admitted to La Salle, and were eager to please the school principal, in the hope that my brother would soon be admitted too.

The Catholic Church in Hong Kong in the 1950's and 1960's was quite conservative and rather insensitive to local customs. My mother was asked to see a nun at Saint Teresa's Church at Prince Edward Road, rather near La Salle Primary School, and it was supposed to be my parish church after my baptism. The Catholic Church wanted to have an understanding of my family background and my parents' attitudes towards my conversion to Catholicism. But the attitude was one of superiority. The nun spoke Cantonese, and my mother could understand her well. Her emphasis was that I should no longer engage in ancestral worship after baptism. I should not kneel and kowtow before my ancestors' pictures and shrines. I must not burn incense. I could burn candles, but they should be white and not red, etc. My mother respectfully agreed.

When I grew older, I resented this attitude of colonial superiority. When I was in senior high school, I read a lot about pseudo-colonialism in China in the late Ching years and how some Western Christian missionaries bullied the local governments. I believed that the essence is to worship one true God, and one should not ask ancestors to grant blessings of wealth, health, babies, success in examinations, careers, etc. Incenses or candles were not an issue; white candles, yellow candles or red candles should not matter.

Years later, I accompanied my mother to visit my father's resting place at a public cemetery twice a year when she could still walk. I helped her light incense sticks and burn paper offerings. It was not that I believed that my father would enjoy the fake paper money that we burnt so that he could use it in afterlife, but simply because my mother was too old and too weak to do it, and I wanted to put her heart at ease. When I visit her, I offer to light incense sticks in front of the ancestral or memorial tablets at her home because my mother expects me to do so, and it pleases her.

Chapter 3

Student Life at the University of Hong Kong

"Universities were very difficult to get in, but very easy to graduate." ...I wanted to understand how governments work and the distinguishing differences between good and bad governments.

I did well at the matriculation examination, and I applied to join the Faculty of Social Sciences. Some of my teachers suggested that I should seek admission to the newly inaugurated Law School. I just did not know what a legal career would be and did not apply. If I had a good understanding of the prospects of a lawyer in Hong Kong, I should and would have applied and got admitted.

My wife, Grace, entered the Faculty of Social Sciences with me at the same time. Before that, she received a call from the Law School suggesting that she should apply for admission to Law School given her results. She said she did not consider it because her parents considered that lawyers were crooks, and decent people should not become lawyers. It was quite easy to get into Law School at that time, and we both could qualify for admission, but we did not apply. Actually the first batch of law school graduates almost without exception did very well in their careers.

The Faculty of Social Sciences offered two streams: one with the disciplines of sociology, economics, political science, social work and psychology, and the other with the disciplines of economics, accounting, business administration and statistics. Those who chose the latter stream probably had the intention of seeking careers in the business world. Those opting for the first stream apparently were more academically oriented. In general, the workload for arts and social sciences students at the University of Hong Kong was quite light, and for me, there was ample time to do part-time teaching.

There were three semesters per annum: ten weeks for the Christmas semester, ten weeks for the Easter semester, and eight weeks for the final semester. Classes began in early October, and final examinations finished in May, hence a very long summer holiday. For students in the first stream, we all had to take four introductory courses in economics, sociology, psychology and statistics. Then in the second and third years, students had to complete four papers each year, normally a combination of two disciplines except Economics where eight papers were available.

I chose political science and economics. The Department of Political Science was launched in 1970, and I was among the first batch of political science graduates. My good friend, Terence Yau, chose the same two disciplines. We were very close during the matriculation years and university years because we had almost identical academic interests; we did the same subjects and papers.

We shared the same naivety too. We had the ambition of joining the governing elite eventually, and therefore we chose political science and economics. At least we wanted to understand how governments work and the distinguishing differences between good and bad governments. We thought that social work was largely remedial work, and could not tackle the major issues of politics and good governance. We both spent a lot of time following the news, and reading newspapers and news magazines. I secretly entertained the ambition of becoming a diplomat, but I understood that the option did not exist for me in Hong Kong. If I were a citizen of a democratic country or of Taiwan and Singapore, I would definitely apply to join the foreign diplomatic service.

The workload was especially light for political science and economics courses, and probably the heaviest for those doing social work and psychology because of the practical work and laboratory sessions. We had to write a small number of essays, sat for annual examinations, and not much more. Skipping classes was a normal practice for ordinary students except the more serious ones.

The joke among students then was if you started working for the examinations when the rhododendron plants began to flower, you should be quite all right[4]. And if you only started working when the rhododendron flowers all fell, you might come under a lot of pressure. Getting first class honours was very, very demanding, but getting a pass in the examinations was often very easy; hence, most students did not work too hard. It was quite similar to the top universities in Japan – very difficult to get in, and very easy to graduate. Graduates then had to work hard in the initial stage of their careers.

The government abolished the system of scholarships for university students based on the results of their matriculation examinations the year I entered the University of Hong Kong. Instead, the government introduced a system of grants and loans for eligible poor students. The scholarship system had offered twenty scholarships each year and I definitely would have qualified for one. A scholarship not only paid for the tuition fees but also the cost of dormitory as well. I thought the government bureaucrats could not even make a distinction between reward for excellence and assistance for the needy. Naturally I was disappointed, but it was difficult to find sympathy.

Again, my application for grants and loans did not fare well because my family owned the flat in which we lived. In the summer of my first year, I was summoned

---

4   In Hong Kong, Rhododendron usually blooms in April, and the university examinations usually start in late May.

by an official of the Education Department who found it difficult to accept that my family of six depended only on the HK$ 120 a month from subletting one room in our flat. My answer was simple, I had to work as a part-time teacher to help support my family. But the amounts of grants and loans I received remained small. There was a lot of cheating of the grants and loans system in its initial years of implementation. The government became aware of the cheating after more than three years, then there was a series of prosecutions that had probably deterred fraudulent applications successfully.

Since leaving La Salle College, I lost my pool of potential private tuition students as I was no longer present at the school. The Chan Sui Ki La Salle Evening Secondary School was about to become the formal Chan Sui Ki La Salle College with proper independent premises, and it would no longer accept part-time teachers, so my only option was to look for part-time teaching positions in the private sector. Respectable private schools would not hire part-time teachers too, and the choices were limited.

I wrote over forty application letters in June/July every year. Though the position was supposed to be part-time, I actually taught twenty-four to twenty-five classes every week, which was the load of a full-time teacher in a proper school. The rate was about HK$ 30 per lesson on the weekly timetable, which would be around HK$ 7.5 per lesson of forty minutes or so. I could secure a monthly salary of slightly more than HK$ 700, which was about half of the earnings of an Executive Officer II in the government in his first and second years of service. Keeping order in class in private schools was a challenging task.

In my first university year, I got a teaching position in a private secondary school at Robinson Road, Mid-Levels. It was notorious for its lack of discipline. Some of the students came from rich families, some did not. The girls often wore extremely short skirts as their school uniform to catch the attention of their male classmates and young male teachers. The latter had to maintain respectable manners in order to survive. University students like me who served as teachers were given Form 4 and Form 5 classes to teach, so as to make good use of our experiences in handling public examinations. I tried to make friends with the students and treat them as equals in order to maintain reasonable order in class and to conduct teaching. The Education Department allowed us to register as "Permitted Teachers" to fill the gap of qualified teachers, and to meet the demand of profit-seeking private schools that paid rather low salaries.

Such schools sometimes played dirty tricks on teachers by terminating their contracts early. Contracts with the "permitted teachers" usually lasted for a year, but the school might not pay them the salary for August (the summer holiday month) if it decided to recruit new teachers for the new school year. Often these university student teachers chose to leave because they had just graduated or wanted to concentrate on the final year examinations. The permitted teachers were not protected as the schools could terminate their contracts by giving one month advance notice. Form 5 class usually ended at the end of April as the English School Certificate Examinations took place in May. In the school year 1970–71, I taught at Mu Kuang English School at Prince Edward Road. It was a decent school despite the small premises, and discipline was very good for a small private school.

My contract was terminated at the end of April 1971 as I was given notice at the end of March. Most of my teaching duties were for Form 5, and the school could easily find a replacement teacher for the limited number of classes for Form 4. The school principal was Elsie Elliott, an elected Urban Councillor who claimed to fight for the rights of the under-privileged. I lost four months of salary, though I taught well, as recognised by my students who invited me to some of their summer holiday activities later. A colleague told me that I antagonised the school principal because I did not help in her election campaign. All teachers were invited to serve as voluntary campaign workers, and apparently all of them took part except me. I had nothing against Elsie Elliott's campaign; I did not take part simply because I was too busy, as I was a full-time university student.

The relatively low salaries accepted by the university student teachers involved a tacit understanding that the school management would adjust their teaching timetables so that they could fulfill their student duties. The university teaching timetables were announced in late September and tutorial arrangements finalised in mid-October; secondary schools, however, began classes in early September. Adjusting school timetables for the university student teachers created difficulties for the school management. As the only university student teacher in Mu Kuang English School, my request for timetable adjustments was resented.

In my final university years, I went to teach in a private secondary school in Kowloon Tong. The standards of the students were not satisfactory, but they behaved well. The school management was fair, and I even received my salary for August, which was quite a pleasant surprise. Though these were annual employment arrangements, and I did not have time to take part in social gatherings, I made many friends with the students and some colleagues, and we met occasionally for many years afterwards.

These students in such private secondary schools often did not do well in the English School Certificate Examinations, and they expected to be so. Though their academic achievements were far from outstanding, they were mature and were ready to join the blue-collar ranks. Some strong male students became construction workers who were paid rather well, although physical stamina was required; it was no joke working for eight hours under the hot summer sun in construction sites. Some became chefs and waiters/waitresses in restaurants, and if they were entrepreneurial they might become small restaurant owners. A lot of them became factory workers, and the pay was low, but they could become sub-contractors or enter the retail trade later. In the beginning of the era of economic reforms and opening to the external world in China, some of them went to the Pearl River Delta and started small factories. A few managed to make a small fortune.

What was significant was that while the majority of the young people could not secure well-defined upward social mobility opportunities through success in the education system, they survived well and were able to improve their living standards through hard work. Hong Kong's rapid economic growth in the 1960s and 1970s generated a labour shortage, which prompted satisfactory increases in wages in these two decades. Opportunities for starting small businesses were plentiful. The general belief then was that there would always be jobs for those willing to work.

As a teacher in these private schools, I was able to have a better understanding of Hong Kong society. In the summer holidays after my second year in the university, I went to work as an unskilled labourer in a textile factory in Kowloon for a week just to experience the hardships of grassroots workers.

University life in Hong Kong was colourful; university students were regarded as the elite of society. The police then exercised considerable restraint in dealing with demonstrators who were university students. Graduates from the University of Hong Kong needed not to worry about job prospects, and they could easily secure jobs offering them middle-class incomes and social status.

University of Hong Kong students were not very keen on sports, but they did take part in student union and student club activities. These activities had their electoral campaign rituals; they offered opportunities for meeting new friends and helped to enhance students' curriculum vitae in job applications. Engaging in no student activities at all looked bad as a record of one's university years.

I met my wife, Grace, when we joined the executive committee of the Sociology and Social Work Society during our first year. So, student activities could be very rewarding in different ways. The new executive committee had to face the electorate, in this case, sociology and social work students, whether or not there was electoral competition. Basically, students came to support the executive committee, but they tried to ask difficult questions as a test of the calibre of the executive committee members. There was a bit of showing off in these question and answer encounters, but they were good preparations for those who later became senior civil servants.

In the social sciences field, students did not find their professors very impressive, especially in the economics and political science disciplines. When I was doing Sociology in the first year, there were two lecturers from Britain who were able to offer liberal and challenging ideas; they did not stay very long at the University of Hong Kong. Then came a very young sociology lecturer from New Zealand. He was dedicated and liberal and was very popular among students, especially young ladies.

The teaching staff of the Political Science Department mainly came from universities in Africa, though they were originally from the United Kingdom. If the department had offered a complete degree programme in political science, I would have taken all its papers, but at that time it only offered half a degree programme. I enjoyed the subject matter, and was probably the top student of the class cohort, but I did not do very well in economics. I received a second class honours, upper division in the end; I heard that the Political Science Department had recommended me for first class honours.

I began to realise my academic inadequacies; I simply did not put enough effort in. I performed very well in public examinations before because I have a good memory, could organise my ideas well and write very quickly. When I sat for my matriculation examinations, for the subject of history, each paper lasted three hours and the candidates had to answer five questions. I could produce an answer of six to seven pages per question.

My speed gradually declined. In the university years, I had to sit for three-hour examinations as before, but a candidate was asked to answer three questions only, and I produced answers of about seven or eight pages each.

So, examination skills were less important in university education; an outstanding student had to read widely and offer independent ideas. My general knowledge of politics from newspapers and news magazines enabled me to do quite well in the political science examinations, but I had not done sufficient reading and thinking. I had to make it up in my postgraduate years. The development of basic research skills at my undergraduate stage was poor, and I could not write research papers of good quality then.

I like to travel, and I visited many interesting places later in my life. But my first overseas travel was to Macau, just before I began university, to give myself some kind of reward. I went with two or three relatives and I appreciated the Portuguese colonial-style beauty of Macau; the brief glimpse of the casino satisfied my curiosity.

Then in the summer holidays after my second university year in August 1971, I joined a Taiwan tour organised by the Social Sciences Society, a student body of the Faculty of Social Sciences. It was all the more enjoyable because my then future wife Grace also went. It was a trip of twenty-six days, and the group visited almost every corner of Taiwan. We boarded Butterfield &

Swire's ten-thousand-ton ocean cruise liner M.S. Taiwan. The boat trip lasted for a little more than a day, but going through the customs at the port of Keelung took more than three hours.

Student tours of this kind were sponsored by the Taiwan authorities. In the Cold War era in 1971, the Taiwan agency in Hong Kong actually sent their staff to make house visits. Those who wanted to join the tour were warned not to display any pro-Beijing newspapers or publications at home, otherwise they might not be granted the travel permit (入台證). The trip tested our Mandarin, and with a few exceptions, most of the Hong Kong university students could not handle Mandarin then.

In those days, a Hong Kong tourist bringing a bottle of expensive brandy, cosmetics of famous brands, or even nylon stockings, into Taiwan could make a bit of money to compensate for part of the travel expenditure. We did nothing of the kind. We did change Hong Kong dollars into the Taiwanese currency at the unofficial foreign exchange market in a few well-recognised streets in Taipei.

In the third year, students had to start applying for jobs. Nobody was worried about this, but securing a prestigious job was regarded as an honour, and students took the exercise as a challenge. Advertisements for government positions appeared in newspapers at the end of the calendar year; applicants had to complete many forms. Written examinations took place around February, and interviews followed in March and April for those who passed the written examinations.

Like most of my classmates, I applied for the positions of administrative officer (AO), executive officer II, and assistant trade officer (ATO) and assistant labour officer. I passed the written examinations for AO and ATO; somehow I did not take the written examination for the assistant labour officer position. In 1972, those who were interviewed for the AO position were not considered for the executive officer II position; the arrangement was not reasonable.

At any rate, I failed to reach the final round of interview for the AO position, but was offered appointment as an ATO. The ATO job offer was respectable. It promised many travel opportunities as trade officers were posted to the territory's trade offices in the major cities of the world. Many years later, I learnt that the then Hong Kong Governor, Sir Murray MacLehose (Hong Kong Governor 1971-1982), was dissatisfied that no AOs had been recruited locally in 1972, and he wanted to step up the employment of local young AOs. In 1973, many more were recruited; quite a number of them had worked in the civil service as executive officers II.

Those with one or two years' experience in the civil service should have distinct advantage over fresh university graduates. Most of the local AOs recruited in the 1970s were subsequently promoted to the highest ranks of the civil service. In the 1960s and 1970s, the British administration maintained a ratio of 1:1 between local AOs and expatriate AOs, and very few of the former could expect to move to the top echelons of the civil service then. The perception was that a "glass ceiling" existed. Within the police force at that time, the colonial regime similarly maintained a substantial proportion of expatriate police officers in the upper ranks.

I applied for some positions in the business sector too. I was offered an executive trainee position at the Hang Seng Bank and also at the Hong Kong & Shanghai Banking Corporation Ltd. In those days, executive trainee positions at the major banks were the best stepping-stones to management positions in the private sector later in one's career development. Many local business groups and foreign banks did not want to spend time and resources on training, and they were often willing to offer much higher salaries to recruit executives with relevant experiences and training from major banks and corporations.

There were ample opportunities available to a decent graduate from the University of Hong Kong then. Most of my classmates had two or three job offers and they could pick and choose. There was an acute shortage of university-trained social workers; many voluntary social service organisations had to accept the requests of their new recruits to go for long holidays before starting work in September.

The traditional "hongs" like Swire Group, Jardine Matheson, and major relatively new entrants into the Hong Kong market like the First National City Bank all engaged in vigorous recruitment campaigns, eager to attract the best people in support of their development. I attended a few interviews and did not perform well. I lacked the aggressive business acumen, and it was probably obvious in the eyes of experienced human resources/personnel experts.

My good friend, Terence Yau, was selected by the First National City Bank as an executive trainee, and he was very happy with the job offer. The American bank offered an above-market-rate initial salary to attract talents, a typical American approach. Terence Yau did not spend much time on academic work, but he was intelligent, observant and had good social skills, qualifications shared by many University of Hong Kong students. He was outgoing, confident, and very knowledgeable of current affairs. He wanted to become a banker, and successfully secured a solid starting position. While I was struggling with earning money through teaching, he wanted to experience university life. He was quite active in student activities, making friends, and even joined a residential hall, the Old Halls, in his third year at the university. University dormitory was expensive, and I never considered it. Terence really intended to enjoy the experience.

Ragging[5] was practised in the residential halls at the University of Hong Kong in those years. Ragging was slightly harsh at the University Hall, and quite mild at the Old Halls. It was against traditional Chinese values, and I personally did not accept it. But new members of the residential halls knew what to expect, and they accepted it. On the other hand, Lady Ho Tung Hall was famous for its aristocratic practices; there were amahs (domestic servants) dressed in traditional, black and white costumes to serve the residents during meals.

Naturally I had to think about my career. In my university years, in contrast to some of the outstanding classmates and seniors, I did not know what constituted an academic career and what the demands of a good academic were. Professor Peter Harris, head of the Political Science Department, recommended me for a postgraduate scholarship at the University of Washington in Seattle in the U.S. I did not expect to get first class honours; my academic performance was quite good, but not outstanding. It was not a surprise that I did not get the University of Washington scholarship.

Unfortunately, the Political Science Department at the University of Hong Kong was a new department. It did not offer a master's degree programme and it did not employ tutors. In the more established departments like

---

5   "Ragging" is a term that is often used in Asian countries to refer to the "initiation ritual" in universities involving the bullying or humiliation of new students by senior students.

the Economics Department, students planning to pursue academic careers and who had impressed their teachers were normally given tutorship while they enrolled for the master's degree programme so that they would have decent incomes and teaching experiences. They would then prepare to apply for overseas scholarships for the Ph.D. programme. This option was not available to me.

I decided to go abroad to study simply because I did not want to serve the colonial government; I did not want to accept a job in the business sector because this did not accord with my interest. Despite my poverty, I was not tempted to become rich. My limited life experiences at this stage certainly made me aware of the humiliations of being poor as well as the importance of making ends meet. I wanted to see the world. I wanted to be free and to have ample time to read and write. Hence, I chose to study abroad and to become an academic later, though at that time I did not even know what academic research and publications were all about.

My parents were disappointed. They expected me to join the civil service or the Hong Kong & Shanghai Bank/Hang Seng Bank, and to pursue a steady civil service or banking career. This would solve the family's financial problems. The pressure on me was especially high. My brother failed to get into the University of Hong Kong in 1971 and 1972; when I graduated, he became a teacher in a private secondary school. My sister Christina did quite well in the English School Certificate Examinations in 1971, and she went on to do Form 6 in a prestigious Catholic girls' school in Happy Valley. But she decided to go to a teachers training college a year later. My decision to go abroad to study would generate considerable economic uncertainties for the family.

Then came the question of my marriage. Grace and I were seriously in love, and we came to the conclusion that we should get married first before I went abroad to study and she would follow me. I was and still am most grateful for her sacrifice for me. She considered herself not ambitious in career development, and she happily worked as a secondary school teacher after graduation. However, the postgraduate student years ahead for us would be uncertain and definitely very tight financially.

Gradually I made up my mind. I wrote to decline the job offers. When I attended the job interview at the Hongkong & Shanghai Bank (now the Hongkong Bank), the personnel manager conducting the interview was quite arrogant and patronising, so in my letter to her declining the offer of appointment, I said I did not want to work in a modern British East India Company. That was a bit immature, but it reflected my political values at that time to some extent.

I ended up working as a research assistant for the political consul at the Consulate General of the Federal Republic of Germany in Hong Kong. This job paved the way for my plan to pursue further studies. In the 1972–1973 period, China established formal diplomatic relations with many countries following the famous Nixon visit to China and the Sino-American Shanghai Communique was released in February 1972. My job at the consulate-general was to collect published information including relevant Chinese newspaper reports and translate them into English. These experiences were useful for me to develop my perspectives and analysis of Chinese foreign policy, which later became the research focus in my Ph.D. programme.

In landing this research assistant job, I had a brief encounter with Rita Fan, the student employment officer of the university at that time. She later became a prominent leader in the pro-Beijing united front during the Chris Patten as well as the post 1997 administrations. I heard about this research assistant position from classmates who said that another classmate, a past university student union president, was going to apply and would likely get it. I was interested in this kind of position then and was surprised that the position was not openly advertised at the student employment service. I went to question Rita Fan and her colleague as to why the job was not openly advertised, and implied that I could complain to the student union newspaper, the *Undergrad*. The job position was soon made open at the student employment office; I applied and got it.

The salary was very reasonable, but obviously there was no career path for this type of position. My choice was a surprise to many of my friends. I started to apply for scholarships, and eventually secured a Commonwealth Scholarship to New Zealand. I was fortunate to some extent. The very limited number of Commonwealth Scholarships available to Hong Kong students normally went to first class honours graduates in the medical, engineering and science fields. With a second class honours, upper division and a mediocre record of student activities, I was quite happy with a scholarship, which would mean that I could be a full-time postgraduate student without having to engage in part-time jobs.

I had some savings accumulated through years of part-time teaching. The money was spent on my wedding to please the families of both sides – fifteen banquet tables of guests for the wedding reception dinner. I had to pay for my wife's airfares to Wellington, New Zealand, which cost slightly more than HK$ 3,000 one way when my monthly salary at that time was about HK$ 1,700.

In 1972, and early 1973, there was a crazy stock market boom in Hong Kong in which a broad segment of the population participated. The Hang Seng Index rose from 323.95 on January 27, 1972, to a peak of 1774.96 on March 9, 1973, and then fell to a low point of 150.11 on December 10, 1974. It was said that some investors could not stand the shock and had to be treated in psychiatric hospitals. This boom and bust cycle demonstrated that the society could be easily influenced by a "herd spirit". Hong Kong people in general had a better knowledge of international stock markets and currency markets than people in most metropolises of the world, though they were not very interested in elections and political developments outside the territory and China.

I did not know the stock market at all, but I joined a lady colleague in the West German consulate-general and invested in shares too without an understanding of the principles governing the working of a stock market. I made some money in 1972 as almost everyone could make money in a boom. But my family later paid a price. I had almost HK$ 15,000 ready to be left to my family upon my departure to New Zealand. My father asked to have the money so that he could invest in the stock market. When prices started to fall later, he was reluctant to sell, and when I returned to Hong Kong for field work and a holiday in late spring/early summer in 1975, the shares were worth only HK$ 1,500, one tenth of the original value.

I should have given the cash to my mother, but I felt a bit sorry for my father at that time. His dream was that I should get a well-paid job, move up in the civil service or major bank, and buy a luxurious flat for my own family and my parents. He was disappointed with my career choice, and he was worried about the uncertainty in family income.

In quick succession, my brother and sisters left Hong Kong to pursue their studies. With the help of a maternal uncle, my brother Philip departed for Sydney in the autumn of 1973 to do a computer programmer course. My sister Christina completed her teacher-training course, served as a teacher in a subsidised school for two years, saved up some money and went to attend university in Sydney too.

My youngest sister, Winnie, did not do so well in the English School Certificate Examinations. But a maternal aunt who was in a divorce and had moved to Prince Edward Island, Canada needed help to take care of her small son. Winnie went to help with the baby-sitting and had the opportunity to do her final year in high school and enter into university in Canada. Due to the acute shortage of opportunities for university education in Hong Kong in the 1970s, young people who did not come from rich families explored various types of opportunities to complete their tertiary education abroad. Our family served as a good example.

The younger generation in our family could not assume the responsibility of supporting our parents as they were all under financial pressure overseas. I occasionally managed to send a hundred Australian dollars home, but this was inadequate and uncertain. Part-time domestic helper jobs were easy to come by in these years though. The younger families usually did not have the space to accommodate live-in domestic maids; they might also want to save money. Hence, part-time domestic help paid at hourly rates met their needs, and the demand grew rapidly. My mother was able to secure such part-time jobs without difficulty, and she was proud of her gainful employment.

So, for those years when I was not in Hong Kong (February 1973 to August 1977), she supported herself and my father in this manner. She continued to sub-let two rooms in our flat. I felt apologetic and there was unease in my heart during these years. After tertiary education, I was supposed to offer my parents a decent life, and yet, after graduating from the prestigious University of Hong Kong, my mother had to work as a part-time maid. She had not worked since her marriage and actually did not have much working experience. In a way, she earned considerable respect from her employer because her four children were all studying overseas. She was very thorough and clean, and was a good cook. I often admired her strong willpower and grit to endure difficulties in her life.

The Middle East war (Yom Kippur War) in October 1973 not only pushed the Hong Kong stock market to a low point at the end of 1974, but the global recession also generated much unemployment in the territory. The famous "hawker street" in Mongkok today was an innovative project then to create jobs and to reduce unemployment.

It was probably the worst economic recession hitting Hong Kong from the end of the 1967 riots till today. The economy started to pick up in late 1976 and early 1977, but the impact was sometimes severe on some young people's careers. Graduates from the engineering faculty at the University of Hong Kong, for example, could not find trainee positions in 1974 and 1975; many of them became secondary school teachers, salespersons, etc. When the economy improved, the construction companies often bypassed them and recruited fresh graduates. They found it very difficult to join the engineer profession subsequently.

Chapter 4

Overseas Study, a New Life

New experiences awaited me and my wife. We faced the interesting issues that Hongkongers encountered overseas.

I got married in February 1973, when we were both twenty-three years of age. This was quite young by the standards then. Young men often got married in their late twenties, and young women about two years earlier. Usually the young couples should be able to find their own accommodation in preparation for their marriages. My wife and I stayed at a hotel for three days before we flew to Wellington, New Zealand, for my further studies. This was a simple and convenient arrangement.

My wife, some of her family members and friends were in tears when they came to see us off at the Kai Tak airport. Airfares were expensive then and we did not know when we could come back to Hong Kong. Very often, overseas students from not so rich families would only go back home after completing their studies. Emails and mobile phones were not yet invented. The common means of communication was by posting letters or aerogrammes (a foldable air letter without an envelope, but with pre-printed stamp, usually light blue in colour). Air letters and aerogrammes usually arrived in a week or so, but there were delays from time to time.

It was a different world then. As students, we did not even have a telephone or television at home during our stay in New Zealand. If we had a lot to talk about, we would make recordings on audio tapes and have them sent by air. Today, overseas students often manage to return home two or three times a year. They usually have smart phones, laptops and other devices that enable them to have real-time and sometimes "face-to-face" communication with their parents, relatives, friends or the world through a variety of ways and means – via IDD's, Skype, emails, live chats and social media, to name but a few.

This trip to New Zealand was the first overseas trip for Grace and me, apart from our tour of Taiwan in the summer of 1971. A lot of new experiences awaited us. We stopped at Auckland first, then took a domestic flight to Wellington. We knew that Wellington is the capital of a Western country, so we were rather shocked to see the small wooden hut as the Wellington airport terminal, which appeared quite like the small military airport in Shek Kong (石崗), Hong Kong. When we reached the hostel in the city centre around 6 to 7 p.m., the streets were quite deserted, and we thought it must have been a public holiday. Later, we found out that it wasn't; it was a normal weekday evening.

Soon we were impressed by the helpfulness and politeness of New Zealanders. The University had been helpful in finding us temporary accommodation. The Commonwealth Scholarship was sufficient for me to lead a simple life, rent my own house, and I did not have to pay tuition fees. There was even a marriage allowance for my wife too if she was not working.

The lady officer from the University Grants Committee who oversaw Commonwealth scholarship matters in Wellington was warm and hospitable. She invited us for "tea" when we first arrived. We were invited to arrive at her house at 6:00 pm; little did we realise that "tea" actually meant dinner for New Zealanders, so we were caught by surprise when a full three-course dinner was served. We were treated with our first taste of Pavlova, a dessert that they were proud to claim as an invention from New Zealand. We were rather amused a year later while we were in Australia that Australians made the same claim as well.

I was quite fortunate as Grace is a very good cook. For the first time in our life, we had an oven. Our flat was attached to the house of our landlord, and we could enjoy his garden too. We had a very spacious bedroom, sitting room, kitchen and a bathroom with a huge old-fashioned bathtub. In comparison with many Hong Kong students who went to New York and Paris for postgraduate studies, our accommodation was luxurious.

Milk was very cheap in New Zealand because it was subsidised (four cents per pint at that time); we soon learnt that the Labour government had been giving school children free milk until 1967. We were also impressed with the ice-cream because it was creamy and had fresh fruits in it. Grace started baking cakes, such as the rich butter cake, and we soon had to tackle the problem of a weight gain.

We faced the usual interesting issues that Hongkongers had encountered overseas. There was only one big Chinese grocery store in Wellington in 1973 where we could get some basic supplies of Chinese food and groceries such as soya sauce. Chinese vegetables were rare. We only went to a Chinese restaurant once during our year in New Zealand. We wanted to save money and the food at Chinese restaurants was far from attractive. Since Grace soon got a job working as a research assistant at the Reserve Bank of New Zealand, I was responsible for shopping as postgraduate students had a relaxed timetable.

We learnt to make salted eggs (鹹蛋) by bottling eggs in saturated salt water and to make the fried dough sticks (油炸鬼), pronounced as Yau^4 ja^3 gwai^2 in Cantonese, to eat with rice congees. My wife could make very good barbecue pork, but she could not always get the skin crispy while making Hong Kong style roast pork. Pork was expensive while lamb was cheap. Fortunately I quite liked lamb and mutton. Vegetables and fruits were cheap in summer and expensive in winter: in the winter months we ate a lot of potatoes and cabbage; tomatoes were expensive. We could easily get a fish head for soup for about ten cents, and occasionally we were asked by the shopkeeper if we kept a big cat.

We shipped a luggage of 150 pounds in a wooden crate to Wellington. Unlike other postgraduate students, we intended to set up home. We brought an electric rice cooker. Grace had a good collection of clothes and shoes. I brought some warm clothing, but I did not have too many books. I had to learn to do some simple cooking. My mother did not allow me to go to the kitchen, which was used by three families, and it was usually very crowded. So I broke my first egg when I was over twenty-three years old and it went right into the kitchen sink. I was the unskilled labourer at home.

I was responsible for shopping and had to carry the groceries back home, up a rather steep slope. Grace's bank was near Aurora Terrace where we lived, so we were able to have lunch together at home. I cooked lunch, i.e., heating up the casserole dish Grace had prepared the day before and the big pot of soup that was meant to last for two or three days. I also cooked rice with the electric rice cooker, fried some omelettes or made a simple salad. For many years afterwards, I was able to make a proud statement that I have prepared lunches for my wife with soup and two dishes while we lived in New Zealand.

Wellington was a small city and we soon met and became friends with the very few people from Hong Kong. There was a group of three Hong Kong doctors who recently arrived at Wellington with their families. They wanted to secure trainee positions in hospitals to become specialists and get New Zealand passports. They took us for picnics by the lake and we often had meals together. Through them, we also met an aunty of Chinese origin who had stayed in Wellington for a long time; she entertained us often and shared some of her recipes with us.

New Zealand people loved picnics and walks in the countryside. Local friends told us that almost every family would keep an old blanket in the car trunk, and wherever they went, they would spread the blanket on the lawn and have tea with cakes, cookies, sandwiches, and a flask of coffee and tea they brought from home. They would not go to cafes in those years. Similarly people brought sandwiches from home for lunch at work; eating out was considered a treat. In contrast, Hong Kong people often went out to eat.

Since I only completed a three-year undergraduate degree in Hong Kong, I was not allowed to do a master's degree right away. I had to do a B.A. (Honours) degree course in Political Science at the Victoria University of Wellington with the right to proceed to M.A. degree by

1973. Overseas study – relaxing in Wellington's park.

thesis in Political Science. The incentive was that if I managed to get first class honours, I could immediately begin my Doctor of Philosophy (Ph.D.) programme. I planned to work hard, and I was grateful that I did not have to worry about money and to spend time on part-time work.

At the end of 1972, the National Party lost the elections in New Zealand, and the Labour Party, after a very long time in the opposition, came to power. New Zealand soon established diplomatic relations with China. There were waves of liberal and progressive ideas in society and especially in the university campuses among the concerned students. Otherwise professors were quite traditional and conservative.

New Zealanders then adored the British royal family, and newspapers and magazines were full of its stories. I remembered that Eugene Rostow, a famous academic and a former senior official of the U.S. State Department, visited the Victoria University of Wellington; he was followed by a group of radical students who tried to embarrass him.

I gradually formulated my area of research for my doctoral thesis, i.e., contemporary Sino-Japanese relations. My undergraduate work was a bit inadequate, and so I worked very long hours every day to compensate for this. I often studied until 3 a.m. in the mornings and got up at 10 to 11 a.m., when I did not have morning classes. There was a lot of reading to catch up. I had to learn to write serious research papers. Grace was very good to me, and she helped me type the research papers.

I had to choose four papers for my B.A. (Honours) degree, with focus on international relations and Asian studies. My teachers found my work satisfactory, and they were aware of my intention to do a Ph.D. They came to understand that I probably had to find another university since the Victoria University of Wellington did not have the expertise nor the library facilities in support of my research work.

I started to prepare for my applications. I naturally started by approaching a small number of prestigious universities in the U.K. and the U.S. In the former case, they advised that they did not have the research nor supervisory resources for my field. I managed to secure admission to one or two of the universities in the U.S., but there was very little financial support. In the meantime, my professors supported my applications to universities in Australia, including the top Australian National University, as well as the Flinders University of South Australia where their friend Dr. Bill Brugger taught.

In January 1974, I was still on the waiting list for a scholarship at the Australian National University; my professors at the Victoria University of Wellington had good contacts there and were able to provide me the information. On the other hand, I was offered a full scholarship by the Flinders University of South Australia. Before Christmas 1973, I learnt that I got distinctions for all my four papers and was awarded a first class honours. Hence, I could start my Ph.D. right away at the Flinders University in Adelaide.

My professors all treated me very well in my year at the Victoria University of Wellington. I was just married, and the year was probably one of the happiest in my life. Life was quite simple then. After the beginning of my academic career, I had the opportunity to return to New Zealand for conferences, and I was very happy to see my old professors again. Quite a number of them came from India.

In Wellington, there were very few students from Hong Kong, and I met only one doing psychology. There were many Malaysian Chinese students in New Zealand then; they were handicapped in university entrance in Malaysia and had to go abroad to pursue their tertiary education. The anti-Chinese riots after the 1969 elections were at the back of their mind. I did not have many in-depth discussions with them. I was their envy though: I was married and had a scholarship. They often had to take up part-time jobs. The Malaysian Chinese students in New Zealand often did not come from rich families; those from rich families usually went to Britain or the U.S.

Grace managed to save some money for a trip to South Island, New Zealand, for the summer holidays. We took the ferry from Wellington to Nelson, and travelled by long-distance coach around the South Island. South Island was most beautiful, and places around Mount Cook and Milford Sound had stunning natural landscapes. What impressed us most was the fresh crisp air and the relaxing atmosphere, which contrasted sharply with the busy urban life in Hong Kong. Our medical doctor friends took us earlier to Lake Taupo, Rotorua and the Waitomo Caves in the North Island. Grace and I went back to New Zealand for two long holidays, the last one in 2019.

So I decided to go to Adelaide. There were very cheap air and rail tickets available in New Zealand and Australia in the summer holidays to benefit university students, so we bought student tickets from Christchurch to Melbourne. We took the overnight ferry from Wellington to Christchurch and flew to Melbourne. From Melbourne we took the train to Adelaide, which took us nearly a day. We spent a day or two in Melbourne as tourists.

The rationale for my decision to study for a Ph.D. degree in Adelaide was similar to that for going to New Zealand. Going to a prestigious university in the U.S. and U.K. had its distinct advantages, but every academic year I had to worry about my financial situation; I had to spend time working as a tutor, etc. I especially did not want Grace to have these worries. Again, the scholarship money at Flinders was enough for a simple life even if Grace did not have a job. I did not have to pay for tuition fees. I received A$50 per week; I paid A$20 for rent, about A$10 for food, and I had A$20 per week for various expenditures. I had plenty of time to concentrate on my studies; unlike the science and engineering postgraduate students, I did not have to consider facilities available at the university laboratory. The scholarship would last at least three years as long as my academic performance was satisfactory.

Australia was considered the "lucky country" in those years by people inside and outside the country. While the world suffered economically from the oil crisis triggered by the Yom Kippur War, the Australian economy was doing very well because of the sharp rise in energy and commodities prices. Australia was relatively egalitarian too; doctors and architects did not earn much more than brick layers. Like in New Zealand, the conservative Liberal Party / National Party coalition lost the general elections at the end of 1972, and the Labour Party, which had been in opposition for a long time, returned to power. The Gough Whitlam government was ready to introduce a lot of reforms, and the same applied to the Labour government in the state of South Australia under Don Dunstan.

Grace soon got a job at the State Library of South Australia; the job also gave her the opportunity to enrol for a part-time post-graduate programme in librarianship at the South Australian Institute of Technology (now the University of South Australia). So she became a professional librarian and stayed that way throughout her career. I understand that her choice of librarianship was intended to help me in my research work and the professional qualification would enable her to transfer jobs more easily, given the fact that my future career was still uncertain at that point. I remained most grateful, especially when I realised that I had not helped her in any significant way.

A car is a must in places that are spread out and public transport is not convenient; it was true of New Zealand and Australia in the 1970s. Besides, the price of petrol was relatively low (about 50 cents per gallon) in Australia compared to Hong Kong. Grace learnt to drive during our stay in New Zealand, and in Adelaide, we bought a car. At that time, most students had a Holden or Volkswagen because they are relatively reliable. Their spare parts came easily and repair work was relatively cheap. We had two Volkswagens consecutively in our three years' stay in Adelaide, a 1962 and then a 1958 model costing $550–$600.

One weakness about Volkswagens in those days was that it was difficult to start in cold weather. On cold winter mornings, I had to go outside to pour hot water around the engine to warm it up before starting the car. We also realised that it could not go as fast as we wanted. In the city area, we could only go 30 miles an hour while the speed limit was 35 mph. It was not perfect, but it was a good means to take us to work and to the university.

We soon found our accommodation, which was half of a normal-sized red-tiled house partitioned into two with gardens in front and at the back. The half house had a spacious bedroom, a sitting-room, a small kitchen (by Australian standard) and a washroom (no bath this time). We shared the garden with our neighbours, Howard and Gwen, who lived in the other half of the partitioned house. We were in a way lucky to have them as neighbours; they were very friendly, invited us for meals, and even offered to help us move in and settle down.

There were big fruit trees in the back garden – apricots and lemons. Coming from densely populated, urbanised Hong Kong, it was the first time that we knew what these fruits actually looked like on trees. In September, the apricot tree started to blossom. It was a beautiful sight. We saw many apricots starting to grow, and we really looked forward to the day when they became ripe so we could pick them. Little did we realise how well informed the birds were. A day or two before the apricots were ripe enough for picking, the birds had their first taste on almost every fruit.

The furniture in the rented house was very old. We bought an old black-and-white television set for A$20. In New Zealand, we did not have a television and often missed the news. We could enjoy movies on television like *War and Peace* during the weekends. We could follow the news and sports programmes conveniently. Soccer was not very popular among the Australian audience and there was no live coverage. Australians loved cricket and tennis, on the other hand, and these sports often appeared live on TV for days and were often hot topics in the daily conversations of Australians.

With Grace working, we occasionally went to the city to watch movies on the weekends. There was an old cinema near our house. It was very cheap and, on Friday nights, it offered discounts for students at 80 cents for 2 consecutive movies. In cold winter nights, people brought blankets with them to watch movies because there was no in-house heating. We watched a few movies. For example, Paul Newman's *Harper* and *The Sting*. By March 1975, colour television was launched in Australia at the time when I returned to Hong Kong for field studies in Taiwan and Guangdong. Grace told me that it was a big event with the launching of colour movies like *"Those magnificent men in their flying machines"* and *"Doctor No".*

We could still remember the special Adelaide event that was held annually in September – the Royal Adelaide Show – an agricultural show organised by the Royal Agricultural and Horticultural Society of South Australia since the nineteenth century. Coming from urbanised Hong Kong, it was fun watching competitions of livestock, and farm skills like sheep shearing. There were foods, joy rides, shows and entertainments for everyone lasting for a whole day. A few South Australian state government departments had their presence there to show support, including the State Library where Grace worked. In the year 1976, she had to be on duty to man the mobile library, which was basically a van with shelves of books and cassettes. She could still recall that people stopped by and showed interest in their collections. She got extra pay and time off later for attending the show!

Food was abundant, fresh and cheap in Australia, and even the postgraduate student's stipend allowed us to eat very well. Hamburger and fruit juice for lunch at the university canteens costed around 75 cents, fish and chips $2.20, steaks $3.50, and dinners at hostels $3. One way of getting bargain food was to go to the Central Market in Adelaide city near Saturday noon. The stalls in those days would close at noon for the weekend and they would like to sell all of their meat, fruits and seafood. So from 11:30 a.m. to slightly after 12, one could get cheap bargains like A$1 per tray of steaks, yabbies (a species of crayfish), and so on. We could have steaks all the time; wine produced in Barossa Valley (South Australia) was cheap too. I understood that my fellow postgraduate students from Hong Kong studying in major European cities found steaks and fresh fruit very expensive.

What was lacking was the Chinese ingredients for cooking such as dried shrimps, shrimp paste and fupi (bean curd skin). There was only one decent-sized Chinese grocery store in Adelaide. From there, we could get essential Chinese food stuff like soya sauce and peanut oil, but the prices were often much higher than what we used to pay in Hong Kong. So every now and then, Grace's family would send us a parcel full of nice treats from home like oyster sauce, rice vermicelli, shrimp flavoured noodles (蝦子麵), but they were often inspected by customs.

Only one Chinese restaurant called Pagoda served Hong Kong style dim sums on Sundays; they offered only four typical kinds: shrimp dumpling, hsiao mai (pork dumpling), roast pork bun, and steam pork rib in black bean sauce.

We also missed the vegetables, since the Chinese grocery store sold only two kinds of vegetables – Chinese broccoli and choi sum. After borrowing a shovel from our landlord, Grace started her adventure in growing our first home-grown vegetables in our back garden, including Chinese cabbage (pak choi), Chinese spinach, spring onions, and coriander. It was hard work in digging up the topsoil and to weed the vegetable patch. Owing to her inexperience, she did not time the planting too well; she ended up having to harvest all the vegetables in one go and had to give them away to our neighbours and friends. We were happy though that the hard work paid off.

The house in South Brighton, Adelaide where we lived was only ten minutes from a long beach with fine white sand. Taking long walks along the beach in the evenings and weekends was very relaxing and enjoyable. Grace and I also discovered ways of introducing varieties in our diet. We found one or two clear river streams where wild water cress was abundant. It was somewhat tough, but if we picked only the young shoots on top, it would be very good vegetable for making soup and hot pots.

We also went to some rocky coasts with shallow reefs to collect palm-size abalones during very low tides in the weekends. Abalones are a Chinese delicacy. They were plentiful along the coasts of South Australia. They usually hid in the shade underneath the rocks, but we did not even have to wade too deep in water to find them. We left the smaller ones untouched when they did not reach the size permitted by the authorities. We even managed to dry some abalones under the hot Adelaide sun and send them home, and our families in Hong Kong were very impressed. When we invited friends for a simple dinner, these two items often appeared on the dinner table and were much to the delight of our guests, be they Australians or otherwise.

Cooking dinners together, helping with the dishes, and sharing recipes from our home countries during the weekends more often than not bound us together and gave foreign students like us a home feeling that we missed from time to time. Grace often shared her favourite recipes: sweet and sour pork/duck with pineapples and green peppers, braised belly pork in soya sauce and "three cup" chicken. We came to learn new recipes from others such as roast leg of lamb from Australia; pork or beef fillet in Satay sauce from Malaysia, and pork dumplings from Taiwan.

In my first year as a postgraduate student at the Flinders, the Politics Department allowed us free access to stationery. I was pleasantly surprised and went to collect some index cards as well as three nice index card boxes. They were very useful for data collection before the computer era. Obviously this generosity only lasted for a few months and had to be stopped. Ph.D. students at that time were given a room each with windows, to the envy of their Hong Kong counterparts today.

There were social experiments in the civil service like allowing morning and afternoon tea breaks and the introduction of flexible hours allowing employees to enjoy a 4½-day week. Grace benefitted from the scheme, especially with her part-time librarianship studies. It was quietly abandoned after a while because of problems of communication among staff members, difficulty in arranging staff meetings, etc. There was a significant interest in trying to help the Aborigines as they were perceived to have been unfairly treated for a long time. The enthusiasm, the idealism and the embrace of humanitarian values were impressive, especially in university campuses.

The radical student movement at that time adopted a strong anti-American position. It opposed American military bases in Australia, like the Pine Gap intelligence facility, and continued to oppose the Vietnamese War and the previous Liberal / National coalition government's strong support for the U.S. war efforts in Indochina. Some students wore "Independent Australia" badges to demonstrate their dissatisfaction with the ownership of Australian resources by major U.S. corporations and their significant role in the Australian economy. In the student dormitories, one could see many pictures of Che Guevara and Ho Chi Minh.

This also meant considerable sympathy for the leftist policies in China in the early 1970s, like young people had to work in farms and factories for some years before applying for university, barefoot doctors, and so on. "White Australia" attitudes disappeared somewhat from university campuses, and became much more subdued in society. In our three years in Australia, we encountered only one or two occasions when some teenagers yelled insulting words at us in the street.

Prejudicial impressions, like Chinese were dog meat eaters, still lingered in the minds of ordinary citizens. Grace's colleague had a bowl of wonton noodles while in Hong Kong, and after she returned, she asked Grace if the dumplings were made of dog meat because the meat did not taste familiar. Grace explained to her that eating dog meat was illegal in Hong Kong and she had never taken any in her life. Otherwise we were usually treated politely. At Flinders, students naturally accepted the values of racial equality and non-discrimination, respect for pluralistic values, etc. The student canteen offered Asian food one day per week.

In August 1974, about one hundred Flinders students occupied the Registry Building of the university where the vice-chancellor's office was located in support of their demands for optional history examinations at the first-year level.[6] Students visited the vice-chancellor's office, sat on his chair for a little while, and examined his collection of wines. It was an unexpected experience for a student from Hong Kong.

At this time, there were some similar occupation campaigns in other Australian universities.[7] There were

---

6 See, for example, https://www.facebook.com/FlindersUniversity/photos/a.424867946169/10152827365806170/?type=1&theater
7 Slightly before the Flinders occupation campaign in July 1974, students at Macquarie University in Sydney moved into the guarded university council building to protest against the partitioning of the student union bar separating students from staff, the refusal of the vice-chancellor to fund student union office bearers, and administration-imposed changes

many mass meetings participated by students and a few professors including my supervisor, Dr. Bill Brugger. A vast majority of the students at the Politics Department and a few staff members were sympathetic to the occupation campaigns. During tea times at the staff common room, there were frequent long discussions going on for two or three hours. As a foreign postgraduate student, I did not have much to contribute to such discussions, and I wanted to discipline myself not to spend too much time on tea sessions in the staff common room. Nonetheless, I very often joined the group discussions and listened for a little while to show my solidarity.

In November 1975, sharp political struggles triggered the sacking of the Gough Whitlam government and led to a constitutional crisis. It was widely debated in the Australian society, and was divisive like the Occupation Campaign in Hong Kong in 2013–14. Almost everyone had a view in the polarised society, and there were demonstrations around the country. Most of the

---

to the student union's constitution. The Builders Labourers Federation in support of the students banned the construction of the partition in the bar.

Later in September 1974, the Assessment Action Group led an eight-day occupation of the Monash University in Melbourne. The Communist-oriented group demanded the abolition of competitive assessment, student-staff control of course content, and open admissions to allow the entry of more working-class students. The university administration subsequently called the police to drag out the occupiers.

See "The history of Australia's student radicalism", *Red Flag*, 17 February, 2014; https://redflag.org.au/index.php/article/history-australia%E2%80%99s-student-radicalism

university students were in support of the reformist Whitlam government.

These events naturally had an impact on my ideas of political participation, democracy and justice. There were many Hong Kong students in Australia, especially in Sydney. Most of them were studying accountancy and dentistry. It would be difficult to find Hong Kong students studying political science in Australian universities. Later in Hong Kong, I had the opportunity of meeting some accountants and dentists who were studying in Australia in these turbulent years; most of them remembered the events but did not think that they had a significant impact on their student life nor their subsequent career development.

There were lighter sides to these student activities too. Some of my undergraduate friends formed a Barossa Valley Study Society. The Society succeeded to get funding support for its activities as part of a Foreign Student Welfare Programme: a free tour of the Barossa Valley, the famous wine district in South Australia. We were invited to join too, and as it turned out, one of the main events was wine-tasting. Free movies were also organised for students; one of them was a movie from China *"The Fiery Red Era" (Huohong de niandai* 火紅的年代*)*. At Flinders, there were many Malaysian students. Those from Sabah and Sarawak seemed to be able to secure funding support from their rich sultans for student activities, which often included barbecue parties at highly subsidised rates. I remembered that I had gone to those parties once or twice.

Library facilities for my research area were limited at Flinders. I had to prove my competence and the availability of relevant research materials before I would be allowed to start my Ph.D. work. The literature review though tedious was essential for doctoral research. My supervisor was sympathetic. I was asked to give two seminars to demonstrate my competence, and I had to go to Canberra, Australia's capital, to review the research materials available.

In those years before the computer age, the Australian tertiary education system mainly supported comprehensive in-depth collections in my field at the Australian National University Library and the National Library of Australia in Canberra. Postgraduate students made frequent trips to Canberra, and they received small travel grants for these trips. This was a sensible policy because it would be very expensive to support the comprehensive development of library facilities in all universities for all specialised fields.

Domestic flights were very expensive in Australia in the 1970s and postgraduate students relied on trains and stayed in student hostels. In May 1974, I made the first three-week trip from Adelaide to Canberra, which took me about a day and a half by train because I had to change trains in between. I made a list of relevant publications available in the two library systems for the bibliography, and it was a pretty boring and tedious task. In the following trip in November in the same year, I spent my time doing photocopying (referred to as making photostats or Xerox copies in those days) so that I could read the materials later in Adelaide.

I had to be careful not to miss any important publications or their citations in those days when digitised library catalogues and databases were not yet available, and the process was laborious. I had eighty-hour weeks while I was in Canberra, but I was lucky that a librarian at the National Library offered me a lot of help. Without him, I had to stay in Canberra for a much longer time. To save time and money, I ate a lot of meat pies during the time in Canberra, which were cheap and filling but certainly not very healthy.

The trips were not without its rewards. I soon learnt that Grace took some of the free time while I was away to knit a blue pullover for me with woollen yarns made in Australia. At the same time, she also helped me search for the journals and the microfilms collections at the Flinders University library. Making copies of journals from microfilms was time consuming and expensive at the time. My wife and I often wrote letters or send aerogrammes to each other on a daily basis. Writing letters to friends and relatives usually occupied most of our weekday evenings while we were overseas. Making IDD calls were expensive in those days.

In the Christmas holidays at the end of 1974, Grace and I went to Sydney by train to meet my brother Philip and my maternal uncle Anthony and his wife Helen. The train trip from Adelaide to Sydney usually took more than twenty hours and there was often a delay of more than three hours. The whole trip usually took about a day.

Adelaide summers are characterised by scorching heat as it is situated at the edge of a vast inland desert. However, it is located right along the coast allowing some moderating effect from the sea. Houses were spacious so that the air inside would not get heated up too much during daytime, and it would usually cool down at night. Windows were closed in summer to keep the heat out. It could get up to 40°C or slightly hotter a few times in summer. Air-conditioning was a luxury then, and people did not use electric fans much. To cool down, people often took showers a few times a day, and perhaps stayed scantily dressed inside the house.

Water in Adelaide was very hard, and often affected the taste of even good quality tea leaf. In many houses, people collected rain water to make tea. We liked Chinese tea and we needed rain water to make tea, otherwise it tasted salty. We used more soap washing ourselves and our clothes. Residents and tenants were supposed to keep the lawn tidy, and people in the neighbourhood believed that everyone had to keep the street tidy. Our landlord left us a very old lawn mower, which was in poor condition and became quite useless; I was unskilled and often lazy, and I kept postponing the task. Eventually our landlord told us that a neighbour complained to him about the condition of the lawn. Since he did not trust us with his new, modern lawn mower, he chose to come to our place to mow the lawn for us. This suited us extremely well.

The demand of workload on postgraduate students was very light; I had to complete a paper and give a seminar once every year. As long as my supervisor was satisfied with my work, my scholarship would continue and I could extend my student visa for another year. Most of my fellow postgraduate students took up tutorships to earn more money; a high proportion of them were married. I did not because the department mainly needed tutors for first-year classes in Australian politics, and I was not qualified. With a salary from Grace, we had no problem with money, and I preferred to finish my Ph.D. degree at the soonest possible time.

The first year of my Ph.D. programme was enlightening, and it was basically reading and reviewing the literature and defining the theoretical framework for my thesis. In contrast to the Ph.D. programme in American universities, Australian universities offered no course work and a Ph.D. student was very much on his own. The advantage was that I could concentrate on my research work with few distractions. I could specialise, write a good thesis and turn it into a book. The disadvantages were that the basic training was weak, and one did not know whether the thesis was a strong one or not. One might enter the wrong track without being given sufficient advance warning. Specialising too early also meant that the young scholars' perspective might not be broad enough.

Top American universities required two full years of course work and a rigorous Ph.D. thesis; the training was well-grounded. But it meant that completing a Ph.D. degree might take up to five or six years, and if one had to spend a substantial amount of time to do part-time tutoring, the time needed would even be longer. Another distinct advantage of studying in a top American university was that there would be a critical mass of talented postgraduate students, and one could learn from each other.

I had two supervisors. Dr. David Plant was a specialist in international relations and Australian foreign policy; he acknowledged right from the beginning that he did not know much about my research area. Dr. Bill Brugger specialised in Chinese politics, and Chinese foreign policy was not his area of research expertise, much less Sino-Japanese relations. I soon realise that doing a Ph.D. thesis was a lonely pursuit. No one else shared the same specialisation, nor much interest in your work. I later learnt that some of my fellow Ph.D. students felt the same way. There was, however, a small group of postgraduate students in the Politics Department working on

Australian politics, and there were considerable group interactions among them.

At the end of 1974, I began to prepare for my field work. It was exciting because it meant one could travel and broaden one's horizon, and I love travelling. In February 1975, I used the Australian student travel system and got cheap air tickets from Adelaide to Kuala Lumpur, but I had to transfer and collect my luggage at Melbourne airport to re-board the plane for Kuala Lumpur.

On the Ansett plane, I met a miner from South Australia on his way to Melbourne. He was very friendly, and he told me about the unemployment situation surrounding the mining and other industries in Australia. Unfortunately, my luggage containing the documents for research was not in the same flight, and I had to wait for the next flight from Adelaide to collect it. I was exceptionally "glad" that my next flight to Kuala Lumpur was delayed, and I got back my luggage in the end before boarding the next flight.

I did some tourist sightseeing in Kuala Lumpur. It was the era of ping-pong diplomacy. I went to watch a ping-pong match there, and despite the very low entrance fees (HK$ 2–10), the attendance was low. I was almost the only one getting tickets fifteen minutes before the match began! The Malaysian Chinese community was apolitical, and not interested in China at all at that time. I was lucky in securing a travel grant from a small British foundation to pay for my airfares, and I received a very small allowance from my department too. I did not have money to go to Japan, which was expensive then; I spent a few weeks in Taipei and Hong Kong, and I managed to visit Guangzhou too.

To save one night's hotel accommodation, I took the overnight train from Kuala Lumpur to Singapore; the train was dirty and overcrowded. A lot of young people from Malaysia went to Singapore for work opportunities, thus enabling Singapore with cheap abundant labour for its blooming industries. I was told that they would get about HK$ 300–400 a month, and hostels were provided by the employer. I wondered at the point if this was a manifestation of the successful Asian economic model that Western economists bragged about, or rather a symbol of the exploitation by multinationals.

In Singapore, I went to talk to a few academics in my field. Although universities managed to recruit a few famous professors, academics were often attracted to teach in Australia. I was not particularly impressed by the university facilities. I met a La Salle College classmate working as an engineer. We went to the street food stalls and I was impressed by the quality and the cleanliness of the food centres there.

The city was booming. Multinationals like Chase Manhattan, Mitsubishi, and FNCB had impressive skyscrapers that dominated the Singapore skyline and reminded everyone of their presence and the success of the Asian dollar market. I was told that the government was clean; drug problems, illegal gambling, and prostitution were minimal. The only complaints came from some of the intellectuals and professionals who viewed Singapore as a police state with limited freedom. My questions were: would Hong Kong lose out? Or would Hong Kong probably do better than Singapore if it were not under the colonial rule?

Then I took the train to Bangkok. I walked through the city streets just to have a glimpse of life there; prostitutes in the streets were not uncommon. For my family, I bought some Thai silk fabric and black obsidian that Thailand was famous for. I wanted to visit Vietnam and Laos as well, but decided not to, as there were still turmoil and conflicts there. The conditions of the places I visited in Asia, the poverty, and difficult life of ordinary people that I came across in the streets made me understand why many people there considered that communism might be a solution.

Malaysia and Thailand established formal diplomatic relations with China in May 1974 and July 1975 respectively. Singapore held back and declared that it would be the last of the ASEAN countries to establish diplomatic relations with China, though its economic ties with China were strongest among ASEAN countries at that time. I walked into universities in these three capital cities and talked to the students about their perceptions of China and Japan. This became a habit in my travels later, I loved to walk into universities and talk to students to enhance my understanding of the countries I visited.

I flew back to Hong Kong to do my research. I made use of the library facilities at the U.S.-funded Universities Service Centre at Argyle Street, Kowloon, where I met the librarian, Liu Yihui, who was very helpful. Later when I joined the Chinese University of Hong Kong, he also worked in the university library there. I met Anita Chan and Jonathan Unger briefly at the Centre doing research; they later became famous Sinologists at the Australian National University.

My visit to Taipei was important to my research work. I used the Institute of International Relations, National Chengchi University as my base. The Institute had a significant group of experts on Chinese foreign policy and Japanese foreign policy; I interviewed most of them and had many informal discussions with them. The discussions were useful.

In Taipei, I normally ate at the student canteens, which were cheap. Dishes were displayed with marked prices; vegetables and bean curd dishes were the cheapest, followed by fish dishes, pork dishes, chicken dishes, and beef dishes. Beef was distinctly more expensive because it had to be imported. A bowl of beef noodles was considerably more expensive than a bowl of pork noodles, and beef soup noodles had no beef, only beef soup. There were usually three respective pots of noodles, rice and buns (饅頭), reflecting the preferences of the Mainlanders who dominated the research institute then. Apparently this was the arrangement for staff canteens in almost all official agencies in Taipei. There were two hours for lunch, and people could take an afternoon nap (a common habit in Taiwan at that time) or have a game of *go* chess (圍棋) with time limits.

President Chiang Kai-shek passed away on April 5, 1975. I was in Taipei then, and I could observe the widespread mourning in the community. Despite his authoritarian regime, his economic policies worked and the people enjoyed the improvement in living standards brought by the economic take-off. I stayed at the National Taiwan University's Chiao Kwang Hall (僑光堂), which is now deemed a historical building. At that time when I stayed there, it was fully occupied with Kuomintang's diplomats and the press attending the funeral; there were refugees from Saigon too.

I then visited Guangzhou (Canton) for a week. As I was not visiting my family in my home village, my application as an overseas scholar took a few months to process. Before I left Hong Kong, I cut my hair very short and bought myself white Hawaiian shirts and cotton pants that were made in China for the trip. I was extra careful not to bring foreign magazines and publications. I stayed at a hotel for overseas Chinese, and walked around the city as a tourist. The state emporiums were well stocked. I watched a game of basketball in the Culture Park.

Hotel accommodation and the food were good, but the rice was stale. In preparations for war with the Soviet Union, the Chinese authorities implemented a scheme of storing grain up to the amount of three annual harvests. Urban residents had to consume rice that was more than three years old, and the quality sharply deteriorated because the storage facilities were poor. I visited Sun Yat-sen University and had good talks with the students. I tried to examine how people lived in Guangzhou; my notes almost filled one whole notebook.

I tried to mail my notebook back to Adelaide as I understood that I might get into trouble at the customs where my research notes might be scrutinised and some of my observations might be found unacceptable. I could not buy a big envelope to send the notebook; a staff member in the hotel suggested that I should buy a piece of thick paper and make my own envelope. I followed her advice and sent the notebook by air mail. I received it six months later, and I believed that it had been examined.

Grace also came back to Hong Kong for a holiday in May 1975; she was very happy to see her family. We also missed the nice cuisines offered at the Chinese restaurants in Hong Kong, such as dim sums and fish ball rice noodles, which were scarcely available in Adelaide. In the spring and summer of 1975, my brother and sisters were all studying abroad and I did not meet them while I was in Hong Kong.

I returned to Adelaide in July 1975, and it was winter in Australia. I had to concentrate on writing my thesis at this stage, and I tried to produce at least ten pages a week. In contrast to the earlier stage of reading and field work, writing was dull and tiring, but it required concentration, discipline and perseverance. In the first quarter of 1976, I almost completed my first draft. Progress was smooth, and I started to look for university positions.

Chapter 5

My Academic Career Began

I delivered my first lecture in Fiji and returned to teach in Hong Kong. An academic career is a lifelong pursuit, requiring commitment and dedication.

In 1976, the economy of Australia was in bad shape. Government funding began to dry up, and there were almost no new job openings in the tertiary education sector. If there were a vacancy for lectureship, competition was keen. The doctoral research students I knew all experienced difficulties in their job hunting and were complaining that job searching was in vain. I applied for two positions at the colleges of advanced education offering sub-degree programmes in Australia and a university lectureship in New Zealand. I was paid to go to Sydney for an interview once, but this was the furthest I could go. My professors admitted that the job situation was very tight indeed.

Almost every Ph.D. student about to complete his degree in Australia applied for positions in Nigerian universities. Nigeria started to prosper because of the sharp rise in oil prices triggered by the Yom Kippur War, and the Nigerian government wanted to develop university education with a plan to establish six new universities. We all applied in early 1976, and received no reply. Then the Nigerian government issued a notice in the *Times Higher Education Supplement* (London) asking applicants to send their applications once again because all applications had been destroyed in a fire. That was quite disappointing. Most of the applicants followed this advice, including me, but I received no news afterwards. I always wondered later how many Australian scholars subsequently secured university appointments in Nigerian universities.

I applied for a lectureship in politics at the University of the South Pacific (USP) in Suva, Fiji, and got an offer of a three-year contract, renewable for another three years. It was a pleasant surprise. Professor Ahmed Ali, then Head of School of Social and Economic Development, took it upon himself to contact me directly with a long letter explaining the offer, the courses I had to teach and the possible research facilities and opportunities at USP. He was most persuasive, especially when he told me that there were 109 applicants for the post, and over 50% of them were appointable. It was only later that I found out that a few members of staff from the School were graduates from Oxford, Harvard and Berkeley.

Few people knew where Fiji was, and I had no knowledge of the island state. Hong Kong was in a serious recession then, the two universities there froze all new openings in 1975 and 1976, and I had to leave Australia upon completion of my studies. Hence, I embraced the position in Fiji as the beginning of my university academic career. The University, which began in 1968, wanted to fill the vacancy in a hurry to teach the first year course in international relations for the coming semester in August 1976, so I had to leave early, while Grace would join me at the end of the year so that she could complete the course and acquire her professional qualification in librarianship. Luckily for us, she got the support of the library school to sit for an early examination especially arranged for her. The examinations accounted for 30–35 percent of the overall assessment and she passed with good results. She managed to join me two months later.

The salary in Fiji was low by Hong Kong or international standards (net monthly salary of 350 Fijian dollars, which was equivalent to about AUD 330). Basically, I could not save any money. Worse still, we only realised afterwards that unless Grace was a teacher, the chance of getting a job was very slim. As the spouse of an expatriate, she would need to apply as one. The employment situation was difficult for expatriates unless there was a definite shortage of skills that could not be filled by locals. There were no vacancies for expatriates in libraries and she failed to obtain a work permit as a librarian during our stay in Fiji. As a university graduate, she could only work for a few weeks at a United Nations agency as a temporary employee. It was not easy to get entry permits for my parents' visit either. We soon realised that Fiji was not the place to settle down.

Nevertheless, my salary was adequate for living comfortably in Fiji. For once in my lifetime, I enjoyed expatriate status, and was part of the expatriate elite in the newly independent state. Fiji was a perfect place to study marine biology or ethnography, but it was almost impossible to do serious work in my research area of Chinese foreign policy. Yet the teaching load was light, so I could spend some time in refining and completing my Ph.D. thesis. I could and did use the research done to publish in academic journals. Teaching was pleasant. It was at USP that I delivered my first lecture on international relations for first year students. It was a good lecturing experience for starting academics like me.

My colleagues were very friendly. Ali and two other colleagues picked me up personally at the airport when I arrived. They invited me to teas, lunches and dinners too. Dining out was cheap. From time to time, my colleagues and I would have a feast at the Bamboo Terrace (a Chinese restaurant) in town. I met students from various islands in the South Pacific, and was guided by my colleagues to observe the cultural differences among them. Students were interested in their studies and were quite articulate. I followed the local custom and invited my students to parties; they would bring their own drinks and I as the host would provide some snacks like chips and nuts. Students understood that their teachers were not well paid.

The University provided a new fully furnished two-bedroom flat at only 15% of my salary and it paid the balance of the rent to the property owner at commercial rates. The flat was located in Laucala Bay where university staff and expatriates lived, and it was just ten minutes' walk from the University. The landlord, a local Indian who lived upstairs of a two-storey house, did a lot of gardening and we came to enjoy the fruits of his labour. There was a banana tree, a coconut tree and a pear tree. Unfortunately, there were quite a lot of insects around the place – cockroaches, small spiders, mosquitoes and lizards. I had to use mosquito repellent at night.

Our landlord was very hospitable and invited us for an Indian meal. It was the first time that we tasted a genuine, home-cooked Indian curry prepared from freshly ground spices. We learnt that there were different kinds of curries from India and there were regional differences in the cooking and the ingredients used. We used only our fingers to scoop up the food, including rice, from the plate. It was quite an experience.

The weather was wet and hot, very much like the rainy days in Hong Kong. I bought an air-conditioner so that I could work better in the cool and kept my windows closed to maintain a quiet environment. It was a luxury in Fiji; the money could have been used to buy an old car, which would have given us higher mobility. Other consumer durables such as washing machines, dryers and vacuum cleaners were also very expensive, even for second-hand ones. In fact, any imported consumer goods and products including soap, shampoos, rubber gloves, coffee, oranges, apples, etc., were expensive. We worked the sums and concluded that shipping them from Adelaide would be more economical than buying them in Suva.

There was no television in Fiji. The local paper the *Fiji Sun* offered limited international news, which was understandable. My sources of news were the one-week-old Australian and New Zealand newspapers in the university library and *Newsweek* magazine, which I had subscribed on my arrival in New Zealand a few years earlier. In September 1976, Chairman Mao died, and I only came to know of his death a few days afterwards.

The news magazine not only served as my important source of international news, but also as the model for my writing style to improve my English. When I started teaching in Hong Kong, I tried to convince my students that this was a good way to sharpen the English language. I guessed not many of them followed my advice. Hong Kong students all understood that a good command of English would be a valuable asset in their career development, but not many were willing to make the effort.

The easiest entertainment was to watch movies at the university campus. I paid 20 to 30 Fijian cents to see two old Western movies once. It was small screen movie though, and it broke down and someone had to rewind the film roll. At any rate, that was what happened when I went, and the only time I did. When I went to town to get *the Australian* (newspaper) on Saturday, I sometimes went to the cinema for a movie. I watched a Vietnamese movie called Hoa Binh (meaning peace); it was very good movie about the war in Indochina. I heard from colleagues that there were a lot of bars in Suva, and alcoholic drinks such as beer and gin were cheap. There was music for dancing too at the bars.

Suva, the capital of Fiji, was rather backward by Western standards, and there was a lot of poverty too. I understood from my colleagues that safety, especially in some neighbourhoods, was in general not satisfactory. There were serious tensions between the Fijian natives and the Fijian Indian community, and they were almost equal in numbers; later the tensions further deteriorated and led to political confrontations and coups. There was a substantial Chinese community in Fiji before its independence in October 1970, but most of them made use of the opportunity offered by the Australian and New Zealand governments to migrate there, especially to the warmer parts of Australia like Brisbane.

In November 1975, Fiji terminated its diplomatic relations with Taiwan and switched to recognise the

People's Republic of China. The last ambassador from Taipei stayed on as head of a trade office, and the new ambassador arrived at Suva shortly before my teaching began at the University of the South Pacific. As the only Chinese teaching staff at the regional university and teaching international relations, I was approached by diplomats from both sides. I had a first taste of united front work there. Suva was a small city, and I understood that both sides knew that I met diplomats from both sides. The Chinese embassy wanted me to help organise a delegation of university staff and students to visit China. I left Fiji after a year and was no longer involved in this diplomatic competition.

I worked 13 hours a day, 6.5 days a week on preparing my lectures and doctoral thesis. At the end of my stay in Fiji, I finished my thesis and I was glad that my supervisors endorsed it. Dr. Bill Brugger had some reservations about my thesis focusing on China's Japan policy in the 1968 to 1974 period; he was sceptical that such a topic might not be able to produce good quality work. I was certainly relieved by then, and I had no serious difficulty securing my Ph. D. degree.

In spring 1977, the Chinese University of Hong Kong and then the University of Hong Kong advertised for lectureships in political science. I naturally applied for both positions in turn and was offered an assistant lecturer post first by the Chinese University of Hong Kong. At that time, the university asked new recruits to serve as assistant lecturers first, and they would be promoted to lecturer positions upon receiving their Ph.D. degrees. Hence, I returned to Hong Kong at the end of August 1977 to begin my long academic career in the territory's universities.

Grace was pregnant and she returned to Hong Kong ahead of me to set up our own home, our first ever in Hong Kong after marriage. My salary was not high, around HK$4,000 per month. Inflation was high though in 1977, especially with consumer goods, furniture, electrical appliances and labour costs. She soon found that our meagre savings in Fiji and Australia could not go very far.

We initially rented a flat in Tai Po. Tai Po was originally a traditional market town in the New Territories, which had been developed as part of the new town development programme in the 1970s. Grace was lucky to get a new three-bedroom flat with an open scenic view of the Pat Sin Range. It was not far from the Tai Po railway station, and it would only take half an hour to travel by train to the Chinese University of Hong Kong in Ma Liu Shui. The rent was $800 per month and amounted to only 60 percent of what we had to pay for a flat in a city district. Hong Kong was developing very rapidly in those years. On our way to the city from Tai Po, new buildings cropped up almost month by month.

Grace went for an interview at the Chinese University Library. She was asked why she would want to get a job so quickly after returning to Hong Kong given her current pregnancy. Later, she was informed by the

Personnel Section that they were very impressed with her qualification and experience, but the Librarian was hesitant in considering her appointment because of the fact that she was pregnant. Soon after, Grace managed to get a professional librarian position at the Hong Kong Polytechnic Library. She was asked to start work right away, even though she informed the Head Librarian during the interview that the baby would be due in four months' time. To this day, she is full of respect for the Librarian who gave her equal opportunities and a non-discriminatory treatment in her recruitment. Not many employers in Hong Kong could do this, even to this day.

Traditional values still predominated in the wish for male offsprings, especially in my parents' generation. My mother commented to Grace that if we had a boy, then "everything will be assured". If we had a girl, we "can still have chances later. So it doesn't matter much". Even though it was put in a diplomatic manner in her own way, we understood her meaning very well.

My daughter was born at the end of 1977 and my son came fourteen months afterwards. I did not spend enough time on the family as I should, and I was most grateful that Grace filled the gap. Before our son's arrival, my daughter stayed at my mother's house on our work days, and then stayed with us for the weekends. She cried a lot when she was with us especially in the middle of the night because of the weekly changes in environment. When our son was born, we employed a live-in Filipino helper to take care of both babies, but my mother still came to help out, and our daughter was obviously her favourite grandchild.

We finally settled down after five years abroad. Most of our university classmates had at least one promotion in their jobs, had a firm grasp of what they wanted to do, or otherwise had changed their jobs. Most of them were confident that they could go much further. Most had already bought their own first homes and cars. It was obvious that those who chose to pursue an academic career were handicapped in the initial stage of career development and had to face considerable uncertainties. I had a late start.

In the late 1970s and 1980s, civil service salaries were adjusted according to inflation every year and increased rapidly. Grace and I were not civil servants, but as public university employees, our salary scales were pegged to those of the civil service. Our incomes rose in a satisfactory manner, as most Hong Kong people did.

I was given college housing after living in Tai Po for one year, then when I reached the fourth point of the lecturer's salary scale, I was qualified for housing allowance. When I was promoted to senior lecturer in January 1986, I was given university housing in the campus, which was very spacious and comfortable. Throughout my academic career, housing conditions for my family had been very good by Hong Kong standards. However, those who had bought their own flats managed to do much better in terms of wealth because of the rapid growth in the price of their properties. University employees and civil servants had to find their own accommodation upon retirement, and they often faced a considerable decline in housing conditions.

I myself faced another handicap. Many of my colleagues at the Chinese University of Hong Kong had received their doctorate from top universities in the U.S. and their supervisors were well-known scholars. Flinders University was a relatively new university in Australia, and some colleagues openly said that they had never heard of the University. My supervisor, Dr. Bill Brugger, was still a lecturer when he provided me reference letters in support of my job applications, although he later became a top China studies scholar in Australia. Fortunately I started publications early, and soon I was able to prove myself with my list of publications in international journals.

In the subsequent decades, I often used my own example to encourage my students who for various reasons failed to do their postgraduate work at the top universities of the world. In comparison with engineering and science postgraduate students, Ph.D. candidates in the humanities and social sciences fields do not need world-class laboratories and equipment, they mainly need a tranquil environment to concentrate on their academic pursuits for a period of a few years. I recognised the advantages of pursuing one's Ph.D. programme in a top international university, but not many students from Hong Kong had these opportunities. The financial costs were substantial in the first place, and even outstanding academic results in universities in Hong Kong at the undergraduate and master's degree levels were often inadequate because of keen competition.

Doctoral degrees from the very top universities and reference letters from well-known scholars and doctoral programme supervisors could be very substantial assets in finding attractive starting positions. But in three years or so, if these were still one's major assets without solid publications, one would lose this advantage. My basic message to my students was this: do not lose heart if things do not go well for the time being, hard work always pays. An academic career is a lifelong pursuit, and commitment and dedication are very important.

Through an unexpected opportunity, I emerged as a media current affairs commentator in February 1979. I was invited as a discussant by Asia Television to comment on the Sino-Vietnamese border war. I probably performed quite well, and there was a vacuum to be filled. Local media were keen to look for commentators, and I was well qualified as I had a Ph.D. degree in political science, I was teaching in a public university, and I could speak Cantonese and English rather well and could explain issues in a concise way. Above all else, I was quite ready to express views critical of the government. Hence, I frequently appeared in the media and gained some recognition in the community. This has been my principal form of political participation till now, though naturally I have been much less active in recent years.

I was asked to serve as Dean of Students at the United College, Chinese University of Hong Kong. It was an annual concurrent appointment, though I served two terms (1980–1982). The arrangement was for a relatively young colleague to guide student activities. It was a recognition, but also a sacrifice. The job was very time-consuming, because the Dean of Students had to take part in almost all student activities, attend university meetings on student affairs, handle student disciplinary cases, etc. Since a vast majority of university colleagues had no difficulty getting tenure, and expectations regarding publications were far from severe at that time, young colleagues were asked to offer their time for college and university services.

My approach towards the college student union and student leaders was quite different from that of my predecessors. The latter adopted a guidance and monitor approach. They wanted to ensure that nothing would go wrong, and they wanted to help train student leaders. I treated the student leaders as equals. I would not interfere in their activities as far as possible, and wanted to secure their understanding and co-operation. I actively introduced some innovations.

In contrast to the student hostel arrangement at the University of Hong Kong, dormitory places at the Chinese

University of Hong Kong were inexpensive and very much sought after since transport to the university was not convenient in the early 1980s. The dormitory places were assigned on a needs basis: students living far away from the university campus and/or in a very crowded environment would be given higher priority. Hence, a student living in Cheung Chau (an offshore island) would almost be guaranteed a dormitory place, while someone living in Shatin (where Chinese University of Hong Kong is located) would have no chance at all unless his housing conditions were terrible.

The allocation of a dormitory place was primarily regarded as welfare, but I changed this thinking as I perceived it as an opportunity to enjoy university life. My plan was to enable every student to have a chance to live in the dormitory for one year so that he would have a better chance of taking part in student activities. At that time the university adopted a four-year system, and I suggested that students should exercise their dormitory options before the final year, as final year students were too absorbed by examinations and job applications and had no time for student activities. The innovation was soon followed by other colleges as well.

The idea of non-residential halls was also introduced while I was Dean of Students. The United College enjoyed the financial support of many rich Chinese businessmen. The latter were not approached by the University of Hong Kong yet; they had accumulated substantial wealth, and were eager to contribute to the upholding of traditional Chinese culture. The leaders of Hang Seng Bank were fine examples. The United College was therefore quite well endowed. Non-residential halls were actually two large rooms for the two respective halls so that non-resident students could have some comfortable space to conduct their activities.

Colleges in those years organised weekly or monthly meetings. The United College held a weekly seminar inviting speakers to talk to students every Friday around 11 a.m. These seminars were supposed to be part of college life and general education. I tried to secure eloquent speakers like Martin Lee to come. Attendance was higher than that in other colleges. But gradually, other colleges made seminar attendance compulsory, i.e., all students had to attend a fixed number of college seminars/assembly meetings per annum, and their attendance had to be formally registered. This solved the attendance problem, and college leaders were no longer embarrassed by the presence of less than twenty students. But the spirit was lost. Later, there were complaints of students reading newspapers while attending the college seminars (those were the days before smart phones). I failed to resist the trend, and the United College was the last to follow the compulsory attendance approach. Gradually I came to understand that student activities that were organised by the university authorities were least attractive to students.

Staff-student relations at the Chinese University in the 1980s were very good, at least at the Department of Government and Public Administration to which I belonged. Teaching load was quite heavy, about twelve hours per week, 50% higher than the local norm today. Research load was not high; some colleagues at that time could still get away with no publications at all. I received my tenure at the end of three years. Even those who did not perform well somehow often managed to secure their tenure with a delay of another two or three years. Under such circumstances, teachers had time for students, and we welcomed students for discussions any time. There were occasional basketball matches between staff and students. Sometimes we invited students for lunch at the staff canteen, and students enjoyed that. More frequently, we had tea in the student canteen. One of my colleagues would often ask students for a beer, though most staff members would not do that.

My political participation took another form. In the autumn of 1979, a friend and a columnist for the *South China Morning Post*, took me for a monthly dinner meeting of the Hong Kong Observers (香港觀察社), a group of local professionals in their thirties eager to demand the British administration to be responsive to the public through well-researched commentaries published in the newspapers. This group was different from the Reform Club and the Civic Association, which had been active in

1978. Staff-student soccer game at the Chinese University of Hong Kong.

Urban Council elections since the 1960s.[8] The Hong Kong Observers was probably a pioneer in the development of political opinion/discussion groups in the community in subsequent years.

This loose group probably had forty to fifty members, with active core membership of about ten including Anna Wu and Christine Loh, who later became members

---

8   The Reform Club and Civic Association were mainly electoral coalitions exploiting the Urban Council electoral system. Voters could vote for the same number of candidates as the number of seats to be filled. Hence candidates pooled their supporters together to vote for each other to maximise the number of common supporters to win the election. Some of the Urban Councillors like Elsie Elliott and Brook Bernacchi (a missionary and a liberal lawyer) emerged as spokespersons for grassroots interests in the 1960s and 1970s.

of the establishment. C.Y. Leung, the third Chief Executive of the HKSAR, was a member of the group for some time. Tsang Tak-sing, who worked for the Beijing backed Hong Kong newspaper *Ta Kung Pao* at that time, often attended the group's meetings without joining the group. He later became Secretary for Home Affairs of the HKSAR government.

The impact of the Hong Kong Observers depended solely on its ability to influence public opinion. At that time, the Murray MacLehose administration (1971–1982) was eager to show that it was responsive to public opinion. Despite the fact that I was quite a new member, I was invited to stand for election as chairman of the group. There were no other candidates, and I served as the group's chairman from 1980 to 1982. Soon after the election, two colleagues and I as the office-bearers of the group were invited to dine with the then Governor Sir Murray MacLehose at his official residence. This was an exceptional honour for young people who had no record of public service to speak of. It was probably Sir Murray's gesture to show the Hong Kong people and his senior officials that his administration was receptive to criticisms and respected public opinion.

There were groups of another kind in the late 1970s and 1980s, which were aimed at exerting pressure on the government through mobilisation of public opinion. These were labelled by the media as pressure groups. They fought for the interests of workers and poor people at the grassroots level, like supporting workers that had been laid off without proper compensation, opposing increasing fees for public utilities, etc. Lau Chin-shek and his Christian Industrial Committee were typical representatives of pressure group leaders and their organisations. These local activists gradually replaced politicians such as Elsie Elliott and Brook Bernacchi. It was significant that these two types of groups did not demand democratic reforms at that time. The Hong Kong Observers did not advocate an accountable government as it was not ready to ask the colonial regime to be accountable to the electorate.

I began to write articles in Chinese for the news magazines like *Ming Pao Monthly* (明報月刊), *The Seventies Monthly* (七十年代月刊), *Pai Shing Semi-monthly* (百姓半月刊), *The Hong Kong Economic Journal Monthly* (信報財經月刊), etc. I perceived this work as a service for the public, and I hoped that my research and academic studies would contribute to the development of civic society through the encouragement of enlightened deliberations. I was one of the first university academics to engage in these publications. Readers of these magazines were intellectuals and the educated public who were interested in current affairs, especially developments in mainland China. The existence of many such magazines demonstrated substantial readership.

Most of the social scientists at the University of Hong Kong were expatriates, and they did not write in Chinese.

At the Chinese University of Hong Kong, many social scientists came from Taiwan with postgraduate degrees from universities in the U.S.; they published in Chinese too, but through publishers and the media in Taiwan. I was among the first batch of political science graduates in Hong Kong, and the first to have completed a Ph.D. degree in political science overseas. Hence, I naturally received many invitations to write.

The incentive was largely a sense of satisfaction and perhaps a little fame. Relative to academic salaries, the fees were very low, sometimes as low as HK$20 per thousand words. In those days, the news magazines listed above accepted ten-thousand word articles, about five pages long. If I received HK$1,000 for such a piece, this would be considered generous remuneration. Usually I received HK$500 to HK$600 per piece. Hence, financially it was not rewarding.

Serious scholars might also think that their precious time should be spent on academic publications, as publications in news magazines were not counted in our annual performance assessment, but only as one's community service at best. In Taiwan and Mainland China on the other hand, academic salaries were low and payments for articles in newspapers and news magazines were relatively high. Sometimes such payments might even constitute a part of an academic's incomes.

In 1980, I was invited to plan a series of articles on Hong Kong for the new magazine *Chung Pao Monthly*

(中報月刊). I invited academic friends to examine developments in Hong Kong in various policy areas, and the articles were later published in 1981 as an edited volume: *Hong Kong in the 1980s – A Society in Transition* (八十年代的香港 — 轉型期的社會). Apparently this was the first serious book on Hong Kong in Chinese, and it appealed to the younger generations of concerned citizens and university students. It was sold quite well by Hong Kong standards, and each of the authors received more than one thousand dollars. As editor, I received no extra money, only six copies of the book. But I considered edited volumes in Chinese on Hong Kong studies met a need of the society, and I continued the venture, producing almost two dozen such edited books in the following decades. I realised that these activities reduced the time available for my serious orthodox academic research, and would handicap my promotional prospects and my university career.

In the era of economic reforms and opening to the external world, universities in Mainland China began to restore their departments in international politics, starting with Beijing University, Fudan University and Renmin University (People's University). The last one at that time was mainly a university for cadres. The discipline of political science was included in the international politics departments.

In late 1981, I was invited by Fudan University for an exchange programme, and I accepted the invitation.

Apparently Fudan University wanted to have a better understanding of the international politics/political science curriculum in Western universities. It could not approach the Western countries then, and it could not contact Taiwan, hence it chose Hong Kong. Regarding the two public universities in the territory, Fudan University avoided the expatriates; it also avoided the political science professors from Taiwan who often held U.S. passports. So I was chosen despite the fact that I was a young lecturer.

I spent two weeks in Fudan University during the holidays at the end of the semester in 1981/82, and I tried my best to help. I was housed in a small villa, which used to be the university president's residence and I was offered good food and services. The hostel staff boiled hot water for my bath in those cold winter days. I had in-depth discussions with three groups: the elderly professors who suffered in the Cultural Revolution and their teaching positions were restored in recent years; the new generation of teaching staff who had been in the research areas of international Communist movement, international labour movement, etc.; and students including postgraduate students.

The first group often included academics who had studied in Western countries before 1949. I could see that they had suffered much in the Cultural Revolution years because of their state of health, and I was impressed that they revealed no complaints nor grudge and were eager to serve with a renewed dignity. I treated them with much respect because of their dedication and commitment, and because of their age too. The younger generation of teaching staff engaged in discussions with me as equals. I could detect a sense of envy from them because of the salary I received in Hong Kong, my ample opportunities of going abroad, my access to research materials, etc. But at the same time they displayed a sense of pride and mission that they intended to serve their country which had already begun the venture into modernisation. They believed that they would be able to make a contribution. Some of them later became senior members of university management and famous scholars.

The students were curious and they did not hide their curiosity; they raised many blunt and honest questions. They demonstrated a similar sense of pride and mission as the new generation of teachers. University admissions were re-introduced in 1977, and the 1977–79 cohorts were mainly young people who had gone to the countryside in the Cultural Revolution era. They were mature students. They began to be aware that opportunities to study abroad emerged as some Western universities initiated the offer of postgraduate scholarships to the top universities in China then.

Beijing University soon approached me too, and I often visited the university in the following years. Universities in China at that time suffered from an acute funding shortage, and they could not pay for my travel, so I had to pay for my own airfares. The Chinese University of Hong Kong supported one overseas trip per annum for junior staff, I naturally saved the funding support for academic conferences in North America and Western Europe. Later, universities in China attempted to offer honours as compensation for scholars who offered help. They were given titles like visiting professors or guest professors (客座教授), and in the 1980s and 1990s, I collected over ten such titles from universities in Mainland China.

Despite my political participation and my role as media commentator, I was proud to say that I had not neglected my teaching duties. I offered my service as dean of students at United College for two years, and I was willing to spend time on students. As a teacher, I was happy to see students coming to me with academic questions. That was rare, but in my days at the Chinese University of Hong Kong, good students did come to visit their teachers with questions intended to initiate intellectual discussions. At the end of the academic year, they came to talk about their career development. But unfortunately, the usual knocks on the door were enquiries about examination syllabi and requests to delay the submission of assignments.

In 1987, I was elected "Best Teacher" of the Department of Government and Public Administration. I dare not say I was the best teacher. Other colleagues were excellent teachers too. Yet I was recognised by students as a caring and dedicated teacher and I was very proud to be a winner in the only competition held in my twelve years at the Chinese University of Hong Kong.

Course preparation was a heavy burden for young lecturers. This was especially so at our department at the Chinese University of Hong Kong. There were about nine colleagues in the department, half in the field of public administration and half in the field of political science. In the political science field, three or four of us had a background in international relations. I was allowed to teach a course in Chinese foreign policy and a half course in Japanese politics, which were my research areas; I also had to teach a first-year foundation courses in political science as well as a political philosophy. I only completed a political philosophy course in my undergraduate years, but in view of the human resource conditions within the department, a junior staff member had to accept teaching assignments quite outside of his research expertise. At any rate, as the teaching duties stabilised, the time needed for course preparation also declined.

In the early 1980s, Hong Kong's future was officially brought up. The times were uncertain: we didn't know where we stood, and what we would be doing in the next five or ten years. It was fortunate for me that I had some good opportunities to travel then. The Chinese University of Hong Kong had established many exchange programmes with foreign universities. Through them I made my first visits to France and Japan.

In December 1980, through the arrangement between the University and the French Foreign Ministry, I visited Paris and delivered talks at the universities and research institutes attended by well-known French sinologists. I was taken to do some sightseeing outside Paris during the weekends, and I visited the Versailles, the Louvre Museum, the Chatres Cathedral, and many other places. I was impressed.

As a political scientist, I certainly treasured these opportunities of learning the politics and cultures of other countries. Besides the exchanges and talks with local scholars, I happened to meet a few graduates from the Chinese University of Hong Kong who had worked in Hong Kong for one year to save up money for the sake of wandering in Europe for half a year. Not many people did that in those days. One of them became a postgraduate student in Paris. It was nice to learn more about post-graduate life in Paris. I did not spend much money on shopping, but I was quite generous when it came to holidays abroad with my family.

In June/July 1982, I went to Japan on an exchange programme with Soka University, which is situated some 30 kilometres from Tokyo. In those days, public transport from the University to Tokyo was not very convenient. It took half an hour by bus to the train station and another 1.5 hours by train to Tokyo. Japanese were very polite; the University sent someone to pick me up at the airport, and gave me a flat for my accommodation. They also arranged for me to meet the university president, the board's chairman, and deans. I also met with professors from the political science department, which was attached to the Faculty of Law.

I used the Metropolitan Railroad system to visit various universities and institutes in Tokyo. The system was complicated, even though I was accompanied by a bilingual exchange student who was supposed to know more about the system than I did. There was the National Rail, then there were various private subway lines. The fares were expensive. The Paris system was by comparison much simpler. It was difficult to navigate the change of railway lines when visiting various places including the Catholic Sophia University, the Hitotsubashi University (a private university) and the Komeito party headquarters.

In August 1982, the U.S. government invited me for a five-week tour of the U.S. through a visitor programme designed for potential political leaders all over the world. The ten members of the delegation included a speaker, members of parliament, academics and civil society leaders from various countries such as Ireland, and India. Some of them were quite experienced or senior in rank.

I felt welcomed as I was picked up personally at the airport of Washington D.C. and driven to the hotel. Two officers from the State Department offered to take me around the capital for a tour. My first impression of Washington D.C. was good, a lovely city with clean and well-planned tree-lined avenues, open air coffee shops, etc. Visitors could often see hordes of office workers starting work at 7 a.m. because of the flexi-time system. People in the streets were often dressed in suits. Later I learnt that the city had its poor neighbourhoods.

The programme especially in the capital was very compact and demanding. We had up to three seminars and two meetings in one day. We had to go through a lot of reading materials beforehand. We were taken to visit the White House and the U.S. Congress. There were valuable exposures to the actual workings of political parties and civic society groups, and there was much to learn from members of the delegation. At the White House, the delegation was greeted by polite, well-dressed and bejewelled ladies often deemed to be rich men's wives recruited by the Reagans. They were good in making polite remarks, but were not able to answer my questions, for example, on the economy.

We received VIP treatments in various places like we were foreign dignitaries: we were occasionally received by the state governors and city majors, as for examples, in Philadelphia and Salt Lake City. There were receptions and visits to NGOs, campaign quarter of a candidate for the Senate race, the trade unions, and the like. Very often, such events were reported in the local media.

The delegation was invited to attend many impressive cultural programmes too. The tour allowed me to see different parts of the U.S. that I had never visited before

– Philadelphia, Utah, Minnesota, Wisconsin, Alabama, and so on. Once we left Washington D.C, we were warned not to wander in the streets alone, especially at night.

I had a taste of family life in the U.S. while we were invited to participate in what they called "home hospitality programmes", and that is, to stay in American people's homes. We stayed overnight with local families in rural areas, and one of the hosts was the local chief of police. The cost of living in major cities was high; eating out was expensive given the relatively low salary of academics (around US$22,000–25,000 a year in 1982). I read from newspapers that unemployment was high among the black population in Washington D.C. – 18% of adults and 88% of teenagers were unemployed at that time. In some cities, I actually saw poor black people wandering in the streets looking like beggars. Dirty work and manual labour were taken up by the non-white population.

There is no denial, however, that the U.S. is a democratic and prosperous country. It is an important leader of the international community and has a lot to offer, though it also has its challenges and problems. It was the time when Margaret Thatcher was about to visit China to talk about Hong Kong's future. Most people I met, especially the well-informed, heard about the expiry of the New Territories lease in Hong Kong. They asked me a lot of questions on Hong Kong's future. I was not able to tell them much. The sense of uncertainty loomed large.

Chapter 6

Hong Kong's Future Was Sealed behind Closed Doors

Confidence crisis 1983. Britain's "honourable" retreat in the Sino-British negotiations. China promised "Hong Kong People Governing Hong Kong". Change was inevitable. Hong Kong's identity, pride and resilience.

In the late 1970s and early 1980s, the lease of the New Territories (which would expire on July 1, 1997) and the future of Hong Kong attracted a lot of attention and discussions[9]. A number of legal experts, academics and civic groups in Hong Kong came forward to suggest ways to negotiate a settlement. Since it was in the interest of all parties concerned to maintain Hong Kong's stability and prosperity, any arrangement reached had to satisfy the demands and wishes of the Hong Kong people.

---

9 See, for example, David Bonavia, *Hong Kong 1997*, Hong Kong: South China Morning Post, 1983; and Joseph Y.S. Cheng, "The future of Hong Kong: a Hong Kong belonger's view", *International Affairs (London)*, Vol. 58, No. 3, July 1982, pp. 476-488.

Otherwise, an exodus of talents and capital would be inevitable, and for those who could not emigrate for one reason or another, their morale and enthusiasm for socio-economic development could not be guaranteed. As such, stability and prosperity could hardly be maintained.

In the early 1980s, the Hong Kong Observers, a political discussion group of local professionals with considerable influence on public opinion, was engaged in the community's deliberations on the territory's future[10]. A public opinion survey, probably the most detailed and the best ever carried out on the subject, was initiated by the Hong Kong Observers and conducted by Survey Research Hong Kong Ltd.[11]. As its chairman, I was responsible for the design and supervision of the poll, which was funded by members' donations. After a year's discussions and preparation, the actual field work was carried out between May 10 and June 11, 1982. One thousand people between the ages of 15 and 60 were interviewed face to face; a total of 71 questions were asked and each interview lasted about forty minutes.

When asked how acceptable the respondents thought each of the five solutions or options, 95% of the people

---

[10] "Pressure Points: a Social Critique by the Hong Kong Observers" is a collection of essays on topics such as the government, law, police, education, etc., published by Summerson Eastern Publishers (Hong Kong) in 1981.

[11] See Joseph Y.S. Cheng, "The Future of Hong Kong: Surveys of the Hong Kong People's Attitudes", *The Australian Journal of Chinese Affairs*, No. 12, July 1984, pp. 113-142.

wanted to maintain the "status quo", which was defined by those polled as "freedom of speech", "comfortable living environment", "freedom of choice", and "economic freedom". Two-thirds felt acceptable about "Hong Kong remaining under British administration but under Chinese sovereignty"; two-fifths thought it acceptable about "Hong Kong becoming a Special Economic Zone"; one-third thought the same about "independence"; and a quarter thought "a return to China" acceptable or alright. The main reasons given for the acceptability of the *status quo* solution were: satisfaction with the existing situation, that there would be no change, and the freedoms enjoyed at this time.

The vast majority of Hong Kong people were politically apathetic and did not like to be involved in politics. They also felt impotent and helpless in deciding their future. In the survey by the Hong Kong Observers, 97% of the respondents revealed that they had made no preparations for the evolution of Hong Kong's future. As for the reasons, one-third indicated that they lacked the capability and were resigned to fate, and one in five responded that they did not know how to prepare. Nearly half believed that China had the largest say in determining Hong Kong's future, and not the Governor of Hong Kong. In fact, over half said they had never discussed the future of Hong Kong. This sense of impotence and helplessness obviously was a major cause of apathy.

As a leader of the Hong Kong Observers and a popular media commentator, I was often presented by the British administration to visitors from Britain as part of the "symbolic opposition", so I came to meet many visiting Members of Parliament, officials from the Foreign Office responsible for Hong Kong affairs, etc. I also had the opportunities of meeting foreign consular officials stationed in Hong Kong, especially those from the U.S. and Japan.

I remained critical of the British government's position and that of the British administration, so the latter had no intention of cultivating me through the process of "administrative absorption". Apparently senior officials of the British administration were eager to have a good understanding of the attitudes of the concerned public so as to better formulate their policies; discussions with the Hong Kong Observers and similar groups were perceived as important arrangements to develop this understanding. Those who were involved in these discussions also valued the opportunities of articulating their views to the British administration. Gradually, I realised that it was almost impossible for us to influence the position of the British administration.

The issue of the territory's future had become an important agenda of the British administration since the late 1970s, and in March 1979, the then Hong Kong Governor, Sir Murray MacLehose, made an official visit to Beijing. In June 1980, in preparation for de-colonisation, the district administration scheme whereby universal suffrage and the elections of district boards were introduced by the then British administration. Existing political groups such as the Hong Kong Observers were encouraged to take part, and there was a promise that a number of elected district board members would be appointed to the Legislative Council, the law-making body in Hong Kong. Further, district board members would receive generous allowances, which would enable them to serve their respective electorates and establish community networks.

My active participation in the Hong Kong Observers, the Hong Kong Prospect Institute and numerous media interviews and exposure in the early 1980s led the public and my peers to believe or expect that I would enter politics. Senior officials of the then Hong Kong government encouraged me to run for District Board elections; I guess that, given time, I could have won a seat in the Legislative Council too. But I was not tempted. I wanted to become an established academic and a respected critic and commentator on the political scene, so as to preserve my integrity, dignity and honesty.

Although my wife Grace said that she would respect and support whatever choice I made in my career, she also made it clear that she did not aspire to become a politician's wife. In the 1983–84 academic year, it was my turn to enjoy my sabbatical year after working six years in the Chinese University of Hong Kong. I went to Australia and managed to do some serious research;

I was concerned that I should produce substantial academic publications[12].

In September 1982, Mrs. Margaret Thatcher, the then British Prime Minister, visited China and reached an agreement with Chinese leaders to "enter into talks through diplomatic channels with the common aim of maintaining the stability and prosperity of Hong Kong". There remained however serious differences between the two sides on the questions of sovereignty over Hong Kong, Kowloon and the New Territories, as well as the "unequal treaties".[13] Chinese leaders declared their resolution to regain sovereignty over all three areas. They would not recognise the unequal treaties signed by the Qing Dynasty government and the British Empire. The British side, on the other hand, insisted that the treaties were valid and legally binding.

In response to the British negotiating stance, the position of the Chinese government hardened and it rejected any suggestion of retaining the British

---

12   My book, *Hong Kong in Search of a Future* [Oxford University Press] was published in December 1984. It became an essential reference providing in depth coverage of official and semiofficial documents of the British, Chinese and Hong Kong governments on the future of Hong Kong. It covers a wide spectrum of views not only from the governments but also from various interest groups at the historical moment on or before the formal signing of the Sino-British Joint Declaration in 1984.

13   For a good analysis of the questions of the "unequal treaties" and sovereignty over Hong Kong, Kowloon and the New Territories, see Anthony Dicks, "Treaty, Grant, Usage or Sufferance? Some Legal Aspects of the Status of Hong Kong", *China Quarterly*, No. 95, September 1983, pp. 427-455.

administration beyond 1997. It presented its own scheme of *"gangren zhigang* (Hong Kong people governing Hong Kong)"; Hong Kong would become a Special Administrative Region (SAR) under Chinese sovereignty, enjoy the privileges of self-administration, and retain its current systems.

The Chinese media naturally lauded Deng Xiaoping's success in the negotiation. After the talk, Margaret Thatcher tripped outside the steps of the Great Hall of the People in Beijing and was reported in the front page of Beijing-backed newspaper Ta Kung Pao as a shock reaction over Deng's "extremely firm and stern words".

The student unions of the territory's tertiary institutions all came out openly in support of Beijing's position regarding the "unequal treaties". I also openly articulated a position similar to that of the university student unions. The vast majority of Hong Kong people held the same view too, though they avoided taking a position publicly. They generally felt very uncertain about their future as change appeared inevitable. In fact, the Hong Kong Observers, in its discussions on the territory's future, came to the same conclusion that change was inevitable, and the group presented this position publicly in its newspaper articles.

The existing political establishment in Hong Kong was worried, and the responsible members of the Hong Kong Observers were invited to dinner at the residence of Legislative Councillor Lydia Dunn before the Sino-British negotiations formally began. Sir S.Y. Chung was present. They were the most important leaders of the Legislative Council and Executive Council who had faithfully toed the line of British administration in Hong Kong. Sir S.Y. Chung asked us if we knew what united front meant; he was obviously concerned that we had been unduly influenced by the Chinese authorities' united front offensive. I offered detailed definitions of the united front concept and strategy, and our group appealed to the two leaders to unite the Hong Kong community to articulate its concerns and demands.

The Chinese authorities' united front offensive was indeed very effective in Hong Kong. In July 1985, when the Drafting Committee for the Basic Law (Hong Kong's constitution) was inaugurated, Sir S.Y. Chung joined the Committee and was seen on television respectfully receiving the appointment certificate. Lydia Dunn instead chose to return to Britain for her retirement. What I predicted about the common interests between Beijing, London and the Hong Kong establishment came true.

The pro-Beijing united front started to approach the Hong Kong Observers in 1982 through Mary Lee, a reporter for *Far Eastern Economic Review*. She was the principal writer of the group's newspaper columns for the *South China Morning Post*, while I was responsible for their translation into Chinese for *Ming Pao*.[14] The group

---

14 See *Ming Pao* (a Hong Kong Chinese newspaper), July 6, 1989.

was invited to the New China News Agency Hong Kong Branch at Happy Valley; our contact was Li Jusheng, a deputy head of the branch.

It was very interesting to see how Li's charm worked on a group of Western-educated elites in Hong Kong. He was very well-prepared, and he spoke Cantonese, the main dialect spoken by most local people in Hong Kong, which made communications much easier. He had been stationed in Hong Kong for a long time, and he understood Hong Kong people's values and thinking well. As the very contents of the Sino-British Joint Declaration demonstrated, the Chinese authorities worked very hard to understand the factors behind the territory's success as well as the worries of the Hong Kong people, and to provide appropriate re-assurances to maintain the territory's stability and prosperity.

Some were disappointed in hindsight at how Margaret Thatcher gradually retreated in Sino-British negotiations and failed to safeguard the best interests of the Hong Kong people. The new British Nationality Act, which came into force on January 1, 1983, was a good example of the minimisation of British responsibility over and commitment towards Hong Kong. Under the Act, Hong Kong's 2.6 million Chinese who were previously registered as British subjects would become "citizens of the British dependent territory of Hong Kong". This meant that when Hong Kong ceased to become a British dependent territory, they would be stateless. It was not surprising that Hong Kong people was not able to develop a sense of identity with the British administration, nor did they feel that they had citizens' rights and responsibilities.

Negotiations between Britain and China on Hong Kong's future were held in secrecy. Hong Kong citizens were not informed at all until an agreement was reached. It was a *fait accompli*. London argued that the complicated negotiation process, if it were public, would merely give rise to unnecessary concern and speculation in the community. The negotiation had to be carried out in secrecy without Hong Kong people's participation. Hong Kong people would simply have to accept this.

Before the formal Sino-British negotiations on the territory's future started, some leading businessmen in Hong Kong approached the Hong Kong Observers through their representatives to deliberate on the idea of a "I love Hong Kong Campaign". The idea was to show China, Britain and the world what Hong Kong people would like to have for their future, and to articulate their demands for freedom of movement and free enterprise. The campaign, with initial support from trade unions and student unions, pressure groups and church bodies, was intended to gather a million signatures and to generate a voice of the Hong Kong community in the international society. But immediately after the announcement of the start of the negotiations, these contacts stopped and the proposal was abandoned. It appeared that the British administration was reluctant to see Hong Kong people getting organised in a mass movement. My term as chairman of the Hong Kong Observers ended in 1982, and Christine Loh replaced me.

As the Sino-British negotiations progressed, more and more Hong Kong people suspected that both the British government and the British administration in Hong Kong had already been preparing for the worst, and meanwhile were making use of Hong Kong and would not make commitments regarding its future. Among the political activists who attempted to promote democracy in the 1980s, there was a general perception that Britain could not be relied upon. There were few fond memories of the British authorities among them, in contrast to the young radicals who waved the British flag and the Hong Kong colonial flag in pro-democracy protest rallies in the recent decade of the 2010s.

The New China News Agency Hong Kong Branch in preparation for the Sino-British negotiations organised many delegations to visit Beijing. This was part of the scheme to consult Hong Kong people and listen to their concerns about the territory's future. But it was also a united front tactic to cultivate support, grant and show recognition to those invited, and build a pro-Beijing united front network. These delegations also facilitated

Chinese leaders to convey messages to Hong Kong people, either directly through their statements made in receiving the delegations or indirectly through the delegations' reports to the media.

I participated in two such delegations, the first a delegation of university academics and professional leaders, and the other a delegation of the Hong Kong Observers. The first delegation arrived at Beijing in April 1983; I was a junior lecturer then and I had time to do ample observations. The New China News Agency Hong Kong Branch sent staff members to accompany the delegation; I suspected that they were responsible for assessing individual members of the delegation too, regarding their political attitudes, views on Hong Kong's future, etc.

April 1983. Hong Kong Academic Delegation to Beijing met with Liao Cheng Zhi.

The head of the delegation, Cheung Yau-kai (張佑啓), was a famous engineering professor, and during the trip, many of his old classmates in Beijing came to see him. One could easily detect their suffering in the Cultural Revolution and their envy for Professor Cheung. I wondered if they had entertained the idea of what would have happened to them had they followed Cheung's example of studying abroad and working overseas instead of staying back in Mainland China.

In December 1983, the Hong Kong Observers delegation headed by Anna Wu visited Beijing in December 1983; I was no longer very much involved because of my sabbatical leave arrangement, but I joined the delegation at the request of Anna. When we arrived at the Beijing airport, there was no one to receive us, and we were uncertain concerning the schedules and agenda of the meetings. We felt that it was a cold reception on Beijing's part.

Ching Cheong (程翔) was the correspondent of the pro-Beijing *Wen Wei Po* at that time; he came to see the delegation and offered some re-assurances. He hinted that the Hong Kong and Macau Affairs Office was not happy that the group's statement had not clearly stated that Hong Kong's sovereignty belongs to the People's Republic of China, and the Chinese authorities wanted to indicate their dissatisfaction.

The subsequent meetings, however, went relatively well. We had many hours of in-depth discussions with

Li Hou (李後) and Lu Ping (魯平) from the Hong Kong and Macau Affairs Office. They were key members of the Chinese government's policy team on Hong Kong issues in the 1980s and 1990s. Though Li Hou was more senior, Lu Ping seemed to lead the discussions. His knowledge of Hong Kong and his Western educational background impressed the delegation. We later learnt that various Hong Kong groups that had met him found his performance impressive too. As a student of Chinese politics, I tried to understand the tactics and strategies of China's united front offensive towards Hong Kong in these two visits to Beijing.

From 1982 to 1985, there was concern for the future of Hong Kong. Many grassroots pressure groups and political organisations emerged from this concern to face the challenge posed by the development of representative government. At the time of Mrs. Margaret Thatcher's visit to China in September 1982, many Hong Kong people preferred a leader like Lee Kuan Yew, the Prime Minister of Singapore.

By 1984, they raised a more sophisticated question: could a strong political party that was acceptable to the Chinese authorities, the British administration in Hong Kong and the local business community be formed? They were hoping that if members of this party could include respected figures from all social strata, it would be able to win the community's trust, to win major elections, and to form a government capable of maintaining the territory's stability and prosperity.

The pro-democracy activists at the time of the Sino-British negotiations shared an ideal, that the return of Hong Kong to the Motherland would offer an opportunity to witness democratisation in the territory (民主回歸). Hong Kong's younger generation and the educated public believed that only an elected government could effectively represent and advance its citizens' interests and sustain the international status of Hong Kong. A close co-ordination between China's central government and that of the Hong Kong SAR would be essential after the handover in 1997. In handling this relationship, the Hong Kong government needed to be directly accountable to its people. I certainly shared this view.

Hong Kong's existing international status and identity would be crucial to its further economic development. To be able to negotiate with other governments on economic and trade issues, Hong Kong, as the SAR under Chinese sovereignty, had to be recognised and accepted by the international community. A representative government would be well placed to gain this recognition, and be able to protect Hong Kong's interests in international negotiations which are unrelated to China's sovereignty. Self-administration would be the most important and attractive element in the return of Hong Kong to China.

This idealistic pursuit of democracy involved considerable trust in the Chinese leadership led by Deng Xiaoping. China began its economic reforms and opening to the external world at the end of 1978. The intelligentsia in Mainland China and the pro-democracy activists in Hong Kong shared high expectations of modernisation, including political modernisation, in China. My understanding of Chinese politics cautioned me that it would not be likely that the Chinese authorities would grant genuine democracy to the territory, but I was ready to support Hong Kong's pro-democracy movement.

The British government at the beginning of the negotiations tried to maintain the position that the British Empire secured Hong Kong, Kowloon and the New Territories lease through legal treaties with the Qing Dynasty. It then retreated to the position of maintaining the British administration in Hong Kong, hoping to exchange sovereignty for administration in a transitional period beyond 1997. China, on the other hand, was fully aware that the resolution of the 1997 issue in Hong Kong would pave the way for the reunification of China and Taiwan. The Chinese government openly rejected this British position in August 1983, condemning its idea in attempting to separate administration and sovereignty, and expressing China's confidence that Hong Kong people could govern Hong Kong. In the same month, the Chinese Communist Party General Secretary Hu Yaobang said that China planned to take over Hong Kong on July 1, 1997.

Hong Kong people were worried about their future. By September 1983, a confidence crisis started to emerge in Hong Kong, which had a toll on Hong Kong's highly open economy. Hong Kong dollar had a dramatic fall against the U.S. dollar and other currencies, and the property prices took a dive. Panic buying of essential food stuff was apparent, especially when people saw near-empty supermarket shelves and long queues in the checkouts with overloaded trolleys of rice, cooking oils, canned food and the like. My mother told me that our neighbour tried to carry home three large sacks of rice weighing 15 kilograms each and twisted her back during the process. (In those days, deliveries from the very few supermarkets were not common in Hong Kong.) The rice would have lasted his family for three months!

In December 1984, after two years and many rounds of arduous negotiations, the Sino-British Joint Declaration on the Future of Hong Kong was signed. From then till June 1997, Hong Kong entered a stage of transition. London had to settle for securing an arrangement acceptable to Hong Kong people, hence the pledges made by the Chinese government to Hong Kong people in the Sino-British Joint Declaration. Hong Kong people, however, did not have a say in the diplomatic negotiations. Many of them were disappointed as the British government was too eager to seek an "honourable" retreat. In ensuring that the retreat was "honourable", the British government and the colonial administration told the community that it had to accept the entire agreement or face the prospects of no agreement at all. Both governments promised continued prosperity and stability. An independent commission was formed to assess Hong Kong people's acceptance of the agreement, and I was surprised that a piece of my commentary was prominently quoted in the commission's report.

My basic assessment was that as far as the articles of the Sino-British Joint Declaration were concerned, there was not much more that Hong Kong people could ask for. The challenge ahead was whether Chinese leaders would keep the promises made. In discussions with close friends then, I often said that there would be an 80% chance that stability and prosperity would be maintained; regarding the freedoms that Hong Kong people enjoyed, there might be some minor erosions, but I was quite doubtful regarding the promise of democracy since there was, as yet, no concrete mechanism to safeguard Hong Kong's autonomy after 1997.

Before the initialling of the Sino-British Joint Declaration, the British administration published a *Green Paper on the Further Development of Representative Government in Hong Kong* in July 1984. The Green Paper presented three objectives. The first of which was "to develop progressively a system of government the authority for which is firmly rooted in Hong Kong, which is able to represent authoritatively the views of the people of Hong Kong, and which is more directly accountable to the people of Hong Kong". To those who supported democratisation and political reform, this stance was a morale booster.

The local business leaders would be prepared to participate in the development of a representative government through political parties to articulate their interests if necessary. In 1984–1985, two members of both the Legislative and Executive Councils, Maria Tam and Allen Lee, made preparations to form political groups which could develop into political parties. Such political groups would include the central figures from the establishment, and representatives from major business conglomerates and rich families. Maria Tam formally launched the Progressive Hong Kong Society. Nevertheless, if the political system of the future Hong Kong SAR did not differ too much from the existing colonial political system, these preparations would become redundant.

After the release of the Green Paper in July 1984, some business leaders openly opposed the proposal to have direct elections to the Legislative Council. A few even went so far as to point out that they would prefer Beijing's appointees to those directly elected to run Hong Kong. They fully believed in the Chinese leadership's sincerity and determination to maintain the territory's stability and prosperity. They were confident that the

Chinese authorities would respect and promote their interests. An elected government, accountable to the electorate and hoping to win the next election, would find it difficult to resist the pressure to offer more social services, which in turn might damage business interests.

Further, many business leaders thought that a Hong Kong government appointed by Beijing would be more predictable and stable than an elected one. (Lee Kuan Yew and his colleagues thought likewise.) They believed that they were capable and experienced enough to deal with Beijing's appointees. They harboured deep suspicion against the leaders of grassroots pressure groups, and felt that they did not have common values with them. They did not like the uncertainty in having to bargain with an elected administration accountable to the electorate. Finally, these businessmen felt that a government appointed by Beijing would be able to maintain a direct dialogue with Chinese leaders and would therefore be in a better position to withstand pressures from the cadres of Chinese organs in Hong Kong, the Guangdong provincial government or the relevant ministries in Beijing.

I had no intention of joining political parties then. But I closely followed the developments as an academic researcher and media commentator. The latter role offered me opportunities to attend some meetings observing the behaviour and thinking of the future political leaders.

Chinese officials responsible for Hong Kong and Macau affairs attempted to dampen the increasing political reform fervour through various channels. Officials of the New China News Agency in Hong Kong tried to convey two clear messages in their contacts with the local community. The first was that, according to the Sino-British Joint Declaration, the British government's commitment was to return the sovereignty and administration of the territory to China, not to the people of Hong Kong; the second was that when the Chinese authorities promised to maintain the *status quo* for 50 years after 1997, they were referring to the *status quo* at the time of the conclusion of the Joint Declaration in 1984, not to the situation in 1997.

The Chinese authorities were not happy with the rapid process aiming at political reforms. They were suspicious of the intent of the then Hong Kong government. Xu Jiatun, then head of the Hong Kong Branch of the New China News Agency, finally issued a public warning in November 1985. In his first press conference held since his arrival two years earlier, Xu warned that political reforms in the transitional period should converge with the Basic Law, Hong Kong's "constitution". Since then, it appeared that both London and the British administration in Hong Kong had abandoned the initiative regarding political reforms in the transitional period, and their officials only emphasised on convergence with the Basic Law.

In July 1985, membership of the Basic Law Drafting Committee was announced. It was obvious that Beijing put top priority on Hong Kong's prosperity and stability over political reforms. In the committee of 59 members, there were twenty-three members from Hong Kong, most of them prominent businessmen and leading professionals. The interests of the establishment apparently were assured, as the Chinese authorities were keen to retain Hong Kong's attractiveness to investors. The approach was very clear in Deng Xiaoping's famous and often quoted reassurance to the Basic Law Drafting Committee members that "Horse racing will continue, as will dancing (馬照跑, 舞照跳)".

The readiness to demonstrate concern for investors' interests had dominated the Chinese authorities' approach to Hong Kong. They realised that as an international financial centre, money could enter and leave Hong Kong very easily. In the 1980s, Hong Kong was the principal source of foreign investment in China, supplying over 60% of external funding in support of China's modernisation, including that from overseas Chinese communities through Hong Kong. I attended and participated in many public forums in the 1980s, representatives of labour groups often shared this view: they indicated that they wanted investors to stay, and they had no intention to scare them away through unreasonable demands. By early 1985, there was a share market boom. Even though British capital was withdrawing, there were acquisition activities, and the local and overseas Chinese capital was returning. Yet the purchasing power of locals was still weak, as most taxi drivers could tell you. Unemployment began to rise.

After the conclusion of the Sino-British Joint Declaration, the emphasis of the Chinese authorities' united front strategy soon shifted from the pro-democracy groups and the universities' student unions to the business community and the existing political establishment. The latter realised that the British administration had to depart in 1997, and accepted the political embrace from Beijing. Many of them received invitations to visit their home towns in Mainland China, and were warmly welcomed by the local cadres. They were generous in making donations to the infrastructural and philanthropic projects there, building schools and homes for the elderly, and so on. The major business tycoons in Hong Kong however avoided serous investment in Mainland China at this stage. They did not invest in major projects in China until the early 1990s.

The professional elites and the middle-class families in Hong Kong responded to the political changes in various ways. A proportion of them chose to emigrate, or planned to emigrate. In some cases, they did so as an "insurance policy". Some moved their families abroad first and the husbands returned to Hong Kong to work. Some young parents attempted to have their babies born in Western countries to secure foreign passports for their offspring.

The majority of the professionals and middle-class families, however, adopted a wait-and-see attitude. 1997 was thirteen years away, and they could still observe for a while. For those who could afford to, they would send their children to study overseas (their favourite countries being Canada, Australia and the U.S.), hoping that they had a better chance to get a job and stay there eventually. Some tried overseas postings in international firms and wished that they would be able to stay there permanently if needed.

Most major business corporations considered that China was such a major market that could not be ignored. There were those who were bold and adventurous and wanted to be ahead of the others in the development of this market. So they sought every opportunity to approach the Chinese authorities and enterprises for business opportunities, though they also understood the risks and difficulties involved. As a result, there emerged a business and professional group of "China hands" or "China experts".

They had a lot of stories to tell. My entrepreneurial school friend proudly related that if he managed to make three long-distance calls from Beijing or Shanghai in a day, he would consider that day well spent. (There were no mobile phones then.) There were worries about frequent business travels to China by air in the 1980s.

The Civil Aviation Administration of China (with its initial CAAC) was given another meaning "<u>C</u>ancel <u>A</u>t <u>A</u>ll <u>C</u>ost" because of the worry about its safety. Challenges and crises give rise to opportunities; this has always been the spirit of Hong Kong people.

Some groups of professionals and academics adopted a positive attitude towards the changeover, and were eager to contribute to the modernisation of China. They were engaged in all types of exchanges with their counterparts in Mainland China, introducing knowledge and knowhow from the outside world, as well as the Hong Kong way of managing and doing things.

I continued my academic exchanges with universities in Mainland China, especially the international politics department of Beijing University. I maintained my dialogue with the elderly academics, the younger generation of university teachers and the students. The latter group was especially impressive, and their command of English was not much inferior to the top students in Hong Kong. They were hard-working and well-read; they mainly had to rely on the Chinese translations of books by famous foreign scholars though. Apparently they were quite attracted by the writings of Henry Kissinger at that time. In preparation for overseas study, they often memorised a small dictionary, doing one or two pages every day. This explained why they did very well in the TOEFL examination but could not speak English fluently.

The waves of emigration opened up promotion prospects for those willing to stay in Hong Kong. Promotions became considerably more rapid not only because of emigration, but also because of the general trend of expansion of the civil service and business corporations. The localisation on the part of the British administration and the major British enterprises such as the Hong Kong and Shanghai Banking Corporation and Jardine Matheson accelerated.

China's economic reforms and opening to the external world offered opportunities to the grassroots workers too. Some factory workers who were entrepreneurial and ambitious went to set up workshops at the Pearl River Delta. With a bit of luck and much hard work, they often managed to serve as sub-contractors and eventually established their own factories in China. Others worked as small traders, which required very little initial capital. Despite the political uncertainties, the Hong Kong economy benefitted from China's economic reforms.

The Hong Kong Observers gradually faded out of the political scene in the mid-1980s. There were some serious internal discussions on its future orientation. Even before the start of the Sino-British negotiations, the group considered that change would be inevitable, meaning that the *status quo* could not be maintained. However, in the transition to 1997, a political discussion group like the Hong Kong Observers would have a limited role to play; it had to be transformed into a political participation group, which was the initial stage of a political party.

The major distinction was that a political participation group had to take part in elections at all levels. Apparently most members of the group were quite successful in their business and professional careers, and they were not ready to pursue an almost full-time political career. In this way, the group was willing to make way for others. I myself understood that one could not try to become an accomplished academic and a successful politician at the same time, and my choice was clear.

Hong Kong People's Association (港人協會) was a political organisation formed in 1984. It was a group of lawyers, academics and professionals who were concerned with Hong Kong's future. Many of its members, like Elsie Leung Oi-sie (梁愛詩) and Anthony Neoh (梁定邦), later assumed important public offices. Audrey Eu (余若薇) who later became a prominent leader of the Civic Party, also participated in its activities. The Association certainly possessed the talents and appeal to become an important political group participating in the coming elections. It produced some publications on Hong Kong law, engaged in important exchanges with the Shenzhen University, and so on. It gradually faded away after an active period in 1984–85. Probably, it had the same weakness as the Hong Kong Observers; its key members were reluctant to opt for almost full-time political careers.

I had another glimpse of how the pro-Beijing united front had been quietly operating. When the Basic Law Consultative Committee was formed in 1985, I was approached by a good friend teaching social work at the Chinese University of Hong Kong. I declined to join and preferred to remain as a commentator. I was a bit surprised though that my academic friend had assumed the role to approach and recruit members for the Basic Law Consultative Committee.

The Hong Kong community demonstrated respectable resilience in facing the challenge of its uncertain future. By the early 1980s, Hong Kong people had developed a sense of identity and pride in the territory's achievements. Everyone could see Hong Kong developing day by day. The rapid economic growth provided ample opportunities for upward social mobility. Housing and basic public services had been improving considerably. The British administration had secured its legitimacy by its performance. Compared with the situation in the Mainland then, Hong Kong people felt very lucky although the issue of Hong Kong's future introduced a new element of uncertainty. For the bulk of the population, emigration was not an option. They considered that life had to go on and continued to work hard and lived the "Hong Kong spirit".

For many middle-class families, moving overseas was a difficult and costly option. It was "costly" not so much in money terms, but in terms of abandoning one's promising, hard-earned career in their thirties and forties. Most professionals and corporate executives who had moved overseas realised that they would receive a reduced remuneration package, and it would be difficult for them to find comparable positions. It was not unheard of that managers and qualified teachers, for example, took up jobs like salespersons, cleaners, cooks and waiters overseas. The issue of pride was significant for some of them.

Some of our friends and relatives who were executives and professionals emigrated and returned after a few years without their families. They soon found themselves working under their former subordinates upon their return to Hong Kong. A few considered the adjustment difficult and regrettable. They also found themselves having to fly frequently between Hong Kong and respective overseas countries in order to see their spouses and/or children. These people were not uncommon, and they were given the name "the space shuttle person (太空人)". Long separation during the emigration process generated marriage and family problems.

Young children in their formative years (or even in primary school age) were often sent overseas for their studies. They were sometimes sent to stay with a relative or friend if they were lucky. Quite a number were sent to private boarding schools in the U.K., due partly to prestigious education system there, and partly to Hong Kong's historical association as a British colony.

Unprepared for the culture shock, they felt alienated and lonely with the sudden change; some coped, but some did not. I heard of a few heart-wrenching stories and I treat them as tests in life.

Young siblings starting up in life often struggled individually to seek chances of emigration through overseas employment or further studies. Brothers and sisters in the same family often ended up as citizens in different countries (usually English speaking countries like the U.K., U.S., Canada and Australia), and they were described as the "United Nations family". We were no exceptions. In the 1980s, my sister immigrated to Canada, my brother to Australia, an aunt and a cousin to the U.K., and my best friends to the U.S. and New Zealand. My wife's brothers stayed in Australia, her mother and sisters in Canada, her first cousins in New Zealand, and her best friend in the U.K.

Some friends and relatives came to me for advice on emigration. My first reaction was, who was I to give advice on this? Then I realised that most of them had already made up their minds, and they basically came to seek some re-assurance. Naturally I believed that optimism and hard work would overcome various challenges whether one were in Hong Kong or otherwise. Basically one had to be sure what one wanted. Above all else, I felt that it was most important to keep the family close together.

Chapter 7

The Intriguing 1980s - Political Participation as a Concerned Academic

Deng Xiaoping: "Hong Kong's previous capitalist system...shall remain unchanged for 50 years" until 2047. The first wave of emigration. Opposing plans between Beijing and London on Hong Kong's future.

The years between the conclusion of the Sino-British Joint Declaration in December 1984 and the Tiananmen incident in 1989 were an intriguing period in Hong Kong.

Economically, we see the shift from manufacturing to services such as trade, logistics, communication and financial services, as the better educated younger generation shunned factory work. In support of China's economic reform, factories together with management and technical knowhow moved up to China.

The "Hong Kong culture" started to emerge in its arts and entertainment scene, both locally and internationally. Town halls in new towns (such as the Hong Kong Cultural Centre, Tsuen Wan and Shatin) sprang up to support local events and performances. Coinciding with the first wave of emigrants from Hong Kong who settled in countries like the U.K., U.S., Canada, Australia and the like, Hong Kong movies, including John Woo's triad film *"A Better Tomorrow"*, Chow Yun Fat's *"An Autumn's Tale"* and kung fu movies made an international presence.

Politically, the introduction of elections facilitated the development of pseudo-political parties, and political leaders emerged in the process. The Chinese authorities attempted to cool down the politicisation of the society and were largely successful; this was especially so because the British government and the British administration in Hong Kong conceded to the Chinese demands. The emerging political elites in the territory cultivated their skill sets to face the new challenges, from election campaigning to the capture of mass media attention and the moderate confrontation with the British administration. Finally the Basic Law drafting process also encouraged rational political debates, at least at the elite level.

Against this background, I remained a concerned academic, trying hard to establish myself as a scholar in political science. I continued to write on Chinese foreign policy, my initial and principal research area. I became interested in political reforms in China, as there were significant proposals and experiments in the 1980s. I naturally published on Hong Kong's political development. This diversification was probably not a good research strategy.

I was still offered many opportunities to meet Hong Kong government officials, though I was no longer regarded as the symbolic opposition since political leaders in the pro-democracy movement were already well established by 1980s. I took part in these meetings as an academic engaged in research on Hong Kong and also as a media commentator. Sir David Akers-Jones, who served as Secretary for the New Territories, Secretary for Home Affairs, Chief Secretary of colonial Hong Kong, and then briefly as the Acting Governor of Hong Kong, was often the host. He organised informal dinner gatherings for academics to meet with the then Governor Sir Edward Youde, and later, Lord Wilson at his official residences. Sir David was not a typically aloof colonial administrator. With his wife always beside him, he played his roles very well with his gentle disposition. He was soft-spoken, unassuming, approachable and a good listener. I learnt a lot from these gatherings.

Despite the increasing pressure to publish in leading international journals to enhance one's academic credentials and support one's promotions, I still spent considerable time writing for Chinese magazines and compiling books in Chinese on political development in the territory. I felt most rewarding when many years later, strangers I met in seminars and conferences approached me with my books asking for my signature.

Almost all of the activists in the pro-democracy movement considered me a friend and a staunch

January 1986. David Akers-Jones introducing British official visiting Hong Kong during the Sino-British negotiations.

September 1991. Dinner with David Akers-Jones & academic friends at his Dragon View villa in Castle Peak.

supporter, and as a media commentator, I often defended their positions. But they knew I had no intention to stand for election, and therefore would not involve me in their organisational work.

In response to the Sino-British Joint Declaration, the British administration released the White Paper on the Further Development of Representative Government in Hong Kong in November 1984, and made preparations for the Legislative Council elections. To meet the challenge of political reform and democratisation, those who had been active in politics began to organise themselves.

Around the time of Sir Geoffrey Howe's (British Foreign Secretary) visit in April 1984, Hong Kong had entered a new stage of political development. The Association for Democracy and Justice and the Hong Kong People's Association were founded. Their platforms and supporters were markedly different, but they had a common objective: to form a pseudo-political party for the coming elections so as to seek various positions in public office. In the summer that followed, the groundwork for Progressive Hong Kong Society was laid under the leadership of Maria Tam. The Society managed to secure the resources and recruit many respectable figures from various social strata and fields. For the first time, core members of the existing political establishment co-opted business tycoons from the major families rooted in Hong Kong to form a political coalition. Those who were involved in Hong Kong politics felt its impact.

In early 1985, three forces seemed to be capable of forming a political group similar to the Progressive Hong Kong Society. The first was formed by elites, with Allen Lee (Legislative Councillor) and the members of his 1983 delegation to Beijing as core members. He was backed by the local Shanghainese business community. Middle-class groups, including the Hong Kong Observers, the Hong Kong People's Association and the Hong Kong Affairs Society might form a possible coalition. To heighten co-operation among them, this group organised a joint committee to discuss the Basic Law and related issues. The third group was an alliance of grassroots pressure groups, including some young District Board members and the Association for Democracy and Justice as foundation members. The last two coalitions needed resources and time to mature and materialise. I maintained close contacts with them and served as a friendly advisor. Such contacts formed part of my research on Hong Kong politics.

In the second District Board elections in March 1985, many intra-district and inter-district alliances appeared. Almost every political group supported a small number of candidates, and most of them achieved satisfactory results. Successful candidates came from a broad spectrum of the community. There were increasing numbers of educators, social workers and professionals; they were younger on average. The elections brought on a higher degree of political mobilisation and political culture. The number of voters was just short of half a million, a milestone in Hong Kong's political scene. The increased participation in the election process reflected a higher degree of politicisation of the community.

By September 1985, elections to the Legislative Council was a first step in Hong Kong's political development. Elections were based on an electoral college, comprising members of the Urban Council, the Provisional Regional Council, the District Boards, and the functional constituencies. Very few people were aware of such elections. Of the 70,000 qualified voters only 25,000 actually voted. Only 24 of the 56 Legislative Councillors had to be accountable to their respective constituencies; other appointed unofficial members had to be accountable to the Governor of Hong Kong who made the appointments. The oath of allegiance was changed, and it could be directed to the citizens of Hong Kong or to the Queen. Most of the newly elected unofficial members opted for the former.

Despite the limited political mobilisation, the elections contributed to the expansion of political groups. Middle-class political groups were prompted to develop and establish close ties with the grassroots pressure groups. They became concerned about local district issues and participated in campaigns for citizens' rights.

This was indeed a significant improvement over the previous decade. In the 1970s, political campaigns focused on two levels: issues affecting people's daily lives and later, problems relating to citizens' rights. People from the lower socio-economic strata gradually learnt to organise themselves in protest activities, to appeal to public opinion and to protect and promote their interests. Social workers from voluntary agencies funded by Western churches and university student activists began to take part. I still remember that the government's clearance of illegal squatter huts was met with protests and petitions by the residents concerned. Other typical examples included protests to bus fare hikes and the monopolistic power of the electric power companies. These were only *ad hoc* campaigns, however, against issues that were directly related to people's daily lives. Grassroots pressure groups were as yet reluctant or unable to fight for their interests from a macro point of view to supervise government's policies or its decision-making process.

Around the same time, student movements started to develop in universities and colleges; they played an important part, for example, in the campaign for Chinese as an official language.[15] Their concerns for global developments and their understanding of their Motherland (People's Republic of China) obviously

---

15   See Chan King-cheung, "Hong Kong's Student Movement" (in Chinese), in the author's edited work in Chinese, *The Political System and Politics of Hong Kong*, Hong Kong: Cosmos Bookstore Ltd., 1987, pp. 289-314; and Hong Kong Federation of Students (ed.), *Review of Hong Kong's Student Movement* (in Chinese), Hong Kong: Wide Angle Press Ltd., 1983.

did not appeal to the grassroots pressure groups. The development of pseudo-political parties and elections in the 1980s enabled these two forces to accommodate each other, and in some cases, merge with each other.

Elections to the Legislative Council based on an electoral college, as well as the elections of District Board committee chairmen within the District Boards, exposed the weakness of independent elected members. The British administration in Hong Kong, through the appointment of one third of the District Board members, exercised important influence in these elections. In fact, the middle-class political groups and grassroots pressure groups had little success in the elections to become District Board chairmen and the subsequent elections to the Legislative Council through the Electoral College.

Such an electoral process encouraged various forms of coalitions within the District Boards. In the 1985 elections, both Allen Lee, who was then trying to organise a political party, and Maria Tam, leader of the Progressive Hong Kong Society and a member of the Executive and Legislative Councils, were actively supporting many candidates. In fact, some of the candidates took the initiative of soliciting their support. Such campaign activities naturally played a role in introducing party politics into the new Legislative Council.

In the mid-1980s, the introduction of Legislative Council elections spearheaded the development of political parties and political participation. It was part of the arrangements to prepare Hong Kong for its return to China. The process attracted the interest of a group of academics who began to specialise in the study of the territory's political development.

To participation theorists, democracy, with the majority of people involved in public policies, has four key objectives[16]: to discover what people want, to take all interests concerned into consideration, to ensure legitimacy and acceptance of policies, to fully develop individual capacities by being part of political life, a central aim of government and society.[17] These objectives, however, did not appear to be the major concerns of the British administration and the Hong Kong community when democratisation was introduced in 1984.

To the government in London, political reforms were a crucial element in the British political tradition in the twilight of the colonial era. They wanted to have an honourable retreat from Hong Kong, and democratisation was deemed an important means by which Hong Kong's autonomy *vis-à-vis* Communist China after 1997 could be enhanced. It was hoped that democratisation could help boost a sense of belonging and confidence in

---

16 See, for example, Richard S., Katz, *Democracy and Elections*, Oxford and New York: Oxford University Press, 1997, pp. 67-68.
17 Peter Bachrach, The Theory of Democracy and Election, Boston: Little & Brown, 1967, p.4.

the community, and as a result slow down or reduce emigration from the territory.

In the first and second District Board elections in 1982 and 1985 respectively, the British administration in Hong Kong were substantially involved. To help build a foundation for representative government after the conclusion of the Sino-British Joint Declaration, they shouldered almost all of the publicity campaigns to encourage qualified residents to register and to vote. In some cases, they encouraged community leaders, some of them I knew personally, to stand as candidates. Given the general political apathy and the lack of well-formed political parties then, the efforts were generally accepted. By the second District Board elections in 1985, various newly formed political groups and the mass media took the initiatives to promote voter registration and voting.

By the third District Board elections in 1988, the British administration's efforts tended to be more low-key and smaller in scale. While routine programmes were organised by government agencies such as Radio Television Hong Kong to promote voter registration, senior government officials generally avoided the subject. The mass media seemed to be less interested too. It was only in the week before the polling day that government efforts were stepped up, and on the evening of the polling day, community workers were sent to low-interest districts such as Mongkok to boost voting. Finally, the voting turnout rate exceeded 30%, as predicted by the government. In that year, the community engaged in heated debates on direct elections to the Legislative Council, and the British administration seemed to have abandoned the initiative to shape political reforms in Hong Kong.

October 1987. Rally at Victoria Park for universal suffrage in the 1988 Legislative Council election.

It was clear from the three District Board elections in the 1980s that the rural areas (for examples, Sai Kung, North and Islands) had higher voter turnout rates than urban areas. In rural areas, there was a traditional system of electing village representatives, and there was peer pressure to vote. In urban areas, more recent new towns (for example Shatin) and districts with high number of public housing estate residents (Wong Tai Sin) had relatively higher turnout rates than the earlier "new" towns (for example Tsuen Wan) and other urban areas (for example Mongkok).[18] The grassroots groups, such as "Concerned Group for the People's Livelihood of X District", were more active in these districts. The candidates from these groups and residents knew each other through district level campaigns such as the "Clean Hong Kong Campaigns". Face-to-face contacts with their electorates turned out to be the most effective channel to mobilise voters to vote.

The District Board election results above revealed a utilitarian element in voting behaviour. Voters in the lower socio-economic strata, in comparison with middle-class, tended to be more enthusiastic in District Board elections. They needed and expected District Board members to explain government policies, seek the right channel to obtain government services, articulate their interests, and help to redress their grievances. It partially explained the motivation to vote but also helped to answer why voter turnout rates were usually lower in middle-class urban districts.

The pro-democracy camp attached much importance to the District Board elections in March 1988, as it failed in its attempt to fight for direct elections to the Legislative

---

18　Emily Lau, "One Point for Democracy," *Far Eastern Economic Review*, Vol. 139, No. 12, March 24, 1988, p. 26; see also *South China Morning Post*, March 16, 1988.

Council in 1988. As political expectations, confidence and morale declined in the second half of the 1980s, the three major political groups in the pro-democracy camp (the Hong Kong Affairs Society, Meeting Point, and the Association for Democracy and People's Livelihood) largely failed to make much progress in expanding their organisations. The District Board elections were vital to a boost of morale and recruitment of new members.

It was in this context that the three groups managed to coordinate nominations to avoid unnecessary clashes among their candidates. While offering their endorsement, limited financial assistance and the general blessing from their leading figures like Martin Lee and Szeto Wah, they could not afford to be too selective in endorsing candidates. Though the pro-democracy candidates lacked financial resources and social status, they had good support from effective grassroots groups. They also managed to recruit well-educated, experienced and professional campaign workers, and as it turned out, the campaign efforts of Martin Lee and company were valuable assets.

My role continued as an academic and supporter. I did research on the District Board elections and Legislative Council elections, and my work appeared in major international academic journals. They still serve as historical records today. I offered media commentaries, as well as my endorsement to candidates from the pro-democracy camp who appreciated such support from an academic cum media commentator. I helped in the actual campaigns in a limited way, partly in response to requests from close friends, and partly to secure some first-hand campaign experiences that had contributed to my research.

The conservative camp was the major opponent to the pro-democracy camp. They were largely represented by traditional neighbourhood groups in the urban areas (called kaifongs) and rural committees (the statutory rural consultative council called Heung Yee Kuk in the New Territories). Typically, they were economically better off businessmen over forty years of age, and professionals like lawyers and accountants with a conservative outlook. Co-opted and appointed by the government, they played a supportive role in campaigns and activities run by the British administration.

The conservative cause was represented by Allen Lee and Maria Tam, Legislative Councillors. When Beijing openly objected to the rapid development of representative government in Hong Kong, the camp adopted a very low political profile. But as political groups, they could not afford to give up the District Board elections in 1988. They supported scores of candidates and actively campaigned for them, enlisting the help of beauty queens and television stars, and imitating many of the tactics adopted earlier by the pro-democracy candidates. They presented a formidable challenge to the pro-democracy political groups since they had at their disposal much more financial resources.

The Chinese authorities started to openly build up their influence and their community network in Hong Kong in 1985. Three district offices in Hong Kong Island, Kowloon and the New Territories were set up by the Hong Kong branch of the New China News Agency. In 1988, a campaign was launched to block the introduction of direct elections to the Legislative Council by the political camp loyal to Beijing.

The considerable scale of involvement by the Chinese authorities in the District Board elections in 1988 was an interesting phenomenon. Supporters of the pro-Beijing camp were mobilised to isolate political opponents and identify their own candidates in the District Board elections. Their participation was subtle though. Many of the pro-Beijing candidates who were professionals emphasised only their local credentials and camouflaged their backgrounds, though a few candidates in the New Territories rural areas openly admitted their connection with China. It was interesting that only two names out of the twelve candidates supported by the pro-Beijing Federation of Trade Unions were disclosed. In some cases, prominent conservative politicians openly endorsed candidates from the pro-Beijing camp; in return, Beijing-loyal organisations as a *quid pro quo* sent letters to their members with an instruction to vote for these conservative candidates.

The Chinese Communist Party was seen to be stepping up its activities in the territory and seeking to establish itself as the dominant political force. It was a cause for concern. They started to organise grassroots neighbourhood groups in districts like Kwun Tong and Wong Tai Sin, for example, and injected considerable resources from China. In some constituencies in Hong Kong Island, China Resources (Holdings) Co., Ltd. and China Merchants Steam Navigation Co., Ltd. (major Chinese corporations in Hong Kong under their respective Chinese ministries) provided transport to support the pro-Beijing candidates on election days.

After the Sino-British Joint Declaration was signed, Beijing-loyal organisations and the local New China News Agency engaged in an all-embracing united front campaign to win the hearts of Hong Kong people. There were numerous rounds of cocktail parties, exclusive receptions and free trips to China. I was invited to a few of them. To a certain extent the Chinese organs in Hong Kong were successful in co-opting professionals, established businessmen, fledgling politicians and grassroots community leaders, who were flattered by the embrace of the Motherland and at the same time afraid or too polite to reject it.

The Chinese authorities in Hong Kong were effectively cultivating the media too, and this approach paid dividends. Top officials of the local New China News Agency branch wined and dined the Hong Kong media proprietors. Middle and lower ranking newspaper reporters, editors and executives were often important targets of the Chinese united front strategy. The operation ensured that, with the exception of a limited number of newspapers and news monthlies, very little harsh criticism was aired against Chinese policies towards Hong Kong or against China in general. The few television stations were especially friendly.

The pro-Beijing united front maintained a constructive dialogue with the pro-democracy groups and remained friendly towards them. Chinese officials responsible for Hong Kong affairs were eager to learn from their assessments of the Hong Kong situation and how to gain public opinion support. But I observed that these groups no longer carried much weight in Beijing's power politics calculations as the Chinese leadership did not have the intention to grant the territory genuine democracy. In early 1985, I was invited to lunch by Yeung Sing (楊聲), deputy head of the co-ordination department (協調部, actually a united front department 統戰部) of the Hong Kong branch of the New China News Agency, and when I arrived at the restaurant of the Chinese General Chamber of Commerce, Qiao Zonghuai (喬宗淮), deputy director of the branch, was there. I was warned in a rather blunt manner that I should respect the position of the Chinese authorities on Hong Kong. I replied that I always respected the interests of China and Hong Kong, and all my political activities had been based on this premise.

Yeung accompanied the academics delegation to Beijing in April 1983, and he served as my link. Qiao was the son of the Chinese foreign minister Qiao Guanhua (喬冠華) and was later promoted as ambassador to Pyongyang.

The warning was an important reason why I declined to join the Basic Law Consultative Committee. My speculation was that the Chinese united front considered that I was interested to be absorbed by it to secure political rewards; my refusal to join the Basic Law Consultative Committee was an indication that I was not interested in these rewards. My friends and I noticed that in our contact with the united front personnel, it was extremely seldom that they came alone and very often came in pairs. We guessed that they could not trust each other.

Local New China News Agency officials in their meetings with the pro-democracy activists in these years often warned them against forming political parties. The warnings were: "There can only be the Communist Party of China and the Kuomintang. How can there be other parties?" There were no satisfactory explanations regarding why there couldn't be other parties in Hong Kong, and there were no hints on what the Chinese authorities would do against the new parties should they be established. Apparently the same warnings were sent to pro-establishment political leaders like Maria Tam and Allen Lee. As far as the pro-democracy groups were concerned, they avoided the use of the label political party because they believed that many Hong Kong people could not accept the idea yet. There was an observation among senior journalists that in the Legislative Council then, there were indeed respective members from the Communist Party of China, the Kuomintang, and the triad organisations.

I did not have much contact with the local New China News Agency at this stage. As a concerned academic and a media commentator, I often had the opportunities to engage the pro-establishment political leaders in political debates on the development of democracy in media forums. I also had many chances to visit universities in Mainland China. The usual topics of discussion were Chinese foreign policy and political reforms in China, but democratisation in Hong Kong was frequently touched upon too. I was fortunate to have many valuable chances of meeting the reformist scholars like Yan Jiaqi (嚴家其). These exchanges helped me to better understand politics in China as well as the rationale and plans for political reforms on their part.

Many of these scholars were heavy smokers. In many of the seminars I participated, the final course for dinner was usually two packets of imported American cigarettes served on a plate. Since I did not smoke, I often offered my share to my friends. Seminar rooms were often full of cigarette smoke, and the smell of tobacco lingered in hotel rooms, beds, pillows and carpets. Grace found this difficult to bear when she travelled with me in China.

I visited China quite frequently in these years, often to Beijing and Shenzhen. To better understand China, I attempted to visit a poor place or province at least once a year. I tried to better understand the different aspects of China's development, and I realised that in the 1980s, there were still many people struggling in poverty in China.

The dynamics of democratisation in Hong Kong were almost unique, as observed by Lo Shiu-hing, because there was no cleavage between conservative or reactionary hard-liners and liberal, reformist soft-liners in the political establishment. There was an absence of any clear-cut elite division. Hong Kong's democratisation process from 1984 to 1988 was the result of opposing plans between Beijing and London on Hong Kong's future polity. It remained colonial in its run-up to 1997[19].

By formally presenting the political reform proposals, and by encouraging community leaders to participate in politics, usually through initial appointments to government's advisory bodies, it had somewhat contributed to the democratisation process. The British administration offered very generous remuneration for members of elected bodies including District Boards, the Urban Council and the Regional Council, as well as the Legislative Council. Hence, elected members were able

---

19   See, for example, Lo Shiu-hing, *The Politics of Democratization in Hong Kong*, London: Palgrave Macmillan, 1997.

to contribute to political groups in the pro-democracy camp for their activities and development. To some extent, this helped the emergence of politicians and a political culture in Hong Kong. Arguably, the British administration was attempting to cultivate a political elite that would help London to retain its influence in the HKSAR after 1997.

While analysing democratisation in the 1970s and 1980s, O'Donnell and Schmitter observed that a democratic opening usually allows social groups led by intellectuals to "press for more explicit democratisation or even revolution". Privileged groups (including landowners, entrepreneurs and so on), being concerned that the democratic process "will not stop at a point compatible with the contractual freedoms of the market or the cosy relations they enjoy with the state apparatus."[20], begin to behave like a *de facto* opposition. In the case of Hong Kong, the privileged groups were gradually absorbed by Beijing's united front since 1984, and they remained in the evolving new political establishment.

In the 1970s, some pressure groups funded and guided by non-governmental organisations (NGOs) in the Western countries began to emerge in Hong Kong. They recruited young staff members who held the ideal

---

20 Guillermo O'Donnell and Philippe Schmitter, *Transitions from Authoritarian Rule: Tentative Conclusions about Uncertain Democracies*, Baltimore: Johns Hopkins University Press, 2013.

of serving the community in a constructive manner. These pressure groups helped to cultivate many of the territory's first-generation pro-democracy activists. Some of them including social workers, as well as activists from the local Catholic and Christian churches, favoured the "conflict approach", and they were involved in the establishment of the Society for Community Organization in 1972, funded initially by donations from various churches and overseas funding sources.

These organisations allowed politically ambitious community workers like Frederick Fung Kim-kee to develop their electoral bases. They worked hard in Sham Shui Po, Kwai Chung and Tsing Yi districts in the New Territories. The strategy was simple, but it was hard work. These activists helped the local residents to articulate their demands on housing and public services, and organised them to exert pressure on the government through attracting mass media attention, presenting petitions, and so on. The hard work paid off, their efforts were appreciated by the local residents who lacked the education, time and resources to get organised, to pursue their demands and redress their grievances.

These activists were able to attract their friends to join their respective groups. They were very successful in the 1985 District Board elections and the 1986 Urban Council/Regional Council elections. Their success set an example for other pro-democracy activists, and their work also established a grassroots work model for activists who planned to stand for elections. Elected offices provided them with respectable salaries and other funding support, and the financial resources enabled them to become full-time career politicians, employ assistants, open district offices, etc. Sham Shui Po and Kwai Chung/Tsing Yi remained strong footholds of the pro-democracy camp until the 2010s.

The strong position exerted by the Chinese authorities and the concessions made by the Hong Kong government successfully suppressed the expectations of a democratic political system by the community. In a 1985 survey, less than a quarter of the respondents believed that China would genuinely let Hong Kong people administer Hong Kong[21]. In the second half of the 1980s, concepts of representative government, democracy, and political participation were well received by the Hong Kong populace because of the concern over the handover, but those who were committed to the cause of democracy were a very small minority.

The community responded to Beijing's opposition to the development of representative government with a sharp increase of interest in emigration. By 1988, a quarter of the respondents indicated the intention

---

21   43.9% of the respondents indicated that they had no faith in the Chinese authorities' promise, and 33.8% remained undecided. See Hsin-chi Kuan and Siu-kai Lau, "The Civil Self in a Changing Polity: The Case of Hong Kong", in Kathleen Cheek-Milby and Miron Mushkat (eds.), *Hong Kong: The Challenge of Transformation*, Hong Kong: Centre of Asian Studies, University of Hong Kong, 1989, pp. 91-115.

to emigrate. It was much higher 45% for those with higher education[22]. The irony was that most people wanted to emigrate because they had little confidence in China's promises on the future of Hong Kong, and not because there would not be democracy in Hong Kong. As previous emigrants from China, they obviously did not accept the socialist system there. Businessmen wanted to emigrate probably for the same reasons and not because they were concerned that Hong Kong might turn into a welfare state as a result of democratisation. From 1980 to 1986, an estimated 21,000 emigrated, and by 1987, some 48,000 left Hong Kong permanently. The vast majority of them were emigrating to the English-speaking democracies of the U.S., Canada and Australia.

Yet, at least 90% of the population could not emigrate, and could only hope for the best. If they could keep their existing lifestyles – without democracy – it was quite acceptable. The traditional political apathy showed signs of return. The voter turnout rate fell considerably in the 1988 District Board elections. There was little participation in the discussions of the development of representative government and the Basic Law[23]. The total circulation of serious local news magazines and political publications was also in decline.

---

22 The survey was commissioned by the newspaper and conducted in early May, 1988.
23 Emily Lau, "One point for democracy", *Far Eastern Economic Review*, Vol. 139, No. 12, March 24, 1988, pp. 25-26.

The controversies arising from political reforms, however, led to a serious cleavage between the so-called "conservative camp" and the "democratic camp", and ruined any consensus regarding the present and future political system of the HKSAR. Moreover, the opposing positions of Beijing and London on Hong Kong left many locals to feel that they had been betrayed. The legitimacy of the existing British administration and the future HKSAR government was damaged somewhat.

As a result, less than half believed that public opinion would influence government decision[24], and even less so with the younger age group (18-24) and those with higher education and income. Why was this sense of political impotence so widespread in a society with freedom of speech and the rule of law? The survey results cast considerable doubt on the Hong Kong government's claim as a "government by consultation", at least when China's interests were at stake.

I was among those who had little confidence in the Chinese authorities' promise of democracy for Hong Kong. I believed that the British government and the British administration in Hong Kong would not confront Beijing on the issue of the territory's democratisation. The former would not want to have to assume responsibility for the confrontation because it would

---

24 On May 31, 1987, *South China Morning Post* published the results of an opinion survey on the released *Green Paper: The 1987 Review of Developments in Representative Government.*

mean commitment to help Hong Kong people, especially granting them the right of abode in Britain. I was willing to contribute to the struggle for democracy because I believed that I should do the right thing irrespective of the chance of success. This has been my attitude until today.

Public sector social services were being consolidated in the 1980s after a rapid expansion of the ambitious programmes of the MacLehose administration (1971–1982) during the rapid economic growth. To a large extent, they satisfied the community's basic demand for social services. Anticipating a slower economic growth in the 1980s, the British administration had to limit its various social service commitments. In addition, owing to uncertainty over Hong Kong's future, Beijing and all parties concerned wanted to maintain the territory's attraction to investors. Thus, more social services and a greater degree of income redistribution were discouraged. The community was aware of Beijing's demand for balanced budgets. The conservative business leaders attacked "free lunches", that is, the social service programmes of the public sector.

At the end of the 1980s, the government indicated that public sector expenditures should be kept at one-sixth of the gross domestic product. The building of public housing flats for subsidised rental to low income families slowed down. Government-run public hospitals were handed over to a new autonomous Hospital Authority.

The proposal for a central provident fund scheme was rejected outright.

Hong Kong's traditional political culture encouraged self-reliance. The spectacular economic growth in the past and the concern over an uncertain future lowered the community's expectations of social services from the British administration. Hence, the slight contraction of the public sector social services did not cause much disquiet in the community. Neither the pro-democracy camp made any specific demand. Many observers considered that the political platforms of the moderate mainstream pro-democracy groups in Hong Kong were similar to that of the moderates in the British Conservative Party.

The drafting of the Basic Law for the HKSAR started since 1985 after the signing of the Sino-British Joint Declaration in 1984. The sincerity of the Chinese leaders in maintaining Hong Kong's stability and prosperity in the transitional period and after 1997 was beyond doubt. Otherwise, they would not have taken great pains to work out the Joint Declaration and the Basic Law. Maintaining the prosperity of the territory, however, clearly had priority over the promises of "a high degree of autonomy" and "self-administration" for the HKSAR.

It was clear then that the Chinese leaders demanded the final say on the important issues. At the time, the vital issues of the constitutional and legal status of the Basic Law remained unsolved. The Chinese authorities refused to revise its Constitution to allow for residual powers within the unitary state and the practice of socialism. This might not pose any problem if the prevalent policy orientation of the Chinese leadership remained unchanged. After all, the reformers in China had also encountered difficulties in finding a convincing ideological foundation to support their reforms. The "primary stage of socialism" argument was obviously not satisfactory. In the event of political uncertainties or major redefinitions concerning existing policies, Hong Kong would suffer considerable shock. The theoretical and constitutional bases of the "one country, two systems" policy would be open to doubt.[25]

The Chinese Government also wanted to retain final control in the amendment and the interpretation of the Basic Law. The result meant that the Basic Law would offer very limited guarantees for the political autonomy of the HKSAR. The instinct of the Communist Party regime in following the Leninist principles of democratic

---

25 Even before the initialling of the Sino-British Joint Declaration, various groups in Hong Kong indicated to the Chinese officials responsible for Hong Kong affairs that the guarantee of a capitalist system in Hong Kong might be in violation of the PRC Constitution; and revision of Article 31 of the Constitution was suggested. The Chinese authorities apparently were reluctant to discuss revision of the Constitution, but they were aware that some form of assurance was necessary.
   See the author's "The Draft Basic Law: Messages for Hong Kong People", in Hungdah Chiu (ed.), *The Draft Basic Law of Hong Kong: Analysis and Documents*, Baltimore: School of Law, University of Maryland, Occasional Papers/Reprint Series in Contemporary Asian Studies, No. 5 – 1988, pp. 7-48.

centralism for maintaining control might well be at work here: when the control of the Party is not secure in the HKSAR, the ultimate control of the Central People's Government has to be defined even more clearly in legal terms. Suspicions over Hong Kong becoming an "independent political entity" (and after the Tiananmen incident, as "an anti-Communist base") were articulated openly by Chinese officials in charge of Hong Kong affairs. They, as well as the Chinese leadership, were constantly aware of the example that the HKSAR set for Mainland China. Chinese leaders were unwilling to dilute the unitary system of the state to accommodate Hong Kong or Taiwan.

Within the HKSAR political system, the appointments by the Central People's Government of the Chief Executive and the principal officials imply that their accountability is to the Central People's Government. This has been reaffirmed by Article 43 of the Basic Law, stipulating that the Chief Executive shall be "accountable to the Central People's Government and the Hong Kong Special Administrative Region". The people in Hong Kong gradually realised that the Chief Executive would have to be someone acceptable to the Chinese authorities. This in return reinforced the general perception in the community that Beijing would have the final say on all vital issues, dampened the community's interest in political participation, and eroded the legitimacy of the development of representative government.

Any concessions made by the Chinese authorities then were of a temporary, *ad hoc* and tactical nature. In the Basic Law draft released in February 1989, Revisions were made in the Basic Law draft in February 1989 on Article 18, the application of national laws in the HKSAR, and Article 19, on an independent judicial authority and that of final jurisdiction of the HKSAR. These revisions went a long way in meeting the demands of the community before the Tiananmen incident in June 1989. Martin Lee indicated that in the Basic Law Drafting Committee, his proposal of involving foreign judges in the Court of Final Appeal was surprisingly accepted by the Chinese authorities.

I took part enthusiastically in the debates on the drafting of the Basic Law as a concerned academic. But I realised then that ultimately, the Hong Kong community might have to rely not so much on the Basic Law but on the other domestic and international factors to ensure that the Chinese leadership would live up to its promises made to the Hong Kong people during the Sino-British negotiations.

Chinese leadership had been assuring the international community that its open-door policy would remain unchanged. Its policy towards Hong Kong was looked upon as a litmus test of its open-door policy. Any violation of the spirit and the terms of its promises to Hong Kong would damage international confidence in China. Hong Kong would set a significant example for

Taiwan. Any variation in China's policy towards Hong Kong might signal a change in its domestic reforms too. Various liberal economic policies in China's special economic zones and the coastal cities would most likely be affected. As long as the Chinese leadership valued Hong Kong's contributions to its modernisation programme, this capitalist enclave might continue to be tolerated.

These factors might be effective in making sure "that Hong Kong's previous capitalist system and life-style shall remain unchanged for 50 years", as promised by Deng Xiaoping. They did not however constitute an absolute guarantee that Hong Kong would remain unchanged up to the year 2047, including the "high degree of autonomy" and "self-administration" promised.

In response to Beijing's strong opposition at the press conference by Xu Jiatun in November 1985, the British government and the British administration in Hong Kong began to tone down their support for democratisation. Timothy Renton, minister of state at the British Foreign Office in charge of Hong Kong affairs, stressed that it would be the British government's job to ensure a smooth transfer of power in 1997, and that to do this, a convergence of the Hong Kong and Chinese systems would be necessary. He stated that political reform in Hong Kong had probably been too rapid. He also agreed to discuss such issue in the Sino-British Joint Liaison Group. Sir David Akers-Jones, the then Hong

Kong's Chief Secretary, also elaborated on the theme that "the systems must converge" in his end-of-year press conference in December 1985. He revealed that the Hong Kong government's political reform proposals would be presented to Beijing before their release to the local community for comment in the form of a Green Paper in May 1987.

Senior members of the Executive and Legislative Councils appeared to feel the pressure. At the end of December 1985, Allen Lee indicated that his plan of organising a political party was to be shelved for the time being. In an interview with the *Hong Kong Standard*, published on December 29, 1985, Lee stated that he did not believe China would allow genuine self-administration. He said that the Chief Executive of the future SAR government would be appointed by the central government in Beijing. A political party, he said, was meaningless. The senior unofficial member of the Legislative Council, Lydia Dunn, also stopped talking about the introduction of a ministerial system to Hong Kong. In fact, the majority of the "unofficials" of both councils had not played a leading role in community discussions on political reform, nor did they carry out much local consultation.

The pro-democracy movement was in a difficult position. It did not have the support of the British government and the British administration on the democratisation process. The dialogue with Beijing was limited. It realised that the Chinese authorities had chosen the local business community as their principal ally. As the pro-British establishment was reluctant to assume leadership, the pro-Beijing united front offensive encountered little resistance. The British administration was much absorbed in the Sino-British negotiations and had no major plans to improve public services, in contrast to the MacLehose era. Fortunately, Hong Kong people still considered the pro-democracy movement a force that would defend their interests despite the fact that they gradually lowered their expectations on democracy.

The movement was led by Martin Lee and Szeto Wah, and it enjoyed strong unity in these years. It started organising protest rallies, but they were usually small in scale. Often a few hundred to a few thousand people participated. I took part in almost all of them to show my support. In articulation of the movement's demand for democracy, the movement organised a mass meeting at the Ko Shan Theatre, Hung Hom on November 2, 1986, with more than one thousand participants. I was honoured as one of the twelve speakers in the meeting, representing the higher education sector.

There were mainly two opposing camps. The 190 pro-democracy representatives from several dozen political groups and civil organisations demanded the direct elections by universal suffrage of the Chief Executive, and at least one half of the seats in the legislature. The functional constituencies and indirect elections by the District Boards and Urban Council/Regional Council should return no more than a quarter of the seats each. Eighty-nine members of the establishment, most of them serving in the Basic Law Consultative Committee, presented basically the Beijing plan. The Chief Executive would be elected by a 600-member electoral college, which would also return a quarter of the seats in the legislature. Half of the seats in the legislature would be elected by functional constituencies and the remaining quarter by direct elections.

Many debates were organised by the media between the two camps. They were civilised, and both sides did not expect to succeed in persuading the other side. Their respective articulations were aimed at influencing public opinion. Making use of the political reform review in 1987, the pro-democracy movement launched a signature campaign in an attempt to exert pressure on the British administration to introduce direct elections to the legislature by 1988.

The British administration pledged to collect public opinion on the issue of political reforms, and employed an opinion survey company, AGB McNair Hong Kong Ltd., to conduct two large-scale polls. However, the interpretation of the data was twisted by treating the 223,696 signatures collected during the signature campaign as one submission, and concluded that the majority of Hong Kong people did not support the introduction of direct elections to the legislature in 1988.

Martin Lee indicated in the Legislative Council debates that nine random-sample surveys conducted by the community came to the opposite conclusion to that reached by the government-sponsored polls. Later the last Hong Kong Governor, Chris Patten, admitted that the British administration had indeed twisted the interpretation of the data. He revealed that a Sino-British secret agreement had been reached before the end of the consultation exercise: if the survey results could indicate that Hong Kong people did not demand direct elections to the legislature in 1988, then the Chinese government would pledge the subsequent introduction of direct elections to the legislature in the Basic Law.

For political reforms, H.C. Kuan and S.K. Lau of the Chinese University of Hong Kong, identified five problems. First, there would be tension between the initiation of reforms and the maintenance of the *status quo*. Second, as Beijing and London competed to take the initiative, the reforms would take shape far too early and would thus tend to be conservative. Third, it would be difficult to obtain a consensus, as local opinions differed. Fourth, political leadership would be lacking. Last, Hong Kong people suspected both Beijing and London. These problems should not be underestimated. I did not disagree with my colleagues, but I decided to continue my efforts.

The Chinese decision to go ahead with the construction of a nuclear power plant at Daya Bay, next to the Shenzhen Special Economic Zone and 50 kilometres from the centre of Hong Kong, further eroded the confidence of the Hong Kong community. Despite the collection of over a million signatures against the plant by a local anti-nuclear group, the Chinese authorities concluded the major contracts in September 1986. The community took the futility of the signature campaign as evidence that Chinese interests would prevail in all future conflicts of interests between Hong Kong and China. Some even suggested that the Chinese authorities had wanted to show that they were the true masters of the territory.

Chapter 8

The Crisis of the Tiananmen Incident 1989

The turmoil of the Tiananmen incident put me at the front rank of the pro-democracy movement. "...as long as freedom, human rights, and democracy could not be guaranteed in China, they could not be protected in Hong Kong after 1997."

In closely following the tragic event of the Tiananmen incident in the spring and summer of 1989, Hong Kong people strongly identified with their compatriots in China. They believed that as long as freedom, human rights, and democracy could not be guaranteed in China, they could not be protected in Hong Kong after 1997. On May 21, 1989, over one million Hong Kong people marched on the streets, and many of them marched for the first time in their lives. They marched for democracy and freedom in China against the suppression of the student movement. Motivated by anger and shock at what was happening in China, they were also struck by a sense of despair and insecurity regarding their own future. Most of them marched again on the following two Sundays.

Before the Tiananmen crackdown in Beijing on June 4, 1989, Hong Kong people counted on China's goal in modernisation, a legitimate objective widely supported by the Chinese people. They believed that Hong Kong's *status quo* would contribute to China's modernisation. The Tiananmen incident showed that power struggles within the Chinese leadership could totally upset this goal and related priorities. The trust in the Chinese leadership, the Sino-British Joint Declaration and the draft Basic Law was badly shaken. This also meant that a meaningful dialogue with Beijing would be difficult and might even lack legitimacy.

On May 20, 1989, martial law was declared in China. The pro-democracy groups immediately organised a meeting at Victoria Park. A friend called me in the late evening. I rushed to the gathering, and we marched to the New China News Agency Hong Kong Branch in Happy Valley. Number 8 typhoon signal was hoisted then, and we all put on plastic raincoats, while some of us had umbrellas.

I was standing right next to Szeto Wah, and I supported him in the gusty wind and rain. I was not a member of his organisation nor one of his protégés, but he was very polite to me; those few hours were my closest moment with him. As a teacher and school principal, he was the most impressive visionary that I know. Leading a simple life, he was selfless and dedicated in his work for the democracy movement in Hong Kong. Known to

Hongkongers as "Uncle Wah", he has worked for decades to fight for Hong Kong's democracy, freedom and human rights. He founded the largest pro-democracy trade union, the Professional Teachers' Union, in 1973 to fight for the teachers' interests, but was forced to disband in 2021 under enormous pressure from Beijing. He was also the Chairman of the Hong Kong Alliance in Support of Patriotic Democratic Movement of China, which was set up since 1989 to commemorate the Tiananmen incident on June 4 every year. This group too was forced to disband after Hong Kong's national security law came into effect in 2021.

On the following Sunday, protest rallies against the Tiananmen incident continued. I was asked by Szeto Wah to march on the front line with him. He said I should represent the higher education sector, as I had a new job in April that year. I assumed the post of the Dean of the School of Arts and Humanities in the newly established Open Learning Institute of Hong Kong (now the Open University of Hong Kong). I normally avoided standing in the front row in rallies, because I did not hold any offices in any organisations then. I was just a concerned academic and a media commentator in support of the pro-democracy movement.

Some relatives and friends warned me against taking such a high profile on the issue; they believed it was unwise for my future career advancement and there could be reprisals from the pro-Beijing united front. I

Speaking at the City Forum as Dean of the then Open Learning Institute.

was grateful for their concerns, though I did not think that such factor should be my consideration under the circumstances. I remembered that on May 28, 1989, when students in Tiananmen Square appealed to Chinese people all over the world to march in their support, Hong Kong people responded and I completed the rally and left. I did not stay like the other activists to receive the cheers of the 1.5 million participants because I believed that I did not deserve the honour.

I was disappointed that almost all senior academics in responsible management positions avoided taking a public stand during this critical moment. I was especially disappointed with the senior academics in the humanities and social sciences fields at the Chinese University of Hong Kong. They were concerned about China's developments, and they were supposed to be committed to the responsibilities of Chinese intellectuals as the conscience of the society. Yet they shunned any public action. Professor Wang Gungwu, vice-chancellor of the University of Hong Kong, declined to comment publicly on the tragedy. On the first anniversary of the Tiananmen incident, he only said that "we all have to learn from history". I considered that they all knew what to say to protect themselves. I suppose too that I would probably be seen by the territory's top academic establishment as imprudent, and lacking in political sophistication like them.

After martial law in Beijing was declared, only half of those surveyed showed confidence in the future of Hong Kong, down from three quarters in January 1989. In the summer of 1989, emigration-related enquiries received by the consulates of English speaking countries like the U.S., Canada and Australia increased markedly. Over one-third of the respondents in an opinion survey indicated that they were actively preparing to emigrate, or had family members who either resided abroad or had secured the right of permanent residence in a foreign country. Three out of four industrialists revealed in another survey held three weeks after the Tiananmen incident that they were either planning or considering to emigrate, while only four out of ten said so in a similar survey held before the incident.[26]

My family and I had already secured Australian passports by then. My close friends knew and some journalists knew too; I did not keep the information a secret. As a Ph.D. student then, and later as an academic, my teaching job was not regarded as a "skilled occupation" in the 1980s. Hence, I was not eligible to apply for a permanent resident visa in Australia. Thanks to Grace and her librarian qualifications and work experiences in the State Library of South Australia, she was able to secure permanent resident status in Australia for the family.

In 1989, I could probably get a university job in Australia. Grace and I decided that since we could leave Hong Kong any time, we should stay until 1996 or so to make our final decision. We both valued our jobs and families in Hong Kong. In practical terms, our annual incomes after taxation would probably be four or five times those we could earn in Australia. Hence, in the worst-case scenario, we could save and retire early in Australia. Our parents were getting old, and my father was in poor health; that was another consideration on our part.

---

26   *South China Morning Post*, June 16, 1989, and July 4, 1989. The surveys was conducted by Survey Research Hong Kong for the newspaper in May and June 1989 respectively.

After serving as United College Dean of Students at the Chinese University of Hong Kong, I had no intention to aim at any management position. I performed my share of administrative duties as a member of the department such as serving at the Hong Kong Examinations Authority and helping in public examinations. I realised that my reformist orientations and my high profile in political participation would not be acceptable to the core management of the university. I was promoted to senior lectureship in January 1986, ahead of a few colleagues many years my senior. I therefore adopted a very low profile within the university. I supported another more elderly colleague to serve as department head so that he might have a better chance of securing his promotion to senior lecturer.

The position at the Open Learning Institute attracted me because it was an innovative idea, at least in Hong Kong, and it aimed to serve those who could not enrol in formal universities but who intended to pursue degree programmes. It was not the orthodox career development path for a scholar, but I wanted to take on a new challenge. My frequent media interviews during the spring and summer of 1989 probably enhanced the image of the new institution.

Given the fears at that time, various demands for the right of abode in the United Kingdom for the 3.25 million holders of British Dependent Territory Citizen (BDTC) passports had stepped up, while attempts were also made to seek some form of international guarantee for Hong Kong people's rights and freedoms beyond 1997. In their panic, Hong Kong people also considered such unlikely options as purchasing a South Pacific Island (in Tonga for example), pleading to place Hong Kong under United Nations Trusteeship, or to go independent, and the like.

China did nothing to help put these fears to rest. When superficial calm was restored in Beijing's political scene, the regime quickly turned its attention to Hong Kong. The initial reaction was criticism, by name, of Hong Kong's mass media by Beijing's *People's Daily* and other official media. Chinese leaders in early June attacked attempts of exploiting Hong Kong as a "counter-revolutionary base". Beijing's Mayor, Chen Xitong, in his report to the Standing Committee of the National People's Congress on the suppression of the student demonstrations, included a detailed account of the news reports on the incident from Hong Kong's mass media as evidence of their collusion with foreign influences in a conspiracy to reduce China to an appendage of international monopolistic capital.

On July 11, 1989, when the new General Secretary of the Party, Jiang Zemin, met the leading figures of the Basic Law Drafting Committee and the Basic Law Consultative Committee, he warned that Hong Kong should not interfere with China. Jiang considered that "according to the principle of one country, two systems, China practises socialism, Hong Kong practises capitalism". "Water from wells should not interfere with river water [井水不犯河水]", an idiomatic expression meaning "I mind my own business and you mind yours". The statements of Jiang and those previously made by Chinese officials responsible for Hong Kong affairs were basically aimed at providing assurances for Hong Kong's stability and prosperity, and at the same time warned Hong Kong people to refrain from acts that would threaten the Chinese Communist regime.

Though the vast majority of Hong Kong people were unhappy with the existing Chinese regime and were willing to severely criticise the regime verbally or through the mass media in the previous spring, they had no intention of taking further action against it. Jiang's statements on "one country, two systems", on the other hand, caused considerable anxiety among Hong Kong people, especially the intellectuals. Though some of them would agree with the analogy that "water from wells should not interfere with river water", they feared that, conversely, when the Chinese river flooded, Hong Kong's well water would be affected. Hong Kong society treasured the rule of law, for one, which was an important pillar supporting the stability and prosperity of the territory. If Hong Kong people, apart from observing the local law, had to exercise various self-restraints in response to the Chinese leaders' guidance and statements, as Jiang indicated, then the rule of law would be much eroded, and people would find it difficult to maintain their existing life-styles.

In media interviews, I often explained that Hong Kong affected China mainly by its objective existence. Hong Kong's economic progress had certainly prompted the Chinese people in the Mainland to cast doubt on the superiority of socialism. Yet as long as Chinese leaders wanted to make use of the territory's resources, they had to accept the compromise of "one country, two systems". Hong Kong people always treasured their freedom of speech and freedom of the media. Up till then, they were able to discuss freely the issues of Mainland China, and the local mass media were able to frankly report developments in China and evaluate them objectively. Such reports and commentaries had a considerable impact on international public opinion, particularly public opinion in overseas Chinese communities.

At the same time, the coverage of world news by the local mass media had much affected China's effective control of information directed towards its own people. Hong Kong's radio and television programmes could be received in many parts of the neighbouring Guangdong province, and the intelligentsia in many major cities in China had access to Hong Kong's publications. As Deng Xiaoping had acknowledged Hong Kong's significance regarding information input for China, the Chinese leadership had to accept the price as well.

In June and July 1989, China's official mass media began to criticise the activities of the Hong Kong Alliance in Support of Patriotic Democratic Movements in China[27] (香港市民支援愛國民主運動聯合會 – 支聯會 in short). On July 21, a signed article of the *People's Daily* criticised by clear implication the leaders of the Alliance, Martin Lee and Szeto Wah. These serious accusations caused much concern in Hong Kong. Pro-Beijing figures and leaders of the political establishment such as Allen Lee made use of the opportunity and appealed to the Hong Kong community to avoid confrontation with China. These accusations, conveyed through the local mass media, certainly created a deterrence effect among ordinary people, and resulted in a temporary setback for the pro-democracy movement's plan to form a political party. But the threat from Beijing simultaneously damaged the confidence of Hong Kong people in the territory's future.

I learnt from the media that while I marched in the front row in the protest rallies in the Tiananmen incident, my academic colleagues Lau Siu-kai, Wong Siu-lun and Lee Ming-kwan were invited for consultation by the Hong Kong and Macau Affairs Office in Beijing on the Hong Kong situation. We continued to meet with Hong Kong government officials together, but our positions clearly differed. They were interested in the maintenance of the territory's stability and prosperity, as well as good

---

27　Set up on May 21, 1989 during the Tiananmen incident in Beijing.

relations between Beijing and the British administration. I naturally focused on the democratisation process and the defence of Hong Kong people's rights. This separation of ways gradually emerged and was further exacerbated in the rest of the transitional period. Friendship was eroded. Worse still, some of my friends might become informal "informers" as they would comment on my political attitudes in their meetings with the pro-Beijing united front leaders. Many of my friends who were pro-democracy activists or supporters/sympathisers of the pro-democracy movement encountered many such cases.

This probably explained why most Hong Kong people avoided serious discussions of politics among friends and relatives. My La Salle College classmates often organised dinners, and I normally declined to present my views on the democratisation process in Hong Kong. Many of my classmates were successful businessmen and senior corporate executives. They were and would not be convinced by my arguments, as their top priority was to enhance their wealth. They were only interested in picking up information from me. So why should I waste my efforts under such circumstances? I participated in these gatherings because I still valued our friendship cultivated since our youth, and I did not intend to damage it.

In response to the crisis, the Standing Committee of the National People's Congress decided to extend the period of consultation on the Basic Law by three months till the end of October 1989. The timetable disappointed Hong Kong people, because it meant that the Chinese authorities were reluctant to revise, in any significant way, the draft Basic Law released in February 1989.

This decision ignored the fact that after the Tiananmen incident, serious differences emerged within the Hong Kong community. In the past, Hong Kong people accepted the Sino-British Joint Declaration. The only worry was that it would not be observed. To some, the Tiananmen incident had just reduced the document to a piece of paper. An October 1989 opinion poll showed that seven out of ten people were not very confident nor even fairly confident that the Basic Law would guarantee that the "one country, two systems" promise would be kept. Martin Lee went so far as to openly ask for a re-negotiation of the Sino-British Joint Declaration. Many then felt that it was meaningless to talk about the Basic Law. Some community leaders, scholars, and others, particularly those who were involved in the pro-democracy movement, refused to maintain contact with Chinese organs in Hong Kong or engage in any formal exchanges. A considerable segment of the population lost its trust in the British government, especially when at this point, the granting of the right of abode to British Dependent Territory Citizen passport holders was rejected.

I did not have much contact with the local New China News Agency even before the Tiananmen incident, so losing contact with Chinese organs in Hong Kong was not an issue for me. In many radio and television forums, I did engage in debates with pro-Beijing united front leaders and commentators. My exchanges with universities in the Mainland naturally stopped. In the public discussions at this point, I indicated that one should not underestimate the staying power of the Party regime. This probably did not please many of the pro-democracy activists, as some famous dissidents predicted the fall of the regime in three months. All these years, I tried to offer the public my objective analyses, though I made my values very clear. Many of my friends who had been engaging in various exchange programmes with Mainland China were disappointed. They had hoped to contribute to China's modernisation and had to terminate these efforts at this stage.

The local establishment, the business community, and some opinion leaders still believed that the Sino-British Joint Declaration must be upheld. They argued that the Basic Law and related discussions had to be treated seriously, and that the British administration in the transitional period had to be supported wholeheartedly. They should maintain contacts with the Chinese authorities at all levels. Such basic divisions of views created difficulties in getting people to discuss the

Basic Law and to reach a consensus that would give it legitimacy.

After the Tiananmen incident, two of the twenty-three Hong Kong members of the Basic Law Drafting Committee, Louis Cha and Bishop Kwong, formally resigned, and Martin Lee and Szeto Wah were removed from the drafting committee by China's National People's Congress. The representativeness of the remaining Hong Kong members was much weakened. They certainly lacked the trust of most Hong Kong people.

It was under such circumstances that a broad consensus in the community emerged that desired the acceleration of representative government in the run up to 1997. The British administration in Hong Kong and the London government showed strong support with a view to minimise Britain's responsibility. In May 1989, the Executive and Legislative Councils reached a consensus on having direct elections of the Chief Executive and all seats of the legislature by 2003. Senior Hong Kong government officials reversed their former position and indicated that the directly elected Legislative Council seats that would be introduced in 1991 would be increased from 10 to 20.

The June 1989 report of the British House of Commons Foreign Affairs Select Committee went one step further and suggested that by 1995, all such Legislative Council seats should be directly elected. The proposal was endorsed by the Joint Committee for the

Promotion of Democratic Government, an umbrella organisation representing the various groups of Hong Kong's pro-democracy movement. The Joint Committee also demanded that the Chief Executive be directly elected through universal suffrage, and a "through train" arrangement for the Legislative Councillors elected in 1995, which meant that they should automatically become members of the first legislature of the HKSAR.

In mid-July 1989, local politicians loyal to Beijing started to express their concern that an acceleration in democratisation might lead to greater confrontation with Beijing after 1997. Many of these figures, including C.Y. Leung and Tam Yiu-chung, had openly condemned the Chinese authorities during the Tiananmen incident. But once they realised that the Party regime had regained full control and Deng Xiaoping was in charge, they returned to the fold of the Chinese Communist united front after a brief period of quietness. Apparently, the Chinese authorities were ready to accept them once again, as many of them had opposed the Chinese leadership during the crisis. When the thirtieth anniversary of the Tiananmen incident approached in the spring of 2019, pro-democracy activists dug up the media coverage of their condemnation of the Chinese authorities in May/June 1989 to mock them.

The local mass media and Chinese authorities with their united front in Hong Kong were not in their best relations in May/June 1989. By mid-June however, united front activities regained momentum and achieved results. While many newspapers in Hong Kong prominently covered reports of political suppression in China, they carried promotional materials from the local New China News Agency and other Chinese organs at the same time. The maintenance of Hong Kong's stability and prosperity came to the fore. Self-censorship, as existed in the past few years prior to May-June 1989, gradually returned and was most prominent with the two major television stations. In the development of the local pro-democracy movement, self-censorship had been a significant obstacle.

Beijing's united front strategy, however, was considerably handicapped. Since the Tiananmen incident, political purge in pro-Beijing organisations in Hong Kong such as Wen Wei Po (a left-wing newspaper in Hong Kong) continued. "Hong Kong's Left has been ripped apart, with many of its stalwarts fleeing and many of its organisations in a state of crisis"[28]. There were suppressed bitterness and resentment among both Mainland Chinese and the Hong Kong Chinese who worked for these organisations. The purge resulted in the loss of many dedicated and competent local talents who joined these organisations, mostly in upper-middle positions, in the mid-1970s.

---

28 K.H. Lau (pseudonym for a former employee of a left-swing organisation in Hong Kong), "The Purge Next Door", *Far Eastern Economic Review*, Vol. 145, No. 36, September 7, 1989. p.77.

Chinese leadership was reluctant to make concessions despite the loss of confidence in Hong Kong after the Tiananmen incident. The deputy director of the State Council's Hong Kong and Macau Affairs Office, Lu Ping, stated in Macau on September 6, 1989: "They (the Hong Kong people) are just making unnecessary worries for themselves. The so-called confidence problem has been created by Hong Kong people, and should be solved by them because they are responsible for the problem."

In recent years, senior journalists and commentators often lament on the low standards of the Beijing-loyal legislators and the united front leaders in Hong Kong. Their performance as politicians hardly command respect. Their dedication and commitment are far from satisfactory, as reflected by their attendance records in the law-making Legislative Council. The Tiananmen incident and the abandonment of political reforms disappointed many idealistic supporters of the Communist Party of China in Hong Kong who had genuinely believed in the cause. Ching Cheong was a typical example. Though he was working in the pro-Beijing newspaper before the Tiananmen incident, his sincerity and concern for Hong Kong people's interests impressed many.

As the pro-Beijing united front gradually became the centre of power in the remaining years of Hong Kong's transitional period, it attracted more and more careerists who sought political gains, social status and/or business opportunities. The tight control of the Party also meant little room for innovations and bold initiatives from members of the united front. As a result, it could not attract outstanding political talents. An easy indicator of careerists would be those political "leaders" who became rich after their active participation in the united front. Their cars and accommodation were the first clues.

On April 23, 1990, the United Democrats of Hong Kong, led by Martin Lee and Szeto Wah, was established. It claimed to be the first political party of Hong Kong. The pro-democracy movement finally had a political party ready to develop an electoral machinery. In the 1991 Legislative Council elections, the pro-Beijing united front lost in the single-seat constituency, first-past-the-post system. But in most constituencies, its candidates managed to secure one third of the votes, revealing its networking and mobilisation power. It was quick to learn from the electoral strategies and tactics of the pro-democracy camp, and it rapidly established its own electoral machinery. Though it suffered from inadequate political talents (lack of attractive candidates), it managed to recruit experts in electoral planning, publicity work, united front work and the like. Some of these experts, for example, worked in the leading advertising firms in the territory. They helped as voluntary workers, and would be rewarded with major contracts from the subsidiaries of state-owned enterprises in Hong Kong.

I returned to full-time academic work at the Open Learning Institute after a hectic period of political activities and media exposure that lasted six weeks or so. The Institute had a small skeletal staff. As dean of the faculty, I was supported by a clerical officer, and the faculty intended to have an establishment of four or five lecturers/senior lecturers besides the dean. We started with three senior lecturers – two of them came from the open learning institution in Macau and they had the experiences. As the Open Learning Institute was not yet a university, it had to go through an accreditation process. The rationale was legitimate: to ensure the upholding and maintenance of standards. But the processes involved concepts and vocabularies that most academics would find foreign and would not be too interested. Hence, there was a danger that going through the accreditation processes was perceived as a necessary evil. There was also a tendency to rely on a small group of colleagues or external consultants who possessed such expertise and experiences.

I was quite an old-fashioned academic. To set an example to students in their learning, I believed in my own dedication and hard work. I had been a teacher throughout my entire life, and I considered that students could easily detect the commitment of teachers. Good teaching skills helped, but it was often not paramount in university education. As dean of the faculty, however, I had to learn the accreditation processes. Fortunately, the faculty performed well in the accreditation exercise.

The first head of the Open Learning Institute was hopelessly incompetent. He soon lost the confidence of the staff and then the Council of the Institute, and he had to resign after about two years. Since academics in Hong Kong did not have the experience of open learning, the Institute had to rely on expatriates who did not have much understanding of Hong Kong.

The chairman of the Council was Cheng Hon-kwan (鄭漢鈞), a structural engineer, and a member of both the Legislative and Executive Councils at that time. He was so over-burdened with a large number of public offices that scheduling meetings with him was a challenge. It was not an uncommon phenomenon. I heard that many of these important public figures did not have time to read the meeting documents. They had to rely on their assistants to highlight the more important paragraphs and remind them when to speak. If you checked their schedules and commitments, you could easily understand why. Under such circumstances, the Council chairman was heavily dependent on the secretary of the Council who could easily steer the chairman to accept his preferred options. The heavy reliance of the British administration on a small group of trusted politicians could hardly lead to effective and responsive governance. The leaders of so many public bodies were in the hands of those who simply did not have the time to study the significant policy issues and to consult the parties concerned.

While the Council members represented the community in monitoring the work of the Institute, the government also appointed senior administrative officers (AOs) to the Council to ensure the Institute's satisfactory functioning. The Hong Kong civil service so far gave the community a good impression, and the elite AOs were generally perceived as clean, competent and efficient. However, the basic flaws of the system also began to show. I had the opportunity of meeting many AOs, some of them were brilliant, most of them were competent, but a small proportion was unsatisfactory. Unfortunately, the staff of the Open Learning Institute encountered a sample from the last group.

The administrative grade recruited predominantly fresh graduates. Hence, those who matured later in life tended to miss out. Normally, AOs moved up the bureaucratic ladder according to a tacit timetable; the outstanding ones naturally advanced considerably faster. But there was no effective mechanism to weed out incompetent ones. The usual weaknesses were that they gradually lost touch with society and they did not have the time to absorb new ideas.

AOs usually worked very long hours, and admittedly they might not have enough time for their families. They attended a lot of official functions and they often went for holidays outside Hong Kong to relax. Basically they had very few opportunities to mix with ordinary people and understand how grassroots families made their ends meet. They did not have time to read broadly, unless they made special efforts. In the end, average AOs did not have a good comprehension of the values and thinking of ordinary Hong Kong people, and they did not manage to catch up with the new global developments. For one, they had not attempted to understand China and Taiwan. Since civil servants had to report to the government for travelling to Mainland China and Taiwan in the 1970s and 1980s, AOs normally avoided going there. Hence, in the early 1990s, senior AOs had to learn how the Chinese political system worked as well as Putonghua through official programmes. Understanding China demanded a lot of efforts, and obviously some AOs did not accord their priority to it.

Within the leadership of the colonial government, there was often a good system to assess the potentiality and competence of AOs. Hence, top government officials could hand pick the cream of the crop as their deputies and assistants. The less brilliant ones were given less important tasks, like joining the Open Learning Institute Council to monitor its work on behalf of the government.

The weaknesses of the Institute's head and management team were soon exposed to its Council, but the chairman and the government officials concerned did not take action promptly. They were too busy and did not want to rock the boat. When they finally decided to act, the government sent an AO to serve as the deputy head of the Institute to supervise the management and the accounts. This intervention alienated the academics in the Open Learning Institute who were concerned with academic freedom and autonomy. The AO who was seconded to the Institute happened to be very arrogant and he certainly made things worse. Throughout the process, the Council and the government officials on the Council did not consult the staff members.

The Council actually had many intelligent lay members. But the advisory committee system of the government did not allow lay members to have much influence. The initiatives were mainly in the hands of the chairman and official members. This was my experience after serving in a number of government advisory committees.

At this stage, the different experiences of various government departments seemed to have an impact on the performance of the civil service. The Housing Department, for example, had to face influential and skilful public housing pressure groups since the early 1970s. The departmental staff therefore became very sensitive to the pressure from public opinion and it also developed competent skills in negotiating with pressure groups. In contrast, the Education Department faced a very deferential clientele, as school principals and teachers at that time would not think of challenging the department. As a result, it was less efficient and less sensitive to the community's demands.

The Open Learning Institute was an innovative project under the David Wilson administration. It was supposed to offer opportunities for those who could not enter the public universities to pursue tertiary education. The Institute was expected to be financially self-sufficient, though the government would encourage institutions like the Royal Hong Kong Jockey Club to make donations to the Institute. No one in the government however had apparently studied the issue in detail. I was the only local among the senior staff, and I was a novice. Hence, there were no local experts who would be able to suggest how the distance learning mode could be adapted to Hong Kong, where people could easily travel from one point to another and they valued face-to-face contact. Worse still, there was no actual plan to cultivate this expertise.

Naturally I was eager to learn, although I was very concerned about the difficult political situation in the territory before and after the Tiananmen incident. I also had to squeeze time for media interviews and writing on current affairs for the local and international media. My media exposure was welcome by the Institute because it helped to remind Hong Kong people of its existence. But my colleagues expected me to concentrate on planning and administrative work and abandon my academic pursuits at least for some time.

The local staff members who shared the ideal of the Institute were frustrated by the incompetence of the management and the lack of channels to articulate their views. I naturally became their representative although as dean of one of the three faculties, I was not even a member of the top management team. This role I discovered was not advantageous for my own career development in academia, but I accepted it anyway.

Apparently my performance at the Institute had a good impression on two lay members of the Council who made me job offers. The first job offer came from Leo Goodstadt, the first head of the Central Policy Unit established by Sir David Wilson, Governor of Hong Kong at that time. I was attracted by the position for two reasons: I would like to make a more solid contribution to the territory, which was in crisis, and I would like to have a close observation of the workings of the Hong Kong government. So I applied for secondment to the government from the Institute for a period of two years. I was grateful that the Institute approved my application.

Chapter 9

At the Central Policy Unit, 1991–1992

Joined the government think tank assessing public opinions on key policy issues, channelling information from all sides: grassroots, tycoons, professionals, legislators, and the pro-Beijing united front. The perks of a senior civil servant.

The Central Policy Unit (CPU) was created as a think-tank for the government. It had a rather small establishment in my days: a deputy head who was a civil servant responsible for liaison with the government to ensure that the CPU had a good understanding of the working of the government and two advisors. I was responsible for political issues and a colleague seconded from the Hang Seng Bank was responsible for economic affairs. Later a third advisor from the British civil service joined us and he was responsible for liaison with London over the transition negotiations and arrangements. We were supported by two senior AOs and a statistician. CPU was supposed to offer a second opinion on government policies, but with this small setup, CPU could not engage in major research projects. It was only a good idea which sometimes had not been effectively implemented.

1990. Interview by Radio Television Hong Kong on the Author's new appointment to the Central Policy Unit.

In the first place, the CPU's small establishment meant that it could not engage in large-scale detailed studies on policy issues. Furthermore, it had to adopt a low profile, and consultation work had to be performed quietly. This meant that those consulted were not given the time and resources to study the issues concerned. They offered their immediate assessments on the basis of their expertise. The CPU did not want to let the public know what policy issues it was studying too, and therefore was in no position to engage the community in deliberations. Finally, the CPU did not have the opportunity to debate with the government officials responsible for the respective policies. It was given assignments by the Governor, to a lesser extent, the Chief Secretary for Administration and the Financial Secretary, and these government leaders then decided what to do with the CPU's assessments and views.

As the colonial civil service had to develop new policy programmes in the 1980s and 1990s, and it did not have adequate policy research resources, it turned to international consulting firms. This was a bad strategy and a waste of resources. In the first place, international consulting firms might have some general expertise, but they did not understand Hong Kong and did not have the time to study Hong Kong people's values. There were numerous examples that Hong Kong people did not get value for money. However, government officials liked to use international consulting firms because some firms would want to please the officials in anticipation of future contracts. Top government officials therefore were confident that these consultancies would deliver what they wanted and would not argue with them.

Local university academics resented this practice. They believed that they had the expertise and a good understanding of the community. Since they were local experts, they often had their own views, and were not eager to please the government officials concerned. Government officials did not have the confidence and expertise to debate with the local academics. Hence, local academics were denied the opportunity to serve the community, and to further develop their expertise so as to secure local and overseas consultancy contracts. Unfortunately this practice remains today. The government's self-protection instinct has been costly from Hong Kong people's point of view.

The CPU's role to offer a second opinion was not well received by top civil servants. They believed that they had the wisdom to make policy decisions, and they did not consider that a small group like the CPU could be wise enough to improve the quality of the decision-making process in the government. Leo Goodstadt was given the nickname of Rasputin by some civil servants as he was compared to the mystic monk Grigori Yefimovich Rasputin who had considerable influence on Nicholas II, the last Czar of Russia. As a CPU member, I did not believe I could command the trust of the senior civil servants I met.

The Unit, however, proved to be valuable in other ways. Sino-British negotiations in 1991 and 1992 were in a difficult period after the Tiananmen incident because of the loss of mutual trust. I spent some time visiting important leaders of the pro-Beijing camp like C.Y. Leung to secure a better understanding of the Chinese position. They were willing to talk to me. Naturally they maintained communications with cadres at the State Council's Hong Kong and Macau Affairs Office like Li Hou and Lu Ping, and I was given messages that they would like to pass on to the British negotiating team.

Apparently both sides appreciated this channel of communication. Confidentiality was maintained, and informal messages could be conveyed without making them public. This channel probably helped to improve Sino-British understanding and facilitated the negotiations. Other messengers came into contact afterwards, those who claimed to be able to deliver messages from and pass on messages to the top leaders in Beijing. I met them without knowing who they were, and I simply passed on information between Leo Goodstadt and these messengers.

After months of contact, we could sometimes exchange casual conversations. A messenger with frequent contact talked about his daughter's education in the Belilios Public School, and I said that my wife also attended the same school decades ago. I came to have the impression that he had come to Hong Kong not too long ago, and like ordinary Chinese parents were very concerned with his child's education.

Later, this messenger casually suggested to me a few times that I should consider becoming a minister after the handover. I replied that I intended to remain an academic, and it was actually my plan to spend only two years at the CPU. I reported this conversation to Leo Goodstadt, and I gathered that probably up to two hundred people had received a similar message.

In the 1980s when I was a media commentator and a critic of the colonial administration, I had many opportunities to meet the leaders of the pro-Beijing united front. We often took part in the media's current affairs panels together. At that stage, I had a healthy respect for them though we did not share the same views. I appreciated their ideals and their sacrifices under the colonial administration before the Sino-British negotiations. In 1991–92, I could detect that their confidence had largely returned after the Tiananmen Incident, and they had high expectations of the new era to come. They certainly did not have a good opinion of the incumbent local civil servants.

I also served as a contact with legislators. I went to meet, for example, Lau Wong-fat, the representative of Heung Yee Kuk, a statutory advisory body that represents interests of the establishment in the New Territories' rural districts and new towns. I met him fairly often to listen to his views. Lau in some ways was a political legend. He was not well-educated, not very articulate, and did not impress people as an effective political leader. Yet he was generous and avoided a high political profile so as not to cause unnecessary jealousy. He offered political donations to the pro-democracy politicians in the New Territories who normally refrained from criticising him. He worked closely as business partners with Li Ka-shing (Hong Kong's tycoon), and this ensured success in his businesses and expanding wealth. He managed to maintain good relations with both the British administration and Beijing, and was largely successful in enabling his son to succeed him. Most people grossly underestimated his political wisdom and skills.

Since Lau did not speak fluent English, and I had some previous contact with him, I was able to solicit his frank views, which he wanted to convey to the government, and which he found difficult to convey to the top government officials he met. I also met pro-democracy legislators who were my friends and brought their views to the government.

As political reforms progressed, the British administration realised that it could no longer rely on a safe majority support in the Legislative Council consisting of official and appointed members. The Wilson administration began to ask senior civil servants to assess support in the Legislative Council for their respective legislative proposals and requests for appropriations. This became a routine exercise after the Legislative Council elections in 1991.

The CPU formed many panels to assess public opinion. There were two groups of top business leaders whom Leo Goodstadt met on alternate Saturdays. Basically it was an arrangement to seek the business community's views on current issues. Gradually there was a certain perception among the concerned public that it was prestigious and influential to join the exclusive club. I attended these panels, and this gave me a very good opportunity to observe the territory's business leaders and learnt their views. Obviously as an academic following Hong Kong politics, this was an important reward for me in joining the CPU.

I was then asked to form a middle-class panel of small businessmen, senior corporate executives and professionals to collect a sample of middle-class views on the performance of the government and its policies. Then there was a panel of grassroots activists. These two panels met once a month. The CPU therefore served as a public opinion assessment centre for the government which had to engage in a competition with the pro-Beijing united front for the hearts of Hong Kong people. Success in this campaign would help lay the foundation for the territory's stability in the final phase of the transition.

April 1993. At the Central Policy Unit's academic forum with Leo Goodstadt.

At the Central Policy Unit, 1991–1992

In 1991–92 when I was with the CPU, this campaign seemed to be easy as the pro-Beijing united front was still suffering from the serious setback of the Tiananmen incident. But the tide was turning. In early 1992, Deng Xiaoping made his famous "southern tour", which marked the beginning of a new round of even bolder economic reforms and opening to the external world. The Hong Kong business community began to respond. Major Hong Kong business groups started to engage in substantial projects in Mainland China. China's annual economic growth rate was able to maintain at an average of about 9% from around 1992 till the global financial crisis in 2008–2009.

While I was working on a research project on the long-term housing needs of the territory, I visited most of the real estate tycoons to collect their views. Soon I was invited to lunch by one of them, and was advised that it was a good time to acquire property. This was in late 1991 and subsequent developments indeed proved this to be the case. I was offered the opportunity to visit one of his company's housing project sites and choose a unit before the open sales. I immediately declined the offer, though I did not report it.

In the 1980s and the 1990s, the last two decades of the colonial administration, most of the privileges enjoyed by senior expatriate civil servants were also offered to local senior civil servants and local senior staff members of public institutions like universities.

As a chair professor and advisor at the CPU, I with my immediate family had a holiday allowance every two years. Hence, my whole family enjoyed some expensive holidays in this period. We once went to a tour of the ancient civilisations in Turkey, Israel, Greece and Egypt, and we were able to visit Bethlehem on Christmas Eve.

One other memorable trip was a tour of Eastern Europe and the Soviet Union in August 1991. In the evening of August 18, 1991, my whole family was taking a stroll at the Red Square in front of the Kremlin. It was shortly after nine in the summer evening, and we saw two black limousines rushing into Kremlin. The curtains were drawn and we could not see the people inside the car. We were a bit puzzled then and wondered why someone obviously important would be in such a hurry to enter the Kremlin at this late hour. The next morning on August 19 before seven o'clock, Grace and I took a walk in the streets near the hotel; my two children refused to get up too early in the morning. We did not notice anything strange.

Later in the morning, soldiers in armoured units and tanks began to appear in the streets. When our tourist bus passed the building of the *Pravda* (meaning "truth", the official newspaper of the Communist Party of the Soviet Union), our Russian tour guide stood up, pointed to the newspaper building, and shouted: "Lies! Lies!" I can still remember that scene. We watched the famous Moscow circus show in the afternoon, and we took the overnight train to Leningrad (soon to be renamed St. Petersburg).

When we walked in the main streets in Leningrad the next morning on August 20, we saw many demonstrators marching peacefully to a gathering. I waved at them and offered some US dollar bills to the leaders of the gathering. He thanked me and we shook hands even though I did not speak Russian. I was probably the only Hong Kong Chinese who made a small contribution to the movement against the Communist Party regime then. This was probably the most memorable encounter in my travels.

August 1991. During the European tour, the author witnessed the crowds gathering in St. Petersburg during the Soviet Coup.

On a less happy note, my father passed away while I was working at the CPU. He had been suffering from diabetes for a long time, and was in and out of hospital for some years. He died of cancer at the age of 84 in June, 1992. He was quite fortunate in that my mother took good care of him. She visited him twice every day while he was in hospital. I only visited him two or three times a week after work. My family concentrated on supporting my mother, while my mother would be responsible for caring for my father. My father's situation reminded me of the importance of family care for the elderly.

My father passed away about 5 a.m. in the morning. My mother and I had the chance of seeing him before he departed. I then returned home to have a shower and went back to work. I did not notify my colleagues and friends, and we had a quiet funeral. Leo Goodstadt learnt about this when he enquired about my father's situation the same day, and kindly suggested that the Governor's private secretary would attend the funeral with the Governor's condolence wreath. I declined the honour but was very grateful for the offer.

Being a CPU staff member brought some unexpected perks. Leo offered to recommend the CPU advisors to be members of the Hong Kong Club. My colleagues welcomed the opportunity but I was not interested. I probably had good social skills, but Grace and I preferred to have a quiet time at home. I always wanted to have some time for reading. Deep down, I realised that I did not enjoy being a politician, and was not very interested in joining the university management. Hong Kong Club membership was a status symbol, and the club house was a good venue to entertain friends. But Grace and I normally did not organise social functions. We only enjoyed going out with the family and very close friends.

Actually, I also let go of the opportunity of joining the Royal Hong Kong Jockey Club, another social status symbol then and now. When I was working at the Chinese University of Hong Kong, the Jockey Club opened a new racecourse in Shatin. But the restaurant facilities were far from being fully utilised in the weekdays in the initial year. Hence, it offered the Chinese University staff the privilege of using the restaurants at very low membership fees. Later when the premise's facilities were fully utilised, the Jockey Club decided to cancel this type of membership. But within the Jockey Club leadership, there were friends of the University who decided to give priority to Chinese University staff to become full members without having to follow the usually long queue. Many of my university colleagues were delighted with the offer, especially those interested in horse races and the Club facilities.

Given my pro-democracy orientations, I speculated that some of my friends in the pro-democracy camp might think I would be co-opted into the government. But the relations between the British administration and the pro-democracy camp were good in the aftermath of the Tiananmen incident. My activist friends were supportive of my work in the CPU, as reflected in their participation in the CPU's panels and our frank exchanges of views in our meetings.

There was an unpleasant incident though. Grace and I were invited to a dinner hosted by Wang Gungwu, the then Vice-Chancellor of the University of Hong Kong, and attended by Prof. John Burns and some of his colleagues in his department. John Burns commented to Grace in a very sarcastic tone that I now had a fat job in the government. I was unhappy with this rudeness. I always believed that criticisms against me should be directed at me, and my wife should not be involved.

In early 1992, I was invited by Patrick Cheng, then president of the City Polytechnic of Hong Kong, to apply for the deanship of the Faculty of Humanities and Social Sciences. I was offered the position, but I wanted to complete my two-year contract with the CPU. I was most grateful that Patrick Cheng indicated that he was willing to wait. After some discussions with Leo Goodstadt, I was able to leave the CPU at the end of June 1992 and returned to a tertiary institution.

Like most Hong Kong people, I felt uncertain about the territory's future. However, since my family could leave for Australia any time, we decided to stay. Grace and I enjoyed our jobs in Hong Kong, and we planned to stay as long as we could. We believed that we probably could find comparable jobs when we were in Australia, but we could never find the kind of job satisfaction that we could get in Hong Kong. Our two children attended an international school run by the English Schools Foundation, and they would most likely go to universities in Australia. There was a worry in my heart that I might have to emigrate before 1997.

I heard many stories from among friends that Hong Kong migrants found it difficult to adjust in Western countries. Occasionally, single female tourists were denied entry because the authorities feared that they might stay or attempt to remain through marriage. The political uncertainty exacted a heavy price on many hard-working families, and I felt sad for the people who had to encounter various types of humiliation and pains of adjustment.

Shortly before I joined the CPU, the United Democrats of Hong Kong was established in 1990 in preparation for the first ever direct elections to the Legislative Council. The Tiananmen incident triggered its formation, as Hong Kong people were eager to support a force and an organisation that would serve as an effective mechanism for checks and balances. Such mentality was described by the media then as "resistance against communism with democracy (民主抗共)". This eagerness overcame the hitherto hesitation and doubt over the formation of a political party based on Hong Kong people, but the organisation still avoided the use of the word political party. Martin Lee served as its chairman and Szeto Wah as its parliamentary whip, a leadership that simply could not be challenged.

In the 1991 Legislative Council elections, candidates of the United Democrats won handsomely. Except for two candidates in New Territories East, all the other candidates won and the group secured fourteen seats altogether. The United Democrats easily emerged as the leading organisation of the pro-democracy movement. It became a dialogue partner of the British administration for consultation in its final years. The pro-Beijing united front could not offer much competition then, because Hong Kong people at that time had lost their confidence in the Communist Party of China due to the Tiananmen incident and the Basic Law drafting process. In comparison with the pro-democracy activists, pro-establishment candidates had not yet grasped the essential campaign skills. They did not take too long to catch up though.

In the few years from 1989 to 1992, I worked as an administrator at the Open Learning Institute, experienced the political turmoil of the Tiananmen incident in Hong Kong, stood at the front ranks of the pro-democracy movement for a while, accepted a civil service job, and finally returned to a normal academic life.

Chapter 10

Life of a Faculty Dean

Quality control mechanisms to upgrade from polytechnic to university status probably created some enemies. Universities' myopic attitude to achieve higher international rankings.

I started work at the City Polytechnic of Hong Kong in July 1992 as dean. The institution, together with the Hong Kong Polytechnic, was in the process of securing university status then. The two polytechnics were degree-granting tertiary institutions, but each degree programme had to go through an external accreditation process first, whereas tertiary institutions with university status could design and offer its own degree programmes. There was obviously a prestige issue, as students and their parents naturally considered a university more prestigious.

As faculty dean, I had to assume the responsibility to help secure the university status for the City Polytechnic. The initial task was to ensure that it had firmly established the quality-control mechanisms and processes. In actual fact, in the eyes of the public and the international academic community, the quality of the staff and students of the two polytechnics could certainly qualify for university status. The funding from the government was generous, and hence as new tertiary institutions, their staffing, facilities and equipment were first-rate by world standards.

The expansion of the tertiary education sector was an important part of the Wilson administration's policy programme to restore confidence in Hong Kong after the Tiananmen incident. The first part of the programme package was infrastructural construction including the new airport at Chek Lap Kok. The second part was to enable 25% of the young people in the appropriate age cohort (18–24 years of age) to enrol in a tertiary institution, about 18% in universities and 7% in teachers training colleges, nursing schools, etc. Upgrading the two polytechnics was an important part of the second policy goal because of their large student intakes.

An intermediate- and long-term task of the City Polytechnic was to encourage its staff members to engage in research and produce publications of advanced international standards. As a new tertiary institution, the City Polytechnic concentrated on degree programme design and external accreditation work, and the staff members had not been expected to engage in research in a substantive manner. The challenge was severer at the faculty of humanities and social sciences.

The initial policy of the government was to encourage the two polytechnics to engage in less academic and more applied degree programmes. The English department, for example, did not offer courses in English literature, but concentrated on courses in teaching English as a second language to help meet the strong demand for English teachers in primary and secondary schools. Similarly, the Chinese department did not offer degree programmes in classical Chinese literature nor modern Chinese literature, but specialised in translation and linguistics.

April 2003. Annual dinner and talk at the CityU Executive MBA Programme's early years.

In those days, most Polytechnic staff do not have doctoral degrees and they were largely recruited for their professional expertise. My challenge was to facilitate them in initiating university level research plans with the objective of gradually producing scholarly publications of international standards. I indicated that pressure would not come immediately, but it would come eventually when all faculty members should be prepared to face the challenge. Admittedly, there were colleagues in their forties and fifties who were afraid to adapt or very reluctant to do so, and some of them perceived me as a threat who refused to recognise their past contributions. Colleagues in the science and engineering faculties were better qualified and equipped to face the new challenge, and they had taken the initial steps well ahead of their counterparts in the humanities and social sciences. As dean, I had to deliver a respectable performance to compete with science and engineering faculties for funding, according to the rules of university management.

I met with a number of interesting and challenging cases during my tenure as dean. When I first joined the City Polytechnic, two law departments belonged to my faculty. I was challenged by one or two colleagues seeking promotion who argued that colleagues in the two law departments had different requirements regarding Ph.D. degrees and publications. In recruiting law professors, especially those responsible for professional training, we had to face the pressure of market forces. It was difficult to attract an experienced practising lawyer earning a much higher income to join a law school in

Hong Kong then. In some cases, I as dean, being satisfied that the candidate could deliver competent teaching, would avoid making demands regarding further degrees and publications in recruitment. This was especially so in the field of conveyancing. Similar issues arose in the recruitment of professors in the accounting and banking fields too. I was quite happy to support their subsequent departure to form a new law school as I had no expertise in the field and I realised that a law school had its own culture and norms. With the departure of the two law departments, it became easier for the faculty to maintain uniform standards and requirements.

In the early 1990s, the City Polytechnic was quite generous in offering full-pay leave for colleagues to study for Ph.D. degrees abroad. This appeared to be overgenerous in the eyes of academics in the established universities. I was sympathetic and simply wanted to standardise the procedures by linking the length of full-pay leave granted to the applicant's years of service. Obviously there was no point offering this benefit to new recruits. I too understood that this would be a transitional arrangement to help colleagues with some years of service to adapt to new challenges.

There were a few cases when colleagues used the leave so granted to fulfill the residential requirements for a foreign citizenship. I did not interfere, and in general I was sympathetic in approving no-pay leave in this connection. There was one colleague who was dissatisfied that he only got no-pay leave without financial support. He was honest in acknowledging that his stay in Australia was intended to acquire his citizenship there. My position was that I recognised his years of service. If he had enrolled for a Ph.D. degree programme, I should be able to offer some full-pay leave according to the recently established regulations. Since he only registered for a postgraduate diploma course, I could not offer any financial support. Subsequently, he acquired his Australian citizenship using no-pay leave, but he still complained often about his heavy financial burden while he was in Australia.

In order to encourage research, I let it be known that at least two pieces of international publications were expected for promotions from lecturer to senior lecturer at the City Polytechnic scale then. This was actually very lenient. Later a colleague came to see me and showed me a publication in a Bangladeshi journal and another in a Filipino journal and claimed that she had fulfilled the requirement. I explained to her that the requirement was set to demonstrate research standards achieved through publications in internationally recognised journals. She was disappointed, but in subsequent years she performed quite well in terms of international publications.

In the expansion of tertiary education and the upgrading of the two polytechnics in the 1990s and beyond, some journalists and commentators observed that Hong Kong academics were the best paid in the world. Hence, a logical demand that their performance should be at the front ranks of the world too gradually emerged. With the establishment of the Hong Kong University of Science and Technology in 1991, which was eager to show its achievements and challenge the leading positions of the University of Hong Kong and the Chinese University of Hong Kong, keen competition among the tertiary institutions in the territory started to surface. International rankings assessed by some international agencies came into the picture. Within a few years, leaders of Hong Kong's tertiary institutions all boasted the improvements in international rankings of their respective institutions.

The competition obviously had some positive impact. University academics in the 1960s to 1980s period in general were not very hard-working. An economics professor at the University of Hong Kong once described to me that a senior lecturer at his university was in the best position to enjoy life: he worked 28 weeks a year (14 weeks for each of the two semesters), 6 years out of 7 (one sabbatical year after six years of service), and only two days a week. He cited the senior lecturer position as an example because an academic usually joined the university at lecturer rank. After many years of service, he normally would be awarded one promotion to senior lecturer despite his lacklustre performance. Further promotions usually demanded recognised achievements in research. In the late 1970s, a few very senior expatriate academics were labelled "furniture" in the university's senior common room because they spent very long hours there drinking.

When I was at the Chinese University of Hong Kong in the late 1970s and 1980s, there was a common saying: "Revise to receive pay, sit comfortably to collect money (溫故'支薪', 坐以'袋幣)". This mocking, twisted proverb in academia depicted that lazy academics not only declined to do research, they also did not spend much time in preparation for lessons and simply relied on their old lecture notes. With the gradual introduction and widespread use of student assessment of teachers' performance in the past two decades and more, teaching standards improved considerably.

Yet the competition in international rankings and student assessment of teachers' performance also had their drawbacks. Political leaders and political scientists understand very well the need to maintain balance. The Ming Dynasty (A.D. 1368–1644) introduced the eight-legged essays (八股文) format in the civil service examinations. The original idea was to demand a formal format so as to facilitate grading. However, the gradual increasing rigidity in following the format eroded creativity and innovative ideas, and historians severely criticised the system.

As international rankings of universities became a significant status symbol, university management teams devised all kinds of staff performance indicators to improve their institutions' respective rankings. Book publications were discouraged, and instead, publications in top international journals were emphasised. Publications in Chinese were normally not counted, while columns in newspapers and articles in magazines were considered community service. These measures were especially disadvantageous for scholars in the humanities and social sciences. It was sad to see that leaders of the local universities were so absorbed in this competition that they refused to engage in an honest and constructive dialogues to restore appropriate balances.

In the beginning of 2000s, the management City University of Hong Kong (CityU, previously the City Polytechnic of Hong Kong, achieved full university status in 1994) attempted to abolish the employment of tutors. The rationale was that they were counted as members of the teaching staff. Their inclusion reduced the number of publications per teaching staff member, and hence lowered the university's relevant score in the assessment of its international ranking. Some disciplines like social work were severely and adversely affected because they relied heavily on field instructors, etc. There were small tactics like attracting top scholars to serve as visiting academics, so much so that their prestigious publications during their brief tenure would be counted as the university's academic output in the relevant years. There was no consideration of the real contributions of the visiting scholars, and whether the university and indeed the Hong Kong community were getting value for money. Rumours were that the Hong Kong University of Science and Technology initiated this practice which was quietly copied by the other universities.

This heavy emphasis on top international journals generated increasing pressure on academics. As the expansion of university education gradually slowed down by the turn of the twenty-first century, and the population trends influenced by the low birth rates meant that the number of young people in the age cohort of 18–24 years of age slowly declined, university recruitment began to slow down. At the same time, the supply of new Ph.D. graduates was expanding as more and more young graduates pursued postgraduate studies. Securing tenure in a local university became more challenging and demands were severe. In the recent decade or so, work pressure was such that young academics often did not have adequate time for their families, especially when they had young children.

This work pressure forced some adjustments and adaptations that might not be beneficial. Many academics privately acknowledged that they had no time for reading. They only read what was required for their research projects, and even then they often glanced through the readings for the purpose of literature surveys. Many academics did not dare move to new research areas because this would involve exploratory work lasting perhaps a year or more, and during this exploration period, publication outputs would drop. When I became a university academic, I appreciated most the opportunity to read and think, and to avoid various work pressures in a competitive economy. I was lucky to have secured my tenure and promotions before the arrival of this tough pressure.

This pressure also extended to Ph.D. students who were often given scholarships or financial support for three years. When the assessment of university performance included the completion rates of Ph.D. students within three years, professors had to exert pressure on them to finish their degrees within the said period. Ph.D. students therefore often opted for safe research topics that could be completed on schedule, and they hesitated experimenting with bold, innovative ideas. In this way, the potential of some good Ph.D. students was not fully exploited.

University professors, especially those who had not secured their tenure or were about to apply for promotions, realised that they needed satisfactory assessment from students. A small number of students who had been reproached by their teachers retaliated by giving them the lowest grades in the assessment. Few teachers wanted to have to explain why they did not secure satisfactory student assessments. Hence, in the recent two decades, university teachers avoided scolding their students, and instead chose to give them high grades, less assignments, short and well-defined reading lists, plenty of lecture notes, etc. These lenient measures were usually adequate to secure favourable assessments. But at the same time, most university teachers would be reluctant to spend time to talk to their students because of work pressure.

When I first started teaching at the Chinese University of Hong Kong in 1976, there were no fixed student consultation hours, and students might knock at their teachers' office doors any time. In my department of government and public administration, most staff members would have occasional afternoon teas and sometimes even games of basketball with their students. These teacher-student social interactions became increasingly rare in the recent two decades. While I was faculty dean and later when I was relieved of my administrative duties, I still spent quite a bit of time with student activists and those planning to pursue postgraduate studies.

In my first year at the City Polytechnic, I started a new journal in Chinese entitled *Hong Kong Journal of Social Sciences (*香港社會科學學報*)*. This was of course a rather idealistic venture, and was initiated by a young academic Law Kam-yee who assumed responsibility for the work involved. I had to secure funding support for the project. The challenge was to convince academics to give their best papers to the journal. Naturally if they had written something outstanding, they would send them to the top international journals, and not to a new journal in Chinese.

We tried to set a good example. Right in the beginning, we relied on young scholars who shared our ideal. We followed a strict anonymous double review process like all important international journals. We therefore did not ask senior academics to contribute on a friendship basis as they might send us commentary-type papers that might not pass the review process. To turn down an invited paper from an established academic could be embarrassing. Some friends suggested that the journal might be used as a vehicle to cultivate ties with Mainland China scholars as they were interested to publish in Chinese outside the Mainland at that time. We refused to do this.

The journal continued to be published under the aegis of CityU for more than twenty years until I retired in June 2015. My colleagues at CityU were not interested because they all realised the pressure among local university professors to publish in top international journals. So Law Kam-yee re-located the journal to the Education University of Hong Kong and resumed publication where he worked. The Education University agreed to provide funding support. Law Kam-yee and I published two issues every year with the exception of one year; the quality of the articles was perhaps not outstanding, but consistently respectable. As editors, Law and I attempted to ensure the academic quality of the journal, but we could not handle the distribution network. The CityU Press attempted to help, but it had to give up soon afterwards. The economy of scale factor had such an important impact that the distribution of academic and professional journals worldwide has fallen into the hands of a few major publishing houses; a global oligopolistic situation has emerged.

We could not break into the Mainland China market, as the Chinese authorities imposed a censorship on sensitive topics like Taiwan and Xinjiang. We were proud that we published articles on the Taiwan independence issue, and explored it from an academic perspective. Before the tightening of the political atmosphere around 2008-9, we could attend the conferences of journal editors in the humanities and social sciences field. Once or twice, I was even elected a member of their board of directors of the association concerned. But the contacts were terminated quietly after the heightened authoritarianism which had emerged shortly before the Beijing Olympics in 2008. We no longer received any invitation letters.

Printing was cheaper in Shenzhen than in Hong Kong. We had toyed with the idea to print the journal there to cut cost. Eventually we abandoned the idea because we were concerned that the printer might not deliver if the authorities found the contents of the journal sensitive. The CityU management could not be bothered with these issues; they would rather focus on the international ranking of the university.

International ranking has more significance for CityU than the Hong Kong Polytechnic University. The latter accepted the mission given it by the government; it was willing to concentrate on certain professions and industries like textiles and clothing, tourism and hotel management, physical therapy, optometry, etc. CityU, on the other hand, wanted to be a research university in competition with the three leading universities, namely, the University of Hong Kong, the Chinese University of Hong Kong and the Hong Kong University of Science and Technology.

Going back to the issue of academic journals, one could easily detect the short-sightedness of the local university presidents. In Singapore, the leading universities there were committed to develop their journals into leading international journals, which could contribute to the establishment of their brand names. Local university academics in Singapore were requested to contribute their very best scholarly works to the selected local journals. Within a relatively short period of time, they successfully achieved the objective. The university management teams in Hong Kong were too concerned with the annual rise and fall in the international rankings. There was no serious plan to cultivate local academic talents. In fact, local universities were quite happy to recruit expatriates because the internationalisation of the university staff would help to improve the relevant score in the assessment exercises.

As Hong Kong approached 1997, localisation was planned not only in the civil service, but also in multinational corporations and the traditional British enterprises. Universities, however, did not have localisation plans, as they intended to recruit the best people globally. In the early 1990s, tertiary education was still in a stage of rapid expansion, and this sector needed to import talents. I accepted this basic position. I accepted that the expatriate staff should stay and should continue to contribute to Hong Kong. I appealed to them to give up their expatriate status and perks, and I planned to treat all staff members equally in terms of tenure, promotion, etc. I considered that it would be unfair for an expatriate to keep his perks and also wanted to enjoy tenure on par with the local staff members. The position was not welcomed by most expatriate staff.

The City Polytechnic in its initial decade and more was very dependent on expatriate staff, especially at the senior management level. Their English language skills were an asset, and their knowledge of and networks with the British accreditation system for tertiary institutions also accorded them a distinct advantage. Most of them did not make an attempt to understand Hong Kong, nor learn to speak Chinese (neither Putonghua nor Cantonese). Quite a few had a sense of superiority.

In January 1995, I was involved in a case of plagiarism. It was a secondary school textbook for the subject of Economics and Public Affairs. In there, there were some excerpts from a book by Norman Miners on the government and politics of Hong Kong. I was asked by the publisher Summerson to write a volume on Public Affairs. I agreed because the publisher was a prominent member of the Hong Kong Observers, and Summerson published the group's collection of newspaper columns. Obviously the high school textbook did not contribute to the advancement of my academic career. It did not offer me much in terms of financial rewards, as the number of students taking the subject was quite small. There was keen competition and Summerson's market share was limited. I accepted the assignment mainly out of friendship. I wrote the volume with the help of a postgraduate student research assistant; I was busy and careless, and had not spent enough time to go over the manuscript very carefully. I had no intention of shifting the blame to the young man, though many of my colleagues could guess the story. I assumed full responsibility for the case.

There were many media reports on the incident, which was embarrassing perhaps because I was a popular current affairs commentator. I was worried about the embarrassment for my wife Grace and my two children who were in secondary school then. Fortunately, the people around them seemed to be quite understanding.

The then president of the CityU, Patrick Cheng Yiu Chung, was very understanding too. To avoid generating trouble for him to whom I was grateful, I took leave and asked for a formal investigation by the University Council.

The verdict of the investigation team cleared me of plagiarism, but criticised me for neglect in the production of necessary references and notes. I was prevented from involvement in administrative duties for two years, and my salary was slightly reduced to that of the average of chair professors in the institution. I never cared too much about university administrative work. When I applied for the deanship position at City Polytechnic and met staff members, I stated that I did not want to be dean for a long time. I would be quite happy to step down to concentrate on research work after my three-year term. I was only forty-five years old in early 1995, and I believed that I could still be very active in scholarly output.

At that point, my plan was simply to go back quietly to research work. There were some job offers, including academic positions in Australian universities and a senior executive position in a newspaper. I was not tempted. My China contact approached me to explore the idea of my joining the pro-Beijing united front; my immediate straightforward answer was that I was glad to be a full-time academic again.

I was grateful that all my friends in the pro-democracy camp treated me kindly in the aftermath of the scandal, and most of my academic friends did the same. Someone, obviously quite close to me at the CityU, went to the police to complain against me for corruption in organising a training event for a group of academics from Zhongshan University in Guangzhou. The police investigation cleared me of any wrongdoing, and I was informed about this only after the completion of the investigation.

I could easily guess who the person was, but I decided to forget about the issue. This colleague did come to me earlier and said that his new superior exerted pressure on him to inform against me. A few newspaper and magazine articles written by authors with pseudonyms criticised me, and I decided to ignore them. I believed that maintaining peace of mind for me was most important. I was most grateful that family life was not affected.

Chapter 11

Quiet Academic Life in the Midst of Change

Academic with a low political profile. Academic exchanges with Finnish universities and Chinese scholars from three generations. With confidence in Hong Kong's future restored somewhat, a sense of uncertainty and a "feel bad" mood prevailed.

In the second half of the 1990s, my research areas were focussed on Hong Kong politics, the development of Guangdong, and Chinese foreign policy. I also wrote about Chinese politics. These have been my research areas all my life. My research on the development of Guangdong started relatively late in the 1990s. I managed to secure a grant from the Research Grants Council to build a Pearl River Delta (PRD) collection at the City University library. Development in the PRD would have an important impact on Hong Kong; proximity to the PRD would give local academics a distinct advantage in doing field work there (one could go to Guangzhou early in the morning, work from lunch hour to dinner time and return to Hong Kong around 8 p.m. or so the same day).

This was a new research area where competition was less keen. I therefore encouraged my young colleagues to explore research on the PRD.

I did my Ph.D. thesis on China's policy towards Japan in the period of 1968–1974 when they normalised their relations. In the following years, I mainly wrote about the broad framework of Chinese foreign policy. In the 1990s, increasingly there was keen competition from Chinese academics from Mainland China. There were also those from the U.S. and other Western countries who stayed abroad but maintained strong networks of ties in Mainland China. They were able to do interviews and had much better access to first-hand information through their informal channels. As a Hong Kong academic without such access and having to rely solely on published materials, I found it difficult to compete.

I therefore moved to new areas where competition was less keen. I began to start my research and to write on China's policy towards Africa, Latin America, the Gulf Co-operation Council, and so on. I enjoyed the challenge of new research areas. Obviously I realised that I could not easily publish on Sino-American relations, as I only had access to second-hand materials.

These years of quiet academic life allowed me considerable time to travel. In the 1990s, I managed to visit all the Chinese provinces. I attempted to go to the poorer places too. I went to some very poor villages in Guangxi in the mid-1990s, where the families had an annual cash income of around 200 *yuan* each. These villages were only a few hundred kilometres from the prosperous PRD. On the other hand, one could see the "new rich" in the major coastal cities in Mainland China who had benefitted from the new round of economic reforms and opening to the external world since early 1992.

In these travels, I often made use of my network of ties with my academic friends in Mainland China. As a chair professor in political science in a public university in Hong Kong and maintaining a low political profile, I was much welcomed in major universities in China. I was able to engage in exchanges with three generations of academics. The first generation was the elderly scholars who had established their reputation before the founding of the People's Republic of China or in the early 1950s. They were often not active in research in the 1990s, but their leadership positions in many leading universities were restored, and their recognition by Western scholars accorded them a respectable role in various exchange programmes with Western universities.

The second generation of university professors were those who completed their postgraduate education and started teaching in universities before the launch of the Cultural Revolution. They suffered during the Cultural Revolution years, and most of them could not cope with the research and publication demands of modern international universities. They felt quite frustrated, but they were the

November 1993. Appointed guest professor by the then Central-South Institute of Politics and Law, Hunan, China.

1995. Training session for China's senior civil servants.

administrators of university departments. Their second language was Russian, and they had very limited English. Sometimes I met them at conferences in the U.S., but they found it difficult to adapt and adjust, and they realised that they could not benefit much from visits to Western countries and the universities there. Naturally they had a good understanding of Chinese politics and Chinese foreign policy, and I learnt a lot from them in our informal discussions. They quite enjoyed visiting Hong Kong though as they were much more at ease in a Chinese society.

The third generation was the young university academics who had benefitted from scholarships from Western universities in the early years of the reform era, mainly in the early 1980s. They acquired their Ph.D. degrees in Western universities and returned to teach in China. They had a good grasp of Western literature and advanced research methods, and they in general performed well. There was naturally a self-censorship. The further they were promoted within the university management, absorbed into prestigious official think-tanks and consulted by senior Party leaders, the less academic freedom they enjoyed. I had many opportunities of meeting them in academic conferences in China in the 1990s, and later, as I became more involved in the pro-democracy movement in Hong Kong, our frank exchanges became rare.

In the aftermath of the Tiananmen incident, many Ph.D. students from China attempted to stay in Western countries and it was not difficult for them to do so then. Actually, the better their academic qualification, the easier it was to secure jobs. Most of my acquaintances in my field taught Chinese politics in second-line universities. They normally had a comfortable life and fruitful academic careers. But since the beginning of the 2000s, their friends who had returned to China and managed to move to important positions in leading universities often came to visit the U.S. and Europe and were received by senior government officials and top universities in the U.S. and other Western countries. I could easily detect the envy of those who did not choose to return to China.

This network of ties with academics in Mainland China was very useful for my travels and research in China. Without a host institution, one would not be able to visit government departments and research institutions and interview cadres and research personnel. The network would also allow me to secure government documents and policy papers of a non-confidential nature, but without the network's official support, they would not be made available for an outside academic from Hong Kong. At a practical level, this network would facilitate me in getting accommodation in university guest houses and transport by university vehicles. Normally, I offered my books as souvenirs, and American cigarettes as small gifts for university car chauffeurs and junior administrators.

Chauffeurs enjoyed a special status in universities and public institutions in China. They were members of the proletariat. As members of the staff establishment, they had a decent salary, accommodation and all social security benefits provided by their work units, as well as extra incomes like gifts from visitors. It was interesting to note that during lunches and dinners, they sat with their bosses and guests. It was widely believed that they knew many secrets of the senior cadres they served, and in turn were well treated by them. In investigations against corrupt cadres in China, the law enforcement agencies often arrested their secretaries and chauffeurs first to squeeze information out of them. These considerations did not apply to visiting academics, but it was wise to placate the chauffeurs who offered services.

In the 1980s when I visited universities in Mainland China, I was very impressed that university presidents, junior clerks and chauffeurs lived in the same type of housing units within the same buildings. This was genuine egalitarianism. In the 1990s, these phenomena gradually disappeared. Expensive furniture, electrical household appliances, cameras, etc., appeared in the homes of senior staff members. The income gaps continued to expand. There was a deliberate policy on the part of the Chinese leadership to reward the intelligentsia. In the years just before the Tiananmen incident, the following complaints often emerged: "those making atomic bombs make less than those selling tea-eggs; and barbers earn more than surgeons (造原子彈不如賣茶葉蛋，拿手術刀不如拿剃頭刀)".

To promote economic development and reward enhanced productivity, the Chinese authorities after 1992 were prepared to offer the professionals and the highly educated considerably higher incomes; egalitarianism in remuneration was no longer practised. At the end of the 1990s, many of the academics in China became car owners and they learned to drive. Car ownership caused a lot of parking problems and traffic jams in the staff residential areas within campuses because car ownership among university staff had not been anticipated.

In the 1980s and early 1990s, Hong Kong people were often embarrassed by their friends in Mainland China who often enquired about their salaries. I felt the same too because my salary was about one hundred times as much as that of my counterparts in China then. Deep down they probably had some doubts about the superiority of socialism. By the turn of the century, academics in China began to talk about their improvements in remuneration and the value of the properties they owned. If husband and wife both worked in the state sector, the family had two flats, sometimes in the centre of the cities where they lived.

I usually explained to my friends in Mainland China that the cost of living in Hong Kong was very high. They enjoyed better housing conditions than us, and they probably ate better. People in Hong Kong normally had more disposable incomes to spend on clothing, household electrical appliances and travelling. But our work pressure was high. At that stage, my academic friends in top universities in China began to complain that though their incomes had much improved, work pressure had become very high for them too.

In my travels to China, I observed the mutual benefits system at work. Within the same policy system, cadres could travel to various parts in China and enjoy the hospitality of their counterparts. Reciprocity was the rule. This was obviously convenient for the cadre corps. As all expenses came from the government budget, the financial burden for the state was substantial. My trade union friends, for example, could send me to their trade union friends in other cities, and there I could enjoy free accommodation, meals, and sometimes local transport arrangements with small payments.

How students treated their teachers in Mainland China was certainly the envy of Hong Kong academics. When university professors in Hong Kong organised functions like academic conferences, we usually could not or would not mobilise our students for help. Postgraduate students on scholarships were asked to deliver a number of hours of work in support of their respective departments, and these work hours were usually calculated in a very lenient manner. In Mainland China, students often considered it an honour to be asked to help their professors and universities. To a lesser extent, this was also true in Taiwan.

When Hong Kong academics visited universities in Mainland China, we were often invited to lavish dinners, and our host institutions would ask junior colleagues or postgraduate students to accompany us to local tours. We were in no position to return these favours. When scholars from our host institutions visited us in Hong Kong, we did not have expense accounts, and we only invited them to simple meals in ordinary restaurants, often in university staff restaurants with no liquor. We did not take them for tours in Hong Kong, nor were we in a position to make such arrangements. So our scholar friends from Mainland China might think we were rude and did not show our respect for them. This was especially so for elderly academics from universities in inland provinces who were not adventurous to move around alone.

In the 1980s, graduates from Mainland China began to come to Hong Kong to pursue postgraduate degrees. This flow much increased in the 1990s and after as local universities began to expand their postgraduate programmes. These postgraduate students were usually quite intelligent and hard-working. To science and engineering professors, they were assets in laboratory work; to teachers in the humanities and social sciences field, they could not offer much assistance. Their English very often were poor, and they were not familiar with the

Western literature. They might be able to demonstrate good scores in English language tests, but their competence in spoken English and their performance in academic discussions were far from satisfactory. They were often late developers, and when they returned to China after graduation to teach in universities, they often became competent academics, especially in terms of publications in academic journals in Mainland China.

There was a case I still feel regretful even today. This Ph.D. student was assigned to me, and his English was very poor. There was keen competition for good Ph.D. students among colleagues; I was normally assigned the less promising ones because I was not involved in the department's management, and because I did not mind accepting weaker students. At the end of their first year during which time they had to do considerable course work, postgraduate students were expected to deliver a seminar. This student panicked during the seminar, and the presentation was disastrous. The department head, an expatriate, decided to send him packing; I advised to retain him. I was confident that he could complete his Ph.D. degree and go back to China to teach in a tertiary institution, but probably not in a top university. The City University of Hong Kong had already granted him one year scholarship, and the department had to assume some responsibility too because he had been given admission without a vigorous English language test. He worked hard in his first year. I was in a minority, and the student had to leave City University in the end. In the mid-1990s, postgraduate students were allowed to write their Ph.D. theses in Chinese at City University, but this practice was terminated later.

There were occasions when Ph.D. students with weak English panicked during their oral thesis defence sessions. I was usually sympathetic. I asked the student to calm down and take a deep breath, then I asked a question speaking very, very slowly. Since this kind of scenario was not uncommon, the examination panels usually avoided pushing the Ph.D. candidates too hard, and the defence sessions often lacked rigour.

In my department at City University, Ph.D. students had to attend a seminar course in which they took turn to present a paper. The idea naturally was to encourage serious scholarly discussions and cultivate the competence to defend one's position logically. But the vast majority of students came to this compulsory course without a sense of participation, they just sat quietly and a few even left at the end of the presentation. They probably had not read the papers in detail before, and had no intention to take part in serious discussions. In this aspect, postgraduate student performance was far from satisfactory.

Since City University was not a research university, the number of Ph.D. scholarships allocated to it was quite small. As a chair professor, I usually had one Ph.D. student only, and sometimes two. I considered this a waste of my expertise. This was also one reason why my colleagues wanted our university to be treated on par with the top three universities in the territory; we should at least be able to engage in fair competition for Ph.D. student enrolments on an equal basis.

My opportunity came in 1995 from an unexpected country – Finland. An academic administrator Marita Siika rang me from Turku after she got my name from the Finnish consulate-general in Hong Kong. She was looking for a Sinologist to help in her M.A. programme in Modern Asian Studies for all Finnish universities. I went there for three weeks and gave a series of lectures. In view of its small population (5.5 million in 2017), the Finnish ministry of education often funded postgraduate programmes on a national basis. Universities formed a consortium to apply for government funding support. Then a university would be selected as the organising institution and an administrator appointed. Students applied for scholarships to take part and they came from the member universities of the consortium.

As a guest lecturer, I was offered economy airfares, full-board accommodation and some spending money (about HK$7,000 for three weeks). Apparently there was a division of labour, University of Helsinki specialised in traditional Asian Studies, and the University of Turku (an old capital city) specialised in contemporary Asian Studies.

My performance probably impressed my Finnish hosts, and they came back for me later when they formed an Asian Studies School for Ph.D. students. The School would recruit four or five Ph.D. students and offer them scholarships, but they would still be affiliated with their original universities. They would meet twice a year, in February and August, for two or three days of intensive seminars. The School would last four years, as students' scholarships would support them for four years during which time they were expected to complete their Ph.D. degrees.

I was appointed academic director of the School, and I attended the seminars, gave a paper each time, read the students' manuscripts and offered them advice and guidance. The remuneration package was similar to what was described above, though the spending money was even less (about HK$2,000 each time) as I stayed only three or four days for each session. Usually one or two more academics were invited to help for each session, often from universities in Europe.

I enjoyed teaching and I was just happy to be able to contribute. The arrangement worked well for both sides and I served as academic director for four terms, altogether sixteen years. Seminars were held in different universities in turn, so I could visit various cities in Finland, a country with beautiful landscape. A seminar session usually included a sauna evening with a barbecue and lots of beer. Often the host institution would organise a traditional sauna in a small log cabin in a forest near a river. After the sauna, the participants were to jump into a nearby river to cool themselves. August evenings were already quite cold in northern Finland, and in winter, it was freezing cold. But I quite enjoyed these sauna sessions. There were plenty of natural forests in Finland, and I loved walking in these forests. One could gather berries and mushrooms in the summer.

Academically, quite a number of the younger generation of scholars in the Asian Studies field in Finnish universities attended the Asian Studies School. Two of them from the first School had become full professors. I was very proud of them. Actually the system was changed after sixteen years, and funding support went to each university directly. That was when my scholarly association with Finland ended. It was not easy for young academics in Finland. University positions were scarce because of almost zero population growth. Competition was keen, and one often had to move from one city to another. For young people, relationships were hard to maintain. Finland was a country without many natural resources, except forests. Per capita GDP was high by world standards, but taxation was also very high due to the comprehensive social security system. Disposable incomes for young academics were quite limited.

During these sixteen years, I visited Finland for more than thirty-two times. Almost every time, I arranged to visit another European country from Helsinki. I visited

Iceland, Malta, Albania, Cyprus, etc., while making use of the Finnair connecting flights. This was the fringe benefit of my academic service to Finland. From Helsinki, there was a ferry service to Tallinn in Estonia, which took three and a half hours. Later there was a hydrofoil service, which took a bit more than one hour only. Tallinn was a very attractive old city, and a day trip to Tallinn from Helsinki was quite pleasant. I often went to Tallinn, and I observed how this small constituent republic of the USSR emerged as a modern, high-tech country. From Turku and Helsinki, there were overnight ferry services to Stockholm too, and I sometimes went to visit Sweden from Finland.

Since 1992 or so, Hong Kong people's confidence was gradually restored and political stability returned. Emigration slowed down in the years to 1997, and emigrants began to return to Hong Kong after they had obtained their foreign passports as an "insurance policy". They probably found it hard to get equivalent jobs elsewhere or they could not fit in very well. The return of some emigrants demonstrated an enhanced confidence in the future of Hong Kong.

The restored confidence coincided with a heightened sense of identity with China. In a university survey, more people than before identified themselves as "Chinese". Hong Kong young people's understanding of China was still unsatisfactory. Understanding China requires conscious efforts that can only be sustained by dedication and keen interest. Hong Kong youth apparently lacked these. They were too preoccupied with their day-to-day life.

With the approach to 1997, Chinese authorities' influence over Hong Kong became increasingly important. The Preparatory Committee for the HKSAR were set up in December 1995. By December 1996, the Selection Committee nominated the first Chief Executive, C.H. Tung, to be First Government of the HKSAR.[29] Later in the month, the Selection Committee also elected the provisional legislature. In February 1997, they announced the team of top civil servants. Both the Chief Executive and the provisional legislature started to work after their elections.

Hong Kong people had no say in all these processes. More important still, the community was not too concerned if they were excluded from these decisions. Few people were interested in these matters, and the media merely speculated on the chances of the potential candidates who had been nominated to fill the post of the first Chief Executive. In September and October of 1996, the media offered many profiles of the declared

---

29 See "Decision of the National People's Congress on the Method for the Formation of the First Government and the First Legislative Council of the Hong Kong Special Administrative Region," adopted by the Seventh National People's Congress at its third session on April 4, 1990, in *The Basic Law of the Hong Kang Special Administrative Region of the People's Republic of China*, Hong Kong: One Country Two Systems Economic Research Institute Ltd., 1992, pp. 67–69.

March 1997. Meeting Hong Kong's first Chief Executive designate, Chee-hwa Tung.

candidates. The pro-democracy political groups did not treat such issues as an important part of their political platforms in the Legislative Council elections in September 1995.

Predictably, Hong Kong people were more dissatisfied with the British administration in Hong Kong, and the then Governor Chris Patten became their target. The community's support for the Governor's annual policy address dropped steadily from 1992 to 1995. A series of polls likewise indicated that the community's evaluations of Chris Patten were becoming increasingly negative. Some even thought that Hong Kong had declined in stature as a result of his years as Governor.

While the Hong Kong community was increasingly frustrated with the British administration, their assessment of the Chinese authorities turned out to be slightly better. Their confidence in the "one country, two systems" arrangement for the 1997 changeover appeared to improve somewhat. Those who wanted Hong Kong to be independent fell from one quarter in 1993 to less than one-sixth in early 1996.[30]

Yet in the few years prior to 1997, Hong Kong people were frustrated with the territory's political, economic, and social environment. They expressed considerable pessimism regarding the future, and a vague sense of uneasiness prevailed in the approach to 1997.

In more specific terms, Hong Kong residents were worried about the spread of corruption. Citing an increasing number of convicted corrupt police officers in the past two years, the commissioner of the Independent Commission against Corruption (ICAC) acknowledged that the uncertainty over 1997 might prompt some officers to make "quick money". Most journalists were disturbed by the phenomenon of self-censorship, another issue of concern. Over half indicated that the pressure of self-censorship came from their superiors. Their outlook was bleak: only one out of ten expected to work until retirement. Six out of ten staff of the government funded Radio Television Hong Kong were worried that

---

30 *South China Morning Post*, February 17, 1996.

they would lose their editorial independence after 1997. In fact, senior police officers, ICAC officers as well as teachers were reported to have high emigration rates.[31]

Such emigration peaked in 1996. Primary and secondary school principals and teachers were worried about their superannuation funds, and therefore opted for early retirement to claim payments before 1997. In those years, teachers between 40 and 50 years old were qualified to apply for emigration to Australia, Canada, and New Zealand.

The "feel-bad factor" was the most striking feature of the public mood since the summer of 1995. The economy grew healthily. Exports remained strong, and massive infrastructure projects continued. Unemployment, albeit at a ten-year high, was only 3.5%. Yet three out of ten employees were concerned that they would lose their jobs, although it was still fresh in their minds that employers acted quickly to retain staff by better remuneration and promotions in the early 1990s. At the same time, personal consumption had been declining.[32]

Most analysts agreed that the "feel-bad factor" was mostly psychological and related to the approach to 1997. Unemployment was due primarily to long-term

---

31 *Ming Pao,* July 29, 1995, August 5, 1995, February 17, 1996, March 16, 1996, June 13, 1996.
32 See *South China Morning Post*, August 9, 1995, November 7, 1995, and November 9 1995.

structural changes in the economy. As labour costs in Hong Kong rose, industrialists shifted their operations to the Pearl River Delta in China and Southeast Asia. From 1980s till the mid-1990s, the rapid growth in the service sector such as finance and tourism was able to absorb the surplus labour. Later, when labour-intensive service industries also moved to China to cut costs (data-processing was a prime example), the unemployment rate climbed slowly. Admittedly, some jobs, for example, in the construction industry could not attract enough local labourers.

Private consumption especially of low-income employees declined as a consequence of wage stagnation. The propensity to spend of the middle class was eroded by the retreat in the real estate and stock markets since early 1994. Some also had to support family members living and/or studying abroad. With the approach of 1997, many families saved more in preparation for the uncertainty ahead. Apparently the airlines and the real estate companies managed to absorb the middle-class purchasing power at the expense of restaurants and department stores.

By mid-1996, the economic situation seemed to improve; economic confidence indicator recovered (from 73 points in January 1996 to 87 in October), after two years of continuous decline. Unemployment rate gradually dropped. Both the real estate and stock markets performed well too.

Trade unions and labourers were unimpressed. The Hong Kong Confederation of Trade Unions complained that 1.5 million employees suffered a decline in real wages in 1995 and 1996 and were unemployed from time to time. Half of the workers and labourers surveyed believed that wage levels, unemployment and social welfare would deteriorate after 1997.[33] Middle-class families expressed concern about the decline in real income and the job situation, especially in employment opportunities for their children. In the midst of these mixed signals in the economy, the Hong Kong government adjusted its forecast for economic growth for 1996 from 5% to 4.7%.[34]

Such are glimpses of Hong Kong people's moods and assessments in the years just before 1997. Confidence seemed to have been restored somewhat, but there was still a sense of uncertainty and a "feel bad" mood. Those who had the means had already acquired an insurance policy through emigration of at least one family member. On the other hand, the wave of emigration generated chances of new upward social mobility. In the years before 1997, localisation plans in the government and major multinationals together with the emigration exodus offered many attractive positions in the middle echelons and above. Those who

---

33 *Ming Pao*, September 12, 15, 1996.
34 *South China Morning Post*, August 31, 1996.

chose to stay and those who could not afford to leave were benefitted.

These opportunities further enhanced Hong Kong people's resilience and pragmatism. Since the vast majority of people could not leave, they had to adjust to the new reality. They therefore did not support confrontations with Beijing, and this explained the decline in the popularity of Chris Patten, the last Governor. Resentment against Chris Patten seemed to be the strongest within the establishment and the business community. The establishment needed friendly ties with and the recognition by the Chinese authorities; the latter desired stability and prosperity. The business ties with Mainland China had been strengthening.

Chris Patten impressed Hong Kong people as a highly skilled politician from a democratic country. He was sophisticated in attracting media attention and building an image of a leader who was close to its people. He was skilled in establishing shifting coalitions with different groups of legislators to ensure the smooth passage of legislation and funding requests. He asked the civil service to set up new performance standards so as to improve its services for the people, and to be more responsive to their demands.

Since the return of Hong Kong to the China, the four Chief Executives so far had not been able to match his standards. Chris Patten's gradual decline in popularity revealed the values of Hong Kong people. While the liberal, democracy-inclined citizens welcomed the new model of political leadership, a majority of Hong Kong people apparently were more satisfied with stability and prosperity, and they wanted to avoid rocking the boat. This mentality facilitated the offensive of the pro-Beijing united front which was carefully rebuilding its networks after the Tiananmen incident.

More significant still, Sino-British confrontations in the 1990s prompted the Chinese leadership to abandon the original plan in working jointly with London for the first Special Administrative Region government, and to start "a new stove", so to speak. The original thinking was that the first Chief Executive would likely be a top civil servant well recognised by the community. Business leaders were not considered then because of competition within the business community, and the impartiality of the Chief Executive was a serious concern. C.H. Tung, who was selected by the British administration to join the Executive Council (the cabinet) in October 1992 was finally selected. The civil service was directed to support the transitional arrangements.

Some journalists and commentators observed that C.H. Tung and Edmund Ho Hau Wah, the first Chief Executive of the Macau Special Administrative Region, shared some similar characteristics. They both came from very rich families and inherited their respective family business empires. Their businesses failed, and were then bailed out with Beijing-backed capital. They owed Chinse authorities serious favours and were therefore considered loyal. The joke was that you had to become bankrupt first before being selected to become the Chief Executive.

Chapter 12

Approaching 1997 – Political Transitions

Prior to 1997, political reforms, if any, were limited. The first Hong Kong SAR government "elected" with Chinese characteristics.

Prior to 1997, the pro-democracy camp was small in scale and fragmented. Despite the fact that over a million people marched during the Tiananmen incident in 1989, the pro-democracy camp failed to unite into a single party. The United Democrats of Hong Kong began with only about 220 memberships in 1990. Around the same time, the Hong Kong Democratic Foundation was formed with a small group of liberal professionals and businessmen. This failure could be attributed to their differences in class interests and their relationship with the Chinese Communist regime.

While the leaders of the Association for Democracy and People's Livelihood attempted to demonstrate their strong commitment to grassroots interests, they were suspicious of the United Democrats of Hong Kong's attempts to strike a compromise between the interests of the grassroots and those of the middle class. The Hong Kong Democratic Foundation, while supporting democratisation process, aimed at promoting the "enlightened" interests of the upper socio-economic strata.

Many leaders of the United Democrats of Hong Kong had a deep distrust for the Chinese leadership, and were eager to exploit for electoral gain Hong Kong people's fear of communism and any future Chinese interference. In contrast, most members of Meeting Point were "nationalist" in their orientation and avoided confrontation with the Chinese authorities. They had a strong interest in the developments in China and were keen to contribute to China's modernisation.

For a short period of time, the Tiananmen incident did heighten the appreciation of democracy by Hong Kong's political establishment. It was known that London and the British administration in Hong Kong supported an accelerated democratisation. Politicians loyal to Beijing however countered this enthusiasm with the view that such a demand was "naïve". They warned that such a move might lead to greater confrontation with Beijing after 1997, and stepped up the publicity to attack such demands.

The decision in January 1990 to adopt a snail pace for democratic reform by the political system sub-group of the Basic Law Drafting Committee came as no surprise. It agreed to keep the number of the 18 directly elected seats in the legislature of 60 seats, only to increase it to

24 by 1999. The Committee proposed that, by 2003, the legislature would comprise an equal number of directly elected and functional group representatives.

By this time, the British government was willing to accept the conservative proposal with minor revisions. While it supported rapid democratisation during the Tiananmen crisis in 1989, it adopted a realistic attitude in its negotiations with China when relative calm returned. Even though London wanted to achieve an "honourable" retreat, it required the co-operation from Beijing.

For the 1991 Legislative Council elections, nearly 2 million voters registered. The British administration spent considerable efforts to encourage voter registration. A large proportion did not register voluntarily and many of them had never actually voted since 1982. The significance of the Legislative Council elections and the publicity efforts failed to mobilise a majority of them to vote. More than 750,000 (39%) eligible voters turned up to vote, that was 330,000 more voters than in the previous District Board elections. It was regarded as a moderate success already.

The pro-democracy camp declared victorious. They won 15 out of the 18 directly elected seats in 1991. They could not claim to have the support of the whole community, but could certainly say that they had the backing of the politically active who supported the cause of democracy. Those who stayed away or refused to register could be interpreted as being apathetic to some extent; they could see no way to change the *status quo* and had little faith in the development of representative government. It could also mean that they were satisfied with the *status quo* and did not want to change it by political means.

The conservative business sector realised that it had to organise itself to articulate its interests. A coalition of 89 businessmen and professionals represented their business interests in the Basic Law Drafting Committee and the Basic Law Consultative Committee. After the promulgation of the Basic Law, some of them formed the Business and Professionals Federation of Hong Kong in 1990 to actively lobby Chinese leaders in Beijing. Others formed a Liberal Democratic Federation of Hong Kong, with the objective of supporting candidates to run for the 1991 elections. In general, their attitude towards party politics was vacillating. They were reluctant to get involved in electoral politics, but preferred to exercise their informal influence through lobbying important British administration and/or Beijing officials. With the lack of commitment, both groups were totally ineffective in the direct elections in 1991, though they managed to secure a few seats in the functional constituencies.

The pro-China groups suffered severe setbacks in the Tiananmen incident since 1989; they were forced to keep a very low profile for some months. The New Hong Kong Alliance, for example, was established in

May 1989 by some leading pro-China businessmen and professionals, who formulated a political model to prevent the pro-democracy camp from dominating the future legislature. Other pro-China figures, who at one stage openly condemned China's suppression of the student leaders in Beijing, soon re-aligned themselves and mobilised support in the elections in 1991.

The pro-China groups were certainly disappointed with the loss of all three candidates in the direct elections to the Legislative Council in 1991. Yet they demonstrated their effective organisation and mobilisation power in the campaigns. The local New China News Agency admitted that it was reluctant to promote political stars, and it had to change immediately. The pro-Beijing united front also blamed the developments in the Soviet Union just before the elections, and cited the mass media's emphasis on the pro-Beijing background of their candidates as the reasons for their failure.

Since the Legislative Council elections in September 1991, the British administration could no longer count on a stable majority support. Senior government officials had to lobby legislators to secure their support of legislative programmes and requests for appropriations. They often complained that they spent up to one-third of their time in the Legislative Council in lobbying. This called not only for commitment and dedication, but also an enthusiasm to adapt to the changing political environment and cultivate new political skills.

On issues concerning the pace of political reforms and the relations with China, the British administration had to rely on the support of the pro-democracy groups as the pro-business legislators were most reluctant to antagonise Beijing after the 1995 elections. Under the circumstance, the British administration might have to take a more radical stance than they thought appropriate. This in turn reinforced the Chinese authorities' suspicion that the British administration colluded with the pro-democracy parties to confront Beijing in the final years of the transition.

On social service issues, the British administration encountered considerable pressure from the pro-democracy parties so much so that its basic political philosophy was sometimes threatened. Its position became more untenable because the pro-business legislators were eager to establish their credentials with Beijing and refused to compromise or engage in serious bargaining with the British administration and the pro-democracy parties.

The bargaining power and the room of manoeuvre for all political parties were strengthened as the British administration no longer enjoyed a complete control over the legislature. The pro-democracy parties and the pro-Beijing groups obviously wanted to establish their clear political identities and often clashed with the British administration. Even the conservative pro-business

Liberal Party did not want to be closely associated with the British administration.

The business community believed that the direct lobbying of Chinese leaders in Beijing would be the best way to articulate their interests. Yet its political party, the Liberal Party, realised that it had to take part in elections, including direct elections, to enhance its credentials in the eyes of Beijing and the British administration. The creation of nine new functional constituencies and ten seats by electoral colleges in 1995 elections provided them important opportunities. The Liberal Party leader, Allen Lee, won a seat in the New Territories Northeast constituency, and it did well in the old functional constituencies as well as in the nine newly created functional constituencies. After 1997, they remained a formidable force in the legislature after 1997 and some were convinced that competing in elections helped safeguard their business interests.

In July 1992, the Democratic Alliance for the Betterment of Hong Kong (DAB), a grassroots political party loyal to Beijing, was formally set up. In a way, it implied that the pro-Beijing united front recognised the electoral system as legitimate. In competing with the pro-democracy camp, the united front with the DAB as co-ordinator hoped to secure a majority in the legislature to order to protect China's vital interests. From an orthodox ideological point of view, the united front had to develop and expand through campaigns while testing the calibre and loyalty of its supporters. From an organisational point of view, it had to cultivate candidates, consolidate and expand its grassroots networks, and refine its campaign strategies and tactics.

I followed these developments closely, did my research and published in international journals as well as the local print media. I continued to serve as a media commentator. A new generation of academics, columnists and media commentators had emerged, and their performance was impressive.

In 1994, the United Democrats of Hong Kong and Meeting Point merged to form the Democratic Party (DP). The leaders and activists of the two groups shared similar backgrounds in terms of participation in the territory's student movement and social movement. Their modes of thinking, values and organisational cultures were quite close. In preparation for the coming direct elections to the Legislative Council in 1995 and the challenges of the transition to 1997, both parties agreed that an amalgamation was the wise move. Meeting Point became a formidable political force in winning four geographical seats in the 1991 elections; among its members, there were many outstanding theoreticians and intellectuals. The negotiations were conducted in secrecy; it was rare that confidentiality was tightly kept among pro-democracy groups. Martin Lee remained chairman of the new party. Apparently the two groups did not actively approach the Hong Kong Association for Democracy and People's Livelihood as they considered that the Association would like to maintain its independence.

In the 1995 Legislative Council elections, the voter turnout rate was 36%, three percentage points lower than the last election, even though the number of registered voters increased substantially, from 1.9 million in 1991 to 2.57 million in 1995. The rate showed that political apathy still prevailed. Hong Kong people realised that most major decisions had to be based the Sino-British agreements, or were actually made by Beijing. Such perceptions reinforced their sense of political impotence. They understood that the Legislative Council elections would have a limited impact on their livelihood (including unemployment and economic growth issues).

Admittedly, many Hong Kong residents had not established a habit of participating in elections. Most of them voted in order to fulfill a civic obligation, rather than to exercise their political right to elect a government. The increase in the number of voters was partly due to the mobilisation power of the Beijing-loyal groups and partly to the lowering of the voting age from 21 to 18.

The performance of the pro-democracy parties was outstanding in the Legislative Council elections in 1995. They controlled from twenty-seven to thirty-one seats, an assessment that was based on the political inclinations of some independents and the Association for Democracy and People's Livelihood. The pro-democracy alliance thus commanded a majority and could therefore oppose positions taken by Beijing, by London, or by both regimes jointly on issues ranging from the further development of representative government to the expansion of social services.

Such victory was obviously embarrassing for the Chinese authorities: voters had supported Beijing's critics. It was natural for the electorate to expect that criticisms and strict monitoring would create checks and balances *vis-a-vis* those in power, and it was a common understanding that Beijing's power over Hong Kong exceeded that of the British administration. Yet Hong Kong people were astute enough not to confront the Chinese authorities. On the other hand, to the Chinese leadership, there was obviously no incentive to accept further democratisation in Hong Kong.

Though the Beijing loyalist groups did not perform well in terms of the number of seats won in the 1995 elections, they secured 34% of the votes. Their mobilisation power was impressive. In the Hong Kong Island East constituency, a relatively unknown candidate representing the pro-Beijing Hong Kong Progressive Alliance competed against Martin Lee, leader of the Democratic Party, and received almost 30% of the votes. This performance indicated the power of the grassroots network of the pro-Beijing organisations.

More significant still, public opinion expressed much sympathy for the leaders of the DAB who lost to the candidates of the pro-democracy parties. Many Hong Kong residents felt that DAB was doing a good job in serving the public, and their presence in the legislature would have contributed to the well-being of the community. If the existing simple majority, single-seat constituency system was replaced by a proportional representation system in medium-sized, multi-seat single-vote constituencies, the DAB and its allies would have been able to win at least five of twenty seats in the direct elections, according to their share of the votes in 1995. Such a change was indeed adopted for the 1998 Legislative Council elections.

The performance of the DAB in the 1995 elections showed that the community services offered by the pro-Beijing parties would be rewarded in the long run. Given their financial resources, they would be able to expand their grassroots network further. They also realised at that stage that they could not toe the Beijing line entirely at all times, and there were sometimes obvious signs of disagreements between the DAB and the Chinese officials responsible for Hong Kong.

By the mid-1990s, Chinese authorities had in place their system of honours to reward allegiance and loyalty in the local community, such as memberships in the National People's Congress and the Chinese People's Political Consultative Conference. Such efforts and resources laid a strong foundation for the pro-Beijing political parties. With a more favourable electoral system and the support of the pro-business groups, the Chinese authorities worked to secure a reliable majority support in the legislature after 1997.

In the District Board elections in September 1994, the Urban/Regional Council elections in March 1995, and the Legislative Council elections in September 1995, the major political groups all demonstrated sophisticated campaign strategies and skills. Most political groups, with perhaps the exceptions of the DAB and the Hong Kong Federation of Trade Unions, were severely handicapped by their relatively small work force and shortage of funds. Consequently, they had to effectively deploy their resources. All political groups had been skilful in attracting media attention and in using opinion surveys. The pro-democracy political parties no longer had the tactical edge they enjoyed in the previous decade.

Hong Kong's elections in this period were remarkably clean if they were judged by the standard of developing democracies. The political culture obviously detested "money politics", and the purchase of votes was unthinkable. Minor violations of electoral rules were common and were usually in disobeying such regulations as in the display of publicity materials, in under-reporting campaign expenditures and the like. Violence was virtually non-existent.

Despite their spectacular electoral victories in 1991, the pro-democracy groups failed to expand their membership significantly. The DP probably did not have more than 200 to 300 active members, nor did it plan to develop into a large party. It depended on the media to maintain an attractive image in the community. Image-building therefor usually dominated the tactical considerations of the DP leadership. The DP had been successful in establishing itself as a staunch critic of both the Chinese authorities and the British administration, and as the most important group fighting for the freedom and rights of the people of Hong Kong. Its efforts had been rewarded at the elections.

The DP, however, was overwhelmed by a number of challenges. In the first place, its concern for publicity often alienated it from grassroots pressure groups who were problem-oriented and wanted concrete solutions. The DP could certainly help to exert pressure by raising grassroots issues in the Legislative Council or with senior government officials. The party's high profile and hunger for publicity often resulted in the failure to compromise and delays in settlements. Many grassroots pressure groups were concerned about being used for publicity's sake and therefore preferred to act without the involvement of political parties.

To attract media attention, the DP legislators often dramatised their gestures and statements. Harsh criticisms of Beijing obviously had a better chance of making newspaper headlines than balanced statements. The DP's success with the media, however, made it very difficult for its leaders to establish a dialogue of mutual trust with senior civil servants. Such political posturing had a negative impact on party support among the intelligentsia. As July 1997 approached, a considerable segment of the middle class in the territory was willing to compromise.

Some leading members of DP were also leaders of the Hong Kong Alliance in Support of Patriotic Democratic Movements in China, which emerged in the wake of the Tiananmen incident. The Chinese authorities regarded the Alliance as a "subversive" organisation and officially ruled out contact with the DP on that basis. They were also unhappy about DP's refusal to support the Basic Law and its opposition to the provisional legislature.

In 1996, however, the Chinese authorities began to soften their stance. When Lu Ping, director of the State Council's Hong Kong and Macau Affairs Office, visited the territory in April to consult the local community on the work of the Preparatory Committee, attempts were made to invite leaders of the Hong Kong Professional Teachers' Union (PTU) to take part in the consultative sessions. Two important leaders of the PTU, Szeto Wah and Cheung Mankwong, were also DP leaders and Legislative Councillors. A formal dialogue between Lu Ping and the PTU leaders therefore could be interpreted as a breakthrough. Subsequently, the PTU leaders made some uncompromising statements, and their invitations were withdrawn. Different views obviously existed among the Chinese authorities on whether to resume dialogue with the pro-democracy groups in Hong Kong.

In the following August, Vice-Premier Qian Qichen, head of the Preparatory Committee, indicated in its fourth plenary session in Beijing that the Chinese authorities were willing to discuss Hong Kong-related issues with people who held varying views on democracy. This was seen as an olive branch from Beijing to the DP, perhaps with a view to involve the DP in the Selection Committee (for the Chief Executive and provisional legislature) soon to be established.

The DP refused to alter its stance, and again Beijing's gesture did not lead to a breakthrough. DP believed that their being in the Selection Committee would not influence the setup of the first HKSAR government. They were wary of Beijing's united front offensive and its divisive tactics. Softening their position might lead to severe challenges from The Frontier, a new political group founded by radical legislators such as Emily Lau and Lee Cheuk-yan, the then leader of the trade union, the Christian Industrial Committee.

I was most impressed by the dedication of Lee Cheuk-yan who led a very frugal life. Despite being a graduate of the University of Hong Kong in the 1970s (the top university then), he could have landed a more ludicrous job. Instead, he chose to dedicate himself to the lower paying trade union work in his early career. Later he became the General Secretary of the Hong Kong Confederation of Trade Unions and a legislator for over ten years. We have had frank discussions on the pro-democracy movement throughout the years.

It was significant that all opinion surveys and poll favoured the participation of the DP in the Selection Committee and a change of DP's stand on the provisional legislature in exchange for a dialogue with Beijing. This would contribute to political stability if DP were to operate within and outside the establishment, especially when there were differing views among the Chinese authorities.

At this stage, DP felt that it should map out its strategy for the post-1997 era. It had no choice but to prepare to survive as the opposition in the political wilderness. It realised that the impact on the HKSAR government's decision-making process would be limited, and its influence very much depended on the extent of freedom enjoyed by the mass media. This new position would require considerable adjustment on the part of the DP leaders. Their electoral successes in 1991 and especially 1995 enabled them to play a key role in the legislature. In many ways they had become part of the political establishment, and their influence was felt through constitutional channels.

The questions still loomed large: would the post-1997 era demand the DP to return to their pressure-group role of the late 1970s? Would some DP legislators opt to stay within the formal political structure, and, if so, would they be absorbed by the pro-Beijing united front?

The formation of The Frontier meant that at least three prodemocracy groups would compete among themselves. The Frontier adopted a staunchly anti-Communist stand, while the HKADPL would be keen to maintain a dialogue with Beijing and to operate within the establishment. The Frontier was founded in anticipation of the transformation of the electoral system into one of proportional representation in direct elections. The radical independents had to work together in order to carve their share of the votes from the DP. There was speculation, however, that the Chinese authorities were pleased with the emergence of The Frontier.

Chinese leaders gave a top priority to the cultivation of the business community since the Sino-British Joint Declaration in 1984. Their rationale then was simple and straightforward: Hong Kong must remain attractive to investors. If investors stay, the stability and prosperity of the territory would be maintained. In both the Basic Law Drafting Committee and the Preparatory Committee for the HKSAR, business leaders dominated the memberships.

Having confidence in China's economic reform and opening to the outside world, the business community in return had been firmly supporting the Chinese government in the Sino-British conflict which they regarded as temporary and irrelevant come July 1997. They were bullish about the economic future of China and Hong Kong's role in China's economic development. Such business confidence explained the continuing boom in the real estate and the stock markets (though with mild adjustments) in the years just before 1997. It was understood that a great deal of money flowed from China into the Hong Kong markets too.

At this time, the richest dozen or so Hong Kong tycoons had the chance to articulate their interests through direct access to the very top Chinese leaders who sometimes visited Guangdong, a neighbouring Chinese province. They believed the best way to cultivate good relations with China was through generous donations to pro-Beijing projects (such as the Better Hong Kong Foundation) and major investments in China. In this way, the HKSAR government would respect their interests. Support for local pro-business political parties was unimportant, and might even be troublesome.

Meanwhile, the existing political system, underpinned by the political philosophy of the British administration, continued to favour the business community. Prominent businessmen continued to dominate the major advisory committees through government appointments. The functional constituencies allowed business interests to be represented in the legislature. Yet, local business leaders opposed the political reforms, and disapproved Chris Patten, the Governor, in his handling of relations with Beijing. It was in the 1995 Legislative Council elections that a group of second-generation business leaders felt compelled to compete for the elections to the nine new functional constituencies to counter the rising demands of the pro-democracy groups and pro-Beijing trade unions.

It was clear from the course of drafting the Basic Law that Chinese authorities often wanted to retain final control, especially in matters relating to the autonomy of the political system' Chris Patten's original political reform proposals in October 1992 to increase substantially directly elected seats in the Legislative Council gave pro-democracy groups a chance to secure a majority and exert control. This was certainly antithetical to the original plan of the Chinese authorities.

To ensure a reliable majority support for Beijing's Hong Kong policy in the legislature and government, the Chinese side cancelled the so-called "through train" approach, "started a new path" and initiated a Preliminary Working Commission in 1993 chaired by Qian Qichen. It has the mandate from the National People's Congress to advise on the formation of the first HKSAR government and legislature, and to nominate members of a Preparatory Committee (150 members from Mainland and Hong Kong was announced in January 1996). The Preparatory Committee was responsible for setting up of a Selection Committee (400 members were announced in November 1996) to select the first HKSAR government and the Chief Executive in December 1996.

The most significant functions of the Preparatory Committee and its Selection Committee were to serve Beijing's "united front" strategy and to legitimise the formation of the first government of the HKSAR. Important interest groups in the territory such as business organisations, professional associations, political parties, and grassroots groups were targeted in the recruitment. From the beginning, the Preparatory Committee adopted the principles of confidentiality and collective responsibility.

Those who had hoped to see more elements of democracy and transparency in the workings of the Preparatory Committee in relation to the Preliminary Working Commission were sorely disappointed. The June 1996 survey showed that four out of ten respondents had extremely low or low confidence and over half had no confidence at all in the Preparatory Committee. The confidence level in the Preliminary Working Commission was even lower.[35]

In recruiting members for the Preparatory Committee, Chinese authorities cultivated a number

---

35   *South China Morning Post*, June 24, 1996.

of pro-Beijing group and avoided dependence on one political organisation. One Country Two Systems Economic Research Institute had eight seats, New Hong Kong Alliance had seven, Hong Kong Progressive Alliance had five, and Liberal Democratic Federation had five. The performance of these political groups in recent elections was not satisfactory. In comparison, the DAB was assigned four seats only, despite the fact that it was able to pose a serious challenge to the DP in the elections that took place in 1994 and 1995. Chinese officials responsible for Hong Kong probably wanted to tighten control of the united front. They did not welcome the development of political parties with strong mass support which was independent of Beijing's control and guidance.

Members of the Preparatory Committee were largely business leaders who had little time for the work, and its Secretariat based in Beijing assumed a heavy responsibility. Participation by Hong Kong experts were limited. The One Country Two Systems Economic Research Institute and Hong Kong Policy Research Institute, both of which were funded by some important Preparatory Committee members, might have played a role in policy research.

In turn, the process taken by the Preparatory Committee to nominate and elect members of the Selection Committee demonstrated a style of "elections with Chinese characteristics". Instead of allowing various important interest groups to nominate their representatives to be elected by the Preparatory Committee, each person took part on an individual basis. It also retained full discretionary power in drawing up the final list of candidates. In the final voting process, all the fifty-six Mainland Chinese members voted alike, and became decisive in the outcome of the elections.

As a result, there were no surprises from the Selection Committee membership. Whether the Chinese leadership designated a candidate for the post of the first Chief Executive was not the question. Similarly, in the election of the provisional legislature by the Selection Committee, Qian Qichen appealed for support for those candidates with experience in legislative affairs. The Committee took the cue and returned thirty-three incumbent Legislative Councillors plus eight former Legislative Councillors. Fifty-one of the sixty members in the provisional legislature were members of the Selection Committee; thirty-three were members from both the Selection Committee and pro-Beijing political groups. Only six were neither members of the Selection Committee nor pro-Beijing political groups.

In the final stage of the transition to the 1997 changeover, the appeal of the British administration weakened. Its consultative system of advisory committees could not compete with the Legislative Council for the limelight. The Sino-British confrontations created difficulties for it to co-opt respectable community leaders into the consultative system of advisory committees. Senior civil servants were inclined to recruit more compliant figures. There was a general lack of initiatives as members of many advisory committees complained about a lack of important papers to discuss, and felt that they could contribute little. A few resigned in frustration.

The original strategy of the British administration was to choose a group of prominent non-politicians – business people, professionals, and academics – to fill the advisory committees so that they could offer civil servants valuable advice and support. Apparently, the emphasis had been too much on support. As a result, advisory committees gradually lost its important function. Given the pattern of China's united front strategy, most community leaders at this stage already displayed an over eagerness to please the Chinese authorities. Membership in advisory committees became a status symbol. It is still the case to this day.

With the approach to 1997, interest groups had to face the new challenges and devise various ways to ensure that their interests were effectively articulated. The Hong Kong General Chamber of Commerce, for example, which was dominated by British *hongs* [36], had to shed its image of having a privileged status

---

36 "Hongs" is a local Cantonese name that refers to major British business houses like Jardine Matheson & Co. established in Hong Kong during the colonial period since 1841.

under the British rule. In the mid-1990s, the Chamber started to elect leaders who could communicate well with the Chinese authorities. They gained recognition and were appointed as members of the Preliminary Working Commission and Preparatory Committee. For the first time in 1995, the Chamber joined in the celebration of the National Day of the People's Republic of China.

With key professional associations, similar changes occurred. While expatriates adopted a low profile, voluntarily or otherwise, leaders had to compete on the basis of their access to Chinese authorities. They wanted to retain their importance in determining professional qualifications. Professional firms who had an early start in the China market in the late 1970s tended to do better in their influence and status. Their chiefs very often received appointments and honours from the Chinese authorities.

Business and professional groups had to work harder to lobby the legislature in order to protect their interest, since the British administration had lost its safe majority support in the Legislation Council in 1991 in the development of representative government. They normally counted on the support of the pro-business Liberal Party. But they found that it was no longer enough. To achieve a majority vote, they also had to lobby the pro-democracy groups. Their dialogues were generally not fruitful and their relationship was frustrating.

There were discrepancies in core value and little incentives on both sides to engage in any give-and-take bargaining. The pro-democracy groups focused on championing the cause of the lower social strata and became quite effective in extracting concessions from the government; any compromises would be perceived as betrayal. The business and professional groups valued efficient government, and they refused to accept the price of democracy in the form of time-consuming debates and delays. For illustration, none of the eighteen proposals put forward by the Legislative Councillors in 1995 came to fruition in January 1996, and only one had a date set for its first reading. The business and professional interests therefore chose to concentrate on lobbying the government. I attempted to follow the dialogue in my research and I was able to attend some of these meetings.

Increasingly, the Hong Kong government played a balancing role in the legislature. It could not afford to be seen to consistently endorse positions of the pro-establishment interest groups. Such groups started to realise in their frustrations that it might be more rewarding to lobby the Chinese authorities, at least with regard to post-1997 scenarios. The Chinese authorities respected business interests and were keen to maintain an executive-led system of government after 1997, which would diminish the legislature's role in the policy-making process.

In the mid-1990s, a significant part of the Hong Kong community, including grassroots pressure groups, still looked with suspicion at politicians and their political parties. Pro-democracy groups, such as DP, neglected to cultivate these groups for lack of time and resources. Their parliamentary work was seen as publicity seeking; this alone further alienated some groups. This neglect sparked initiatives among groups of radical social workers who were disappointed with the lack of progress in the democratisation process. Consequently, they became confrontational, resulting in further polarisation. Many small radical groups emerged to protest against the Chinese authorities.

The Christian community too was faced with the divisive issue of how to prepare for the approach to July 1997. The Catholic Church wanted to serve as "the conscience of society". While running a large number of Catholic schools, hospitals, and charities with heavy government subsides, Catholic Church leaders needed to maintain good relationship with the incoming HKSAR government. Other Christian groups bickered over such issue as China's National Day. The Lutherans and Methodists were most amenable to co-operating with the Chinese authorities. Some of their leaders argued that "Hong Kong is returning not only to China but to the People's Republic of China". Conversely, local evangelical churches that had strong links to China's secret "house churches" began to move underground.

The Chinese authorities began publicly building their community network and local influence in Hong Kong in the decade before the changeover. The Hong Kong government apparently did not see this as a serious threat. Since the later 1980s, people complained about District Officers from the Home Affairs Branch, that they were unable to speak Cantonese (local Hong Kong dialect), were too young and immature, and were insensitive to local traditions. Posted for only two to three years, they were unable to build strong ties with community leaders in their districts. Since the early 1990s, the funding for the Branch was reduced.

Many district-based Beijing loyalist groups emerged since the 1991 elections. Though their development was still handicapped by the Tiananmen incident, they were regaining momentum with the approach of July 1997. While they did not seem to be very active, their names, such as the Kwun Tong Munching Friendship Promotion Association, appeared in advertisements in support of the work of the Preparatory Committee. Funding came mainly from pro-Beijing business community, and their leaders were often honoured with appointments by the Chinese authorities. At this stage, such groups tended to concentrate on social activities.

The mobilisation power of those groups loyal to Beijing was mixed, despite the financial and political resources at their disposal. In the 1995 Legislative Council elections, for example, Fung Chi-kin of the

DAB competed in the financing, Insurance, real Estate and business services functional constituency and lost badly to the DP candidate, Cheng Karfoo. Fung was assumed to have the firm endorsement of all the Chinese enterprises and their friends in these sectors. His failure indicated that many employees of Chinese enterprises refused to deliver the votes as directed by their superiors.

By early 1997, both Chinese leaders and Hong Kong people showed a higher level of confidence in the stable transfer of power. People began to accept that the post-Deng era had begun, and the leadership succession in Beijing was no longer a threat. Chinese leaders emphasised Hong Kong's value to China and worked hard to retain investors. The compositions of the Preparatory Committee and Selection Committee were evidence. China's economic reforms and openness to the outside world were shown to be irreversible. Soon a provisional legislature in 1997 "elected" by the Selection Committee replaced the 1995 legislature which lasted only 21 months.

Hong Kong professionals, if they had to choose between unemployment in Canada or Australia and a job comparable to their own in Shenzhen, would opt for the latter. Their worry over 1997 was much overshadowed when they realised that there were no greener pastures elsewhere. The return flow of former emigrants was indeed mounting as Hong Kong approached July 1997. It was reported that six of ten former emigrants returned from overseas in 1995. In 1992, it was only one in ten.

I had a lot of discussions on such issues with my friends as they came for advice, and I valued their trust. These dialogues proved to be useful for my understanding during my research. By this time, the people of Hong Kong lowered their expectations of the future. Not too many demanded a high degree of autonomy for the HKSAR. Most people accepted the stationing of the People's Liberation Army in the urban areas. They no longer demanded a say in the selection of the first Chief Executive. In sum, they accepted stability and prosperity as the substitute for democracy and autonomy. Slackening economic growth and unemployment became Hong Kong people's foremost concerns.

Hong Kong's 1997 handover attracted so much international media attention. When my family and I were touring Europe, Asia and North American countries in the 1990s, we were often asked by fellow tourists about the same questions: Will Hong Kong be OK after the 1997 handover to China? What are your plans after 1997? Will you be leaving? My wife stuttered. The situation was complex and we were bombarded by mixed messages from all sides. We, like many of our friends, had mixed feelings too about our future, a future not only for us, but also for the next generations.

In approaching 1997, the uncertainty about Hong Kong's future gradually faded. Hong Kong residents increasingly believed that all would go well in 1997, given Chinese leaders' concern about their image. However, this belief might be just pragmatism at work, or rationalisation to allay fears. Fear of a major upheaval by 1997 were diluted and replaced by mere concerns as to whether they continued to enjoy the rule of law and the freedoms, and, indeed, if the way of life in Hong Kong would slowly be eroded.

These rationalisations meant that the Chinese authorities were given the benefit of the doubt to make "one country, two systems" work. They were also given a vote of confidence by local and international investors. Less reassuring though were the estimates at that time that 700,000 members of the local population held foreign passports, and that probably another 500,000 possessed the right of abode in a foreign country. It was believed that they were largely well-educated, middle-class families who adopted a "wait-and-see" attitude.

I interviewed the Preparatory Committee members in early October 1996. While Hong Kong people understood very well that the Preparatory Committee was not accountable to them, they watched closely if the rule of law and freedom of the media were respected in their operations. The Chinese authorities were largely satisfied with the situation, especially with the fact that about 6,000 applied to join the 400-seat Selection Committee. Applicants were elites from all sectors, including retired politicians and former senior civil servants.

In regard to the first Chief Executive position of the HKSAR, various opinion surveys were engaged in an informal public selection exercise. The then Chief Secretary, Anson Chan Fang On-sang, was consistently the most popular choice, securing 50 to 60% of the respondents' support. Her support declined to 40% in October 1996. Martin Lee, leader of the DP, was not a popular choice. His support dropped gradually from 16% in December 1995 to 5% in October 1996.[37] To avoid confrontation with Beijing, the public apparently preferred an experienced senior civil servant to a pro-democracy leader. Still, pro-democracy leaders remained very popular among the Hong Kong populace.

For the actual election of first Chief Executive of the HKSAR government, Sir Ti-liang Yang and Che-hwa Tung[38] were endorsed by China as the final contenders and they competed vigorously. They were both considered acceptable to the Hong Kong community, with an approval rating of 73% and 56% respectively. Such contest reduced the suspicion that the Chinese authorities completely controlled the election process. In general, the election of the first Chief Executive went smoothly and the China

---

37 *Sunday Morning Post*, October 6, 1996.
38 Ti-liang Yang was the Chief Justices of Hong Kong from 1988 to 1996 then. Chee-Hua Tung is a businessman who assumed leadership of the family's shipping business from 1982. The shipping company went bankrupt in the mid-1980s, and was believed to be rescued by Chinese government enterprises through Henry Fok in 1986.

side was pleased to see the pragmatism in society in avoiding direct conflict with Beijing.

The election of the provisional legislature of 60 members however did not go that well. Governor Chris Patten in his final policy speech argued for non-cooperation with the provisional legislature even though 33 of 34 existing members were previously elected. He strongly defended his unsupported reform package back in 1992 which drastically increased directly elected seats. Soon in an opinion survey, eight out of ten expressed their belief that the Hong Kong government should help the provisional legislature if it were to operate in early 1997.

Hong Kong people generally frowned upon violence and open conflict. Politics in post-war Hong Kong were characterised by a combination of pressure group lobbying, public opinion initiatives and legal means. Bargaining, long-term negotiation and conflict resolution permeate all levels of Hong Kong's political culture.

Before the Sino-British Joint Declaration in 1984, neither the colonial government nor the community wanted a fundamental change in the political system, as it might attract interference from Beijing. Since 1984, Hong Kong people understood that they either "accepted the "one country", two systems" option or to emigrate. At the grassroots level, petitions and protest rallies were usually conducted peacefully and in an orderly manner. Protesters and the police were willing to co-operate to avoid clashes.

In the process of drafting the Basic Law, for example, political groups and the concerned public seriously debated every controversial clause in the document. Though many in Hong Kong had doubts concerning the binding power of the Basic Law on the Chinese authorities, there was general acceptance that securing a Basic Law acceptable to the community was almost the only option available. The hope was also expressed that the serious debates would have an educational effect on all parties concerned.

Most Hong Kong people adopted a utilitarian attitude towards democracy: they viewed it as a means to realise practical, concrete objectives. Many voted for those pro-democracy candidates who were severely critical of the Hong Kong government and the Chinese authorities, because they hoped to achieve a certain degree of checks and balances. They neither expected nor wanted them to be the government. They were prudent in calculating the cost of political participation. While they perceived democracy as an important means to guarantee their freedoms and their lifestyles, they also considered that their own individual efforts were more reliable in improving their own livelihood. Such were their approach and attitudes towards political participation in Hong Kong in the mid-1990s.

In the 1990s, I was an observer of Hong Kong politics. I had no intention of joining a political party nor taking part in elections. I did serious research on the political developments of the territory and published in international academic journals. In this decade, more academics from the younger generation engaged in research on Hong Kong's political and social developments. They were in general well-trained, competent and hard-working. As discussed in the previous chapter, the pressure to publish gradually increased. As the number of prestigious international journals remained largely stagnant, and the number of articles about Hong Kong that these journals would accept was not large, competition became increasingly more severe. Those working on China were in a slightly better situation, as China studies attracted much attention in the international community including the international academic community then.

I contributed often to *The Other Hong Kong Report* book series launched in 1989 by the Chinese University of Hong Kong Press. It was a pet project of its director then, T. L. Tsim. He intended to produce an annual volume of critical studies of the territory's various policy areas alongside the official yearbook released by the Government Information Services. The initial responses were very good; however, as the university management teams emphasised international journal articles and ignored book chapters in their assessment of teaching staff performance, the book project found it increasingly difficult to attract contributors. The last issue was published in 1998. It was the outcome of the publication pressure I mentioned earlier. I felt it was quite a pity.

As a senior academic engaged in research on Hong Kong politics and a media commentator and columnist, I was often invited to attend gatherings by top government officials and leading figures of the pro-Beijing united front. These meetings offered good opportunities for me to enter into dialogues with government officials and leading politicians, and to learn from the views of other commentators. They constituted a part of my research work. I also made my preparations so that I was in a position to make a contribution to the discussions.

The most rewarding kind of dinner party was a gathering of serious discussants who had worthwhile views to offer so that all participants felt that they had learnt a lot from each other. If the hosting government official had an important message to offer and when at least different types of views were articulated, this would not be disappointing. Sometimes these gatherings were simply social events, without much to offer in terms of discussions. The worst case was when one or two arrogant figures tried to dominate the discussions with their views; it was a time wasted. In sum, this was research work and political education for me.

In the early 1990s, I came across one or two occasions when some senior government officials invited visitors from Mainland China for lunches or dinners at Western restaurants in some expensive five-star hotels. Typical of China's stage of development at the time, the visitors could not read the English or French menu, nor handle the cutlery properly and were quite embarrassed. The insensitivity did not help to promote exchanges and understanding between Hong Kong's civil servants and their counterparts from the Mainland.

There was another side to the story too. I heard rumours that in early 1997 when senior civil servants attended Preparatory Committee meetings in Shenzhen, they were scolded by Shiu Sin-por. Shiu served as deputy secretary-general of the Basic Law Consultative Committee and the chief executive of the Beijing-loyal One Country Two Systems Economic Research Institute, and apparently was trusted by the leading cadres of the State Council's Hong Kong and Macau Affairs Office. The arrogance of people like Shiu reflected the distrust and even lingering ill feelings between the leaders of the pro-Beijing united front organisations and officials of the British administration. The former believed that they had been unfairly treated by the latter in the years after the 1967 riots.

Notes:

If readers want to have an in-depth understanding of the political developments in Hong Kong during this period, please refer to the following list of references:

Cheng, Joseph Y.S. "Hong Kong Legislative Council Elections: Review of 1991 and Planning for 1995," in Benjamin K.P. Leung and Teresa Y.C. Wong (eds.), *25 Years of Social and Economic Development in*

Hong Kong, Hong Kong: Centre of Asian Studies, the University of Hong Kong, 1994, pp. 291–313.

Cheng, Joseph Y.S. "Political Participation in Hong Kong – Trends in the Mid-1990s," in Warren I. Cohen and Li Zhao (eds.), *Hong Kong Under Chinese Rule*, Cambridge: Cambridge University Press, 1997, p. 170.

Cheng, Joseph Y.S., "The Basic Law: Messages for Hong Kong People," in Richard Y.C. Wong and Joseph Y.S. Cheng (eds.), *The Other Hong Kong Report 1990*, Hong Kong: The Chinese University Press, 1990, pp. 29–63.

Cheng, Joseph Y.S., "Political Modernization in Hong Kong," *The Journal of Commonwealth and Comparative Politics*, Vol. 27, No. 3, November 1989, pp. 294–320.

Cheng, Joseph Y. S., "The Political System," in Peter Wesley-Smith and Albert Chen (eds.), *The Basic Law and Hong Kong's Future*, Hong Kong: Butterworths, 1988, pp. 141–171.

Lee, Jane C.Y. and Ng Chi-sum, "The Nationality and Right of Abode Policy for Hong Kong Residents – Political or Pragmatic Consideration?" *Hong Kong Journal of Social Sciences* (in Chinese), No. 7, April 1996, pp. 192–211.

Tang Tsou, *Twentieth Century Chinese Politics* (in Chinese), Hong Kong: Oxford University Press, 1994.

For the 1991 and 1995 Legislative Council elections, see all major newspapers in Hong Kong in September 1991 and 1995, such as the *South China Morning Post, Ming Pao, and Wen Wei Po.*

Chapter 13

Power for Democracy, Building a Mediating Platform for Electoral Candidates

I was the first convenor with no conflict of interest. Principles, conventions and compromises the keys to success. Strong sense of solidarity in 2003 against the backdrop of Basic Law Article 23 legislation.

This chapter and the next present in great detail the work of Power for Democracy (the group) and my involvement. The intention is to show what a very small civil society group with limited resources set out to do (and has done) to promote political participation and democratisation in Hong Kong. Since the group did not support its members in standing for elections, the voluntary work of its executive committee was largely motivated by idealistic and altruistic considerations. This was especially so because the group normally did not seek media exposure. The contributions of the young members were truly laudable.

The establishment of the Power for Democracy on June 8, 2002 marked my return to more active political participation. As a new and unique pro-democracy group in term of its functions and services in Hong Kong, the group served as a mediating platform dedicated to the co-ordination of electoral candidates from amongst political parties within the pro-democracy movement.

Albert Ho Chun-yan and Emily Lau Wai-hing were the initiators of the group. Albert Ho, my best friend in the movement, is a human rights solicitor and former Democratic Party chair. He was also a founding member of the New School for Democracy (Chapter 16) and the Hong Kong Alliance in Support of Patriotic Democratic Movements of China. As an avid reader, he has always in mind the broader picture. I often helped to organise academic seminars and activities together with him. He is keenly interested in international issues such as the Diaoyutai Islands disputes with Japan. As a Chinese patriot, he believes in China's sovereignty and the pursuit of peaceful settlement with Japan. Owing to his involvements in numerous activities and commitments, he seems to suffer from an occasional lack of sleep.

The original rationale to set up Power for Democracy was simple. In the previous District Council elections, there were some constituencies in which two (in rare cases more than two) pro-democracy candidates competed against each other. Such contest divided the votes and allowed the seats to go to pro-establishment candidates. Such cases were severely criticised by supporters of the pro-democracy movement, hence the damage was more than a loss of seats. Ho and Lau hoped that some co-ordination work could be done to avoid the kind of negative competition within the pro-democracy movement.

I was approached by Ho and Lau to serve as the new group's convenor because of my long years of association with and service to the pro-democracy movement. As a senior academic and seasoned media commentator, I was well-known to activists in the movement. They knew that I had no political ambition and would not run for public offices; there would not be any conflict of interest.

The first executive committee of Power for Democracy consisted of fourteen members, including five Legislative Councillors such as Albert Ho, Emily Lau and Lee Cheuk-yan. Typical of pro-democracy groups in Hong Kong, funding was a serious challenge. Basically the major expenditure item was the employment of an assistant who supported the group's day-to-day work as an executive officer. We were looking for a fresh university graduate who was interested in non-governmental organisational work. Naturally, we expected the candidate to share our values and belief in democracy. The salary we could offer was not high, about HK$13,000 a month, which was slightly above the median starting salary for a fresh university graduate at that time. We were very fortunate to have recruited a recent graduate from the City University of Hong Kong, with a first class honours degree in the social sciences.

Sometimes I wondered why such a promising young lady would like to join our organisation as we could not offer any clear career path for her. But she indicated that she was not interested in the civil service nor a trainee position in a major multinational corporation. On the other hand, there were no promotion prospects, and salary increases while working for Power for Democracy were limited. We were very grateful for her service. She proved to be a most dedicated and meticulous organiser. She left us after a few years, and became an assistant to a deputy convenor of Power for Democracy who was running for a seat in the Legislative Council then.

Later, Power for Democracy recruited another young lady who just graduated from the Hong Kong University of Science and Technology, again with a first class honours degree. She too proved to be a valuable asset of the group. Similar to her predecessor, she left us after a few years of service and became the staff of a Democratic Party legislator. I mentioned these two young ladies because I believed that the pro-democracy movement owed a lot to these talented young people serving various organisations in a very low-key manner. Without their dedicated service, these organisations could not have functioned effectively.

They did not have a very comfortable or stable working environment. She had to share her office and had to move her office twice. The group had to pay a rent of HK$2,000 a month for a small office space and the use of office facilities. When the second young lady was working for us, Power for Democracy was in financial difficulties. Each executive committee member contributed HK$500 a month (and for Legislative Councillor members HK$1,000 a month each) to pay for her salary. Her morale and performance did not seem to have been affected.

Other than salary and office rent, there were only minor expenditure items. Any concerned citizen who are aware of the modes of operations of both the pro-democracy movement and that of the pro-Beijing united front would appreciate the cost efficiency of the former. Occasionally, I sought donations from three rich friends, but there were limits because these three donors were well-known to all pro-democracy groups that also sought contributions from them. Power for Democracy did not hold any fund-raising dinners because many of its executive committee members belonged to political parties that conducted their own fund-raising activities. The group did not want to add to their burden.

In 2003 and 2004, Power for Democracy held street stalls for fund-raising purpose, and collected almost HK$40,000 and HK$15,000 respectively in the two years. It also made use of the candle-light vigil in commemoration of the Tiananmen incident in 2004 to do fund-raising in the streets and collected slightly over HK$30,000. In

2018, the pro-Beijing propaganda machinery *Ta Kung Pao* and *Wen Wei Po* attacked Power for Democracy for receiving foreign money from agencies in the U.S. These attacks were groundless. Power for Democracy had been a registered company. Its incomes and expenditures could easily be monitored by the public.

In its initial years, Power for Democracy did a lot of advocacy work promoting democratisation and political reforms together with other civil society organisations. Basically it adopted the usual strategy of attempting to exert pressure on the government through influencing public opinion, by releasing public statements, holding press conferences and lobbying government officials. Hong Kong Democratic Foundation was the group's usual partner at this stage. In December 2003, the two groups released a "Civil Society Green paper on the Political System", which was compiled by Dr. Sonny Lo Shiu-hing and myself.

In those years, government officials were polite in maintaining a dialogue with civil society groups. Power for Democracy was able to meet Stephen Lam Sui-lung, Secretary for Constitutional and Mainland Affairs, two or three times a year. In February 2004, it was received by members of the Constitutional Development Task Force, namely Donald Tsang, then Chief Secretary for Administration, Elsie Leung Oi-sie, the then Secretary for Justice, and Stephen Lam. Even though the pro-democracy movement failed to press its demands, there was a polite dialogue and the government officials were willing to explain their positions. The relationship deteriorated gradually afterwards.

In believing that the group should be in touch with the grassroots, it organised street forums on Sundays at the pedestrian area in Mongkok. Emily Lau was especially interested in the human rights issue, and on International Human Rights Day on December 10, 2003 she involved Power for Democracy and other groups to organise some activities. In February 2004, Power for Democracy was offered a weekly column by *Apple Daily*. It was considered a good forum, especially for the group's younger members and a way to earn a little money. Similarly in the following April, it was asked by the *Hong Kong Economic Journal* to contribute a column every three weeks.

In its advocacy work in the early years, Power for Democracy approached the Catholic Church and the Christian churches as well as the pro-business Liberal Party. It was in this connection that I first met Bishop Joseph Zen Ze-kiun in November 2002 (he became Cardinal in 2006). It is worth noting that a pro-democracy group at this stage could engage in a dialogue on political reforms and democratic elections with the Liberal Party; the group met its leaders in July 2003.

In preparation for the District Council elections in November 2003, Power for Democracy met in February 2003 all the major political parties in the pro-democracy

July 2003. Speaking at the Hong Kong Junior Chamber seminar – "You and I bring HK back".

movement that intended to present candidates. The fact that almost all political parties were willing to engage in co-ordination was an initial success. The group in its preparatory stage managed to recruit key members of these political parties to join its executive committee. This laid the foundation for the subsequent co-ordination work. No one had any relevant experience then, and the approach adopted was straightforward. Every political party presented its list of candidates, clashes were identified and negotiations were initiated on each constituency with more than one candidate. In most cases, it was a clash between two potential candidates; in a few cases, there were three to-be candidates.

November 2003. At the District Council election Rally.

The incentive for agreement was obvious. If two or more pro-democracy candidates competed among themselves in a single-member, simple-majority constituency, it was quite likely that the votes would be split and they would lose; as a result, the seat would go to a pro-establishment candidate. They and their respective organisations would also be condemned by supporters of the pro-democracy movement, as shown by past experience. Moreover, while there were four hundred constituencies, the movement could only field

264 candidates in the end. Many constituencies were still untouched by the movement.

Power for Democracy basically provided a platform for these negotiations to take place. Often, the major political parties might clash with each other bilaterally in a number of constituencies, so there would be much room for give-and-take compromises. Power for Democracy only offered its good service; it would not and was in no position to intervene or take sides. When a small radical group challenged a major party in one constituency, there was less room for give-and-take, and reconciliation and compromise would be difficult. In some cases, when there were accumulated ill feelings between two candidates, mutual hostility would prevent rational decision. In the extreme case, a candidate might leave his/her party in order to continue to compete against his/her rival from the pro-democracy camp in the controversial constituency. Power for Democracy could not function as a platform in these scenarios and had to admit failure.

In presenting their respective claims, the candidates concerned normally would indicate that they had started work in the constituency in question for a long time already, and it would be unfair to ask them to withdraw. These candidates could often establish their presence in the respective constituencies since certain dates, though it would almost be impossible to ascertain or substantiate their continued service records.

To make compromises and concessions work easier, Power for Democracy started to solicit lists of candidates from political parties earlier and earlier. In the November 2019 District Council elections, for example, Power for Democracy began work in the spring of 2017. The idea was that when registration of interests took place well before the election date, candidates involved in clashes could not claim that they had already done much work in the constituencies in question. They (and their organisations) would have ample time to make adjustments and find other appropriate constituencies. This strategy proved to be effective, though more work would be needed for the group.

To reduce differences, Power for Democracy stipulated the principle that the incumbent pro-democracy District Councillors should not be challenged by other candidates within the camp. In subsequent years, the principle was extended to include pro-democracy candidates who had secured 35% or more of the votes cast in the previous election. The rationale was that the candidate was already enjoying majority support from voters in the pro-democracy camp, and this often meant that he/she should be able to secure 55%–60% of the votes in direct elections to the Legislative Council according to previous experience.

These conventions were criticised by the small political parties taking part in the co-ordination exercise as they said that such conventions would favour the largest party, i.e., the Democratic Party. Yet at the same time, they also wanted protection for their candidates who were incumbents or who had secured 35% or more of the votes cast in the previous election, though the number of their candidates to be thus protected was relatively smaller. There were some suggestions later regarding the raising and lowering of the 35% threshold.

Power for Democracy made every attempt to remain neutral and usually did not take part in the voting in the decision-making process. For important issues, decision was made by consensus, allowing each political party, no matter big or small, to have a veto power. The impartiality of Power for Democracy was thus maintained; it had not been accused of favouritism.

There were accusations against another type of favouritism though. Some district-based groups had not been involved in the co-ordination exercise and they complained. This was natural because negotiations could not possibly involve every single potential candidate. The rule of thumb adopted was that any pro-democracy political party with a Legislative Councillor would be invited to take part.

The co-ordination exercise thus involved only the more established political parties in the pro-democracy movement. There were some attempts to remedy the approach. When the co-ordination exercise had been completed among the member groups, Power for Democracy then contacted the small, district-based groups and individuals with an attempt to avoid clashes.

The incentive for the district-based groups to take part in co-ordination was that they also wanted to avoid clashes with other pro-democracy candidates. Further, they would like to be included in the list of candidates representing the pro-democracy movement that Power for Democracy presented usually in a press conference and in an advertisement in *Apple Daily* on the day just before the elections. If money was sufficient, there would be one more advertisement. Since most voters in District Council elections did not know their candidates well, especially those challenging the incumbents, the list presented by Power for Democracy was a reliable guide for voters supporting the pro-democracy movement.

In the November 2003 District Council elections, the sense of solidarity was strong. Power for Democracy was able to organise a campaign rally for the 264 candidates on its list with about two thousand participants near the Tsim Sha Tsui Cultural Centre. For the independents and those from the small district-based political groups, there was no thorough screening process as Power for Democracy did not have the resources to check their records and credentials. The basic demand was that they accepted the common platform agreed upon by the groups within the pro-democracy movement.

A senior member of the Democratic Party and member of the Central and Western District Council publicly criticised Power for Democracy for including a candidate in the list and allowing him to take part in the campaign rally. His public accusation resulted in a small dent to the image of the candidates' list presented by Power for Democracy and the solidarity of the movement. It was totally unnecessary; the accused candidate had voted against the pro-democracy movement's position in an important vote on a democratisation issue. Power for Democracy did not have a plan nor the manpower to check the voting records of every candidate. In this controversial case, the group only asked for support of the common pro-democracy platform, and the accused candidate met this minimum requirement. He certainly could argue that he had abandoned his previous stand. This was a case of personal ill-feelings. Narrow election considerations were unfortunately accorded higher priority than the broad interests of the pro-democracy movement.

Subsequently, I served as co-ordinator and mediator on a number of occasions for the pro-democracy movement, and these incidents were not rare. I normally avoided any public reactions to criticisms from people whom I considered supporters of the pro-democracy movement, so as not to intensify the "contradictions among the people". I just tried to use quiet persuasion, which often was not totally effective, but at least it would not exacerbate the damage. I often appealed for help from the leaders of the parties concerned. Unfortunately they usually placed party interests first. They normally did not want to confront their own party members because this would cost them their internal party support.

The pro-democracy movement performed well in the November 2003 District Council elections. The most important contributory factor came from the massive protests against the intention of the Hong Kong government to legislate the Article 23 national security law on secession, subversion, terrorism and collusion with foreign forces. More than half a million people took part in the protest rally on July 1, 2003. It was within this context that voters tended to accord more political considerations than it was normally the case to District Council elections.

The overall voter turnout rate was higher than the last District Council elections (see Appendix I. The District Council election results). The Democratic Alliance for the Betterment of Hong Kong (DAB), the pro-Beijing party that aspired to become a ruling party in Hong Kong, lost 21 seats, and suffered the largest electoral setback since its establishment. It had had high expectations in the elections because of the huge resources spent.

In contrast, the established pro-democracy political parties achieved a 67% success rate as a whole (151 of the 226 candidates won). The Democratic Party was the major beneficiary, gaining an additional 17 seats compared with the last election. The results were particularly impressive when the popular votes gained was actually less than those for DAB, while the seats secured were much higher. The pro-democracy camp's electoral victory emboldened it to be more ambitious in the coming Legislative Council elections in September 2004.

September 2004. At the Hong Kong Legislation Council elections rally.

Some executive committee members congratulated me on my coordination work. I told them that there were a number of other factors that were also responsible for the good results. Personally I thought it was primarily the fact that voters were awakened or even shocked by the government's intention to legislate the security law (Basic Law Article 23) and they tried to express their disapproval through voting, even though they realised that District Councillors had very little influence in political decisions of this kind.

Thus, higher voter turnout rates proved to be more favourable to the pro-democracy camp. DAB and the Hong Kong Federation of Trade Unions had by the turn of the century established effective and reliable grassroots networks with substantial mobilisation power. In contrast, such networks were much more limited with the pro-democracy camp. Political climate at the time of the elections and the actual weather on elections day affected the voter turnout rate, which in turn impacted severely on the pro-democracy camp. The phenomena were similar to those in Japan where higher voter turnout rates favoured the governing Liberal Democratic Party, while the Japan Communist Party as well as the religion-based Komeito could count on the loyalty of their respective party members to deliver reliable votes to their respective party candidates.

The Beijing-loyal grassroots networks were often given the label "snake soup, vegetarian meals, moon cakes and rice dumplings (蛇齋餅糭)". In practical terms, the network organisations would visit the elderly, especially those living alone in public-housing estates, on a monthly basis, each time with a bag of rice, a bottle of soy sauce and a bottle of edible oil. There were moon cakes for the Mid-Autumn Festival, rice dumplings for the Dragon Boat Festival, and special gifts for the Chinese New Year. Occasionally, banquets with snake soup, vegetarian meals and the like were organised for the neighbourhood to enjoy.

But they did more than merely presenting these gifts. They represented a meticulous, long-term strategy of the pro-Beijing united front to cultivate voters and build a powerful electoral machinery. The gifts were a channel to enable district-based intermediary organisations to reach people at the family-level. In recent years, this delivery system was modelled after the good, old traditions of the Communist Party of China.

The new immigrants from Mainland China were another one of their important target groups. Right at the Lo Wu railway station at the border, there were posters and pamphlets advising new immigrants to seek help from the pro-Beijing united front. Naturally the new immigrants who were often not well educated needed help to find school places for their children, queue up for public housing, and know the ins and outs of public sector social services available to them. The united front was patient enough to wait for seven years till they were qualified to become voters. By then the bondage had become quite strong.

The protests against the Article 23 legislation in 2003 shocked the Chinese authorities in realising that though Hong Kong had returned to the Motherland, the hearts of Hong Kong people had not. This meant more resources and greater support for building these grassroots networks. Though the DAB suffered a serious electoral setback in 2003, it largely maintained its position in the September 2004 Legislative Council elections, and more than recovered its losses in the 2007 District Council elections.

The gradual building up of these grassroots networks and the associated electoral machinery increasingly challenged the pro-democracy camp's electoral opportunities in the District Council elections. In the 2000s, the traditional type of District Council leaders (such as *kaifongs/neighbours* running small businesses in the district) had largely disappeared. The expectations and demands of the voters were such that District Councillors had to work almost full time. In fact there were more and more full-time District Councillors. I often served as a voluntary campaign worker for my friends in these elections. The major purpose was to be in contact with the electorate, and to learn the moods and demands of the voters.

The pro-democracy groups encountered substantial difficulties in recruiting candidates. The ideal would be to encourage young professionals to stand. They could deliver their professional services at the grassroots level and enjoy a good image among voters. But doctors, lawyers and accountants in their thirties and early forties, for instance, were usually too busy in advancing their careers, often had young children to take care of, or mortgage to pay off. So it was almost impossible to persuade them to run.

District Councillors have to work hard when they are elected. But challenging a pro-establishment incumbent was very difficult. Pro-establishment incumbents worked rather hard. With more resources and subsidies at their disposal, they usually could employ one or two more assistants. They could raise money more easily from the pro-establishment business groups. As civil servants became increasingly less and less neutral, pro-establishment incumbent District Councillors could get better support from the civil service in handling their constituents' requests and complaints. Since they were in a majority in every District Council, they could almost monopolise the government funding allocated to the District Councils for district work. For those who were wealthy businessmen or concurrently Legislative Councillors with less time at their disposal, they normally would employ a team of assistants to ensure a satisfactory delivery of services.

The pro-democracy challengers received little support from their political parties, which usually did not have the financial resources. The would-be candidates often had been assistants working in the legislators' and District Councillors' offices, and they served their apprenticeship there. They were usually very good candidates, calling themselves community affairs officers before declaring their candidacies. But the pro-democracy movement obviously needed more candidates. In the elections in the 2000s, it could only field around two hundred and fifty candidates out of more than four hundred constituencies, allowing dozens of pro-establishment candidates to be elected without opposition. The recent District Council elections in November 2019 was certainly a significant breakthrough.

Candidates from the pro-establishment camp, on the other hand, were usually given ample resources to develop new constituencies. Their patience, resources and support from the pro-establishment grassroots networks often proved to be effective. From the 2007 District Council elections onwards, the pro-establishment camp each time attempted to unseat about six to ten promising young leaders of the pro-democracy movement who would soon run for the Legislative Council, and with careful preparations, their success rates were not low. The casualties sometimes included established legislators holding concurrent District Council seats such as Lee Cheuk-yan and Albert Ho. Such electoral victories well demonstrated the effectiveness and sophistication of the pro-establishment camp's electoral machinery.

Recruitment of young professionals to stand for District Council elections was relatively easier for the pro-establishment camp, which could offer them lucrative business ties. They understood that services to the establishment would be rewarded. Budding lawyers might wish to seek favours in being included into the recommended list of legal firms kept by the

Chinese state-owned banks in Hong Kong for their clients. Outstanding District Councillors in the pro-establishment camp enjoyed a good chance of co-optation into the government as political assistants and deputy secretaries. They had better opportunities of joining the government's appointed system of advisory committee too. Professionals in Hong Kong often had to go to work in the Pearl River Delta and other parts of Mainland China. If they were members of the DAB and other groups loyal to Beijing, they would indicate their memberships in their name cards in anticipation of more friendly treatment from the local cadres in Mainland China; in contrast, their counterparts affiliated to pro-democracy groups would often avoid disclosing their ties while working in Mainland China.

There were less-than-legitimate measures adopted by the pro-establishment camp. Power for Democracy approached the Electoral Affairs Commission a number of times to launch its complaints and asked for law enforcement actions, but failed to secure active responses from the government authorities. In the elections in the recent two decades or so, the elderly living in old age homes were mobilised to vote. Initially, they were taken for a one-day trip on Election Day, offered a good lunch and then brought to the voting station. Then on the tour buses, the tourist guide or the staff member from the elderly homes would tell the senior citizens to vote for a certain number assigned to a candidate on the ballot papers.

The practice was obviously unethical and unlawful if these elderly voters had no plan to vote for any particular candidate in their respective constituencies and they had no knowledge of the candidates. There were many media reports on such practices. In recent years, instead of using tour buses bringing scores of elderly voters to the voting stations, they were brought there on an individual basis and they received guidance to vote in support of number X on the ballot papers. These phenomena again were reported by the media, but apparently no serious investigations and prosecutions had taken place. Such inaction was disappointing, to say the least.

Over a decade ago, some organisations began to hold voting-station surveys, or exit polls. There were strong suspicions against these self-claimed research groups as the community was not aware of any of their research publications or their research papers on elections. There were doubts on whether their findings would be passed straight onto the political parties which would then use the information to guide their electoral strategies. Nonetheless they were still allowed to operate. Subsequently, as it became public knowledge, a lot of respondents chose not to give an honest answer in response to their surveys. The surveys became unreliable and useless, and they then disappeared.

I stepped down as convenor of Power for Democracy in June 2004 after a term of two years. Richard Tsoi Yiu-cheong was elected convenor. There were few changes in the executive committee as it wanted to retain an influential member from each major political group within the pro-democracy movement. I always wanted to make sure that I had adequate time to do a good job as a university academic, and I always believed in making way for the younger generation.

Richard was a student activist in his university student years, and he was a key organiser in the July 1, 2003 massive protest rally against the legislation of the Basic Law Article 23 security law. He was a recognised leader among the second-generation political activists, but he was unsuccessful in his bids to the Legislative Council. I was ready to stay in the executive committee to continue to support the work of Power for Democracy.

The success of the co-ordination in the District Council elections in November 2003 encouraged the pro-democracy movement to repeat the exercise for the September 2004 Legislative Council elections. I was asked to again assume this responsibility, together with Rev. Chu Yiu-ming and Father Louis Ha Ke-loon. Although I was involved in my personal capacity as an academic, I received administrative support from the group, like organising the final campaign rally meeting. The executive committee usually enjoyed pleasant co-operation, as there was no competition and no personal rivalry. The members knew each other for a long time, and there was substantial mutual respect.

Our team of an academic (myself) plus two religious leaders supporting the pro-democracy movement were chosen to approach various political groups within the movement to achieve optimal numbers in the lists of candidates in the five geographical constituencies under a multi-member constituency, single-vote system. The rationale was that if the pro-democracy movement presented too many candidates in a constituency, the supporting votes would be divided too thinly and reduce the number of seats that could have been won.

The process was supposed to be confidential; somehow there were leaks to the media. Hence, there were complaints from the candidates and political groups concerned. I was mainly responsible for releasing information to the media and answering their queries, but I was never doubted as the source of the leaks. I was proud to say that I retained the trust of the movement. One could easily imagine the challenges of the co-ordination work that had to deal with the stars and leaders of various political parties who were very concerned with their images and media exposures. My approach was that I never publicly criticised members of the pro-democracy movement and quietly absorbed any blame myself. This explained why few people would be interested in the coordinator role.

There were massive turnouts in protest rallies against the then proposed security law (Article 23) and protesters demanded democratic reforms on July 1, 2003, January 1, 2004, and July 1, 2004. More than half a million people participated. In the aftermath, there were high expectations that the pro-democracy movement might secure majority seats in the Legislative Council. My assessment and that of most experts were that this would be a very tall order because the electoral system stipulated in the Basic Law had been so designed to ensure a majority of seats for the pro-establishment camp[39]. The goal might be reached if the voter turnout rate could be raised to about 70%, which might show that a lot of the less than enthusiastic voters had been mobilised to come out to vote to bring about this breakthrough. My estimate was that the pro-democracy movement probably would capture 25–26 seats out of 60 in the September 2004 elections.

The voter turnout rate was 55.64% (with 1.78 million voters voting), surpassing the previous record of 53.29% in 1998, but it was not high enough to give the pro-democracy camp the breakthrough it desired. The pro-democracy camp secured 59.9% of the votes in the direct elections, winning 18 seats in

---

39 In the 2004 Legislative Council elections, there were 60 seats, in which 30 seats were directly elected from geographical constituencies, and the other 30 were functional constituencies elected by professional or special interest groups.

the geographical constituencies and 7 seats in the functional constituencies. But the pro-establishment camp maintained its 39.6% share of the votes in the geographical constituencies, successfully preventing a landslide victory for its opponents.

The co-ordination task force could claim that it had achieved the target in reducing competition within the pro-democracy movement and avoided mutual attacks within the camp. It was not responsible for the actual campaign work however. In the co-ordination exercise, there were many considerations regarding the chemistry among the candidates, especially that among candidates on the same slate[40]. Naturally I did not reveal these issues then, and I have no intention of discussing them now. This was the responsibility of a coordinator, and I intended to strictly observe the tacit ground rules. Gradually, journalists realised that it would be futile to seek extra information from me, and they wisely turned to other sources.

The arrangement for the New Territories East, a seven-seat constituency in 2004, attracted a lot of criticisms as only one slate of candidates was presented. According to the electoral rules, the first to the second last winning member on the slate of candidates had to secure a full quota of votes in order to secure a seat. Thus the full

---

40 A slate is a group of candidates that run in multi-seat or multi-position elections on a common platform.

quota of votes for a seven seat constituency amounted to 14.29% (100% / 7) while a single-candidate slate could win a seat with 10–11% of the votes. In order to win four seats for the pro-democracy movement in New Territories East, the slate might have to secure 53.87% (3 x 14.29% + 11%) of the votes; and similarly to win five seats, the slate had to win 68.16% (4 x 14.29% + 11%) of the votes. To the critics, this did not seem logical and represented a waste of votes under the system.

I had consulted the experts and the candidates concerned, single slates in the New Territories East might be able to win four seats, but most unlikely five. The pro-establishment camp would at least secure one seat, and James Tien Pei-chun, leader of the Liberal Party who led the party to withdraw its support for the Article 23 legislation, was very popular and expected to win a seat too. The presentation of one single slate would reduce pressure on Leung Kwok-hung (nicknamed "Long Hair", a more radical democrat), who was running as a single candidate, and hopefully would facilitate the maintenance of friendly relations with the radical wing of the pro-democracy movement.

A more logical way would have been to present two slates, one consisting of candidates from the Democratic Party, and the other led by Emily Lau from the then Frontier, followed by Ronny Tong Ka-wah from the then [Basic Law] Article 45 Concern Group. The disadvantages were that the Democratic Party slate might attract severe competition and criticisms from Leung Kwok-hung's supporters, and I was not sure that Emily Lau could co-operate well with Ronny Tong. The advantage of a single slate was that it would free considerable resources to support the pro-democracy candidates in other geographical constituencies. This was especially so for the Article 45 Concern Group. I could not offer a detailed explanation of the above considerations to the public, and had to absorb criticisms of the apparently 'unwise' arrangement (or a "tactical miscalculation" according to some media reports) to present a single slate for 7 candidates from the pro-democracy movement including those from the Democratic Party, the Frontier and the Article 45 Concern Group.

In the end, the pro-democracy camp secured 58.7% of the votes in New Territories East, and it was able to claim four seats. The single slate only attracted 39.2% of the votes; Leung Kwok-hung won 14.14%; and Andrew Wong Wang-fat, an independent who might be persuaded to support the pro-democracy cause, 5.36%. Campaign co-ordination among the single-slate candidates had some room for improvement. But the pro-democracy camp won four seats, saved considerable resources, and avoided difficulties with its radical wing. It was obvious that Leung Kwok-hung and Andrew Wong could not be persuaded to take part in the co-ordination exercise.

There was a controversy with the electoral outcome in Hong Kong Island. The general assessment was that the pro-democracy movement should be able to win four seats out of six in the Hong Kong Island constituency. The DAB should have no problem securing one seat, and the other pro-establishment candidate Rita Fan Hsu Lai-tai should be popular enough to retain her seat. So the initial agreement was that the pro-democracy movement would present two slates, one consisting of Yeung Sum followed by Martin Lee Chu-ming, the other led by Audrey Eu Yuet-mee followed by Cyd Ho Sau-lan,

To maintain a balance in the distribution of votes, an appeal was made to the voters that male voters would vote for the Democratic Party slate, and female voters would vote for the slate led by Audrey. In the course of the campaign, it was perceived that the Audrey Eu slate seemed to be very popular, and the Democratic Party in the second slate might be in danger of losing its second seat. There were some discussions between Audrey and the Democratic Party, and the former abandoned their campaign in some areas in the final days of the campaign period. The Democratic Party also released an emergency call for support on Election Day. This was almost standard practice, but this time it was very effective as a substantial number of pro-democracy voters turned to vote for the Democratic Party slate because they did not want to see Martin Lee defeated in an election.

The outcome was disastrous for the pro-democracy camp. The swing was so strong that the Democratic

Party slate had a surplus of 13,756 votes after securing two seats (it won 131,788 votes altogether). The Audrey Eu slate had a surplus of 14,828 votes after winning one seat (it secured 73,844 votes altogether) and Cyd Ho surprisingly lost as the second candidate under this slate. If the Democratic Party had halted the emergency call for help earlier, the Audrey Eu slate could have easily secured one thousand more votes and retained the seat for Cyd Ho. If the swing to the Democratic Party had been slightly stronger, the Democratic Party could have won two thousand more votes and secured the third seat, thus at least won four seats for the pro-democracy camp in the Hong Kong Island constituency.

The pro-democracy camp and the Democratic Party did not accurately assess the swing of the vote. It was indeed very difficult to know when to halt the emergency call for help. The Audrey Eu slate slowed down in the final days of the campaign out of good will. Cyd Ho successfully made a come-back after four years. Tsang Kin-shing also stood as a candidate on behalf of the pro-democracy camp. He asked to be placed on the Audrey Eu slate. I delivered his message twice to Audrey's team. The candidates concerned declined without giving a reason. I could not persuade the team to accept Tsang Kin-shing. Tsang was dissatisfied, and there was an unpleasant encounter between him and me in a casual meeting among campaigners. He accused me of dishonesty, and I strongly refuted as this involved my integrity and reputation. Tsang's slate subsequently won 5,313 votes. The encounter illustrated the difficulties of serving as a co-ordinator.

The pro-Beijing DAB slate enjoyed a surplus of 15,643 votes after winning one seat (it secured 74,659 votes altogether). Choy So-yuk, the second candidate on the DAB slate, emerged as the winner. It was said that DAB's Choy So-yuk had made her holiday plan after the election, as she had not expected to win.

There was a pleasant surprise in the 2004 elections for the pro-democracy camp. Mandy Tam Heung-man won the accountancy functional constituency seat as the pro-establishment camp's eight male candidates divided the votes too thinly among themselves. The pro-Beijing united front did not intervene because it was certain of victory and probably did not want to favour any of the candidates. This neglect allowed Mandy to emerge as the winner, and the pro-democracy camp met its basic target of twenty-five seats.

The election results were acceptable to the supporters of the pro-democracy movement especially for those who had a realistic assessment of the actual political situation. With a voter turnout rate of 55.64%, the movement gained around 60% of the votes in the direct elections (the percentage varied a little depending on whether or not some independents were considered members of the pro-democracy camp). The pro-democracy camp could expect to do well (18 seats out of 30 in the geographical constituencies), but could not achieve the breakthrough of winning a majority of seats in the Legislative Council that could successfully challenge the Beijing design of the political system. Many supporters of the pro-democracy movement had high hopes of achieving this significant breakthrough, and they were disappointed.

Despite the good performance of the pro-democracy movement in the 2004 elections, the Democratic Party won fewer seats (reduced from 12 in 2000 to 9), and it lost its position as the largest party in the Legislative Council. Actually, it had lost its predominant position in the movement.

In the first place, new radical political groups all targeted against the Democratic Party. In 2006, the Civic Party was formed, and it obviously competed for the moderate, liberal voters who had supported the Democratic Party before. With the split within the pro-democracy camp, basically every political group hoped to win a seat in each geographical constituency, and there was no incentive to engage in co-ordination. The two major parties, namely, the Democratic Party and the Civic Party, might attempt to secure two seats in a favourable geographical constituency. At any rate, no party would seriously support attempts at co-ordination under such circumstances.

Under Richard Tsoi's leadership, work continued along similar lines as before. Lobbying work with the government declined because they were less and less interested in a dialogue with the pro-democracy movement, but a dialogue was still maintained. Power for Democracy and other pro-democracy groups jointly initiated a plan to propose reforms of the District Councils on their composition, organisational structure and operations, with a view to promote democracy at the district level. Another project proposed was the cultivation of a new generation of activists for the pro-democracy movement. The advantage for Power for Democracy to assume this role was the pooling of resources in serving all the groups to achieve a certain economy of scale. Interactions among activists from different groups hopefully would improve their mutual co-operation in the future.

Power for Democracy was in financial difficulties in these years. It continued to raise funds at the street level. On July 1, 2004, the group raised HK$21,842; and on July 1, 2005, HK$33,511; and on July 1, 2006, HK$67,362. Without exceptions, I helped, but the group's political stars had commitments to their respective political parties. The group's quiet political work was not glamorous, and was not well understood by people in the street. Our experience was that in the absence of significant political events, fund-raising at the street level might not be very rewarding.

Chapter 14

Power for Democracy, Successes and Failures 2006-2019

Overall interest of democracy movement versus individual gain. Discord between moderates and radicals surfaced. Advocacy work in modelling a primary for Chief Executive election. Electoral reforms rejected by Beijing. Strategic voting in Legislative Council elections.

In July 2006, I was elected deputy convenor in the third executive committee of Power for Democracy while Richard Tsoi remained convenor. There was not too many changes in the executive committee, though it absorbed two young men.

Power for Democracy started work early on the co-ordination of the District Council elections in 2007. Co-ordination work which began in early 2006 went relatively smoothly among the political groups engaged in the co-ordination exercise. But some individual candidates claiming to support the pro-democracy cause challenged the list of candidates endorsed by the co-ordination mechanism. It was difficult to ascertain their true intentions. Further, Power for Democracy failed to organise a campaign rally meeting for all pro-democracy groups because some candidates preferred to concentrate on their own individual campaigns. Solidarity and the image of the entire pro-democracy movement thus became secondary considerations for quite a number of candidates. Inter-party competition was also a factor. Power for Democracy managed to offer services like organising two photo sessions with political stars for all the candidates of the pro-democracy movement to be used in their publicity materials.

March 2007. Discussion Forum organised by Power for Democracy.

The pro-democracy camp encountered a setback in the 2007 District Council elections. The gains secured in the previous elections in 2003 were lost (see appendix); the established political parties within the camp only won 95 seats, compared with 151 seats last time. The voter turnout rate was 38.8%, some 6% lower than that in 2003. However, the number of registered voters increased substantially to 2.95 million, hence actual voters amounted to 1.14 million, a record high.

The Democratic Party lost badly in the number of seats and the success rate also dropped. Party chairman Albert Ho offered to resign, but the party asked him to stay. The chairman of its election committee resigned to assume responsibility.

The newly established Civic Party won eight seats with a success rate of 19%. Its good image and territory-wide popularity were not reflected at the district level. It realised that much more grassroots work had to be performed.

The Chairman of the Hong Kong Association for Democracy and People's Livelihood (HKADPL), Frederick Fung Kin-kee also offered to resign for the poor election results, and his resignation was accepted. Fung acknowledged that the electorate had changed, and his party's traditional participatory political culture had not been able to adapt to the changes. The radical League of Social Democrats did not do well either, and its Chairman Raymond Wong Yuk-man, emphasised the impact of new immigrants on the change in the structure of the electorate. He criticised the ill-defined role of the pro-democracy movement, and indicated that it should re-examine its mode of political struggle against Beijing.

The offer to resign on the part of Albert Ho and the actual resignation of Frederick Fung were significant. The 2007 election results signalled the dissatisfaction of the younger generation with the traditional position and mode of operation of the established political groups within the pro-democracy camp. Wong Yuk-man's criticisms were also worth noting. The emerging differences between the moderates represented by the Democratic Party and the radicals represented by the League of Social Democrats had significance. Co-ordination in elections became more difficult.

The pro-establishment camp won a major victory; its meticulous grassroots services were finally rewarded. Its electoral success demonstrated that services plus avoidance of unpopular political issues could be a formula for success during normal times of relative political stability. It also showed that voters might have a short memory.

The DAB had a record high success rate for the party. Its vice-chairman indicated that the party's outstanding results were due to its emphasis on people's livelihood issues, as well as the high quality of its new candidates. He was careful to say that the connection between District Councils elections and Legislative Council elections might not be strong.

The Hong Kong Federation of Trade Unions won seventeen seats, with sixteen of the successful candidates carrying its banner and that of the DAB. It also secured a satisfactory success rate of 53.1% with 32 candidates. The Civil Force, a group led by a vice-chairman of the DAB concentrating its work in New Territories East, achieved the highest success rate of 90%, the highest among all political groups.

In sum, the effectiveness of the pro-Beijing united front was fully demonstrated. The weaknesses of the pro-democracy camp were exposed, and more importantly, there was not much they could do to reverse the situation. In the following District Council elections in 2011, the pan-democrats had to be satisfied if they could minimise their loss to a few seats. Liberal middle-class voters had no strong interest in district issues, and they did not need services from their District Councillors. The pro-democracy camp did not have the financial resources and manpower to compete with the Beijing loyalists' service machinery at the grassroots level.

From late summer till the end of 2006, Power for Democracy organised a number of street seminars in Mongkok (one of the most densely populated and busiest retail districts in the world), on the issues of democratic elections and the significance of the democratic election of the Chief Executive. These seminars continued into mid-2007.

In August 2007, a seat happened to be vacant with the death of Ma Lik, the then chairman of the pro-Beijing DAB, and a by-election would be held in the Hong Kong Island constituency. It offered a good chance to experiment with the implementation of primaries. So the group supported a primary election to elect a standing candidate from the pro-democracy movement. In September, Anson Chan Fang On-sang won the primary against a candidate of the League of Social Democrats. On December 2, 2007, she defeated Regina Ip (then founder of Savantas Policy Institute) to win the seat with a 54.5% majority.

George Cautherley, a leader of the Hong Kong Democratic Foundation, had been advocating serious policy studies on the part of civil society and the pro-democracy movement. In February 2006, the Hong Kong Democratic Foundation, Power for Democracy, the Society for Community Organization, as well as a group of Legislative Councillors, academics and concerned citizens, formed a forum to study the territory's medical and health policy. Cautherley provided generous funding support, and a detailed report on the reform of Hong Kong's medical and health system was released on June 2, 2007. In the following August, the forum commissioned a territory-wide opinion survey on the issue to be conducted by Lingnan University, and the results of the survey was publicised on January 20, 2008.

I was involved in the forum and made considerable efforts. I had no expertise on the health and healthcare issue, but I firmly believed in serious policy studies on the part of civil society. The pro-democracy movement in general did not have the resources to engage in detailed policy research. Even when the movement produced a policy report based on serious efforts, they often complained that it was neglected by the mass media. Hence, opposition parties had no incentives to engage in serious policy studies.

In this case, the forum's report was objective and thorough. It certainly achieved a standard considerably higher than those accomplished by foreign consultancy firms. It had no political overtones. Nonetheless, it did not receive serious attention from the government. Senior government officials simply preferred to work according to their own agendas and schedules, and were not enthusiastic about any input from civil society. Hong Kong's media tended to ignore policy proposals from civil society too. The forum's policy report did not succeed in attracting media attention and stimulating much community discussion on medical and health policy. One explanation was that the media did not expect that policy research on the part of civil society would make an impact. Hence, a vicious circle was established.

In December 2007, Power for Democracy helped to organise a delegation of representatives of Hong Kong's pro-democracy political parties to study and observe Taiwan's legislature elections. The trip was hosted by the Friends of Hong Kong and Macau Association in

Taiwan. Since the early 1980s, I had been invited to visit Taiwan at least two or three times a year and had established a good network of ties with the academic community, civil society, media and government agencies there. Hence, Power for Democracy was entrusted this assignment. I believed in the value of mutually-supportive ties between the civil society organisations in both places.

Before 2000, academics and the pro-democracy political parties in Hong Kong mainly met their counterparts associated with the governing Kuomintang. In the 1980s and 1990s, the Kuomintang government was interested in Hong Kong because of the 1997 issue. The regime was keen in its attempts to meet the challenges of diplomatic isolation, as well as to define a new approach in dealing with Beijing. The economic prosperity in Taiwan in these two decades allowed the Taiwan authorities considerable resources to cultivate ties with the overseas Chinese communities including Hong Kong.

Bilateral ties between Taiwan and Hong Kong cooled during the Chen Shui-bian administration because Chen's Democratic Progressive Party was less interested in Hong Kong and had a narrower definition of Taiwan's priorities in external affairs. Economic growth in Taiwan began to slow down in the twenty-first century too. An indication of these changes were the dwindling financial support given by the Chung Hwa Travel Service (the unofficial representative of Taiwan in the territory) to Hong Kong's activists. Before 2000, academic conference organisers could approach the Chung Hwa Travel Service and obtain a few airline tickets to bring Taiwan academics to Hong Kong. This financial support very soon disappeared after the advent of the Chen Shui-bian administration. I was concerned that civil society ties should be maintained between Hong Kong and Taiwan, and I was glad that Power for Democracy could play a role.

The introduction of democracy in Taiwan in the late 1980s facilitated the rapid development of its civil society. Elections at various levels had generated an industry which specialised in the provision of electoral campaign services. At the same time, political parties big and small also became highly sophisticated in electoral campaign tactics. The Taiwan experience showed that democracy could definitely function well in a Chinese society, and Hong Kong's political activists were eager to learn from them.

In July 2008, Power for Democracy elected its fourth executive committee. The group managed to persuade two young men who had joined the executive committee two years ago to serve as deputy convenor and secretary, while Albert Ho and I stepped down to become ordinary executive committee members. Attracting young talents was a severe challenge for a low-profile civil society group like Power for Democracy; for those interested in a political career, they would prefer joining political parties and prepare themselves for elections.

In the absence of elections, Power for Democracy would concentrate on the advocacy for political reforms and democracy. At this stage, there was almost no dialogue with government officials. Its relations with both the Donald Tsang administration and the C.Y. Leung administration deteriorated.

In July 2010, Power for Democracy elected its fifth executive committee. There were more young people to take up the responsibility. Like many political groups in these years, Power for Democracy experimented with a web television project in co-operation with OurTV starting in September 2010. The idea was to promote political participation and democratisation through current affairs and educational programmes. Young members of the executive committee were mainly responsible for the weekly programmes. The attempt was not a spectacular success, and the lessons learnt were that the group had to make more substantial efforts in cultivating the expertise to be effective. Competition was keen too.

Another project was initiated in September 2010. The forums on people's livelihood issues started by involving the new generation of activists from various political groups in the pro-democracy movement. The idea was to provide training for them in policy analysis and debates. The forums were edited for web television by OurTV. The differences between the moderates and the radicals in the pro-democracy camp exacerbated at this time, and it was hoped that the initiative would help reduce these differences, to improve ties with new generation of activists from various political groups and to promote solidarity.

In February 2009, the group, realising the advantages of starting early, started its co-ordination work on the 2011 District Council elections. In this connection, it published *Chinese Election Engineers* released in July 2011 at the Hong Kong Book Fair. The book was supposed to be a pioneering volume on actual electoral campaign work in Hong Kong, with practical discussions on the selection of constituencies, organisation of campaign workers, community services, preparation of publicity materials, use of public opinion surveys, presentations in election forums, and arrangements on elections day. It was supposed to be a guide book for those interested in taking part in elections, especially District Council elections.

The 2011 District Council elections represented a low point for the pro-democracy movement (see appendix: District Council election results). The structural difficulties were far from being overcome, as the pro-establishment camp had mobilised even more resources in the past four years. To add to the challenge, the pro-democracy movement was sharply divided over the government's legislation to bring about Hong Kong electoral reform on the election of the Chief Executive and the Legislative Council in 2010[41].

During the government's consultation period, the Democratic Party and the HKADPL supported the government legislation. The radical groups (for example, People Power, the League of Social Democrats) opposed the agreement these two parties reached with the Central Liaison Office, the then representative of the Chinese government in Hong Kong. The quarrels became open.

For 2011 District Council elections, People Power, led by Wong Yuk-man at that time[42], presented 62 candidates, and many of them competed against those of the Democratic Party. The radical groups, People Power and the League of Social Democrats, refused to participate in the co-ordination exercise of the pan-democrats. These radical groups failed badly in the elections of District Councils because their candidates often failed to deliver solid grassroots services.

The Neo Democrats, a splinter group originally from the Democratic Party established in October 2010, secured 8 seats with a success rate of 80%, because of

---

41   The 2010 electoral reforms included: 1. membership of the election committee to select the 2012 Chief Executive was increased from 800 to 1,200; and 2. ten more seats were added to the 60-seat legislature.

42   In name, Wong Yuk-man was just an executive committee member of People Power, not its chairman. But it was commonly recognised that he was the group's *de facto* leader. People Power split from the League of Social Democrats and was inaugurated in January 2011.

its agreement with the Chinese authorities on political reforms. The political parties in the pro-democracy camp taking part in the co-ordination exercise altogether won 82 seats, down from 95 in 2007.

On the other hand, the DAB won handsomely. Some of its candidates also carried the banners of the Hong Kong Federation of Trade Unions, and/or that of the Civil Force, though they were not on their lists of candidates. They secured about one third of the elected seats in all District Councils. Such Beijing loyalists presented confusing pictures of their affiliation in the election. For details, please refer to Appendix: District Council election results.

The divisions and quarrels within the pro-democracy camp considerably weakened the pan-democrats. People Power openly attacked the co-ordination mechanism for the District Council elections 2011. Although the Neo Democrats stayed within the mechanism, its differences with the Democratic Party often created difficulties for Power for Democracy to reach decisions by consensus. I was an executive committee member all the time, but I mainly helped with the street forums and fund-raising at this stage. I received so many phone calls from my colleagues engaged in co-ordination work, and I understood their frustration, especially that of our convenor, Richard Tsoi.

The government's election reforms in June 2010 introduced five new seats (referred to as The District

Council (Second) functional constituency) to be elected from incumbent District Councillors on a territory-wide basis in the Legislative Council elections in 2012. The pan-democrats, usually with a 55–60% share of the votes in direct elections, felt confident to win three seats if it could minimise its number of candidates to three. An assessment would be the pro-establishment camp should be able to concentrate on two slates of candidates and safely secure two seats. The pro-democracy camp should avoid a scenario of too many candidates which might divide the votes too thinly among themselves and thus failed to win three seats.

Some kind of consultation and co-ordination exercise were called for. Richard Tsoi attempted to arrive at a consensus among the Democratic Party, the Civic Party, the HKADPL, and the Neighbourhood and Worker's Service Centre. [These four parties were interested in presenting candidates in the District Council (Second) functional constituency election.] Three meetings were held in April and early May 2012, but no agreement was reached on the presentation of pro-democracy candidates.

For the Chief Executive election in 2012, I was invited to preside over the primary election to select the candidate representing the pan-democrats, even though I was not much involved in the co-ordination work relating to the District Council elections in 2007 and 2011. An organising committee was formed, and

I served as its chairman. The political parties involved wanted to secure the service of a political science chair professor to enhance the impartiality of the primary election, and I gladly agreed to help.

As the Chief Executive were to be officially determined by a 1,200 member Election Committee, the objective of the primary election was largely educational – to involve ordinary Hong Kong people who had no role to play in the formal Chief Executive election. It was to set an example or a model for the pro-democracy movement in an optimistic anticipation that the democratic election of the Chief Executive would come soon, hopefully by 2017.[43] The project demonstrated considerable optimism and commitment on the part of the moderates in the pro-democracy movement. Election of the Chief Executive by universal suffrage remained an ideal, but the gesture appealed to the public for support and hoped to offer some civic education at the community level.

The University of Hong Kong Public Opinion Programme was also interested and it offered its services at cost. The primary election took slightly more than four weeks beginning with the press conference on December 3, 2011, announcing the arrangements and ending with the actual voting on January 8, 2012.

---

43 By November 2021, Hong Kong's Chief Executive is selected by the Election Committee of 1,500 members (an electoral college), and appointed by China's State Council. The composition of the Election Committee favours pro-Beijing and business interests.

The operation of setting up voting stations in various places in the territory was very challenging, especially when there were severe resource limitations. Voting stations were established in or near 74 Mass Transit Railway stations and a number of busy spots. It was quite a challenge in picking exact spots for the polling stations, since some of them had to compete with other vendors in the busy streets in Hong Kong while at the same time they must ensure personal safety and decent working environment. Fortunately for the volunteers manning the voting stations, the December weather in Hong Kong was mild, and they did not have to endure extreme weather conditions in the open.

There were two debates between the two candidates, one of which was televised by a local television station. The organisation work was challenging and complicated, ranging from the usual press conferences, debates between candidates to the setting up of voting stations, training of personnel working for the voting stations, and publicity work encouraging people to vote. It was surprising that basically no major mistakes had been made, and the project was completed satisfactorily.

In the end about 34,000 people voted, exceeding the original target of 20,000. Results were announced in the evening of the voting day. 50% of the weighting went to a public opinion survey, and another 50% went to the actual voting. Albert Ho from the Democratic Party defeated Frederick Fung from the HKADPL. Ho secured two-thirds of the votes in the actual voting, and Fung almost one-third. Among the 1,008 respondents in the public opinion survey, slightly over half indicated that they would support neither candidate.

The most serious weakness of the project was that it was criticised by the radical pro-democracy groups like the League of Social Democrats and People Power. They went as far as to physically disrupt the voting process. The differences between the radical wing and the moderate wing of the pro-democracy movement further deteriorated, and became very open.

A surprising outcome awaited me at the sixth Power for Democracy executive committee election in the general meeting on July 7, 2012. Richard Tsoi had earlier indicated that he would like to step down as convenor, though he would be willing to stay in the executive committee. There were some initial discussions on Tsoi's successor, and some executive committee members and I were ready to support Li Yiu-kee, a former student activist, to serve as convenor.

During the exchanges of views at the meeting on the future of the group, members expressed doubts on the group's role and contributions in the future. Emily Lau even suggested that the group should be disbanded. Ronny Tong, a Legislative Council member of the Civic Party, attended the meeting. He alluded to an earlier assurance by the Chinese authorities that the election of the Chief Executive by universal suffrage would be possible by

2017, and that of the entire legislature soon after this. Ronny believed that the entire pro-democracy movement should be mobilised to demand political reforms in 2013 and this would pose an important challenge; Power for Democracy could make a contribution. He suggested that I should serve as convenor and that he would also serve in the executive committee.

Ronny's suggestion won the support of the members. I realised then that the group could be in a crisis, and under these circumstances, I agreed to serve. I was subsequently asked to serve as the convenor of the Alliance for True Democracy, the umbrella group in the pro-democracy movement co-ordinating the campaign to demand political reforms in 2013–14. This is covered in detail in chapters 17–18.

My first task was to raise money, and a substantial donation from a rich friend ensured funding for the group's activities in the coming two years. Fundraising at the street level continued all these years. We made use of the opportunities offered by the protest rallies organised by the Civil Human Rights Front. Money thus raised was an important source of funding for the group. It also represented the recognition of its work by the supporters of the pro-democracy movement. On July 1, 2012, and July 1, 2013, the group collected HK$9,847 and HK$65,058 respectively.

The new executive committee had many young people, which was a good sign. As convenor, I was responsible for the co-ordination of the 2015 District Council elections. We started work early, and I much relied on the assistance of Andrew Chiu. There was a mutual understanding that I would step down as convenor in July 2014, and he would take over the responsibility. Naturally I would offer him my strong support. In September 2014, I stepped down as convenor, but I agreed to serve as deputy convenor to be responsible for fundraising and would jointly complete the co-ordination work for the 2015 District Council elections with Andrew. In 2016, I resigned from the executive committee so as to leave Andrew a completely free hand. I was very happy that someone could ensure that Power for Democracy could continue to function effectively. As a pro-democracy activist, I always tried to cultivate young talents and support their work. I do not believe that a good leader would be indispensable.

Co-ordination work proceeded smoothly as the rules and procedures were widely accepted by the political groups engaged in the exercise. The only concerns were the departure of the radical groups and the potential impact of the quarrels within the pro-democracy movement.

In August 2014, Beijing rejected political reforms and stated that Hong Kong's Chief Executive would have to be backed by a majority in a nominated election committee. The nomination rules for the committee made it difficult for the pro-democracy opposition to get in. Election of

Hong Kong's Chief Executive and legislature by universal suffrage would be an 'ultimate aim". The development triggered "Occupy Central"[44], a protest movement initiated by Benny Tai (a university academic), and taken over later by other young and more radical protesters in other districts (mainly the Admiralty, Causeway Bay, and Mongkok).

Hong Kong society became highly polarised as a result of the Occupation Campaign. There was fear that voter turnout rate would be low. During the Occupation Campaign, the young activists openly challenged Benny Tai and his associates, and the traditional pro-democracy political groups were sidelined. The young activists believed that the peaceful approach was ineffective, and they were prepared for bold confrontations with the authorities. How this would impact the 2015 District Council elections was unknown then.

In view of the polarisation in the society, the splits within the pro-democracy movement, and the general pessimism regarding the prospects of democratisation, most leaders in the pro-democracy movement believed that it would lose some more seats in the District Council

---

44   Facing Victoria Harbour, Central District is the business and retail hub on Hong Kong Island with iconic skyscrapers, high-end shopping malls and hotels. The movement became better known as the Occupation Campaign or occupation movement since other districts were also occupied later. It was also labelled by the media as the "Umbrella Revolution" or umbrella movement for the umbrellas carried by protesters to ward off tear gas and police batons.

elections, some of them even predicted that it would lose twenty to thirty seats. I had no reason to be optimistic, but there was no excuse to give up and I believed that serious efforts would yield satisfactory results. The candidates and their political parties simply had to work harder.

A new development emerged in late spring 2015; many political groups formed by young activists in the wake of the Occupation Campaign demonstrated an interest in taking part in the District Council elections. I made substantial efforts to contact them and initiate a dialogue with them. They did not want to take part in the co-ordination exercise, and they wanted to avoid co-operation with the traditional pro-democracy political parties. I showed respect and tremendous patience in my dealings with them. I offered them our list of candidates in various constituencies without asking for any information in return, and I invited them to take part in the training sessions that Power for Democracy organised for the candidates of the political parties engaged in the co-ordination exercise. These training sessions should be valuable to those who had no experience in election campaigns and no support from established political parties.

I tried to talk to these would-be candidates. A few of them did not make up their minds until early September, two months before the elections. My first question was: did they really want to be District Councillors? I explained that this called for substantial commitment. If they intended to serve in District Councils, they should choose constituencies suitable for them, that they should be prepared to stay in the constituencies after losing in the elections and continue to do grassroots work. If they had no plan to become District Councillors and simply wanted to take part in the elections and make a contribution, they could choose to challenge the political leaders of the pro-establishment camp so that their resources could not be diverted to other pro-establishment candidates. I offered to show my support for them in their campaign publicity materials.

My efforts helped to reduce conflicts between the established pro-democracy groups and the new post-Umbrella Movement groups. The success was far from complete. There were still six candidates from the post-Umbrella Movement groups who competed against those from the pro-democracy camp, mainly against those of the Democratic Party. But at least there were very few open attacks which would definitely have been exploited by the pro-Beijing media to discredit the pro-democracy movement as a whole.

I was very happy that the pro-democracy movement performed surprisingly well in the 2015 District Council elections. The success allowed the movement to claim that the support for democracy and the movement had strengthened after the Occupation Campaign which had lost the community's support in its final days. This was significant evidence against any attempt to discredit the campaign and a considerable boost of morale for the movement in its low tide. The most important factor for the electoral victory of the pro-democracy groups was the high turnout rate, a record high of 47% (1.467 million people voted). Despite this relatively enthusiastic participation, there were still 66 uncontested seats. Almost without exception, they came from the pro-establishment camp.

The pro-democracy coalition participating in co-ordination secured 104 seats, compared with 82 seats in 2011. (See Appendix I: District Council election results, 1999–2019.) Other pro-democracy groups that had not joined the co-ordination mechanism secured 11 seats, and the post-Umbrella Movement groups won 9 seats. The pro-democracy movement, however, was still in a minority in all eighteen District Councils. But the turning of the tide was important for the pro-democracy movement, and for Power for Democracy as well. It was indeed encouraging to see many new groups of young activists willing to take part in elections. Some of these new post-Umbrella Movement groups subsequently decided to join the co-ordination mechanism, though by then I had left the work entirely to Andrew Chiu.

Compared with 2011 results, the Democratic Party did not perform too well. The HKADPL and the Civic Party did better. The Neo-Democrats' performance was probably the best among all pro-democracy groups, but it mainly concentrated in the New Territories East. The League of Social Democrats returned to the co-ordination mechanism this time; it presented five candidates but failed to secure any seat.

None of the pro-democracy groups which were outside the co-ordination mechanism and the post-Umbrella Movement groups won more than one seat. In fact, quite a number of them failed to secure seats. But their participation probably helped to raise the voter turnout rate, especially that among young people.

There were also a number of relatively new political groups which claimed to adopt a middle-of-the-road political orientation. Path of Democracy led by Ronny Tong established in June 2015 was an example. Altogether these groups claimed 8 seats. In the eyes of the supporters of the pro-democracy movement, they were not pan-democrats, and treated as pro-establishment groups.

The pro-establishment camp did not perform too badly, though it failed to score a sounding victory as had been expected. The DAB secured less seats compared with the last election. Two of its elected District Councillors carried the banner of the Hong Kong Federation of Trade Unions as well, and they subsequently left the DAB. It appeared that the Federation increasingly wanted to present itself as an independent political group, and, to a limited extent, even engaged in competition with the DAB.

The New People's Party had a high success rate. Some of its elected District Councillors, however, also carried the flag of the Civil Force. In general, the pro-establishment parties had high success rates. Altogether the pro-establishment camp won 299 seats, and it enjoyed a majority in all eighteen District Councils. This meant that it could control the government funding allocated for district-level projects; when the government wanted to mobilise public opinion support, it could easily claim that all District Councils agreed with its policy positions.

Since the Sunflower Student Movement in Taiwan in March-April 2014 and the Occupation Campaign in the autumn of the same year, interactions between the pro-democracy groups in the two places much increased, especially between the more radical wings of the respective pro-democracy movements. There was a strong sense of mutual support. The slogan "Today's Hong Kong, Tomorrow's Taiwan" emerged in the regional elections in Taiwan at the end of 2014, and vividly demonstrated their solidarity. The ruling Kuomintang suffered a huge electoral defeat.

Both Power for Democracy and the New School for Democracy avoided contacts with groups advocating for the independence of Taiwan. In January 2016, the two groups organised a delegation of civil society groups and university student unions from Hong Kong to visit Taiwan and observe the presidential and legislature elections. The delegation was received by the mayor of Taipei, Ko Wen-je.

Power of Democracy did not assume an important role in the elections to the Chief Executive Election Committee[45], an electoral college responsible to select Hong Kong's Chief Executive, held in December 2016. The pro-democracy camp however performed well, despite the systemic limitations. Over three hundred seats (of over 1,000 elected seats) were won. The campaign was co-ordinated by the Professional Commons. I personally helped to organise the group of candidates for the Health Services functional constituency, and performed some liaison work on an individual basis.

In lining up support for the candidacy of the Chief Executive, the enthusiastic participation of the younger generation of professionals was impressive. The Professional Commons helped to line up the support for John Tsang, a former Financial Secretary, as a candidate to challenge Carrie Lam. The pro-democracy movement in general agreed to support John Tsang as the movement could not present a candidate this time.

There were differences of views within the democracy camp though. Some opinion leaders and moderate leaders believed that John Tsang would have

---

[45] The Election Committee is formed every five years to carry out its selection function. In December 2016, it comprised 1,200 members, and over 1,000 were elected from various functional sub-sectors, and was responsible to select the Chief Executive in 2017.

a reasonable chance of defeating Carrie Lam. This was not realistic. My understanding was that he depended largely on the pro-democracy camp for his votes. The Chinese authorities should still be able to command the loyalty of a safe majority in the Election Committee, and one should not have false expectations.

There were some moderates who treated John Tsang as a hero and an ally. Again I considered this an unrealistic assessment of the political situation. John remained a member of the establishment and he had never supported the pro-democracy cause while he was a senior member of the government. While he might have more liberal views than Carrie Lam, his support for the pro-democracy movement after his electoral defeat was extremely limited.

This position on the part of the moderates did not bode well for co-operation with its radical wing which always had reservations about taking part in the Chief Executive election under the existing system, especially when the pro-democracy movement did not even have a candidate.

There was a view among some commentators and supporters of the pro-democracy movement during the election campaign that John Tsang was backed by Xi Jinping, while Carrie Lam was supported by the Jiang Zemin faction. I was shocked by such views.

Power for Democracy in late January 2017 organised a platform for citizens who wished to articulate their views on the choice of the Chief Executive for the reference of the Election Committee members, especially those of the pro-democracy camp. I was very much involved in the project. On February 25, 2017, Power for Democracy organised a deliberation day for the Chief Executive candidates, but only Regina Ip and Woo Kwok-hing turned up. Woo was a former vice-president of the Court of Appeal of the High Court. The group was instrumental in helping Woo to secure adequate support from the pro-democracy Election Committee members to make him an official candidate. The rationale was to enhance competition in the election, and I tried my best to help.

The Hong Kong's Legislative Council elections were held at around the same time. The electoral system is characterised by a single-vote multi-member constituency system. Hence, every party coalition would try to formulate an electoral strategy to optimise the votes distributed to promising candidates within the coalition. In preparation for the 2016 Legislative Council elections, Benny Tai initiated a plan "Project ThunderGo" to guide voters to distribute their votes strategically among an optimal number of promising candidates in each geographical constituency, so as to increase the number of seats won by the pro-democracy camp.

Benny Tai's proposal was to form a strategic team to study the opinion surveys and various trends so as to issue guidance to voters supporting the pro-democracy camp to engage in strategic voting. This plan encountered quiet but strong opposition from the established pro-democracy political parties. I supported the idea of strategic voting and agreed that efforts should be made to optimise the number of candidates. The objective of democracy movement (and voters in support of democracy) as a whole might differ from that of individual candidates: the former naturally wanted to win the maximum number of seats. Individual candidates on the other hand would like to persist till the very last moment in their campaigns to enhance their respective chances, albeit in the next elections, even though that they recognised that their defeat would be highly probable earlier on in the campaign. Established political parties were opposed to the proposed interventions by Benny Tai's project which might generate unpredictable outcomes.

 I accompanied Benny to visit the leaders of almost all mainstream pro-democracy political parties. I understood that Benny Tai would not abandon his campaign, and the latter would not accept his plan. But a dialogue at least would improve their mutual understanding; otherwise open mutual criticisms would discredit the entire pro-democracy movement and might even generate confusion and opposition to the plan leading to uncontrollable distortions. I could only say that Benny Tai was willing to make some adjustments taking into consideration of the political parties' concerns.

 Meanwhile, to handicap strategic voting, the pro-establishment camp succeeded in blocking almost all large-scale public opinion surveys by the media and other agencies on the 2016 Legislative Council elections, so that the general public would have no reliable data to gauge the support levels of the candidates to engage in strategic voting. A few friends kindly offered to help, their funding support allowed Power for Democracy to commission the University of Hong Kong Public Opinion Programme to conduct a series of surveys on the candidates in the five geographical constituencies and the District Council (Second) Functional Constituency (actually the territory-wide constituency) just before the elections. This series of surveys emerged as the most comprehensive and reliable poll data for the reference of the entire community, and was obviously a service to Hong Kong people. I am glad that I was involved in the fund-raising and the organisation of the surveys.

Strategic voting probably became quite widespread among supporters for the pro-democracy movement in the 2016 Legislative Council elections. A few candidates like Suzanne Wu Sui-shan of the Labour Party and Sumly Chan Yuen-sum of the Civic Party withdrew just before the elections so as to avoid dispersing the votes too thinly among the pro-democracy candidates. The worst fears of the leading candidates were that voters thought that they were safe and went to vote for other pro-democracy candidates. For those who were lagging behind, their concern was that they would have little chance to catch up because voters would not like to "waste" their votes on candidates without much chance of winning.

Benny Tai's team issued a message of guidance informing people how to engage in strategic voting just before the Election Day. This was controversial and was criticised by some pro-democracy candidates, though his team subsequently conducted a survey which revealed that the guidance was not very effective. Power for Democracy and I did not want to offer guidance to voters because of the very nature of its work.

Somehow, it might have produced an educational effect on the voters. Most people who became aware and engaged in strategic voting consulted among family members, and often they followed decisions made within their families. I knew that with most families supporting the pan-democrats, an agreement was reached for a family member to vote for candidate A, and another to vote for candidate B, and so on. With roughly the same share of the votes, the pro-democracy camp did quite well in the elections, gaining twenty-eight seats, and the medical functional constituency seat was won by a doctor who supported pro-democracy policy positions. Geographically, the camp secured six out of nine seats in New Territories East and only four seats out of nine in New Territories West.

After the Legislative Council elections in 2016, four pan-democrat legislators were unexpectedly disqualified for their mocking behaviours and political posturing during the oath-taking ceremonies. They were following two precedents in the past when the "offenders" were simply asked by the president of the Legislative Council to take the oath again. This time, the Secretary for Justice challenged the president's decision, and the High Court's ruling followed the latest interpretation of the National People's Congress Standing Committee on Article 104 of the Basic Law which requires oath-taking to be mandatory, accurate, complete and solemn for assuming office. According to the interpretation, Oath-takers are not allowed to retake their oaths.

These cases were symbolic of the increasing political pressures on the pro-democracy movement after the Occupation Campaign. It was especially significant when the executive branch of the government challenged the autonomy of the legislature and the Standing Committee of the National People's Congress actively intervened through its unilateral interpretation of the Basic Law. The well-established precedents established in the legislature and understood by legislators and the Hong Kong community as a whole were overturned by the executive branch.

Since two disqualified candidates would like to appeal the decisions, and the other two indicated that they had no intention to compete in the by-elections, there were two vacancies at the Kowloon West and New Territories East constituencies in the by-elections scheduled in March 2018. In this single-member, simple majority election, we realised that if the pro-Beijing united front would present only one candidate, more than one candidate from the pro-democracy camp might most likely lead to defeat. The camp decided to conduct co-ordination exercises in both constituencies to select one candidate each in the by-election. Power for Democracy accepted this responsibility. I had left Power for Democracy in December 2016, but I still offered to help Andrew Chiu, my successor, in the co-ordination exercise where necessary.

We started work in the summer of 2017. Different candidates had their individual strengths and weaknesses, and thus would prefer an assessment formula that would work best for them. After much consultation, disagreements and arguments, we reached a consensus in the formula to be used in the selection, and announced the list of participating candidates and election procedures on December 7, 2017. The initiative consisted of public telephone survey (45% weighting), actual voting at the district level (45% weighting), and voting by 250 representatives of the participating groups (10% weighting). I believed that the participation was satisfactory, and fortunately the exercises proceeded smoothly.

Finally, Gary Fan came first in New Territories East, (and subsequently won the election to the legislative Council). Edward Yiu Chung Yim, an architect professor, won in Kowloon West. But he and his supporters were worried that his nomination might be invalidated because of his political position at the time[46]. At a January 2018 meeting, a plan B was discussed. One way would be to ask Frederick Fung who received the second highest support to run. Supporters of Yiu felt that Fung's political position was too moderate and pragmatic to represent Yiu's relatively radical views. Leaders of the democracy movement expressed concern about his weak appeal and proposed to persuade a heavy-weight politician Alan Leong Ka-Kit to run as a back-up should Edward Yiu be disqualified.

Even though I was not present in the plan B meeting, I was requested to contact Frederick Fung to deliver this message. Alan Leong would like to have the agreement and open support of Fung first. In the presence of Andrew Chiu and two other pro-democrats, I told Fung that such backup plan would only be adopted with his public blessing. I also pledged support should he still decide to run as backup candidate. I also pointed out

---

46   Around that time, the Hong Kong government made use of a number of technicalities to disqualify candidates during the process of nomination for the Legislative Council elections. A few pro-democracy nominees were disqualified by middle-ranking returning officers who made the decision by examining the statements made by and deeds of the candidates concerned. The mechanism was introduced without consultation and adequate early warning. The disqualified candidate could appeal through a judicial review of the returning officer's decision, but it would be meaningless, since the court ruling would come after the election. If the court overturned the returning officer's decision, the election that had taken place became void, and a new election had to be organised. Such cases in fact emerged in 2019.

that the radical wing of the pro-democracy movement might attack him, and he might be defeated because of this division. Fung queried the assessment that he would lose, but declined when I offered to do a public opinion survey. It was a frank conversation, and as a messenger, I had no personal interests or gain. I wanted to protect Andrew Chiu too so that his co-ordinator role for Power of Democracy would not be tarnished.

Later, Frederick Fung's party, the HKADPL, held a meeting and refused to endorse Fung's candidacy in the event of Edward Yiu's disqualification. It was then that Fung had no choice but to drop his plan. He then publicised the contents of our conversation and severely attacked me for putting pressure on him. The radical wing and supporters of Edward Yiu were ridiculing Fung on the Internet, and Fung did not openly respond to these attacks. It was quite obvious that no one could have forced a candidate to withdraw from an election through a meeting.

For some weeks, I kept quiet to protect the individuals concerned and to avoid giving the pro-establishment camp a chance to discredit the electoral campaign of the pro-democracy movement. I did not criticise him publicly before the elections in March. I only explained to the media that I had been asked to deliver a message. Power for Democracy later approached a candidate who came third in the exercise and he was kind enough to become the backup candidate and registered himself on the final day of the registration. Later in the day, Edward Yiu received notice that his candidacy had been validated.

Yiu was defeated by a Beijing loyalist from DAB in the March election however. This shocked the pro-democracy movement, which was supposed to command the support of 55–60% of the votes. There were many criticisms of Yiu's handling of the campaign, and he could not attract the votes of grassroots residents of the public-housing estates. One important factor was the division between the moderate segment and the radical segment of the movement. It was difficult to find a candidate who could appeal to both.

Fung continued his unreasonable attacks on me in his autobiography. I began to realise then that he was actually helping the pro-Beijing united front to discredit me, so much so that I could no longer engage in the promotion of solidarity within the movement. From then on, I knew that he was no longer a member of the pro-democracy camp. Fung this time ran as an independent candidate, as he chose to withdraw from the HKADPL after they refused to endorse him. By this time, his credibility within the democracy camp had gone.

The second Legislative Council by-election in Kowloon West took place in November 2018, and a similar difficulty re-emerged. Lau Siu-Lai, an incumbent legislator was disqualified after the oath-taking controversy, and it was agreed by the pro-democracy camp that she would stand again in the by-election. Her back-up was Lee Cheuk-Yan, a veteran Labour Party leader.

Again, Lau Siu-lai's nomination was invalidated by the electoral office and Lee Cheuk-yan took her place. Lee lost this time to an independent candidate Rebecca Chan Hoi Yan, a nonpartisan firmly backed by the pro-Beijing camp. It was difficult to find a candidate who could appeal to both the moderate and radical segments of the supporters; it appeared also that the young voters wanted to see new faces. The mobilisation power of the pro-democracy camp weakened, and the turnout rate was a low of 44.5%. The pro-democracy camp saw Fung's candidacy as a ploy to split votes with Lee. It had to be admitted though that votes to Rebecca exceeded those of Lee and Fung combined. The pro-Beijing united front won two single-seat constituency, simple majority electoral contests consecutively. Its mobilisation power and campaign strategies were superb. This was seen as the political depression for the pro-democracy movement until the political crisis in the second half of 2019.

Fung continued to compete in the District Council elections as an independent candidate in November 2019. He scored a dismal 154 votes in the Tsim Sha Tsui District Council constituency. It was sad to see him fall to such a level. After all, he was among the first generation political activists who pioneered grassroots services in the Sham Shui Po district in the second half of the 1970s and 1980s.

There were no more co-ordination exercises for the pro-democracy camp in the 2020 Legislative Council elections. In recent years, although I no longer served on the executive committee of Power for Democracy, I always offered my support when I was called upon.

Chapter 15

I Joined the Civic Party

Dual leadership structure and "blue blood" political stars. The schism deepened. Intra-party competition. Pushing the "Alliance for Universal Suffrage" with de facto referendum, a taboo to China. To negotiate or not to negotiate was not the question.

I accidentally joined the Civic Party. I was neither a member of the Article 23 Concern Group nor the Article 45 Concern Group, foundation groups on which the Civic Party was established. Among the core founders of the Civic Party, I only knew Margaret Ng Ngoi-yee. We usually met for a certain purpose relating to the political development in Hong Kong. I was invited to dinner in late 2005, and I understood that it probably was an invitation to join the party. As a researcher on Hong Kong politics, I was curious to better understand the emergence of a new party.

I decided to join because I believed that I could make a contribution. The establishment of a moderate, pro-democracy party with a strong appeal to the community would be an asset to the territory's political development. The Democratic Party had gradually lost its undisputed leadership of the pro-democracy movement. It increasingly came under attack from the movement's radical wing. There was a considerable demand for an alternative to the Democratic Party among the moderate supporters of the pro-democracy movement. Obviously the Civic Party could broaden the spectrum of the political base for the movement.

2005. I joined the Civic Party.

I did not join the Democratic Party in its inauguration because I had no intention to pursue a political career then. I had not changed, and the Civic Party understood very well that I had no plans of standing for election. But I considered that I could contribute to the new party's relations with the other political groups as well as its organisation work. I realised that I was not among the core leaders of the party.

By that time, I had reached an implicit understanding with the management of the City University of Hong Kong where I taught that I would not seek any administrative position within the university. In return I would accept more teaching duties, and I would like to be left alone to engage in activities within the pro-democracy movement. The arrangement worked quite well until mid-2013 or so.

Before the Civic Party's formal inauguration, a series of meetings were held. I was asked to preside over the first meeting, and I believed that I had performed well. Margaret Ng then asked me to take detailed minutes for the next meeting; I understood the message. But I had not thought of seeking any leadership role within the new party, and I was seriously considering not joining the executive committee.

It was actually Margaret Ng who came to me and asked me to serve as the first secretary general of the party. I agreed to serve as my general contribution to the territory's political development. I believed that I was well qualified for the position. My first important proposal to the party was on its structure. I suggested a dual leadership: the party leader who served as the convenor of the parliamentary group, responsible for the current legislative and policy issues; and the party chairman, who assumed the responsibility of the overall development of the party in the long term. The party at its founding stage promised to devote half of its resources to community work including political education, and the party chairman with his/her status had a special duty to ensure its implementation. The model to a considerable extent was based on the British Labour Party. This had relevance for the pro-democracy parties in Hong Kong, as there was a tendency for them to be dominated by one or two political stars, and the party organisation was too focused on short-term Legislative Council work. The party's founding leaders chose Professor Kuan Hsin-chi to be its party chairman, a fine choice; Kuan certainly would not challenge the parliamentary group.

A small incident occurred during the Sunday before June 4, 2006, when the Hong Kong Alliance in Support of Patriotic Democratic Movements of China organised its annual protest rally demanding the reversal of the verdict on the Tiananmen incident. Journalists observed that I was the only one among the party's executive committee present. In actual fact, I went to support the cause every year on a personal basis. The absence of the party leaders caused a small controversy, which largely disappeared when they all showed up at the candlelight vigil at Victoria Park later in the evening on June 4.

The party applied to join the Civil Human Rights Front soon after its inauguration on March 19, 2006. At that time there were some radical groups within the umbrella organisation which considered the Civic Party too elitist and intended to reject its application for membership. This would not damage the party in any substantive way, but its image might be tarnished somewhat. Before the Civil Human Rights Front's meeting, I did some lobbying work, and I represented the party to present its case at the meeting. Fortunately, the lobbying succeeded. I certainly believed that it was ridiculous to reject the application of the Civic Party which had stated publicly its mission to promote democracy and social justice. But these were signs of the rise of radicalism and the lack of consideration for the solidarity of the pro-democracy movement.

In its early years, there were some party leaders who talked about its ambition of becoming the largest party in the pro-democracy movement. Many party members naturally shared the view that their party was superior to the Democratic Party. It was legitimate to entertain the objective, but at the same time we should be concerned about our relations with the Democratic Party. In one or two radio interviews when I was asked these questions, I stated that the Democratic Party was a well-established party. It had many strengths like its grassroots organisations that new parties could not compete with. Political parties usually had ups and downs, and I was sure that the Democratic Party would have many successful years ahead. My statements partly reflected my assessment of the weaknesses of the Civic

Party. I certainly would like to see close co-operation between the two major parties of the pro-democracy movement.

In contrast to the early political parties of the pro-democracy movement, key members of the Civic Party did not know each other well. It was therefore suggested that the executive committee should have dinner together after its weekly meeting at the party office. It was a good idea, but unfortunately committee members were usually busy and the practice was abandoned after some time.

Wong Yuk-man, the then leader of the League of Social Democrats, openly attacked the Civic Party as a "blue blood party" in its very early years. This image of the Civic Party had its advantages and disadvantages. Lau Siu-kai, head of the Central Policy Unit then and a former colleague of mine at the Chinese University of Hong Kong, offered me his observation: "People think that these senior barristers are really serving the people, because they can earn much more by staying in their practices". People had a lot of respect for the leaders of the Civic Party. Some senior civil servants and top professionals looked down on the grassroots politicians of the pro-democracy camp whom they considered unqualified as executive officers in the civil service. They certainly would not feel the same about Civic Party leaders.

There were distinct disadvantages. Grassroots voters found it hard to identify with a party whose representatives were wealthy professionals. That was exactly the objective of Wong Yuk-man's attacks. People might have doubts whether the party leaders could understand their daily problems and would dedicate their precious time to struggle for their causes.

This image affected party support and its recruitment of party members. I came across some people who were considering joining the party and they asked me if party members had to speak good English. There were some young party members who believed that one had to have a very good command of English and had to be members of the legal profession in order to have a bright future in the party. Naturally I tried to offer my re-assurances.

The significance was that the Party faced considerable difficulties in expanding its appeal to a broad spectrum of Hong Kong people. The Civic Party certainly enjoyed a strong attraction to the liberals among the middle-class groups, but it was here that it encountered strong competition from the Democratic Party. There were some challenges from the pro-establishment camp too, like for example, from Regina Ip's New People's Party. As reported by party chairman Kuan Hsin-chi, the party had 106 founding members, and the membership expanded to 292 in September 2007. By October 2008, the membership growth slowed down to 349.

The weaknesses were exposed in the 2007 District Council elections. The party was ambitious and it presented 42 candidates with a target of fifteen seats.

The candidates included four barristers, three lawyers, two accountants and three engineers. Hence, the new party had been successful in mobilising professionals to stand as candidates. But many candidates did not spend enough time and efforts on grassroots services, and the period of preparations was relatively short. The appeal of the party's political stars failed to be translated into votes at the grassroots level for the candidates.

District Council elections in 2007 was a comeback for the pro-establishment camp and especially for the Democratic Alliance for the Betterment and Progress of Hong Kong (DAB) (see the chapter 14 on Power for Democracy). There was a considerable electoral setback for the entire pro-democracy camp. At this stage, there were no more easy seats to be won. Incumbent District Councillors exploited their advantages, and they normally worked hard to satisfy their constituents. At least their respective teams of assistants managed to deliver the services essential to keep the incumbents' seats. In this context, winning eight seats plus one District Councillor who was later absorbed into the party was not too bad a result.

I was responsible for the campaign and I had to assume responsibility for the lacklustre performance. I was a good organiser, and I managed to make the arrangements for the elections. But I obviously did not have the talent to brighten up the campaigns with various innovations. I campaigned hard for the candidates, and the party leaders in general worked hard for the candidates' campaigns. However, the entire party lacked experience in District Council elections, in contrast to the Democratic Party and the Hong Kong Association for Democracy and People's Livelihood (HKADPL). Subsequently the party was less ambitious in District Council elections, and it became more demanding on the candidates in preparatory work. But it also encountered the usual difficulties of mobilising promising professionals to stand.

The earlier Chief Executive election in March 2007 was a success for the Civic Party though. The Democratic Party agreed to support a Civic Party candidate to represent the pro-democracy movement. It presented its party chairman Lee Wing-tat as the candidate in the by-election in 2005, but Lee was not qualified as a candidate because the pro-democracy camp did not have one-eighth of the seats in the Election Committee necessary for a formal nomination. Party members had expected Audrey Eu to serve as the candidate, but she already declined to stand when she accepted the position as party leader. The party then endorsed Alan Leong Kah-kit.

In preparation for the Chief Executive selection by the Election Committee in 2007, the pro-democracy camp had to gain sufficient seats in the Election Committee (at least 100 out of 800 seats) in order to nominate its own candidate to stand. The movement mainly targeted the professional sub-sectors (with 200 seats) in the Election Committee. Altogether the pro-democracy camp endorsed 137 candidates in 12 sub-sectors and secured 114 seats (83% success rate) in the Election Committee. They did well to ensure that Alan would become a formal candidate to challenge the incumbent Donald Tsang Yum-kuen.

This was the first time that the pro-democracy movement could have a formal candidate in the Chief Executive selection, and the honour went to the Civic Party. The outcome of the selection was not unexpected: Alan secured 123 votes while Donald won 649 votes. The winning of more than half of the seats in the professional sectors in the Election Committee was already an achievement for the pro-democracy movement. Alan's performance in the electoral debate was highly satisfactory. In subsequent elections in the professional sectors to the Election Committee, the pro-democracy movement managed to do quite well, especially in the accountancy, education, engineering, health services, higher education, information technology and law sub-sectors.

I helped to co-ordinate the election campaign for the higher education sub-sector. Enthusiasm was not particularly high, because at the time, the Election Committee members were only responsible to cast their votes twice during their terms, one in the Chief Executive election and one in the election of the Hong Kong deputies to the National People's Congress. Typically university academics were not interested in administrative work and campaign activities. The registration of candidates, preparation of publicity materials, reporting of electoral expenditure, etc., required considerable time and efforts. In response, I recruited a young academic who was interested to stand as a candidate to serve also as co-ordinator. I also managed to enlist the service of a consultancy firm to handle all the campaign work at a charge of about HK$7,000 per candidate. In this way, the administrative work of the candidates was much reduced and they managed to save considerable time.

Regarding campaign work, I tried to set an example and visited every tertiary institution including small ones like Chu Hai College of Higher Education. I realised that sincerity and commitment were needed to mobilise the staff members of the tertiary institutions to vote. To be realistic, our voters understood very well that supporting us to become members of the Election Committee would not change the outcome of the Chief Executive election under the current election system. Candidates therefore had to demonstrate the need to take joint action to show Hong Kong people our values. I tried to persuade a few more enthusiastic candidates to visit a number of universities, and that each candidate should at least be responsible for campaigning in his/her own institution. Under this arrangement, at least a small team of candidates visited every tertiary institution in our campaign.

The team of candidates for the higher education sector managed to secure a seat for every candidate on its slate. In contrast, all the senior members of the universities' management who were candidates lost. The results certainly demonstrated university staff's resentment against their management teams at that time. There were twenty seats for the higher education sector, but we had a slate of only fifteen candidates, partly because we failed to attract more colleagues to serve as candidates and partly because we wanted to leave other options to the voters. I was happy to be elected with the highest number of votes among all the successful candidates.

Two young candidates approached me for financial support. It was true that I lobbied them to serve as candidates, but I had not expected that they did not want to pay for their own electoral expenses. So I approached Kuan Hsin-chi and we each paid for one candidate's electoral expenses without any discussions with the team. Punctuality also posed a small problem. Since the candidates had very little interest at stake, a few were often late, and I had to remind everyone to be punctual. This obviously was not a popular task. Minimum discipline was essential, but there was no means to enforce it.

Voting for Hong Kong deputies to China's National People's Congress was a controversial issue. I stated at the very beginning that we should not take part in the voting. The voting system was such that an Election

Committee member had to choose 36 candidates in total from the official list of candidates. The Chinese authorities' stipulation was so designed to demonstrate healthy support for all successful candidates and to ensure that candidates not acceptable to them would not get elected. My position in not participating was exactly because I believed that we should not get involved in the election of Hong Kong deputies eager to toe the line of the Chinese authorities. But many influential politicians and rich businessmen would reach out to the pro-democracy Election Committee members for support, and they would implicitly offer rewards for such support.

When I hosted the first meeting among the team of candidates, I formally made such a proposal and nobody expressed any dissenting views. A lady colleague at my university who was on the team's slate came to see me and argued for her participation in voting for the Hong Kong deputies. She said she would like to send some decent people to the National People's Congress. I asked her if she could find 36 candidates worthy of supporting (otherwise the ballot would be invalid), and I reminded her that she had not said anything when I proposed non-participation. Any rate, I accepted that I could not enforce any decision of the team. Subsequently this colleague joined the management of the university.

The Legislative Council elections in September 2008 was a major test for the Civic Party. The party took part in all five geographical constituencies and four functional constituencies, and it hoped to secure seven seats, one seat more than before. In the end, it secured only five, one less than before, which was not very satisfactory. As secretary general, I was responsible for the elections again. But each candidate would be responsible for his/her own campaign. I had to take care of the distribution of party resources, arrangement of publicity for the entire party, and general co-ordination and administrative work. The tasks were many, but the responsibility was limited. Resources at the disposal of the party was far from adequate, fortunately the candidates themselves were able to mobilise financial support and voluntary workers.

Audrey Eu's performance was outstanding in the Hong Kong Island constituency; she placed herself second on the list and successfully secured two seats for Tanya Chan and herself. Alan Leong and Ronny Tong retained their respective seats in Kowloon East and New Territories East, but their rankings among successful candidates were not impressive. Claudia Mo and Fernando Cheung lost in Kowloon West and New Territories West respectively. Fernando originally represented the social workers in his previous term, but he opted for direct election in the geographical constituency in 2008. New Territories West was a huge area, and he was especially tight with resources. I tried to help, but there was a limit to what I could do. Claudia Mo came under severe attack from Wong Yuk-man, and the Civic

Party attributed her failure to this. It reflected the schism between the moderate wing and the radical wing of the pro-democracy movement. The radical wing at this stage seemed to treat the Civic Party as the principal target; this was partly related to Alan Leong's candidacy in the earlier Chief Executive election. The radical wing of the movement strongly opposed participation in the Election Committee elections and the Chief Executive election.

In the functional constituencies, Margaret Ng representing the legal profession easily retained her seat. Mandy Tam Heung-man lost her seat in the accountancy constituency; this time the pro-establishment camp was much better co-ordinated and Mandy could not secure a simple majority of the votes in the constituency. Civic Party candidates also failed in the tourism and engineering constituencies. This was not too surprising because these two constituencies were quite conservative. The election within tourism constituency was not on a one person, one vote basis, only the owners of hotels, tourism agencies, and airlines were qualified to vote; and engineers tended to depend on major contracts from the government.

When the party was first established, I proposed that Claudia Mo and Kenneth Chan Ka-lok should be responsible for the Kowloon West and New Territories West party branches. The party did not have Legislative Councillors in these two geographical constituencies; the responsible persons had a very good opportunity to serve as the party's candidates in the coming elections. I believed these two executive committee members were appropriate candidates. The party had to assume responsibility for the expenses of these two party branches though. I was a bit surprised that Kenneth chose not to stand; I approached him and indicated that I would support him if he wanted to stand. But he declined.

Mandy Tam's candidacy resulted in a serious difference between me and the parliamentary group. Apparently the group decided to replace Mandy as the party's candidate for the accountancy constituency in 2008 with Amy Yung Wing-sheung, an accountant and a District Councillor in the Islands District Council. I was not informed and no one had discussed the issue with me, though I was the secretary general and was supposed to be responsible for the party's campaign. I later discovered that Mandy did not get along with the founding leaders of the party, and her style did not meet their approval.

Mandy approached me and Claudia Mo for support. The executive committee was scheduled to vote to elect the candidates should competition emerge; otherwise it would simply vote to endorse the candidates in the absence of competition. I had supported Mandy in the 2004 Legislative Council elections as a co-ordinator of the pro-democracy movement, and had contributed to her electoral campaign. I had not contacted her after the elections before joining the Civic Party, and I did not know her well.

In the executive committee meeting, I clearly stated that I supported Mandy's candidacy and I hoped that the executive committee would do so. My rationale was based on the simple principle that the party should support the incumbent legislator if she had made no serious mistakes and had implemented the party line all the time. I indicated that it was the party's founding leaders who had invited her to join the party. They had the moral responsibility to support her candidacy after she joined the party, and Mandy certainly had expected that. Finally I said that the chance of Mandy winning the seat this time would be low, and the same applied to Amy. The party should review the choice of candidate again after the election.

Those who supported the replacement of Mandy did not offer any explanation. They never openly revealed their rationale. The executive committee voted in support of Mandy by ten to nine votes. Many party members tried to guess how each executive committee member had voted. Audrey Eu later asked if I was concerned about a split of the party. I said I was not worried; at worst one member would leave. I truly believed so, because this type of competition was common in almost all political parties. But I realised that the party leadership felt threatened. In fact I had formally proposed earlier that the party's candidates in the District Councils and Legislative Council elections should be approved by the party's general membership as part of the democratisation of the party's decision-making process. But my proposal was not accepted; the founding leaders wanted to retain control. Actually the Democratic Party had adopted this democratic procedure.

A very important mission of the Civic Party was the promotion of democratisation in Hong Kong. In the second half of 2000s, there was still considerable optimism in the pro-democracy movement. In March 2007, the twenty-two pro-democracy Legislative Councillors arrived at a consensus on the future electoral systems for the Chief Executive and the Legislative Council. The Civic Party was part of this "Alliance for Universal Suffrage". Regarding the Chief Executive election, it was proposed that the existing 800-member Election Committee would be expanded with the addition of 400 directly elected District Councillors to form the Nomination Committee. Any 50 Nomination Committee members would be able to nominate a candidate, and the election would be based on universal suffrage. The Legislative Council elections would adopt a hybrid model: half of the members would be elected from single-member constituencies by simple majorities, and half would be elected by a proportional representation system on a territory-wide basis. It was proposed that the Alliance should strive for the implementation by 2012.

According to seven public opinion surveys by the University of Hong Kong Public Opinion Programme since June 2007, support for the proposed future electoral systems had been positive and steady. Regarding the electoral system for the Chief Executive, over half of the respondents gave their support while one-sixth opposed. Regarding that for the Legislative Council, nearly half supported while one-sixth opposed. Regarding the date of implementation, the last of the seven surveys revealed that nearly two-thirds of the respondents hoped that the electoral system for the Legislative Council would be implemented in 2012, and over half of them hoped that for the Chief Executive would be implemented in the same year.

As a new party, the Civic Party was naturally concerned with its image and Hong Kong people's assessments of its performance. Synergy Net, a think tank, observed in its 2009 research report that both the Democratic Party and the Civic Party stood out in terms of overall performance among all political parties. The Legislative Councillors from the Civic Party performed well in the six performance areas, especially their work in the Bills Committees. This was not surprising because four of the party's legislators were outstanding barristers in the territory and they were hard-working. The party's concern about environmental protection also won appreciation[47].

In terms of popular support, the Civic Party ranked third among ten parties/political groups, lagging behind

---

47 See Report of the Civic Party Chairman to the Annual General Meeting, December 5, 2009.

the Hong Kong Federation of Trade Unions and the Hong Kong Confederation of Trade Unions. Civic Party leaders Audrey Eu topped the list of legislators in popularity throughout the year while Alan Leong came second three times and third once. One-tenth of respondents felt that the Civic Party represents their interests best; it was third in rank, behind Democratic Party and DAB. Nearly half were very satisfied or satisfied with their performance.[48] It was observed within the Civic Party that although the party and its leaders were enjoying a very good image, the general public might not be able to identify with the party.

In the broad picture, the political reality was far from favourable for the development of a new political party in Hong Kong. As the pro-Beijing camp well realised, it would be difficult for one single party to appeal to the entire community. Hence, Beijing camp supported the Hong Kong Federation of Trade Unions for its appeal to the grassroots, the DAB for its coverage of various socio-economic strata, Regina Ip's New People's Party for its attraction to the middle-class, especially the civil service and the disciplinary forces, and the Liberal Party and the Business and Professionals Alliance for Hong Kong for their business interests. There was also the

---

48 See the website http://hkupop.hku.hk/ of the University of Hong Kong Public Opinion Programme, which ceased operation on 30 June 2019. This was continued by the Hong Kong Public Opinion Programme http://www.pori.hk/.

consideration of the "divide and rule" tactic to maximise control by the united front.

The Civic Party had to compete with the Democratic Party for the support of the liberal middle-class and the very small segment of the business community willing to endorse a pro-democracy political party. Radical parties like the League of Social Democrats adopted a radical political platform and also attempted to appeal to the grassroots. Then groups like HKADPL chose to concentrate on grassroots services in districts like Shamshuipo, and the Hong Kong Confederation of Trade Unions naturally had its base among workers.

Where were the natural support bases for the Civic Party? The support from the liberal middle-class helped the party to establish a good image, but it was inadequate for it to develop into a broad-based party with a substantial membership. Despite the weaknesses of the Democratic Party, it had an early start and therefore a firm foundation. The party's nearly one hundred District Councillors at its peak provided an electoral support network that far exceeded that of any other pro-democracy party.

Financial resources posed a serious challenge for the Civic Party. Well-established professionals appeared to have the capacity to make donations, and some of the party leaders like Audrey Eu were indeed very generous. But their wealth could not compare with that of the major business groups. The party headquarters operated on the basis of an annual budget of around HK$3 million. Legislators used their salaries and allowances to support their own constituency offices.

The party could only provide very limited subsidies for its candidates in District Council elections, usually a few thousand Hong Kong dollars. Those interested to run had to find their own resources to do constituency work in preparation for the campaign, and it was extremely difficult to unseat pro-establishment incumbents in this manner. The latter might not be as hard-working and dedicated, but they made it up by employing at least two or three assistants to deliver services in their names to ensure the satisfaction of their constituents. Under normal circumstances, over 80% of the District Councillors were re-elected, like local representatives in most democratic countries.

In the eyes of Beijing, the Civic Party was considerably radicalised in late 2009 and the first half of 2010, through the formation of an alliance with the League of Social Democrats in a pseudo-referendum on democratisation. The Civic Party released its declaration on democratic elections on September 6, 2009, and then its proposals on the roadmap of political reforms three days later. The party intended to join hands with the other pro-democracy parties to exert pressure on the Donald Tsang administration to promote political reforms. If the Tsang administration failed to produce a roadmap leading to full democracy when it released its intermediate political reform plan for 2012, then the pro-democracy camp would ask one of its legislators to resign in each of the five geographical constituencies, forcing by-elections allowing the entire electorate to vote as a de facto referendum on the political reform plan of the pro-democracy camp mentioned earlier. And if this de facto referendum (also known as the "Five Constituency Referendum") did not work, all the pro-democracy legislators would resign by July 1, 2011, in protest.

The Donald Tsang administration refused to communicate with the Civic Party. On December 5, 2009, the party held its annual general meeting and decided to move into the second stage of the campaign, i.e., promoting the de facto referendum and calling this the "New Pro-Democracy Movement". The emphases were to explain to Hong Kong people the absurdity of the functional constituency system and the strong relationship between democracy and people's livelihood. The Civic Party provided two resignations in the five geographical constituencies, namely, Alan Leong in Kowloon East and Tanya Chan in Hong Kong Island.

I was not much involved in the decision-making process on this matter. I could not understand how the Civic Party could co-operate closely with the radical League of Social Democrats under Wong Yuk-man. In the first place, I was not optimistic regarding the attainment of full democracy for Hong Kong although I genuinely believed in the cause and had been working for it since the days of the Sino-British negotiations on the territory's future. But my understanding of the Chinese Communist Party regime was that it would like to remain in full control and would not allow Hong Kong people to choose their own leaders who would be accountable to them.

I also cautioned the Civic Party that support for the de facto referendum would likely make the party the principal target of attack by the pro-Beijing united front. The party should be aware of the danger and should be prepared for it. I did not want to see many party members to expect that the Donald Tsang administration would yield, and that the democratic election of the Chief Executive would come soon. Some party members considered that Audrey Eu should be the ideal candidate in the democratic election of the Chief Executive and that she would be supported by a majority of Hong Kong people. I did not dispute this assessment; I only thought that Beijing would not grant Hong Kong genuine democracy, and that we should be aware of the severe challenge ahead.

Though I had not been much involved in the decision-making process, I was determined to help. I contributed to Alan Leong's campaign in Kowloon East as Tanya Chan enjoyed the support of Audrey Eu. I could claim that besides the two candidates, I spent more hours in street campaigning than any other party member. I was usually very serious with my campaign work, I spoke for three hours using a loudspeaker with few resting periods in between. I responded to the very occasional phone calls, but otherwise I did not use the mobile phone at all. I observed that many campaign workers spent more than thirty minutes on their mobile phones in the two-hour sessions scheduled specially for them. I was frequently asked to campaign for District Council candidates; I often arrived before the candidates and was more concentrated than the candidates themselves in street campaigning.

The pro-Beijing camp boycotted the de facto referendum since the Chinese authorities were very sensitive regarding any referenda; they were especially concerned that a referendum might take place in Taiwan. Hence, it treated referenda as taboos in Hong Kong too. It chose to discredit the by-elections which were meant to pose as a de facto referendum, rather than to mobilise its supporters to vote for its candidates. Fortunately the university student unions offered candidates to compete so as to avoid the scenario of having unopposed elections when all were pro-democracy candidates. Admittedly the electorate was not very enthusiastic. The voter turnout rate was only 17%. But the participation of 570,000 voters was nonetheless impressive; they came out to vote in support of the pro-democracy movement's political reform proposal. These were the hard-core supporters of the pro-democracy movement.

The de facto referendum attempt resulted in a severe division within the pro-democracy movement. The Democratic Party and the HKADPL decided to enter into negotiations with the Central Liaison Office. The Democratic Party was subsequently severely attacked by the radical wing of the pro-democracy movement. These attacks lingered on for almost a decade, though of course became much weaker subsequently. I certainly did not believe that the Democratic Party would betray the pro-democracy movement. I knew the leaders of the party very well, and my trust and friendship with them had never been affected. But I considered that they had made a bad mistake.

During the de facto referendum campaign, I maintained contacts with the Democratic Party mainly through Albert Ho. I made clear my position to him, and I listened to his explanations. I invited him and other Democratic Party leaders to come and help in the campaign work as a symbolic gesture. Albert Ho came once or twice. The Civic Party did not publicly criticise the Democratic Party, but close co-operation became more difficult.

I always believe that solidarity within the pro-democracy movement is very important, and it would be very damaging for the movement if one half of the movement was ready to negotiate and the other half refused. The Democratic Party considered that it could secure significant concessions from the Chinese authorities on the issue of democratisation; I never entertained such optimism. The Democratic Party also neglected the usual tactics of the pro-Beijing united front in splitting the pro-democracy movement, and it subsequently paid a heavy price. Joseph Wong Wing-ping, former Secretary for the Civil Service, told me that he believed that the Democratic Party had secured too little from the negotiations. I replied that since the movement had been split and the Democratic Party had agreed to engage in secret negotiations, its bargaining power was much weakened. Joseph Wong became a media commentator and a critic of the government after his retirement, and he came to the City University of Hong Kong to do some part-time teaching. I therefore had many opportunities to discuss such matters and to learn from him.

The leaders of the Democratic Party at that time were probably too eager to demonstrate its leadership within the pro-democracy movement in view of the keen competition from the other pro-democracy political parties. It accepted the Central Liaison Office's condition that negotiations should be confidential, and it therefore could not discuss with and inform the other pro-democracy parties. The Democratic Party considered acceptable to enter into negotiations even when other pro-democracy political parties refused, provided that they kept others informed.

I, too, considered that they should reject the meagre concessions made. But in the end the legislators of the Democratic Party and the HKADPL supported the Donald Tsang administration's political reform bill, and the government secured the two-thirds majority support in the Legislative Council as required by the Basic Law.

The Democratic Party formed a policy-making group consisting of its heavyweight leaders to handle the issue[49]. Martin Lee strongly opposed the proposal of this group while Ronny Tong also objected to Civil Party's participation in the de facto referendum. Hence, commentators said that Martin Lee should join the Civic Party, and Ronny the Democratic Party. The Democratic Party argued that public opinion surveys in June–July 2010 indicated that over half of the respondents supported the Democratic Party's compromise formula of political reforms, but this also reflected that the majority of the supporters of the pro-democracy movement did not support it. If the party's proposal received a majority endorsement among pro-democracy community, then it should have attracted a predominant support, not just half of it, from the public.

On the part of the pro-democracy movement, the initial plan was the resignation of all the pro-democracy legislators after the referendum. This was opposed by the Democratic Party, and the plan was abandoned. This was probably too drastic an act at that stage. I guessed

---

49   Lee Wing-tat, 判刑前的沉思 *(Meditations before Sentencing)*, Hong Kong: Lee Wing-tat, 2019, pp. 70-72.

some pro-democracy legislators were secretly happy to see that the Democratic Party refused to accept the plan.

Lee Wing-tat in his memoirs admitted that a major mistake of the Democratic Party was the lack of effective response to the attacks (especially those on the Internet) from Wong Yuk-man and his supporters. I certainly objected to those who spent greater efforts in criticising fellow organisations and members of the pro-democracy movement than they did on the government and the pro-establishment camp. As a rule, I never openly criticise specific individuals and groups within the pro-democracy movement. It was sad that many radicals in the pro-democracy movement severely attacked the Democratic Party for betraying Hong Kong and the cause of democracy.

Lee Wing-tat further revealed in his memoirs that what probably prompted the negotiations with the Central Liaison Office was a formal letter from President Hu Jintao to Albert Ho through an intermediary. This indicated that the Chinese authorities maintained contact with the leaders of the party, or at least with some important leaders of the party. In the eyes of Beijing, the Democratic Party was perceived to be an important force within the pro-democracy movement ready to negotiate and co-operate with the Chinese authorities. Obviously the Chinese authorities were on more friendly terms with the Democratic Party than the

Civic Party. I was rather proud of this fact as a Civic Party member.

Lee Wing-Tat further revealed that in the negotiations with the Central Liaison Office, its responsible persons indicated that they would like to continue their discussions with the Democratic Party on future political reforms. Lee said that the promise was soon forgotten. In fact the pro-Beijing united front severely attacked the Democratic Party in the 2011 District Council elections and the 2012 Legislative Council elections. The Democratic Party obviously did not do well in the latter, winning only one seat in New Territories East and failing to secure any seat in New Territories West. Lee admitted that he had been naïve in trusting the Communist Party of China. Chan Kin-man, a sociology associate professor from the Chinese University of Hong Kong, also took part in the negotiations. He was considered a moderate at that time, but he later chose to lead the Occupy Central Campaign with Benny Tai in 2013 to 2014. I sometimes wondered if his subsequent radicalisation had been related to his experiences in the negotiations.

The Civic Party suffered in terms of its image and representativeness through its participation in the de facto referendum and its close co-operation with the League of Social Democrats. The report of its chairman to the annual general meeting in January 2011 acknowledged that its image declined to a rock bottom in 2009, but it was much saved by the open debate between

Audrey Eu and the Chief Executive Donald Tsang on June 17, 2010. There was no satisfactory explanation as to why Tsang initiated a directly televised debate; debate was not his strong point and he did not have much time to prepare himself. Audrey Eu performed extremely well and her performance facilitated the Civic Party to return to the top as the political party which could best represent or uphold the interests of the pro-democracy movement[50].

At the end of 2010, the Civic Party had to prepare for its elections of the office bearers. Kuan Hsin-chi planned to step down after two two-year terms and he asked me to stand for election as party chairman[51]. I believed that I was a good candidate and agreed. I soon discovered that the party leadership intended to support Kenneth Chan Ka-lok as the new party chairman. Kuan Hsin-chi later told me that he could no longer support my candidacy. He gave no reason and I did not ask. The vast majority of the executive committee came out openly in support of

---

50 See Report of the Civic Party Chairman to the Annual General Meeting, January 8, 2011, p.2. See also *Racing for the Gold: The 2008 Hong Kong Olympic LegCo Elections:* a report commissioned by Civic Exchange, conducted by Hong Kong Transition Project under Michael DeGolyer, p.47, Table 55. Available at https://issuu.com/civic-exchange/docs/200809_08legco; *Calm after the Storm: Hong Kong people respond to reform*, a report commissioned by the National Democratic Institute, conducted by Hong Kong Transition Project under Michael DeGolyer, p.46, Tables 61 and 62. Available at https://www.ndi.org/node/21546

51 Chairperson of the Civic Party is responsible for the overall development of the party, and therefore he or she typically does not run for elections to the Legislative Council.

Kenneth Chan and this was widely reported in the media before the election.

The writing was on the wall. Audrey Eu and her inner group did not trust me and did not want me to serve as party chairman. My support for Mandy Tam's candidacy in the 2008 Legislative Council election had antagonised her. Alan Leong wanted me to stay in the executive committee; I counter proposed that if I won in the election, Kenneth Chan would serve as a vice-chairman and vice versa. Kenneth Chan rejected my proposal. I expected to lose in the coming election and therefore declined to serve in the next executive committee, as I perceived that there was no tolerance for different views.

I soon discovered that my candidacy became the focus of those party members who were dissatisfied with the party leadership, especially in regard to the elitism in party work. Basically I did not consider that these were very serious issues, but they had to be addressed, and explanations and adjustments had to be made. Complaints of patron-client relations, inadequate attention paid to the leaders' contacts with rank and file members, etc., were common in all political parties. I was probably perceived as someone outside the party leadership's inner core, and I attempted to set an example of always working at the front line with the staff members and voluntary workers while avoiding the limelight.

The obstacles I encountered during my campaigning for chairmanship disappointed me. I tried to ask from the party headquarters for party members' contacts and was denied; they also refused to distribute my campaign materials. A member of the Kowloon East branch requested a meeting with both candidates competing for the party chairmanship; the request was turned down. Unlike me, the party leadership enjoyed full access to the entire list of members and their contact information, including the list of founding members, and it was able to exploit the use of proxy votes. The Civic Party's mission was to fight for genuinely democratic elections; it should set an example in its own elections. I had to count on the efforts of Claudia Mo and others to make contacts on my behalf. I did not do much campaigning myself, I chose to concentrate on articulating the reforms needed within the party. I did not lobby the staff members who were party members because I did not want to create difficulties for them.

The election was held in early January 2011, and I lost by a very narrow margin of eleven votes. This was again widely reported in the press. The result to me was satisfactory, not only in terms of the level of support I got, but also in terms of my other considerations. The results meant that my past service won recognition. I avoided the challenging scenario whereby I had to serve as party chairman without the party leaders' support, which would be very difficult for me and the party publicly.

When I was interviewed by the press, I openly denied the existence of any differences in party line. It was true: the differences were on intra-party work styles. I had not criticised any member/s publicly. I declared that I would stay in the party and continue to contribute to its work.

I kept my promises. I have not been involved in the party's subsequent policy-making processes. I usually attended the annual general meetings, fundraising dinners, and I helped in the election campaigns of the party's candidates. I believe I have maintained a cordial relationship with the party. Later, Kenneth Chan broke his electoral pledge and chose to stand for a Legislative Council seat in Hong Kong Island in 2012 and became a legislator before his term as party chairman ended. His action caused some complaints within the party, but I said nothing.

In November 2016, Claudia Mo announced her withdrawal from the Civic Party. The root cause could be traced back to the support for Mandy Tam's candidacy for the Legislative Council elections in 2008. I had tried to persuade her to stay till her political retirement. The withdrawal was completed amicably without mutual recriminations. I was glad that it happened that way.

I have some disappointments with the party, certain reforms were needed for it to develop and become a formidable political force in Hong Kong. But its leaders and a vast majority of the members have been idealistic and ready to work selflessly for Hong Kong. I never want to do anything to damage their contribution. In the Legislative Council elections in 2016, a new generation of candidates successfully secured seats in the Legislative Council and they soon proved themselves. The Civic Party continued to serve in the difficult struggles of political development in Hong Kong.

Chapter 16

New School for Democracy: What Democracy Means

Non-violent political struggles through education and publicity in the pursuit of human rights, freedom, the rule of law and democracy in Chinese societies. Power struggles among the overseas pro-democracy groups not uncommon.

The New School for Democracy was formally established on June 1, 2011. The initiative probably came from Wang Dan and Andrew To Kwan-hang. They knew each other during the Tiananmen incident in June 1989. At that time, Andrew To was a student activist and secretary general of the Hong Kong Federation of Students. Andrew To approached me and Albert Ho. I was attracted by the idea of working for political development in Mainland China and co-operation among the political groups within the pro-democracy movement in Hong Kong.

I left the executive committee of the Civic Party in January 2011, and I was in the final years of my university academic career, scheduled to retire in June

2015. I obviously had to deliver in terms of teaching and research publications, but for a senior professor without administrative duties, I could devote some time to the New School for Democracy. I approached two rich friends in Hong Kong and raised HK$0.8 million which served as the initial funding for the School.

Andrew To was a leader (former chairman) of the League of Social Democrats; Albert Ho had been a prominent leader of the Democratic Party and the Hong Kong Alliance in Support of Patriotic Democratic Movements in China. At that time, the radical wing of the pro-democracy movement was severely attacking the Democratic Party in the aftermath of the de facto referendum in 2010, hence a joint venture involving Andrew To and Albert Ho was significant. The cooperation was planned to extend to Taiwan and overseas.

Ma Ying-jeou was president of Taiwan at that time (2008–2016) and his administration was keenly interested in improving relations with Mainland China. The Blue Camp in Taiwan therefore did not intend to support an organisation dedicated to the promotion of democracy in Mainland China. Since there were three activists from Hong Kong, Wang Dan and Andrew To decided to invite three activists each from Taiwan and from the overseas pro-democracy movement.

Tseng Chien-yuan was an academic and a recognised human-rights activist in Taiwan. Ku Chung-hwa was an established sociology professor in Taiwan and had been very active in the human rights movement there. Lin Chia-lung was a Democratic Progress Party member of Legislative Yuan from Taichung at that time; he later became mayor of Taichung and minister of transport. This was an impressive list. It was a bit unfortunate that we could not recruit someone from the Blue Camp. Part of the reason was that there was much tension between the two camps at that time, and it was difficult for their members to work together in the same civil society group.

This reflected the changing political situation in Taiwan. When my generation of pro-democracy activists first approached Taiwan, our contacts were mainly from the Blue Camp. It had traditional ties with Hong Kong and the Kuomintang had its party organisation in the territory; there were some pro-Kuomintang media and trade unions too. Staunch anti-communists had considerable influence as political commentators and columnists as well as in literary circles. The Kuomintang government maintained an unofficial organ in Hong Kong, the Chung Hwa Travel Service. It was very interested in the Hong Kong future issue, and many Hong Kong academics and activists were invited to Taiwan for conferences and observation tours in the 1980s and 1990s. The Kuomintang government then had a generous budget for these exchange activities.

The Chen Shui-bian administration (2000–2008) was not interested in Hong Kong, and the Democratic Progressive Party did not have an established network in the territory. The Green Camp had some supporters among the local Taiwanese business community, but these businessmen had strong business ties in Mainland China and were not interested in Hong Kong politics. Hence, the New School for Democracy managed to make a contribution in connecting the political activists and civil society between Hong Kong and Taiwan.

My ideal was to recruit leaders from various groups of the overseas pro-democracy movement to join the New School for Democracy. Wang Dan invited his good friends Hu Ping and Wang Juntao to join; I failed to persuade Wang to recruit Yang Jianli, another prominent pro-democracy human rights activist based in the U.S. I continued to persuade the two to co-operate but was politely ignored. As a pro-democracy activist in Hong Kong, I was often approached by various overseas pro-democracy activists and groups. I always tried to avoid criticising them publicly, or getting involved in their quarrels and disputes. Apparently this was also the approach of the Hong Kong Alliance in Support of Patriotic Democratic Movements in China.

As an academic, my resources were naturally very limited. I could help them organise seminars, invited them for one or two simple meals, often in my university's staff restaurant, and put them in contact with other activists and academics in Hong Kong in accordance with their requests. Occasionally I helped them to secure university venue for academic conferences and contributed a little in organising work in terms of inviting local speakers and participants.

There was one serious omission in the board of directors, all nine members were males. Later when I travelled in Europe introducing our group and attempting to raise money, the local activists often criticised us for neglect of gender equality. Later the School managed to recruit Lu Ping to join the board in May 2014; she was an excellent choice as a famous author and a former head of Taiwan's Guang Hua Information and Cultural Centre in Hong Kong. Unfortunately she had to resign later because of a government appointment, and the School still has to recruit one or more lady directors to date.

The launch of the School attracted severe criticisms from Hong Kong's pro-Beijing newspapers, *Ta Kung Pao* and *Wen Wei Po*. The media attacked the School as a coalition of activists promoting the independence of Taiwan, Hong Kong, Xinjiang, Tibet and Mongolia. These attacks were ridiculous because we had no connections at all with the pro-independence activists from Xinjiang, Tibet and Mongolia. We were careful in avoiding contacts with the deep Green Camp, i.e., the groups advocating for the independence of Taiwan. Albert Ho and I have been the most ardent supporters of Greater China within the pro-democracy movement in Hong Kong. We accept China's sovereignty over Hong Kong, and struggle for genuine democracy within the "one country, two systems" model. Wang Dan and his friends all the time have the democracy of China in mind.

Our directors from Taiwan carefully toe the line of the Democratic Progressive Party which avoids support for Taiwan's independence. Hence, since mid-2011, support for independence has become merely a convenient label to justify the condemnation and political suppression in Hong Kong, at least by the pro-Beijing united front.

The School's inaugural ceremony was held in Taipei for the simple reason that Wang Dan, the School's founding chairman, could not come to Hong Kong. It was not too difficult for the three Hong Kong directors to go to Taiwan. Later even Tseng Chien-yuan was denied entry into Hong Kong, and the board could only meet in Taiwan. Top leaders of the Democratic Progressive Party attended the School's inaugural ceremony through the efforts of Lin Chia-lung, and the Blue Camp was not represented.

This symbolised the changing pattern of ties between the civil society in Hong Kong and its counterparts in Taiwan. The Mainland Affairs Council of the Taiwan government in the Ma Ying-jeou administration years still maintained an exchange programme with Hong Kong. Seminars and academic conferences were organised on Hong Kong issues, and delegations of Hong Kong political groups were invited to observe elections in Taiwan. But it was obvious that the Ma administration was eager to cultivate good relations with Beijing, and did not want to alienate Beijing and the HKSAR government. In fact, its representative in Hong Kong was upgraded to Taipei Economic and Cultural Office in Hong Kong in July 2011.

Formal channels of communication had been established too. In April 2010, the Hong Kong-Taiwan Economic and Cultural Co-operation and Promotion Council was set up to engage in negotiations with its Taiwan counterpart, the Taiwan-Hong Kong Economic and Cultural Co-operation Council. This arrangement was described by the media as the "white glove" policy. The two councils were incorporated as legal entities, and would be authorised by the two governments to conclude agreements; government ministers served as members in both councils. As trade and investment activities across the Taiwan Straits expanded rapidly in this period, Hong Kong's role as an intermediary also developed and the presence of the Taiwan business community in the territory became more prominent, though its interactions with the local civil society remained limited.

Priority of the Ma Ying-jeou administration's approach to Hong Kong was naturally turned to the official level as well as trade and investment activities. The holding of Taipei-Hong Kong inter-city forums in 2000, 2001 and 2013 were indications of the success of the approach at the official level. While the Kuomintang did not enjoy much appeal to the younger generations in Taiwan, it was not attractive to the young student activists and those of the pro-democracy movement in Hong Kong too. Visitors to the Kuomintang headquarters easily observed that the officers and staff members were elderly people, usually retirees from the civil service and various official/semi-official organs. At least at the turn of the century, Hong Kong visitors to the Democratic Progressive Party's office in Taipei were impressed by the fact that young people were holding important positions. They were often informed that the average age of the officers at the party headquarters was in the mid-thirties. The New School for Democracy's directors and staff members in Taiwan enjoyed excellent networks with the civil society groups there and the Democratic Progressive Party, and it was able to make a contribution in linking the civil society groups between the two places.

I was asked to serve as the Rector of the School, so I assumed the administrative work as the other directors were quite occupied. The plan was to start activities with the money raised by me from Hong Kong and that raised by Lin Chia-lung in Taiwan. Lin was a much more effective fundraiser than I, though he had a lot of other important commitments. Besides the ideal of promoting co-operation among pro-democracy groups in Hong Kong, Taiwan and overseas, I intended to set up a model for the overseas pro-democracy groups. Naturally the School required a high standard accounting and auditing system. Andrew To as a professional accountant offered much assistance as I was totally ignorant of accounting systems. This proved to be a valuable asset, and the School slowly established its good reputation in this area among overseas pro-democracy groups.

Right at the beginning, I stipulated that the School would not assume financial responsibility for meals and entertainment of its directors. Directors from Hong Kong paid for their own airfares and accommodation when they went to Taiwan to attend meetings. I had to reject a director's request for re-imbursement for his expenditure on drinks in hotel bars with his friends. The directors from Hong Kong often paid for the meals of the board members in our meetings. When I went overseas, I spent my own money and did not ask for financial support from the School.

My belief was that responsible persons of pro-democracy groups should not benefit in any way financially from the groups concerned. They could opt to serve as staff members of the groups and receive salaries, in that case they should be accountable to the respective groups' governing bodies.

The School decided to have its main office in Taipei, partly because Wang Dan and the three Taiwan directors were there, and more important still because rents and staff salaries were considerably cheaper there. The Hong Kong directors would fly to Taipei a few times per annum. Eventually the School could even secure discounted accommodation offered to non-governmental organisations; this would be unthinkable in Hong Kong.

As the political situation later deteriorated in Hong Kong, the decision proved to be wise.

When Wang Dan and Andrew To initiated the organisation, they had a school in mind, i.e., its mission would be to promote democratic education in China and in various Chinese communities. The original plan was very ambitious, the School would offer courses comparable to those offered by internationally recognised universities and eventually even sought accreditation from universities in various countries. I set up a fourteen-week course on Chinese foreign policy in English; Wang Dan's course was abandoned after producing lectures for three weekly sessions. This work was soon terminated and the School had to seek alternatives.

The three directors representing overseas groups suggested to charge tuition fees for the School's courses, and they expected that the students would be Chinese in the U.S. attempting to seek permanent residential rights through applications for political asylum. This had been the practice of many overseas pro-democracy groups, as services provided in support of such applications would generate much-needed incomes for the activists and their groups concerned. This explained why in U.S. cities there were usually a few groups organising protest activities on the June 4 anniversaries, and they refused to collaborate because they were competing for clients.

My position was a firm rejection of getting involved in the application for political asylum "business". I would not openly criticise such businesses, but I would withdraw from the School if it got involved. I became isolated in the board because the other directors wanted to avoid disputes and therefore would not articulate their views. I was ready to allow free use of and free access to our courses, and other pro-democracy activists and groups might make use of our courses in their business activities.

On one occasion in the School's early years, when an activity was conducted in Taipei, a prominent first-generation pro-democracy activist from China then in exile overseas came with the intention to embarrass Wang Dan. I approached him and tried to persuade tolerance. Fortunately he accepted and did not take further action. I realised that usually people would not intervene for fear of embarrassing oneself, but I certainly had the reputation and image of the School in mind.

Albert Ho once shared a story with me. He was visiting the U.S. some years ago and engaged in a meeting with some overseas pro-democracy activists. One of them approached him and said that the president would like to meet him. He was surprised because he did not think he was that important so much so that the U.S. President would want to see him. He soon discovered that the president was actually the self-proclaimed president of the Chinese government-in-exile.

I was once approached by a prominent pro-democracy activist based in the U.S. asking me to support one of his activities in memory of the Tiananmen incident. I said I did not have the organisational resources and indicated that I would contact the Hong Kong Alliance in Support of Patriotic Democratic Movements in China for help. I rang Richard Tsoi for assistance; he was a bit upset because the Alliance had long planned a similar activity and he thought that this activist based in the U.S. simply wanted to steal the limelight from the Alliance. I always supported my good friends in the Alliance and replied to the activist that I could not help.

Hong Kong activists supporting the pro-democracy and human rights movements in Mainland China fully understand that our role is a supporting one and it is only secondary. Ultimately the political struggles would be decided by the people and the activists inside Mainland China. This understanding meant that we would never compete for leadership and would simply offer assistance and support within our capabilities. It helped us to avoid getting involved in the disputes among the overseas pro-democracy groups.

I was often invited to attend the conferences of various overseas pro-democracy groups. I usually paid for my airfares and offered payments for the conferences as ordinary participants. I prepared myself for my presentations, usually I talked about the situation in Hong Kong or my analyses of the political developments in China. I carefully avoided getting involved in the disputes among individuals and groups. I could not accept most of my invitations because I could not afford the time and expenses. I tried to attend one every one or two years so as to follow the developments of the overseas pro-democracy movement. I sometimes asked Andrew To to represent the School if he could spare the time.

The School made good use of Wang Dan's reputation and supported his lecture tours among universities in Taiwan. Wang held academic positions in Taiwan's universities, but at this stage the pressure for serious academic publications rose. The academic tolerance for politicians who were defeated in elections and sought temporary shelter in tertiary institutions declined sharply. Wang was not in this category, but nonetheless he felt the pressure too; it was obviously very difficult for him to be a serious scholar and a political activist at the same time.

The School gradually re-defined its work programme. Exploiting its networks of ties in both places, the School organised conferences and talks in Taiwan and Hong Kong. Since it was not a political party and presented no candidates in elections, it was widely accepted among civic society groups in both places. The most significant activity developed was the organisation of training courses for activists from Mainland China; they were activists without much experience and reputation yet, hence training and exposure were valuable for them. In the beginning, these training sessions took place in Hong Kong because it was easier for the trainees to come to Hong Kong from Mainland China. Later they were moved to Taiwan because of tight surveillance in Hong Kong, and trainees could be stopped upon entry into the territory.

The School was established first and delivering work programmes before it approached donors. Its high-standard accounting and auditing system was helpful. It was able to prove its appeal because it held fundraising dinners in Hong Kong and other fundraising activities in Taipei; it collected donations at the street level on June 4 every year in Hong Kong. It proved that it had a good reputation as it could appeal to ordinary people for donations.

The School's mission was to engage in non-violent political struggles through education and publicity work in the pursuit of human rights, freedom, the rule of law and democracy in China and other Chinese societies. The School realises that the most effective struggles would be those carried out inside Mainland China; those outside can only assume a secondary role. This is exactly why human rights activists and dissidents in China are very reluctant to leave the country, while the Chinese authorities are willing to accept their departures, including those of their family members. Hong Kong activists in support of the pro-democracy movement in China are perfectly willing to accept their secondary role; those exiles originally from China are less willing. Hence, there are much more competition and power struggles among them.

The Sunflower Student Movement in Taipei in March-April 2014 occurred before the Occupy Central Campaign in Hong Kong. A coalition of students and civic groups against the cross-Straits trade agreement in services occupied the national legislature and successfully forced concessions from the Ma Ying-jeou administration. The movement obviously won the support of the people and further damaged the popularity of Ma. The student leaders in the movement also emerged as heroes. The demonstration effect on Hong Kong was significant.

In turn, the impact of the suppression of the Occupy Central Campaign by Beijing and the C.Y. Leung administration and their rejection of Hong Kong people's demands for democracy was also felt in Taiwan. In the local elections held at the end of 2014, the slogan "Today's Hong Kong, Tomorrow's Taiwan" first emerged, and the Kuomintang lost heavily in the elections. There gradually developed a strong sense of mutual support between those who opposed interferences from the Chinese authorities in the two places.

The School occasionally organised exchanges programmes between Taiwan and Hong Kong, including the Hong Kong delegation to observe elections in Taiwan. My principle was to maximise the number of visitors by minimising the amount of subsidy for each invited visitor. Sometimes we asked the visitor to pay for his/her airfares which were not expensive, and the programme would pay for the visitor's expenses while in Taiwan. They would also be asked to share rooms between two people in three-star hotels. They could pay for the extra costs themselves to secure an upgrade to enjoy single rooms. When directors from Hong Kong joined these delegations, they paid for their own expenses. On one occasion, a pro-democracy activist from Vancouver, Canada asked to join the delegation, and he complained about the hospitality we provided. I offered my explanation and ignored such complaints.

Normally these delegations lasted for a week (or three or four days) including the Election Day and the day after voting. The attraction was that one could experience the final campaign activities which might include hundreds of thousands of people. The disadvantage was that the electoral candidates and their staff members were extremely busy and they could not afford the time for in-depth discussions. We suggested that these delegations might take place two or three months before the Election Day so that there could be more meaningful exchanges with the candidates and their key campaign staff members. This arrangement should be more appropriate for those who wanted to learn from the campaign organisations and techniques of the candidates in Taiwan. But this was never realised;

somehow the dramas of Election Day and the evening before were too powerful an attraction.

The School through its connections was often able to organise very good seminars involving academics, senior journalists and public opinion survey experts for the delegations to enhance their understanding of the politics in Taiwan, and I found them quite informative. In this way, the School hoped to offer more for the delegations. It also avoided contacts with the pro-independence political parties and politicians, for example, the New Power Party. The School does not support Taiwan independence, but recognises it as a legitimate political demand in a free society. Moreover, since some of the delegation members had plans to stand for elections in Hong Kong, contacts with the pro-independence politicians and political parties might be troublesome for their future candidacies. Personally I am not against these contacts, though my position of not supporting Taiwan independence is clear.

As the Rector and director of the School, I was often approached by human rights activists and dissidents from Mainland China as well as those in exile. I could not refuse to meet them, but there was often the danger that they might come from China's intelligence apparatus. My normal approach was to meet them and treat them as journalists; I had no confidential information to offer and I did not attempt to collect such information. My resources were limited, and I usually offered to have afternoon tea together. I did not hesitate to offer my views on Hong Kong politics and the political developments in Mainland China, they could easily be found in my writings. I was prepared to listen carefully to show my respect for my visitors. But these meetings took up quite a bit of my time. I understood that Albert Ho had this challenge too.

Among these contacts was Li Dan, who ran the 1908 Bookstore at Peking Road, Tsim Sha Tsui, Hong Kong. In the early years of the School, he approached its staff member and proposed to offer a joint programme of talks as a salon activity in his bookstore. I had no objection to this type of joint cultural activity as long as our staff member could handle it. Then Li suggested that he had a similar operation in Beijing, and my Western academic friends visiting Beijing could also use this venue to offer talks. I brought this suggestion to Jean-Philippe Beja, and apparently he gave one or two talks in Li Dan's bookstore.

Li claimed to be the responsible person of a human rights non-governmental organisation in China. In the mid-2010s, I discovered that Li Dan was involved in the publication and sale of a book in slandering a group of pro-democracy activists including me. I did not think this was a very serious matter because I was already familiar with this type of defamation tactic. I naturally discussed this with my colleagues in the School who also found Li questionable. Later I met him in Taipei as member of a visiting delegation, I asked why he participated in such a book project. Li replied that these books produced by the Chinese propaganda machinery usually had the opposite effect of making the people being attacked more famous. I found him totally shameless and walked away. Naturally I had no more contacts with him.

As a rule, I did not intend to occupy any responsible position for a long time. I believed that I should pass on the honour and responsibility after I had done my part. Hence, I was very happy to support Andrew To in taking up the position of Rector in May 2014. Andrew is seventeen years younger than me, and since he was a Hong Kong student leader at the time of the Tiananmen incident and had served as an active member of the Democratic Party as well as the Hong Kong Alliance in Support of Patriotic Democratic Movements in China, he knew the overseas pro-democracy activists well. He enjoyed my full support and that of Albert Ho, so he was very happy with his new responsibility.

The School's board of directors did not have any formal re-election process since its establishment in 2011, and this is not proper. In early 2019, I resigned as director of the School because of health reasons, though I remained a keen voluntary worker. I hoped that this would be an opportunity to initiate a formal election process, and I also hoped that one or two ladies would join the board to secure a more politically correct gender balance. Wang Dan left Taiwan for the U.S. in

2017 because he believed that in view of the political changes in China at that stage, he could contribute more through his lobbying work in the U.S. He established a new organisation Dialogue China (對話中国) there in June 2018, and he wanted to focus on his new think tank. He stepped down as chairman of the School while continuing to serve as its director; Tseng Chien-yuan served as the new chairman.

Despite the fact that I had resigned as the School's director earlier, I was still responsible for organising the international academic conference for the thirtieth anniversary of the Tiananmen incident in May 2019. Previously, I was asked by the Hong Kong Alliance in Support of Patriotic Democratic Movements in China to organise similar conferences on the twentieth and twenty-fifth anniversary of the tragic event. It was not too difficult for me then, as I could use the university facilities and I had the support of my sole research assistant. This time was a bit different, I was already in retirement and had no help. More important still, the Alliance decided to hold the conference in Taipei as it wanted to have a larger-scale conference and it believed that many guests could not secure entry into Hong Kong. The organisation work started in mid-2018. The leaders of the Alliance and I managed to raise the money by August or September, and I could then start inviting speakers. The original budget was HK$0.7 million, but eventually it exceeded HK$0.8 million. We were fortunate in obtaining some funding support from the Hong Kong Federation of Students and another student group at the Chinese University of Hong Kong. They had raised some money in 1989 and did not have the opportunities to spend all the money. In recent years, the local student groups were much less interested in activities relating to China, and they were quite happy to let us spend the money on a worthwhile event.

The student group at the Chinese University of Hong Kong warned us against spending money on entertainment in social gatherings. I felt a bit funny to be cautioned in this manner; nonetheless I seriously explained to the group my conference plan, and I highlighted my good record in organising serious academic conferences. For those for the twentieth and twenty-fifth anniversaries, I produced a serious scholarly volume each. At a later formal meeting with the student group, I together with a young staff member of the New School for Democracy in Hong Kong went to the Chinese University and found no one in the meeting room. We rang our student contact, and were told that they could not get a quorum for the meeting and therefore had to cancel the meeting. They had forgotten to inform us. I asked this responsible person of the student group to meet us since we had arrived at the Chinese University; he declined because he was having a date. So we wasted more than three hours of travelling and waiting time for nothing. I thanked my colleague for his troubles, and he lamented on the falling standards of university student activists at this stage. I understood I had to be very patient with student activists.

There were naturally discussions and arguments on whom we should invite. Albert Ho, Lee Cheuk-yan and I finally agreed that we should invite all the prominent activists in the Tiananmen incident to come irrespective of their subsequent political positions and performance. Due to budgetary considerations, the organising committee would offer them economy airfares if they were ready to present serious papers of 8,000 words in length minimum, otherwise they would be offered hotel accommodation and meals only during the conference period. My position was that we should take no consideration of their quarrels with each other as well as their moral standards, changing political values and reputations. We would not offer special treatment for any guests.

I received one request that he should be invited as the honourable guest of the conference, I declined indicating that the conference had no such arrangements. I received two or three requests that as prominent Tiananmen incident activists, they should be accorded significant roles in the conference. My reply was that all paper presenters and participants would receive equal treatment as members of the two respective categories; efforts would be made to attract media to cover the conference and facilities would be arranged for the journalists to do interviews. The conference fully respected the choices of the journalists. There was one request from an overseas director who wanted airfares without writing a paper. I felt very disappointed, but subsequently found another source of funding to pay for his airfares without making exceptions to the conference budgetary rules. I presented a paper, but I paid for my own airfares. In the final four weeks, I still received suggestions from the co-sponsoring organisations in Taiwan on an extra keynote speaker; I explained that whatever the value of the suggestion, it would be rather impolite to send an invitation to a prominent scholar in less than four weeks before the conference. These are questions one had to tackle in organising a conference which involves overseas pro-democracy groups and activists.

The responses were better than expected. The conference had to expand from two days to two and a half days. We were able to raise more money by inviting pro-democracy parties in Hong Kong as well as groups in the U.S. and Canada to serve as co-sponsors of the conference. These overseas groups were associated with the cause to reverse the Chinese authorities' verdict on the Tiananmen incident, and they contributed US$1,000 each. In view of the potential risk that the pro-Beijing united front activists in Taipei might attempt to disrupt the conference, the organising committee decided to employ security guards. They appeared quite credible as a deterrence as the four security guards deployed all looked very strong. Apparently they were ex-servicemen. Recruiting strong, well-built security guards for events in Hong Kong was often more difficult.

The conference went well, and the groups concerned were happy with the results. I adopted a very low profile in avoiding the limelight, and tried to facilitate the international media to interview the paper presenters. I managed to publish all the papers in English in an electronic journal in late August, and some academic colleagues led by Professor Huang Mab of Soochow University in Taipei were responsible for the formal publication of the papers in Chinese, including some Chinese translations of the papers in English. I was glad that the task was completed without serious mistakes. I realised that somebody else would have to organise the conference for the thirty-fifth anniversary. It would be too optimistic to hope that it would take place in Beijing in 2024.

By the time of my resignation as director of the school, it was well established and enjoyed a good reputation in Hong Kong, Taiwan and overseas Chinese communities, not so much as a major non-governmental organisation of ample resources, but as a respected group doing constructive work, and could easily be accepted as a partner by non-governmental organisations and political parties in these places. It was difficult to assess the School's impact on Mainland China, but the frequent condemnations of the School by the local *Ta Kung Pao* and *Wen Wei Po* and the occasional attacks against it by the mainstream official media in Mainland China probably suggested that the Chinese authorities were concerned about its work.

As civil society groups in Taiwan and Hong Kong engage in more frequent exchanges, and the people in both places share a stronger sense of solidarity against the threat of interferences from the Chinese authorities, the School would have a useful role to play.

Chapter 17

Alliance for True Democracy: the Fight for Universal Suffrage amidst Contradictions

A thankless task in resolving structural contradictions and hostilities among parties and individuals while formulating political reform proposals towards universal suffrage. First sign of trouble from Beijing's united front.

In late February 2013, I was approached by the leaders of the Democratic Party and the Civic Party to form a platform for pro-democracy parties to promote democratic elections of the Chief Executive (CE) and the entire legislature by universal suffrage. The initiative was sparked by a decision of the Standing Committee of the National People's Congress in December 2007. The Committee rejected the demand for the democratic elections of the CE and the legislature in 2012, but promised that the election of the CE by universal suffrage could be implemented in 2017, and following that, the election of the entire legislature by universal suffrage.

One could find no further satisfactory elaboration of this promise. The logical explanation, with the benefit of hindsight, was that while the election of the CE by universal suffrage could be allowed, control of the nomination process would still be retained by the Beijing authorities. But there were no discussions of the scenario in 2007 nor in the years that followed.

At that time, the pro-democracy camp was quite divided because of the negotiations in 2010 between the Democratic Party and the Central Liaison Office on the issue of political reforms. The platform needed a convenor acceptable to both the radical wing and the moderate wing of the camp, and I was considered probably the only candidate; at least that was the position of the Civic Party. When I stepped down from the executive committee of the Civic Party while remaining as an ordinary party member, I had no strong identification with any single party in the pro-democracy movement, and therefore relatively neutral.

I accepted the invitation to be the convenor of the Alliance for True Democracy with some difficulty, though I considered it an honour. In the first place, I never entertained much optimism that the Chinese authorities would willingly grant Hong Kong genuine democracy. In other words, the platform was given a mission impossible. I also realised the tremendous difficulties in reaching a consensus among the pro-democracy political parties and in generating sincere co-operation among them. Any open quarrels among them and the breakup of the platform would be part of my responsibility, and I had to absorb the blame. It would be therefore a thankless task, and I had ample experiences before. Finally, I understood that financial resources and even manpower resources of the platform would be a serious problem.

The Democratic Party offered a staff member to assist in the administrative work like liaison and minute taking while the Civic Party promised the help of one staff member responsible for the accounts of the platform. I was grateful for the support of the party leaders and the staff members concerned who were already over-worked, like almost all staff members of the pro-democracy groups. There were actually no arrangements made, however, to relieve or reduce their original responsibilities so that they could serve the platform.

Fortunately, a well-off friend offered his financial support. He offered a donation to the platform and I could employ one full-time staff for administrative work and later another half-time staff for publicity work and management of the platform's website. The total monthly bill came to about HK$20,000, and I estimated that his donation could last for the entire functioning period of the platform. The issue of fundraising was never mentioned in the invitation, but subsequently I was the only one in the platform approaching individuals for donations. Every member group believed that it had financial difficulties, and wanted to minimise its financial contributions to the platform to a minimum.

My wife Grace was the only one to whom I raised these complaints, and she asked the sober question: why should I do it? It was my naive idealism of course. I just wanted to make a contribution to the territory's pro-democracy movement. I explained that it was like a protest rally, one individual's participation was certainly insignificant when hundreds of thousands of people were involved. If everyone thought that the protest rally could do without him or her, it could never draw a big crowd.

Just before the launch of the platform, I went to an academic conference in Paris together with Chan Kin-man. We had a long lunch on the day of my departure and we discussed the political situation in Hong Kong. We both said that we wanted to make our contributions as concerned scholars. Soon afterwards, he announced that he was joining Benny Tai's Occupy Central Campaign.

The platform had its first formal meeting on March 13, 2013. It was nominally initiated by twenty-four pro-democracy legislators, while waiting for the decisions of the three legislators from People Power. The name Alliance for True Democracy (ATD) was adopted; the choice of words was limited since alliance and democracy were the essential words. Gary Fan Kwok-wai of the Neo Democrats was well recognised for his talents in design, and he was asked to design the ATD logo. I planned to meet weekly on Wednesdays at 6 p.m. at the Legislative Council building to facilitate the attendance of the legislators so that they could easily rush back to the council chamber if they had to speak or to vote. I promised to ensure that meetings should normally last no more than ninety minutes, and I asked participants to be punctual as everyone acknowledged that lateness was a very common bad habit. I usually started the meetings at 6:05 p.m. and managed to end them at 7:30 p.m. or before.

This demanded careful preparations. The participants were all very busy, they normally did not come well prepared. So as convenor, I had to have a good understanding of the agenda; I had to assess the key issues to be settled, and which decisions I could seek endorsement relatively easily. The meetings had to stay sharp and focused; I had to identify the options clearly to facilitate choices. Naturally care had to be taken to allow people to have their say; otherwise they would feel a loss of face. On the whole, I managed to gain a good reputation in chairing meetings. At a higher level, I had to plan ahead and lay out the work programmes step by step for approval in meetings.

One of the first agenda items was raising the initial funding. I offered to donate HK$10,000 myself, and asked each group to contribute HK$5,000 or HK$10,000. Democratic Party, the Civic Party, the Hong Kong Professional Teachers' Union, etc., were categorised as major groups, and they agreed to contribute HK$10,000 each. Smaller groups including the Neo Democrats, People Power, and Hong Kong Association for Democracy and People's Livelihood, etc., agreed to contribute HK$5,000 each. The Hong Kong Social Workers General Union initially applied for an exemption of payment. When rejected, it then offered to contribute HK$1,000; this proposal was found unacceptable too. Ultimately it did not pay up and opted to attend meetings without the vote in the decision-making process.

I mentioned these matters mainly to demonstrate the financial challenges of running a loose pro-democracy coalition or platform, and certainly the ATD had not received any funding support from external governments or agencies. Every donation secured was reported back to all the member groups. In the period from March 2013 to August 2014, the convenor issued more than ten financial statements detailing all items of incomes and expenditure to all its members. I was sure that they soon fell into the hands of journalists and the pro-Beijing united front.

To show solidarity, I was very keen to involve the more radical political groups of the pro-democracy movement. We were fortunate that eventually all pro-democracy legislators joined except Wong Yuk-man's League of Social Democrats. In view of his subsequent political position, it was not surprising. People Power, another radical group, accepted the ATD's invitation to participate. In its letter to ATD, People Power indicated that it would uphold its position in the platform's deliberations including its demands that all functional constituency seats should be abolished in the 2016 Legislative Council elections, and that the ATD could only negotiate with the Hong Kong government on political reforms, and should reject direct negotiations with the Central Liaison Office or the central government in Beijing.

These demands were found unacceptable by some hardliners in the Democratic Party, and they often believed that the platform should exclude the radical political groups to facilitate unity and smooth progress. They were concerned that People Power would confront the Democratic Party within the ATD. I went to consult People Power, and secured a compromise understanding that: its demands were not pre-conditions for joining the ATD, but were mainly a declaration of the group's political position; it would withdraw from ATD should the platform's subsequent development deviate from its position. A delicate balance had to be maintained between the Democratic Party and the radical groups right from the start.

In its second meeting, the ATD discussed the arrangements for its first press conference. I indicated that I needed only five to six minutes for my opening statements in both English and Chinese, and two minutes would be given to each legislator and group representative. The speakers would register with the staff members from 9 a.m. onwards on the next day to determine the order of the speakers; whoever called first would speak first and so on. The arrangement was needed to avoid criticisms that legislators from major parties like the Democratic Party always got to speak ahead of representatives of smaller groups. Later I set the rule that speaking order would be determined by the arrival times of the invited speakers to encourage punctuality and avoid controversies over the order. This practice was sometimes followed in other functions of pro-democracy groups.

The ATD in its third meeting deliberated on its voting mechanisms and the voting rights of the member groups. I offered three options for the members to consider; naturally the groups' representatives had to go back to their organisations for decisions. Eventually it was decided that each legislator had one vote, and each member political party or organisation would also have one vote each. This favoured major parties like the Democratic Party which enjoyed seven votes with six legislators; the small political parties favoured one organisation one vote. They were willing to concede because we all realised that political reform proposals would be determined by a two-thirds majority in the Legislative Council, hence legislators should be accorded a heavier weighting. Small groups also understood that they could always withdraw from the platform if they opposed the majority position.

Proxy votes were accepted, so the Democratic Party representative Sin Chung-kai would have seven votes in his hands. Ordinary matters would be decided by a simple majority of the representatives and legislators present; important matters would be determined by a two-thirds majority of all members. The designation of an important matter would be decided as an ordinary agenda item. Important matters in everyone's mind would be the ultimate decisions on the political reform proposals and negotiations with the Hong Kong government.

As convenor, I indicated that I would be contacted by the local consular community and the pro-Beijing united front. I offered to present written reports concerning these contacts as practised in the Civic Party. But members agreed that written reports from the convenor might easily be leaked and they suggested that I might exercise my discretion in reporting back these contacts to the platform. I kept my promise.

The platform encountered strong hostility from the pro-Beijing united front right from the beginning. ATD's first public seminar was held on April 7, 2013, at the City University of Hong Kong. Some "patriotic" organisations came to disrupt the seminar, and it could not be conducted. This was the first time in my political participation experiences in Hong Kong that a normal open seminar could not be held due to a disturbance. This was certainly not a good sign.

As the convenor of the ATD, I later attended a public City Forum discussion on the political reform issue organised on Sunday noon at the Bandstand of Victoria

Park, and broadcast live by Radio Television Hong Kong. During the session, one or two dozen Beijing-loyal activists (referred to as "uncles of Victoria Park"[52]) kept on yelling with their hand-held loudspeakers and shouting constant and abusive expletives while I spoke. Worse still, they followed me when I left to get a taxi home, and they used foul language against my mother, my wife and my daughter. These attacks in the streets outside the Civic Forum venue were exceptional. I recognised that among the mob was Fu Chun-chung, head of Defend Hong Kong Campaign which was later formally established. To me, the opposition to the pro-democracy movement by the pro-Beijing united front heightened to a new level. This posed a serious threat to the freedom of expression we used to enjoy and the development of civil society in Hong Kong.

The general dissatisfaction of the Hong Kong community with the lack of progress in reforming the electoral system was accumulating. Severe criticisms from Beijing's united front did not help. The two major tasks facing the ATD platform were the formulation of

---

52   "Uncles of Victoria Park" is a colloquial term that refers to a group of usually retired pro-Beijing men who were stationed near the venue of the public City Forum, and caused disturbance and disruptions by yelling and shouting foul language at pro-democratic politicians or speakers while the event was on air. The City Forum, Hong Kong's current affairs debates programme, ended in July 2021 after 41 years, as a "normal programming rearrangement", according to RTHK, Hong Kong government's broadcasting service.

At one of the City Forums in Victoria Park, Hong Kong.

political reform proposals and the related publicity work to mobilise the community's support for democratisation.

On another front, the Occupy Central Campaign initiated and led by Benny Tai attracted a lot of attention. With a view to mobilise public support for democratisation, Benny developed an innovative programme, a series of deliberation days with the intention to stimulate the enthusiasm of the concerned public who wanted to become active.

The ATD platform came to an agreement with the Occupy Central Campaign on a division of labour. We both remained entirely separate organisations. If the Chinese authorities agreed to negotiate, then the ATD would be responsible for the negotiations. If the negotiations led to a satisfactory outcome, the Occupy Central Campaign would be disbanded. If there were no negotiations or should they end in failure, the Occupy Central Campaign would be activated. This agreement was based on the assumption that the Chinese authorities would refuse to recognise the Occupy Central Campaign and negotiate with it. The agreement was announced to the public at an early stage. There and then, I made it known publicly that I had not been involved in the Campaign; if I participated in any Campaign events should political reforms fail, it would be in my personal capacity. My contacts from Beijing warned me that this declaration was unwise and politically incorrect.

Beijing authorities refused to respond to the call for negotiations. After the launch of the actual Occupy Central Campaign, I took part just as an ordinary citizen; I did not participate in the discussions among the leading activists nor in their meetings with the media on the understanding that the platform might function again if the Chinese authorities were willing to negotiate later. Naturally, I understood that the possibility was very low. Since I was not involved in the decisions among the leaders during the actual occupation, I was able to offer some objective commentary as an academic to the international media.

The platform had very limited resources for publicity work. It worked along the traditional lines of organising seminars, setting up street stations to engage the public at the grassroots level, holding press conferences, and so on. These activities did not cost much money: setting up street stations relied on the voluntary work of the member organisations. Conducting public opinion surveys and producing short publicity video-tapes, however, were expensive, at least from the point of view of the platform's limited budget. In publicity work, the platform secured the valuable help of expert volunteers.

In formulating political reform proposals, the platform decided to seek the inputs of academics who had the expertise and whose proposals were above party interests. An academic advisory group was formed and it consisted of nine university academics. Some of them were recognised as moderates and this was considered a good thing.

Besides the threat of disruptions from the "patriotic" organisations, the platform failed to secure the presence of the politicians from the pro-Beijing camp while organising seminars. ATD decided not to invite the representatives of those "patriotic" organisations though. The platform would send representatives to seminars and forums organised by the pro-Beijing camp, including those conducted by the "patriotic" groups.

The government chose not to take the platform seriously. The platform throughout its operational history had only been invited to meet government officials once. I went to see Raymond Tam Chi-yuen, the Secretary for

Constitutional and Mainland Affairs, with two or three members of the platform. The meeting lasted for about forty-five minutes. I was invited to offer an introduction of the platform's political reform proposals, and the officials present asked for some clarifications. Basically it was a formality for record keeping purpose. I tried to show good will in avoiding to meet the press afterwards nor to voice any criticisms of the contents of the meeting. My contacts with members of the pro-Beijing united front were discussed in the chapter on the united front (Chapter 19).

In sum, the platform had no opportunities to engage in serious discussions at all on the subject of political reforms with the HKSAR government nor with the Chinese authorities. The nearest thing to serious discussions were the public debates I had with senior government officials including the Secretary for Justice Rimsky Yuen Kwok-keung in forums that were organised by the television stations and some prominent groups of the pro-Beijing camp. I went into such details to demonstrate that the Chinese authorities had no intention to negotiate nor think about serious political reforms. Gradually, Hong Kong people knew it very well.

The ATD released its preliminary views on the election of the CE to solicit views from the community on May 8, 2013. The common objective was to secure the election of the CE by universal suffrage. There was broad consensus on adopting the French presidential election system in which the top two candidates would enter the second round should no candidate secure more than half of the votes in the first round. The deliberations therefore concentrated on the nomination process.

Within the pro-democracy movement, there were considerable resentment against the existing system whereby the nomination of the CE by the Election Committee (an electoral college) was dominated by the pro-establishment camp. Under the existing system then (i.e., for the CE election in 2012), of the 1,200-member CE Selection Committee, 1,044 members were elected from 35 subsectors, 60 nominated by the religious subsector and 96 were ex-officio members of the Legislative Council or Hong Kong deputies to China's National People's Congress. The pro-democracy camp could at best secure a little more than a quarter of the elected seats. To become a CE candidate, at least 150 nominations from members (one eighth) of the Election Committee must be received. The CE candidate should not have party affiliation.

In the 2002 CE election, for example, the Chinese authorities wanted to ensure the re-election of C.H. Tung and a handsome electoral victory for him. They first changed the rules to make the nomination process open. Since the pro-establishment camp Election Committee members all understood the Chinese authorities' intentions and were reluctant to confront them, C.H. Tung secured so many nominations that there were not enough votes left to nominate another candidate. Another example was in the 2005 CE election; Lee Wing-tat of the Democratic Party failed to gain even one-eighth of the votes to secure a formal nomination, because the pro-democracy camp did not accord a high priority to the CE Election Committee election to nominate a candidate. The camp knew that having minority seats in the CE Election Committee, their candidate would not win.

Regarding the nomination process, members of the ATD easily came to a preliminary agreement on certain ground rules. It rejected any primaries or restrictions on nominations. To avoid domination of the nomination process by the pro-establishment camp, each nominating committee member can only nominate one candidate, and each candidate should not present nominations exceeding one-sixth of the nominating committee membership. Moreover, nominations should not require more than the support of one-eighth of the nominating committee membership. There should be no further requirements regarding the sectoral categorisations of nominating members, in view of the concern that the industrial, commercial, and financial sectors might be able to block the nomination of a pro-democracy candidate. The most significant provision was that candidates may be nominated by a defined number of registered voters through the civil nomination channel. This nomination method was strongly favoured by the more radical groups within the ATD. Finally, the preliminary views also allowed the future CE to have political party affiliation.

The academic advisory group worked on the premise of the ATD's preliminary views. The concept of civil nomination was strongly supported. It was efficient and soon presented three options. Option A involved the formation of a nominating committee consisting of the original 2012 Election Committee membership sectors and election methods plus all the District Councillors to be elected in November 2015 (slightly more than 400). The nominating committee would then have around 1,500 members (the original 1,200 members of the 2012 Election Committee already included more than one hundred District Councillors). Formal nomination of a CE candidate might then be secured through the support of one-tenth of the members of the nominating committee, or at least 2% of the registered voters for the geographical constituencies in the Legislative Council elections (about 70,000–80,000 people at the existing level).

Option B proposed the election of a nominating committee by universal suffrage. The territory would be divided into twenty constituencies each returning about twenty committee members on a proportional representation basis. The constituencies would try to follow the boundaries of the existing districts for District Council elections. Formal nomination would require the support of one-tenth of the members of the nominating committee.

Option C suggested the formation of a nominating committee consisting of all the District Councillors and Legislative Councillors, about five hundred members in total. Formal nomination might then be secured through the support of one-tenth of the members of the nominating committee, or at least 2% of the registered voters for the geographical constituencies in the Legislative Council elections.

The proposals from the academic advisory group and the deliberations of the ATD did not consider if the Chinese authorities would accept the proposals or not. The proposals reflected the hitherto strong condemnation of the Election Committee as a "small circle election", and the demand for the participation of Hong Kong people in the nominating process. There was also the general understanding that in the negotiation process to come, one would receive the views of the Chinese authorities and they should be assessed then.

The hostility between the Democratic Party and People Power created considerable difficulty for the functioning of the ATD. On August 7, 2013, the executive committee of People Power formally wrote to me as the ATD's convenor complaining against Emily Lau of the Democratic Party. Emily was accused of stating in an interview by ATV in mid-July that People Power intended to leave the ATD and hijack the coalition. She also indicated in an interview by *Ming Pao* that civil nomination was not the baseline in the demand for the democratic election of the Chief Executive, and thus differed from the ATD's position.

The challenge for me was that if the disputes and the hostility could not be contained, the ATD would split. After some consultation, I offered the position that the public documents released by the ATD would be its position, principles and baseline; it would not retreat from them in the course of the negotiations with the Hong Kong government, but adjustments could be made based on the trends of public opinion. Actually the principal document released so far was the ATD's preliminary views on the 2017 CE election publicised on May 8, 2013. While the ATD planned to release its final proposals on democratic elections before the end of 2013, naturally member groups could discuss various proposals, but the discussions did not mean that they could neglect the coalition's baseline.

The differences between the Democratic Party and the radical groups of the pro-democracy movement had its roots in the secret negotiations between the Democratic Party and the Central Liaison Office in 2010. The Democratic Party was seen to be too eager to compromise with the Chinese authorities. In the eyes of the Democratic Party, on the other hand, many radical groups in the pro-democracy movement had been infiltrated by the pro-Beijing united front which would attempt to sow discord within the pro-democracy movement so as to weaken it. There were elements of truth in this analysis.

There were, however, deeper structural reasons for these political differences. Within the movement, many people, especially the younger generation, were getting increasingly impatient with the mainstream political groups. They considered that the latter's peaceful, moderate, non-violent approach could not bring about the reforms which were the original ideals of the movement. They believed that the leaders of these mainstream groups had been too absorbed in the work of the Legislative Council and behaved like part of the political elite. Hence, the radical groups managed to appeal more to the young people, and those at the grassroots level. Since Hong Kong's return to China, these socio-economic strata had been suffering from the decline in real incomes, the expanding gap between the rich and poor, the reduction in upward social mobility opportunities and the rising housing prices.

The Occupy Central Campaign initiated by Benny Tai attracted the radicals as they were eager to do something different. The Democratic Party realised that it had been losing its electoral support to the radical groups. It obviously could not easily win over the supporters of the radical groups, and all pro-democracy political parties could not easily win over the supporters of the pro-establishment camp. The Democratic Party criticised the radical groups for spending more efforts attacking it than they did against the pro-establishment camp. This was to some extent true because the radical groups understood very well who their potential supporters were.

On the democratisation of the Legislative Council elections, in comparison, member groups within the ATD did not have too many arguments. The ATD's fundamental position was that all functional constituency seats in the Legislative Council should be abolished in the 2016 Legislative Council elections, or in the 2020 Legislative Council elections at the latest. In its preliminary views on Legislative Council elections to solicit the views of the community released on October 3, 2013, it proposed mixed election modes with a) single-seat constituencies returned by simple majorities; b) treating Hong Kong as one constituency adopting a proportional representation system; and c) dividing Hong Kong into a number of multi-seat constituencies adopting a proportional representation system. The preliminary views remained open on all three modes with a) + b) or a) + c), accepting that in either way voters would be given two votes. The ATD also appealed for the abolition of the existing practice that passage through the Legislative Council had to secure a majority of votes both among the geographical constituencies and functional constituencies, which in practice accorded a veto power to the majority of the functional constituency seats.

The ATD proposed that an increase of seats in the Legislative Council might be considered, though this increase in seats must not apply to the functional constituencies. No solution was offered on the securing of a two-thirds majority in the Legislative Council to eventually abolish all functional constituency seats, though the ATD suggested that functional constituencies might be combined so as to reduce their proportion of seats in the Legislative Council.

The final proposal of the ATD on the CE election was released on January 8, 2014. On the nomination process, it proposed three channels: civil nomination, political party nomination, and nomination by the nominating committee. Civil nomination would demand a candidate to secure the signed endorsement of 1% of registered voters; political party nomination would require a political party or a coalition of political parties receiving 5% or more of the total valid votes in the last Legislative Council direct elections. The ATD deliberately avoided the stipulation of the percentage of members of the nominating committee needed to endorse a formal candidate. The idea was, if other more democratic channels for nomination were available, the coalition would not set the conditions for nomination by the nominating committee.

The ATD's final position paper on Legislative Council elections was released on March 19, 2014. It proposed the maintenance of seventy seats in the Legislative

Council, and avoided the suggestion of additional seats. This was based on the consideration that there was a view in the community that the pro-democracy movement wanted more seats for the benefit of its politicians. It adopted the combination of 35 single-seat constituencies by a simple majority system, and 35 seats to be elected by a territory-wide constituency adopting a proportional representation system. The ATD proposed the adoption of the d'Hondt method in the proportional representation system, i.e., on the basis of the votes secured by each slate of candidates, the first candidate would be deemed to win all the votes, the second candidate one half, the third candidate one third, the fourth candidate one quarter, etc.; and seats would be awarded to all candidates on all slates in the order of the number of votes won. All functional constituencies, including those of District Council (Second), where five seats were to be returned by territory-wide direct elections with District Councillors as candidates, would be abolished.

The coalition believed that the mixed election mode would facilitate the Legislative Council to better balance the consideration of territory-wide issues and district-based issues. The ATD offered a plan for the transitional arrangements in the 2016 Legislative Council elections. The plan proposed to retain the 35 directly elected geographical constituency seats, to adopt the d'Hondt formula, and to reduce functional constituency seats to 20 through amalgamation of the existing ones. The reduced 15 seats would be elected by a territory-wide constituency based on a proportional representation system.

While the coalition platform managed to deliver its political reform proposals, the contradictions between the Democratic Party and the radical groups continued to sharpen. Besides the more fundamental factors analysed above, face-to-face encounters in meetings did not help. Representatives from the radical groups at the ATD's meeting often attempted to score points off the Democratic Party's representatives who did not take these criticisms kindly. The atmosphere was often tense. While I tried my best to maintain peace and solidarity within the platform, I was aware that some members of the Democratic Party believed that I tended to favour the radical groups. This was an exaggerated view; the truth was every political party fought for its own position and interests, and I could not influence them much.

The Democratic Party participated in the platform on the premise that it genuinely wanted to achieve further democratisation through negotiations with the Chinese authorities. There was a contradiction here: the ATD agreed that it should negotiate only with the Hong Kong government, not with the Chinese authorities, but all parties concerned realised that on the issue of the democratisation of the electoral systems, the Chinese authorities made the final decisions. The other contradiction was that at the very beginning of 2014, our united front contact already informed me as well as a group of pro-democracy legislators whom he met as a group that the Chinese leadership had rejected the demands of the pro-democracy movement (see Chapter 19 *Experiencing China's united front*). Hence, the Democratic Party leadership should not have high expectations by then.

The Democratic Party and Ronny Tong held the view that the ATD's proposal should be reasonable and as far as possible acceptable to the Chinese authorities, and that they should not be perceived as too radical. Most important of all, the ATD's position should be flexible and ready to compromise. Ronny Tong was straightforward and articulated his views in the ATD's meetings, though the Democratic Party representatives did not speak in such explicit terms in the platform's meetings. I tried to meet their demands by often stating openly that while the published documents represented the ATD's baseline, it was ready to adjust its position according to the trends of public opinion. The understanding was that if the Chinese authorities were willing to agree to the democratic election of the CE and they could persuade the majority of Hong Kong people to accept their proposal, then the ATD or at least a majority of its member groups would be ready to go along.

Some leaders within the Democratic Party were concerned that the ATD's position might become too radical and inflexible so as to make negotiations with the Chinese authorities impossible. That was why Emily Lau had indicated that the ATD might have been hijacked by People Power. On the other hand, the radical groups might have very low expectations that the Chinese authorities might grant Hong Kong people the right to elect their Chief Executive. They chose to insist on a radical position with the expectation that the more moderate groups within the ATD would accept a reasonable offer by the Chinese authorities. They wanted to participate in the ATD because it was a good platform to articulate their views, and they could always withdraw, a position which would give them valuable publicity. They might also want to monitor the moderate groups' approach to negotiations with the Chinese authorities on political reforms.

I was well aware of these contradictions and difficulties. I indicated that I was ready to resign after the ATD had released its final electoral reform proposals. Member groups of the ATD could then find a better convenor for the platform in its next stage of operations. I wanted them to have this option so that the pressure on me would be reduced.

The first challenge came with the release of the ATD's final proposal on the CE election in early January 2014. I was very careful and checked with the member groups' representatives on exactly what to say at the press conference when the proposal was presented. I explained that the proposal with the three channels of nomination was a well-integrated proposal. The problem was that the Civic Party and the radical groups insisted on civil nomination, but the Democratic Party's position was that civil nomination was not essential as long as the electoral system could meet recognised international standards and would not involve unreasonable restrictive elements amounting to a selection process of formal candidates. I followed the exact script, emphasising that the proposal was a well-integrated proposal, and any omission would not be the ATD's original proposal, but I avoided the statement that omitting any one track of nomination was not acceptable. Though I escaped any blame as convenor, the radical groups openly criticised the public statement made by the Democratic Party leader which implied that the Party could accept the omission of the civil nomination channel.

The differences were related to the severe attacks by the pro-Beijing united front that the civil nomination of CE candidates would go against the stipulation of the Basic Law and its relevant appendix. Hence, it was a matter of whether or not one should avoid potential confrontation with the Chinese authorities at this stage of public deliberations. I managed to persuade all ATD members to commit to the same position, to avoid the controversy as to whether dropping one channel of nomination was acceptable or not. I attended a number of media interviews explaining the ATD's common stand, including a RTHK radio talk show with Emily Lau, chairperson of the Democratic Party.

I was quite frank in these media interviews. I indicated that if the Chinese authorities offered a truly democratic electoral system of the CE without the civil nomination channel, roughly one half of the twenty-six pro-democracy legislators within the ATD would endorse it, and the proposal would have the essential two-thirds majority support in the Legislative Council. I did not name the thirteen or so pro-democracy legislators, but I stated that senior journalists would have no difficulty identifying them.

The ATD avoided a split this time, but it was less fortunate in the next round of the controversy.

Chapter 18

Alliance for True Democracy: a Mission Impossible

ATD's reform proposal gained popular support in a referendum, but ignored by authorities. China's new definition of one-country-two-systems model for Hong Kong. "Mobilising the masses to struggle against the masses", a Communist tactic.

The Occupy Central Campaign led by Benny Tai was an elaborate programme of mass mobilisation through community-wide deliberations. The campaign planned to select eventually three political reform proposals for final endorsement through a referendum. The Alliance for True democracy (ATD) regularly invited the leaders of the Campaign for consultations, although the two organisations remained separate.

On February 12, 2014, Benny Tai and Chan Kin-man came to the ATD's meeting to brief ATD member groups on the Occupy Central Campaign's plan. They indicated that they had collected sixteen political reform proposals, twelve of which from individuals and groups with pro-democracy background, and four from individuals and groups with pro-establishment background. It was their plan to complete stage two deliberations in March, and hold stage three deliberations in April-May 2014. At the stage three deliberations, three to five proposals (eventually it was decided that three would be chosen) would be selected for the final choice at the referendum. There would be twenty meetings at the stage three deliberations, with five hundred participants each. The referendum was scheduled in June to choose a political reform proposal, and they planned to use the following July 1 mass rally to demonstrate support for the chosen proposal.

The challenge for the ATD was to ensure support for its political reform proposal to be included in the final three options at the stage three deliberations and to secure its endorsement at the referendum. Otherwise it would be placed in a very awkward position. Hence, the ATD would have to spend its very limited financial resources to promote its political reform proposal; it also committed to conduct a series of public opinion surveys to ascertain the level of community support for its political reform proposal.

There were three major elements in the ATD's publicity programme. The first was a "One Person, One Letter" campaign staged at street stations and manned by ATD's member groups. This was first held on March 2, 2014 and repeated on April 20, 2014. This publicity mode exploited the manpower of the member groups and was relatively cheap in budget terms. The second element was newspaper advertising which was relatively costly and it was only used on a limited scale. The group also produced some video programmes to be placed on the Internet. Production relied on volunteer work to cut costs, but YouTube refused to distribute the video in June 2014, because it considered that the publicity video contained political information which might be considered politically sensitive by the Chinese authorities.

In the voting at stage three deliberations of the Occupy Central Campaign held on May 6, 2014, the ATD's political reform proposal came third, after that of the Hong Kong Federation of Students and Scholarism[53]. More significant still, the League of Social Democrats and People Power campaigned hard in support of the proposals of the two student groups and not that of the ATD. The two radical groups explained that their tactical action was aimed at ensuring that all three proposals endorsed for the final selection at the referendum would contain the civil nomination element and that all other proposals would be excluded. The Democratic Party decided to withdraw from the ATD, while other member groups were dissatisfied with their action.

The ATD could choose to expel People Power in an attempt to retain the Democratic Party. But a split at this

---

53 Scholarism is a student activist group in Hong Kong founded in 2011 by Joshua Wong.

stage would be very damaging; the platform needed a good image to secure the endorsement of its political reform proposal at the referendum. The two radical groups pointed out that four legislators, namely, Ronny Tong, Dennis Kwok, Charles Mok and Kenneth Leung were also involved earlier in promoting political reform proposals contrary to that of the ATD, and the platform only sent formal letters reminding them of their obligation to support the platform's proposal. Hence, the platform should be consistent in its disciplinary actions.

After consultations with other member groups, I was able to secure agreement from all of them that the platform would inform the public that it had not been engaging in discussions to disband ATD. At this stage, all groups would declare that they would continue to work hard on the promotion of the platform's political reform proposal for the referendum. The understanding was that the Democratic Party would formally leave the ATD should it continue to function after the referendum. I was happy that at least the platform could last until the completion of the referendum, and that all member groups would re-assess their respective support for the platform's proposal until the government formally presented its own proposal.

The Occupy Central Campaign's referendum was successfully held. Online voting started on June 20 and ended on June 29. Voting took place at several voting stations from June 22 to June 29. Altogether 787,000 citizens took part in the referendum, and this was a path-breaking record for the territory. The ATD's proposal came first with over 331,000 votes[54]. I worked extremely hard for the stage three deliberations voting and the referendum, and I was satisfied that I had delivered as the convenor of the pro-democracy movement's platform. All the groups worked together, arrived at consensus formulae for the democratic elections of the Chief Executive and the Legislative Council, and the formulae were endorsed by Hong Kong people. I managed to retain the trust of all the member groups.

The broad picture was far from optimistic though. The Chinese authorities formally ignored the platform, and so did the Hong Kong government. They had no intention to negotiate with the pro-democracy movement, and they had no plans to promote democratisation. With the benefit of hindsight, since the facade had been broken, Beijing would further tighten its policy towards Hong Kong. Although the formal decision on political reforms was to be announced by the Standing Committee of the National People's Congress on August 31, 2014, the writing had been on the wall. The Chinese leadership would nominally keep its promise of allowing Hong Kong people to elect their Chief Executive by universal suffrage.

---

54   Cheung, Tony and others, "Alliance for True Democracy proposal wins Occupy Central poll as nearly 800,000 Hongkongers vote" *SCMP*, 29 June 2014. Available at https://www.scmp.com/news/hong-kong/article/1543231/alliance-true-democracy-proposal-wins-occupy-central-poll-nearly.

It would, however, tightly control the nomination process so that the community could only choose from a list of candidates approved by Chinese leaders.

This was not acceptable to the entire pro-democracy movement. The British consul-general and the U.S. consul-general had actually privately and publicly advised the pro-democracy movement to accept the decision of the Standing Committee of the National People's Congress. There was a certain logic in their appeal: that it was a step towards universal suffrage, and Hong Kong people could choose the lesser evil. This argument exerted some pressure on the leaders of the pro-establishment camp. Further, the relations of the pro-democracy movement with the Chinese authorities could be maintained; the movement could continue to bargain for further concessions in the near future, especially regarding the electoral system for the Legislative Council.

I tried to explain to them that acceptance of the Chinese authorities' decision would be the end of the pro-democracy movement, and the movement would be badly split. The movement would lose its dignity and the trust of its supporters. The Chinese authorities had not made acceptance of their decision easier: they did not discuss subsequent arrangements for further democratisation, and they rejected all suggestions for minor adjustments from the moderate pro-establishment camp. It was obvious that Chinese leaders adopted a "take it or leave it" attitude, and the decision of the Standing Committee of the National People's Congress was imposed on Hong Kong.

The pro-Beijing united front demonstrated its mobilisation power against the demands for democratisation and the Occupy Central Campaign. It organised a signature campaign and a mass rally in support of the Chinese authorities' position. The resources spent were substantial. John Y.S. Lau, an experienced journalist who well understood the operations of the pro-Beijing united front, revealed that the Chinese authorities had established four to six thousand united front organisations in the past three or four years. They were usually in the names of the alumni bodies of universities in the Mainland, the traditional clan and hometown groups, and so on. They were registered as companies, which was the normal and convenient way to set up shop in Hong Kong, even for non-governmental organisations.

The normal registration cost for a new incorporated company would be at least HK$ 30,000 to HK$ 40,000. There were the annual expenditures on tax returns by an accountant and company registration fees, which would amount to HK$15,000 at the minimum. These organisations organised many dinner gatherings to maintain their contact networks. When I was still at the City University of Hong Kong in the first half of the 2010s, I observed that many Mainland China university alumni organisations held their dinner meetings at the staff restaurants in the university campus. Astute observers would also notice that an increasing number of sign boards and placards were being posted on the exterior walls of buildings, bearing the names of various Chinese university alumni and neighbourhood associations of some remote Chinese districts that they never heard of.

During 2013–2014, I gradually realised that the relations between the pro-democracy movement and the Chinese authorities had entered a new stage. Basically the latter were no longer interested in maintaining a cordial relationship with the pro-democracy movement because they refused to make the necessary concessions. The general approach was to make Hong Kong people understand that the territory's economy was highly dependent on China, and therefore they had little bargaining power. Hong Kong people therefore should learn from their counterparts in Macau and stop behaving like a crying child asking for something that his parents would not give. The Chinese authorities would define the parameters of the "one country, two systems" model, and the Hong Kong community should learn to accept them.

The pro-Beijing united front had abandoned the "gentle persuasion" approach, i.e., it would no longer preach its gradualist road, that democracy would be implemented when conditions were ripe. They understood that this approach had lost its credibility and persuasive power. Hence, it would no longer engage in deliberations on the subject nor in a kind of "give and take" negotiation process. The united front, however, would continue to infiltrate the pro-democracy movement and absorb the people who would abandon the cause for personal gains.

This hard-line approach coincided with the change in political environment in Mainland China. Most China experts agreed that the Chinese leadership began to exert increasing suppression against all types of critics and dissidents since the Beijing Olympic Games in the summer of 2008, especially in view of the troubles in Tibet in the previous spring and the riots in Xinjiang in the following year. The underground churches, the autonomous labour groups and the human rights lawyers especially came under severe pressure. This suppression has been intensifying during the Xi Jinping administration.

While the ATD was happy with the results of the referendum, the Democratic Party held a press conference on June 30, 2014, indicating that it would withdraw from the platform. I secured the ATD's authorisation to invite the Democratic Party to continue its co-operation with the platform. The pro-democracy movement also found satisfaction in the fact that more than half a million people took part in the traditional protest rally on July 1 demanding political reforms. The general understanding was that the Chinese authorities would not concede and the Occupy Central Campaign would soon be activated.

In its meeting on July 10, 2014, the ATD invited the representatives of the Hong Kong Federation of Students, Scholarism and the Occupy Central Campaign to discuss the entire pro-democracy movement's response to the situation. In its meeting on July 23, ATD decided to further involve the Democratic Party and the Civil Human Rights Front. The six-party format was maintained till the end of August 2014 upon the announcement of the decision of the Standing Committee of the National People's Congress.

The student groups were eager to initiate actions before and after the end of August, while members of the ATD wanted to study the formal resolution of the Standing Committee of the National People's Congress first. These differences largely arose from the self-defined roles of the actors concerned; everyone knew for certain that the Chinese authorities would not grant Hong Kong people genuine democratic rights. Though there were no illusions, the student groups wanted strong actions from the community to exert pressure on the government before the announcement of the formal decision, while the mainstream pro-democracy parties respected the Occupy Central Campaign's position that the civil disobedience campaign should start only after the exhaustion of all legal means.

The words of Alex Chow, the then Secretary General of Hong Kong Federation of Students, best summed up the frustrations of the activists especially those of the younger generation.

"In the past 30 years, the democracy movement has been too slow and too painstaking. The power of civil disobedience lies ... in the blood and tears of everyone who is behind the struggle."[55]

As ATD's convenor, I realised that my role was to co-ordinate these meetings in the short period before the actual launch of the Occupy Central Campaign. After that, ATD would be in retirement according to the broad agreement on its division of labour with the Occupy Central Campaign reached in early 2013. As far as the convenor was concerned, he would not be involved formally in the Occupy Central Campaign, because if the chance for negotiations emerged later, ATD would then be responsible for the negotiations. For members of the ATD, they would take part in the Occupy Central Campaign under the names of their respective political groups concerned and they would be represented in the decision-making processes of the Occupy Central Campaign.

The absence of a decision-making mechanism on the part of the Occupy Central Campaign (which involved various groups in the pro-democracy movement) soon became an issue in July and August 2014. While the ATD served as a temporary platform involving almost

---

55   Julie Makinen and Violet Law, "2 Hong Kong college students emerge as leaders in mass protest", *Los Angeles Times*, October 5, 2014. https://www.latimes.com/world/asia/la-fg-hong-kong-leaders-20141006-story.html#page=1.

all relevant stakeholders, it had no role in the civil disobedience campaign to be launched. The Occupy Central Campaign led by Benny Tai had developed its own decision-making process accountable to its defined membership, but could not easily absorb the various political groups in the broad pro-democracy movement.

With the benefit of hindsight, this was an important factor which had led to the loss of the leadership initiative on the part of Benny Tai and his colleagues almost immediately after the launch of the Occupy Central Campaign in the early morning of September 28, 2014.[56] The Hong Kong Federation of Students and Scholarism refused to accept the leadership of Benny Tai, as they were impatient and more inclined to take radical action. The generational differences among leaders of the pro-democracy movement were exposed.

In a meeting in mid-July 2014, there was still a suggestion that the ATD should meet the Chief Secretary for Administration. Though many members agreed that it would not achieve anything, a majority still considered that the gesture would be necessary in terms of accountability to the moderates in the community. There was also a

---

56   It is also worth noting that when Benny Tai initiated his campaign in early 2013, it was called Occupied Central Campaign, modelled after the Occupy Wall Street Campaign in 2011. After the Campaign had actually been launched in late September 2014, the media simply called it the Occupation Campaign, as it had been taken over by other protesters, and the sites of occupation were not only the Central District as originally planned, but also the admiralty, Causeway Bay and Mongkok.

proposal that the ATD should be involved in the Occupy Central Campaign. As convenor of the ATD, I explained that I did not support this involvement because of the previous agreement on the division of labour between the ATD and the Occupy Central Campaign. I also realised that the student groups desired independent action and did not want to be constrained by a broad platform including the established pro-democracy parties. The Occupy Central Campaign had its own decision-making and accountability mechanisms and it too did not want to be bound by a coalition of various groups.

My intention was to allow the ATD sufficient room for manoeuvre so that it could still engage in possible political reform negotiations in the future, though the probability was very low. Meanwhile I attempted to facilitate the ATD to serve as a platform for contacts and deliberations for all concerned groups before the launch of the Occupy Central Campaign, and avoided being too ambitious and entangled in the competition for initiatives in the Occupy Central Campaign.

I was prepared to participate in the Occupy Central Campaign right at the beginning, but only in the capacity of an individual citizen. I went to Admiralty in the very early morning of September 28, 2014 in response to Benny Tai's announcement of the launch of the campaign. I had packed a bag for the purpose as guided by the campaign organisers. Shortly before noon, the police stopped the transport of sound equipment into the occupied area. I went to negotiate with the police, together with Emily Lau, Lee Cheuk-yan, Albert Ho and Fernando Cheung Chiu Hung. I explained to the police officer that we needed the sound equipment for the co-ordination of activities and it would be dangerous if there were no means of communication, especially in the darkness of the night.

One of the police officers stood aside and was seen making a call. He was apparently consulting his supervisor. To our surprise, he announced that we were under arrest. We were taken to the premises of the Hong Kong Police College in Wang Chuk Hang. Simple statements were taken from all of us without the presence of lawyers, nor did we ask for any. At that moment, having a few legislators among us, we were quite sure that we would not be ill-treated. But we felt humiliated by the fact that the police had to take our photos, front and side, as well as detailed fingerprints like we were suspected criminals.

A lawyer friend of the Civic Party came to see us, but his service was not needed at that stage. Any rate, his visit provided us information on the developments outside. We were allowed to stay together in the same room and talk, and throughout the detention, we tried to follow what was going on at the protest site through the Internet.

We were treated decently and were given two meals. In the evening, we were sent to a locked classroom-size room with beds, and we expected to be detained for 48 hours according to the law. We were about to go to sleep when we were told by the supervising officer that we would be released without bail. This was again a surprise for us. When we left the police station, it was about 11 p.m. We all went home by taxis as it was too late and too difficult to go back to the Admiralty protest site because the roads were blocked. Only then did we realise that protesters had clashed with the police and tear gas had been used.

With the benefit of hindsight, we speculated that we had been arrested without cause probably because the police wanted to remove the "influencers" or whom they perceived as leaders before they would intervene in the protest activities in a heavy-handed manner. We were subsequently released because by then the police had switched to a softer approach, probably on the instruction from Beijing. At the same time, the student activists including Joshua Wong and Alex Chow Yong-kang, who were arrested earlier were also released.

During the Occupation Campaign, I went to take part in the protest activities as an individual participant. I did not approach the platform at Admiralty to speak. I just sat there to show my support, and I always tried to talk to the young protesters to learn about their thoughts. I normally went in the evening after work, did not spend the night there, and I returned home around midnight.

I learnt from my friends and from media reports about the difficult relations among the Occupation Campaign leaders, the student activists and the pro-democracy political party leaders. I did not get involved since I did not take part in the decision-making processes at all. The pro-independence sentiments rose quite dramatically during the Occupation Campaign. The student activists rejected their Chinese identity because they valued their freedoms and their lifestyles more. They were deeply frustrated with the situation and had the perception that there was no way out. In sharp contrast to the traditional pro-democracy party leaders, the young protesters valued their experiences of participation more and did not consider it important to formulate strategies and define campaign objectives.

Given the priority accorded to their own experiences of participation, there was an inclination among the young protesters to reject organisation and leadership, an inclination shared by participants in the radical movements in Western Europe, like the Five Star Movement in Italy in 2009 and the Yellow Vests Movement in France in 2018. Since they had no confidence in the existing political system, they viewed the pro-democracy parties as part of the establishment in Hong Kong. A popular slogan in the protest activities then was "you do not represent me", and since the young protesters did not trust anyone who claimed to represent them, they naturally rejected leaders and formal organisations. I did not share such values, but I could understand and certainly respected their stand.

All the time, I do not believe that the Chinese Communist regime would grant Hong Kong people genuine democracy. But I am convinced that the struggle for democracy has been a worthwhile pursuit. This struggle demonstrated that supporters of the pro-democracy movement did not bow to pressure nor abandon their ideals; the struggle at least helped to prevent serious deteriorations in the territory in terms of the maintenance of the rule of law and our freedoms, and thus avoided turning Hong Kong into Macau. I was ready to talk to the Chinese government and the Hong Kong government because they were in effective control and accepted by the bulk of the population as well as by the international community. They were the authorities I had to deal with on a daily basis. In these ways, they were legitimate.

I had earlier entertained hopes that the Chinese leadership might eventually change and become more democratic; this evolution would be the best scenario for all parties concerned. I often told others that Hong Kong would not have democracy until China has it too. These considerations plus my lifelong interest in China's developments and China's history, meant that I had been very concerned about the political evolution in China and ready to contribute to the development of democracy there. My friends Albert Ho and Andrew

To shared these values and political orientations, and that was why we were directors of the New School for Democracy.

In the wake of the Occupation Campaign, the young activists represented by the student unions of the territory's tertiary institutions refused to take part in the annual June 4 candlelight vigil held in Victoria Park. This was a symbolic act to demonstrate their rejection of their Chinese identity, and to show that they were no longer concerned about China and treated China like any other foreign country. This political posturing was similar to that of the pro-independence movement in Taiwan. The Hong Kong Alliance in Support of Patriotic Democratic Movements in China and the Democratic Party were angry, and many older supporters of the pro-democracy movement also resented this attitude. There were arguments and quarrels over the Internet, and the differences were fully exposed to the public.

I never take part in these quarrels, and I firmly believe that democracy means respect for pluralistic views, and tolerance of differences. My leadership position in the New School for Democracy obviously demonstrated my political stand, and I considered that open attacks and bickering should be avoided. In the evening of June 4, 2015, I took part in the School's fund-raising work outside the Victoria Park as usual. Ten steps away from our street station was another fund-raising station of a radical student group which earlier declared that they would not take part in the June 4 vigil. There was naturally the question raised by the participants of the candlelight vigil as to why the said student group should take advantage of the occasion to raise money given their refusal to participate in the memorial function. I simply said hello to the students and avoided further contact.

My general approach is to appeal for mutual understanding and mutual support. The question of the principal contradiction has been my usual line of argument. All types of pro-democracy groups face the common threat of suppression from the Chinese authorities, we therefore have a common enemy and we should contain our differences and attempt to co-operate whenever we can. Once Hong Kong achieves full democracy, we can settle our differences through the ballot box. I dare not say that I had convinced the young activists, but at least I managed to talk to them as in the case during the District Council elections in 2015.

The position and strategy of the Chinese authorities clearly indicated the difficulties ahead for the pro-democracy movement. The British and American consul-generals openly and privately appealed to the pro-democracy movement to accept the proposal from Beijing. Their position was shared by Western governments in general. In 2014, Hong Kong was not yet on the White House's agenda on Sino-American relations, and President Barack Obama apparently did not intend to allow the Hong Kong democratisation issue to interfere with his agenda. Britain at that time was eager to improve relations with China which in turn was prepared to cultivate better ties with the David Cameron government by offering attractive packages of trade and investment. The new Chinese leadership was probably re-assessing its Hong Kong policy at this stage, in line with Xi Jinping's policy of suppression against the human rights lawyers, the autonomous labour groups and the underground churches as well as the Tibetans and Uighurs in Xinjiang.

Young activists and young people in general therefore became alienated from the Chinese authorities. They refused to identify with China, and they had no expectations from the Chinese authorities. The two was self-reinforcing. A dialogue with Beijing would be futile and meaningless, defining strategies and objectives and co-ordination with them would be irrelevant. Confrontation was meaningful and the personal experiences of participation were highly valued. In these ways, the inter-generational gaps within the pro-democracy movement deepened during and in the wake of the Occupation Campaign.

The supporters of the pro-democracy movement became divided along generational lines too. Middle-class liberals tended to support the traditional pro-democracy parties like the Democratic Party and the Civic Party. They were usually above forty years of age, well-educated and enjoying above average incomes.

They probably constituted about one-half of the 55 – 60% voters supporting the pro-democracy movement in elections. Supporters of the radical groups were usually below thirty-five years of age, with tertiary education background and earning around HK$20,000 a month. They constituted 20–25% of the voters in support of the movement. They tended to vote for the League of Social Democrats, People Power and other radical groups, as well as independent candidates. They might also refuse to vote as they perceived Legislative Council work ineffective and meaningless.

The two broad generational groups represented different formative experiences. The relatively older generation usually had poor childhood years, but they grew up during the economic take-off of Hong Kong. Steady employment was not a problem. Acquiring one's accommodation was within easy reach; at least one could secure public housing. They had a more realistic assessment of the British colonial administration. In the years after 1997, they suffered a general decline in real incomes. Take myself as an example, when I retired in 2015, my salary was about 150% of that in 1997; obviously inflation was much higher than that, which meant my real income had dropped. Most of my counterparts owned their accommodation, and their assets appreciated. This offered comfortable compensation for the general decline in incomes. Their identification with China was fairly strong, and they appreciated its achievements and improvement in international status. Naturally they shunned any violence in political participation.

The younger generation, in contrast to their elderly counterparts, often failed to secure an improvement in socio-economic status over time. They found it extremely difficult to buy their own accommodation due to the highly inflated property prices. In fact, they had to live with their parents or in rather poor housing conditions if they moved out of their parental homes. Hence, they felt they had failed to achieve the living standards and lifestyles that their educational qualifications and exposures led them to expect. They tended to enjoy what Haruki Murakami called "the small concrete fortunes" like an overseas trip with their boy or girl friends, an expensive dinner, etc. This meant that they had no saving plans nor did they believe in savings. Naturally they resented the establishment, and some of them perceived the moderate pro-democracy parties and politicians as part of the establishment.

Hong Kong's younger generation was not very different from that in East Asia and the Western world. They encountered very similar frustrations and challenges. The gap between the rich and poor in the territory was larger than that in other parts of the world; in fact Hong Kong had the largest wealth gap among all major cities in the world, and housing conditions probably were among the worst. Hong Kong did not have democracy, and the young people had a national identity dilemma. They started bringing colonial flags to protest rallies in the early years of the 2010s, and the strong negative reactions from the pro-Beijing united front gave them much encouragement. These flags appeared more and more often in the protests.

Actually, around this time, Hong Kong people had been actively differentiated themselves from those from Mainland China. It first began when China relaxed its overseas travel restrictions following China's economic boom. In the 1990s and later in the 2000s, Chinese tourists began to flock to Hong Kong, and later to Western countries such as Europe and the Americas. While Hong Kong's retail trade welcomed them, there were no lack of commentaries or reports in social media and the press ridiculing what were regarded as "uncivilised" behaviours of Chinese tourists including smoking indoors, spitting on the street, rowdy manners, obsessive buying (thus causing shortage of supplies such as baby formulae to locals) and the like. The behaviours of Mainland tourists aroused local resentment in Hong Kong, as well as a sense of unease in overseas countries.

When my wife and I were visiting Kinderdijk, a famous historical windmill and a UNESCO World Heritage site in Holland, she saw to her big surprise, a conspicuous notice written only in simplified Chinese and prominently posted inside a paid toilet for tourists. The notice in Chinese said, "Do not stand on the toilet seat". And this was not a single incident. As we went to other European countries and visited the popular tourist destinations, she also found other notices written only in Chinese: "Do not smoke inside the toilet", "Do not spit", and such like. The press also reported that some tourist agencies in China had to issue a set of detailed instructions to inform Chinese tourists what not to do while travelling overseas.

Hong Kong tourists wanted to be differentiated; one way of demonstrating the distinction was to speak good English in front of the local Europeans. Then T-shirts with slogans like "I am a Hongkonger, not Chinese" began to appear. But the articulation of the Hong Kong identity was most prominent among young people in the wake of the Occupation Campaign.

My conversations with the young protesters offered me some enlightenment on their reasons for rejecting their Chinese identity. They certainly explained to me that they felt no emotional ties with China, that they strongly believed that they were Hongkongers and would like to have nothing to do with China. They condemned the Chinese Communist regime and its policy towards Hong Kong. They were dissatisfied with the general situation in Hong Kong, and considered that the Chinese Communist regime had to be responsible. But they also refused to acknowledge the objective fact that Hong Kong people could not afford to ignore the Chinese authorities, and that to have nothing to do with

China might not help to reform Hong Kong and bring it closer to their ideal scenario of the territory.

In their frustration and anger, they were critical of the moderates in the pro-democracy movement, and especially their leaders. The lack of tolerance and respect for different views went against the spirit of democracy. There was a conspiracy theory among some supporters of the pro-democracy movement that the attacks against the Democratic Party and the Hong Kong Alliance in Support of Patriotic Democratic Movements in China by the radical groups were actually organised by the Chinese Communist intelligence apparatus to sow discord within the pro-democracy movement. The conspiracy theory especially focussed on some prominent radicals who spent greater efforts criticising other pro-democracy groups and leaders rather than the pro-Beijing united front. I avoided such speculations myself, though I always preached solidarity within the pro-democracy movement and considered those who severely criticised fellow activists openly as a liability to the movement. Undeniably supporters of the pro-democracy movement were worried about the infiltration of various pro-democracy groups by the Chinese Communist intelligence apparatus.

The C.Y. Leung administration changed course abruptly from the initial harsh crackdown to a cool treatment of the Occupation Campaign. The lack of effective leadership and the division between the Benny

Tai group and the student leaders meant that there could be no strategic planning. There were sensible moderate voices from Cardinal Joseph Zen Ze-kiun appealing for an early termination of the occupation because the community increasingly resented the campaign for the daily inconveniences it caused. Such an appeal made no impact because no one was in a position to make such a decision when most of the protesters claimed that none could represent them. The 79-day occupation ended when opinion surveys indicated that roughly four in five Hong Kong people wanted it to stop.

Obviously the C.Y. Leung administration succeeded in containing the occupation without making any concessions. In its final stage, apparently the occupation could no longer command the community's support. The pro-Beijing camp interpreted this as a major victory and a significant defeat for the pro-democracy movement. The latter in the following years suffered from a serious depression when its various protest rallies lacked mobilisation power. The C.Y. Leung administration however made no attempt to reduce the contradictions in the society; the anger of the people continued to accumulate. The District Council elections in November 2015 (Chapter 14: Power for Democracy, successes and failures 2006–2019) should have been a warning sign to the C.Y. Leung administration and the Chinese authorities, but they ignored the signal.

The Occupation Campaign represented the first major attempt on the part of Hong Kong people to seek political reforms through concrete action to exert pressure on the government. They realised that the usual ways of public opinion pressure and massive peaceful protest rallies would not work. This attempt was countered by the Chinese authorities' inclination to teach Hong Kong people a lesson so that they would learn to accept the baselines of the "one country, two systems" model as defined by Beijing. As explained earlier, the general political climate in Mainland China under the Xi Jinping administration was tightening since the Beijing Olympics in 2008.

In the Occupation Campaign, both sides gradually lost patience and sought a showdown. On the part of the pro-democracy movement, it demanded results and refused to tolerate indefinite delays. This impatience was obviously stronger among the young activists. On the part of the Chinese authorities, they probably considered that the chips were down this time, and it would not be worthwhile to continue with the persuasion tactic. This hard line approach was reflected in the fact that there were no negotiations with the ATD and no further negotiations have been held with the pro-democracy movement since. The hard-line approach was accompanied by tactical patience, waiting for the inconveniences of the community to generate public opinion pressure to end the Occupation Campaign.

The Occupation Campaign therefore marked the beginning of a new phase in relations between the pro-democracy movement and the Chinese authorities. Hong Kong media reported that in his informal conversations with friends, Chief Executive C.Y. Leung described his administration's relationship with the pro-democracy movement as one of "contradictions between enemies". This was certainly reflected in the way he handled the relationship. The Xi Jinping administration has also been emphasising political struggles. C.Y. Leung was eager to toe the Beijing line.

From 2013 to 2014, the pro-Beijing united front fully demonstrated its mobilisation power. It organised mass gatherings and pro-government rallies, engaged in signature campaigns, and it placed advertisements in newspapers in support of the government position by numerous business and community organisations. Gangsters were seen in threatening the protesters' gathering in Mongkok. Later, the organisers of the Occupation Campaign had to face prosecutions. In sum, the pro-democracy movement had to expect considerably greater pressure in the years ahead. Some commentators described these measures as the usual Chinese Communist tactics of "mobilising the masses to struggle against the masses".

Chapter 19

Experiencing China's United Front – Best Friend or Worst Enemy

United front overtones during invited visits to China. "...the hearts of Hong Kong people had not returned" – turning point in the Chinese authorities' policy towards Hong Kong. Deep infiltration into civil society groups.

As a pro-democracy activist, I had many opportunities of being contacted by the pro-Beijing united front. In the Sino-British negotiations in the early 1980s, Hong Kong's elites became aware of the concept of united front as they were contacted through introduction by their friends. Typically these contacts were in the form of dinners and meetings initially, with a view to learn the political attitudes and orientations of the people contacted and then to persuade them to accept the Chinese authorities' position on Hong Kong.

The united front work sounded like a simple operation, similar to salespersons of insurance companies who are trying to establish contacts with the intention of selling insurance policies. Like top salespersons, united front personnel were well-trained, well-mannered and patient. The first objective was to maintain contact and engage the targets in in-depth discussions. Depending on the perceived value of the targets and the necessities of the times, the frequency of contacts might subsequently be much reduced. But like businessmen, united front personnel normally did not want to break the contacts, as they could become useful at a later stage. After all, resources had been spent in cultivating the contacts.

Chinese Communist Party considered that the united front strategy as one of three significant weapons in securing victory and achieving the establishment of the People's Republic of China in 1949 (apart from the Leninist party organisation and the Party-led People's Liberation Army). Apparently, there was some kind of apprenticeship arrangement: junior personnel accompanied their seniors and learnt by observation.

The basic idea of the united front was to win over people who could be won over, including enemies, or to undermine individuals or groups who were critical of Beijing's policies and could not be "persuaded" otherwise. There probably were concentric circles of people involved in the united front, with front organisations or their affiliates in China and abroad who might appear to be unconnected to the Communist Party.

Take the example of Hong Kong - the staunchly anti-communist literary figures and columnists were approached in the early 1980s. When Xu Jiatun, the then first Party secretary of Jiangsu arrived at Hong Kong in 1983 as head of the Hong Kong branch of the New China News Agency (NCNA), he sent lychees to these columnists just before the Dragon Boat Festival with a very traditional and polite note (愚弟家屯百拜). Obviously this was a friendly gesture and one could not return the lychees because they were not expensive gifts. Xu wanted to demonstrate that he was ready to contact those who were most hostile to the Communist Party of China for ideological reasons. While he could not expect to win over these public opinion leaders, at least he wanted to reduce their enmity.

An outstanding success of the united front strategy in recent years was the winning over of the old generals of the Kuomintang regime in Taiwan. Some of these military leaders had participated in battles against the Chinese Communist forces, and were involved in the defence of Taiwan in the Cold War years. Yet in the recent decades, there were frequent stories of their visits to their counterparts in Mainland China, to play golf with them, and so on.

This was a good example of the exploitation of human weaknesses where money and sex probably did not apply. These military leaders in their retirement were often lonely. In the processes of democratisation in Taiwan since the end of the 1980s, they were neglected by the government and the community, especially when the Democratic Progressive Party was in power. They were then approached by their pro-Beijing contacts through friends. The visitors as a rule did thorough research and were able to discuss the campaigns in which the generals had taken part. Naturally the visitors showed a lot of admiration for their military leadership as well as their moral characters. Then they were invited to visit Mainland China after a time when they became familiar and trust was built up.

Typically, the ex-military leaders from Taiwan would visit their respective hometowns, and the local cadres in China were mobilised to show respect for their visitors. Again, the cadres had made the efforts to study the life histories of their visitors and therefore were able to impress them. They would be taken to visit historical sites to show that the achievements of the Kuomintang were remembered. This was made easier in the recent decade as cross-Straits relations improved. The Chinese authorities at various levels had more room of manoeuvre in demonstrating a more favourable recognition of the Kuomintang rule before 1949. Usually the united front paid for these trips. In the end, these retired military generals became strong advocates of peaceful reunification, since they were convinced of China's remarkable achievements in various fields. Naturally they supported the general improvement of cross-Straits relations.

My very first encounter with the pro-Beijing united front was at a meeting organised by the Hok Yau Club[57]. Contact was made probably because I had participated in one or two activities organised by *The Chinese Student Weekly* of which I was a fervent reader. I was keenly interested in Chinese history, and the meeting was in form of a movie followed by a talk on contemporary Chinese history. It took place in an old building in Kowloon Tong. I was a Form 4 student then, and I received more attention because I came from La Salle College, an elite English school. The man who adopted a teacher role was kind and sincere, and he asked many questions about me. Any rate, I did not take part in any further activities because I was too busy with part-time work.

In the summer of 1971, I went to Taiwan for a tour/visit organised by the Social Sciences Society of the University of Hong Kong Student Union. This was probably a united front activity supported by the Taiwan authorities. The student group visited the legislature, one or two government ministries, many universities and infrastructural projects. We were shown the building of an experimental nuclear facility in National Tsing Hua University. The student group was interested in the

---

57 Hok Yau Club in Hong Kong is a non-profit organisation operating under the guidance of the Chinese Communist Party. It is aimed at supporting and recruiting students and youth. Some Club members claimed in his autobiography to be "underground recruiters" of the CPC in 1960s and 1970s.

political institutions and the infrastructural projects as Taiwan was in the stage of economic take-off. The group was also grateful for the hospitality of the host institutions. I was impressed by the schools; they had a lot of space and large playgrounds. The Kuomintang government allocated substantial funding in support of the education system which in turn served as the foundation for its economic development.

During my postgraduate years in New Zealand and Australia, I did not come into contact with the united front. In those years, there were rarely any students from Mainland China, and only a few students from Taiwan. A couple from Taiwan became our good friends, and we often discussed political developments in China. I had brief encounters with the embassy of the People's Republic of China in Fiji, as well as the informal representatives from Taiwan. I did not have deep impressions of these encounters. I certainly found both sides skilful in making contacts and building trust, though I did not know whether they were equally sophisticated in approaching the local community.

After joining the Chinese University of Hong Kong in September 1977, I became a current affairs commentator with some reputation, especially in the wake of the Sino-Vietnamese border war in February 1979. I probably attracted the attention of the local NCNA, and my contacts were cadres from its co-ordination department, including Yeung Sing. I soon learnt that the co-ordination department of the Agency was actually the united front department, and there were three or four of its staff members responsible for the higher education sector. Many of my friends teaching in local universities came across the same people. These were local Cantonese-speaking cadres, and they were as usual skilful in making contacts and building trust. They took us to certain restaurants which served rather good but not very expensive food. I guessed they had budget considerations in those years. They always came to see us in pairs then, though this practice was relaxed in the 1990s. I wondered if they had reasonable career paths.

In view of the economic reforms and opening to the external world, the local NCNA organised some tour groups to China in 1979. Yeung Sing approached me and I helped to gather a group of colleagues at the United College of the Chinese University of Hong Kong. The group toured China for more than two weeks in July 1979, and we had glimpses of China emerging from the Cultural Revolution. Someone from the local NCNA accompanied us, and with the benefit of hindsight, I believed that he had been closely observing our behaviour to ascertain our individual political attitudes.

We took the train from Canton (now Guangzhou) to Zhengzhou, China's railway hub then. The trains left Canton in the early evening. The train had been under the sun the whole afternoon, and without air conditioning, it was very hot inside the train. I had the upper bunker bed near the ceiling of the train cabin, and it did not cool down till early morning. Obviously the tour was intended to give us a good impression of China, but services for tourists were still very backward. While in Xian, a day trip to Yan'an was scheduled. The local tour guide who was a very enterprising young lady had considerable difficulties arranging lunch for the group. Finally we visited a people's commune on our way and enjoyed a good lunch there. We also visited the famous Shaolin Temple in Zhengzhou, and I discovered some destroyed Buddha statues in some closed rooms. The legacy of the Cultural Revolution had not yet been completely removed.

The Democracy Wall in Xidan Street, Xicheng District in Beijing was still there, although the high tide had gone by July 1979. I visited the site, and, as an observer, I mainly asked the people around simple questions like where they came from. I told them I came from Hong Kong. The group went to a local opera in Luoyang; we tried to follow the singing by watching the subtitles on a piece of white cloth on the far side of the stage. In the middle of the opera performance, there was a technical problem, and the subtitles disappeared. There were some low grumblings among the local audience, and the Hong Kong group discovered that even the local people too had to depend on the subtitles to understand the singing.

Though tourist services were far from being developed as there were still not many tourists in China then, the Summer Palace in Beijing had a restaurant offering the Chinese Imperial cuisine. This was an encouraging sign in the development of the tourism industry. While we were in Luoyang, the group visited a major industrial plant. At that time, these large state-owned enterprises operated hospitals, schools, etc. We were shown the kindergarten operated by the factory, and the teachers made tremendous efforts to prepare a student performance for us. I felt very embarrassed that we gave them so much trouble.

I enjoyed the trip very much; it helped me in my understanding of China then and strengthened my identity with the Chinese nation. I was always ready to go and teach in China in subsequent years. When visiting various historical sites, we were given a lot of freedom to wander about. In my later trips to China, more and more restrictions were established as more and more tourists, domestic and foreign, came.

My colleagues from Taiwan received special treatment because the Chinese leadership just initiated a new peaceful approach to Taiwan. The letter released to the compatriots in Taiwan by Ye Jianying, chairman of the Standing Committee of the National People's Congress, on January 1, 1979, symbolised the new approach. When attending a performance in Beijing, the master of ceremony specially welcomed the visitors from Taiwan in our group, but Hong Kong was not mentioned. The united front overtone was never lost.

In my previous chapters, I mentioned my academic visits to China in the 1980s. There was not much united front element in these scholarly exchanges though. I was truly impressed by the superb qualities of the students in the top universities in China. They were proud of themselves, and they were confident that they could make a contribution to the modernisation of China. This kind of devotion to the country and nation was extremely rare among Hong Kong students who were usually planning their own personal careers. They were eager to seek knowledge and information not available to them, and they were keen to go to the U.S. to pursue their Ph.D. work. Hence, visits of famous professors from the U.S. to the universities in China usually attracted a big crowd.

It did not appear that the academics I came across in the universities were involved in united front work. Sometimes as a gesture of honour, I would be invited to meet a vice-president or the president of the university I visited. Apparently, there was a strong sense of hierarchy in treating visitors, especially among university presidents. Presidents of top universities were accorded a vice-ministerial rank, and presidents of lesser universities were given a bureau head rank, deputy bureau head rank, and so on. Hence, I was never received by the president of Peking University or Tsinghua University. Occasionally one of their vice-presidents might meet me briefly out of courtesy. I realised that the larger universities had a number of vice-presidents, and there was a certain pecking order among them too. A more prestigious visitor naturally would be received by a vice-president of a higher rank. But I never bothered with such protocol.

A vice-president in a top university affiliated to one of the eight "democratic parties" and serving as a member of the National Committee of the Chinese People's Political Consultative Conference (often the China Democratic League) would often be responsible for the university's united front work. On one occasion in the latter half of the 1980s, before the Tiananmen Incident, I was given the honour of meeting one such vice-president of Peking University. I was a senior lecturer at the Chinese University of Hong Kong then, rather insignificant in the eyes of the Peking University leadership. I was asked to wait outside the library building of the university, and the vice-president would pass by to greet me. Naturally I was accompanied by two colleagues from the international politics department of the Peking University who were responsible for my exchange programme at the university. I had five minutes of polite conversation with this leader of the Peking University. It was a bit like the U.S. President bumping into the Dalai Lama in a corridor while the latter was visiting the White House, but of course protocol wise, we were much, much lower in the hierarchy.

In the previous chapters on the Hong Kong Observers (chapters 5–6), I mentioned Li Jusheng, then deputy head of the local NCNA, and I could observe that his elderly charm had a positive impact on the key members of the group. Typically, united front cadres tended to be older and more experienced in life; their age and life experiences were assets. They were able to demonstrate a sincere understanding of their targets while they articulated the Chinese authorities' position in a friendly way, and emphasised on the rationale of the Chinese leadership. We had a few meetings with Li at the NCNA office in Happy Valley, often in the afternoon, and Cantonese dim-sums were served as afternoon tea. We had to avoid the use of English words to show our respect for Li, who apparently did not speak English. This proved to be a bit difficult for some members of the Hong Kong Observers whose importance naturally declined, as it had no intention to take part actively in elections, and probably too sophisticated to toe the Beijing line.

In the first half of the 1980s, the Hong Kong Observers often met Szeto Keung, who was nominally a journalist of the NCNA. He was a younger brother of Szeto Wah, a prominent leader of the territory's pro-democracy movement, and he often reminded us of this fact. Szeto appeared in some of our informal meetings. He adopted the role of a friend, and he would inform us how we were perceived by the Chinese authorities, and what the united front expected us to do. He was careful to indicate that he would like to inform us about the thinking and strategy of the united front only, but not to advise us what we should do.

As the united front expanded rapidly to meet its increasingly important role in the 1980s, there were other types of actors besides cadres of the local NCNA. Dorothy Liu Yiu-chu (廖瑤珠) was an interesting figure. She was very active in the 1980s during the Sino-British negotiations on Hong Kong's future and the drafting of the Basic Law (as she was a member of the prominent Basic Law Drafting Committee). She organised meetings and luncheons for senior journalists, columnists, public opinion leaders and leading professionals. People came because she was known to have good relations with the united front, and her meetings might serve the purpose of informal briefings. These meetings also offered opportunities for the participants to exchange views. I was invited to these meetings and attended them a few times. Some of the participants including myself felt a bit embarrassed that Liu paid for all the expenses.

Typically Liu and others adopting this role bragged about their severe criticisms of the inflexible positions of the Chinese authorities and their sharp encounters with some senior Chinese officials. In this way, they were also showing off their importance. When the British administration was still the official authority, these gatherings played a fairly effective role in conveying messages from the Chinese authorities and influencing public opinion. These meetings probably played a role in the united front's recruitment, especially when the leading professionals who attended the meetings were the targets.

My role as an academic and a media commentator meant that I remained at the fringe of the pro-Beijing united front in the 1980s and 1990s. At the same time I was contacted by the consular community in Hong Kong, notably the diplomats from the U.S., Britain, Japan and occasionally some European countries. As I hold an Australian passport and had studied in New Zealand, I occasionally met their consular staff in Hong Kong too.

It was obvious that I did not possess any confidential information. All I could offer was my objective academic analyses as a political scientist, and I did not hide my position as a pro-democracy activist. I could not present misinformation, because my views appeared in media interviews and my publications, academic and otherwise. I avoided the mention of any gossips that I came across, and I refrained from discussing differences among leaders of the pro-democracy camp.

It was relatively easy for me to resist temptations from the united front. In 1985, I declined to join the Basic Law Consultative Committee, and I had received no appointments from the Chinese authorities ever since. I am always faithful to my wife. I did not engage in business activities on the side, and was basically happy to remain a salaried academic. I very seldom engaged in real estate and stock market transactions. I had no intention to join the government; I left the Central Policy Unit as a D3 official (which was equivalent to a junior Deputy Secretary of the Policy Branch) to return to academia in

June 1992 after one and a half years of service. All these meant that I had no desire for "carrots" from the pro-Beijing united front. In recent years, I encountered the "stick" though when they launched a smearing campaign against me.

In the early years of the 2000s, my relations with the united front had been cordial, partly because the Chinese authorities were still tolerant with the pro-democracy movement, and partly because I was not very active in the movement. Our interactions were at a low level because of my insignificance.

Regarding my academic activities in Mainland China, I was usually on the "give" side. My trips to China was paid by my university according to its rules. I sometimes helped to organise academic conferences in China and I usually provided the funding support. Again I applied through the normal university channels and often had to seek extra funding from foundations and major corporations. It was usually cheaper to hold conferences in Mainland China because accommodation and meals were much less expensive. The other attraction was that universities there had ample administrative resources. As a chair professor without administrative positions, I had very little help in organising conferences. I insisted on producing a book from the conference papers each time, to make sure that participants had to make efforts to write papers and that the conference would not just be a gathering for friendly conversations.

In the recent two decades, academic conferences were less attractive to scholars on both sides. University teachers in Hong Kong were under heavy pressure to produce papers in prestigious international journals; conference papers did not carry weight in their performance evaluations. Famous academics in China were no longer interested in conferences; they much preferred talks with substantial remuneration. But in some of the conferences I attended, I was able to meet scholars who served in the most influential think-tanks that provided advice to the top leaders. To be able to have in-depth discussions with them was helpful for my research.

As my participation in the pro-democracy movement intensified, and relations between the Chinese authorities and the movement deteriorated, the opportunities to engage in academic exchanges were no longer available. Later, I was able to visit these think-tanks and meet these scholars as a member of the Finnish National School of Asian Studies delegation though. My host institutions had not expected a pro-democracy activist from Hong Kong in the visiting group. Under such circumstances, I could still conduct some meaningful discussions.

In the late 1990s when the HKSAR was established, I was invited by the office of the Commissioner of the Ministry of Foreign Affairs for discussions on China's foreign policy in Hong Kong. There were very few scholars in Hong Kong specialising in China's foreign policy; I was often the only Hong Kong academic whom they invited. The other three or four participants were professors who taught in local universities but originally came from Mainland China. Later I was dropped from such dialogues as I became more involved in the pro-democracy movement. These meetings were actually quite interesting for me as a researcher.

In these cordial years when I was at the fringe of the friendly contacts of the united front, I was occasionally approached by *Ta Kung Pao* and *Wen Wei Po*. The latter even asked me to write a weekly column once when it attempted to soften its image as the mouthpiece of the Chinese authorities, and I did write for it a few times. They called me for comments when they knew that I was critical of the position of the U.S. government. A good example was the Edward Snowden affair in 2013, when, to my surprise, a reporter of *Ta Kung Pao* rang me. I discovered that while Hong Kong pro-democracy activists were sympathetic towards Snowden and critical of the Obama administration, our U.S. counterparts who had left China had almost opposite views.

When I met my counterparts in Mainland China, I usually presented my publications as gifts since I edited two journals, and I always had some books to give away. I received publications in return from my academic friends in China. When they visited me in Hong Kong, they often brought me tea leaves. As long as they were not expensive, I happily received their gifts and offered simple lunches and dinners. I often had more tea leaves at home than I could consume. When my brother and sister abroad returned to Hong Kong for a visit, they often had some tea to bring home.

I was on the "give" side in another way. Many of my scholar friends in Mainland China loved to visit Hong Kong. If they were competent research workers, I normally would like to help. I introduced them to my friends who happened to be organising conferences, and I applied on their behalf for academic exchange programmes at my university. The City University of Hong Kong had ample funding for this purpose; the offer was economy return air fares, one week of ordinary hotel accommodation and a small stipend. The visiting scholar had to give a seminar.

Serious discussions were usually avoided in letters and emails. I was told by an academic friend at the international politics department of Peking University in the mid-1990s that he had been warned for being too friendly with me. I then realised that my letters to him had been monitored.

Just after the turn of the century, I was invited to visit the Nanjing University of Aeronautics and Astronautics. My host warned me beforehand not to talk about Hong Kong politics because the University had close ties with the People's Liberation Army. I agreed and chose a topic which steered clear of the sensitive area. In the question and answer period, a student commented on Martin

Lee and criticised him, and then he asked for my views on Martin Lee. I tried to defend Martin in an objective manner, indicating that the pro-democracy movement had its supporters and Hong Kong society was politically divided. I thought that my answer was quite harmless.

After the seminar, I was severely rebuked by my host. The academic told me that discussing such a topic was politically very sensitive and that I had breached my earlier promise. I said I had chosen a politically neutral topic, but I could not refuse to answer a question posed at a seminar. My host indicated that he might get into trouble for arranging my seminar, and he observed that his department head left the room when I talked about Martin Lee. I apologised to him and offered to explain to his department head.

Since the 2000s, before visiting my academic friends in Mainland China, I always asked if it was inconvenient for me to see them. This would hopefully avoid any trouble for them. Occasionally, I received an angry reply severely criticising my political stand. I interpreted such acts as attempts to demonstrate their loyalty to the authorities, and I never bothered about them anymore. I have never visited Mainland China since mid-2014.

The pro-Beijing united front established contacts with almost every single activist with some weight within the pro-democracy movement. I was accorded such treatment when I began to serve as the convenor of Power for Democracy in June 2002. Then when the

Civic Party was formed in March 2006 and I became its first secretary general, these contacts multiplied. I and my fellow activists never understood why we had three or four contact lines. Often, when there was a major crisis or development in Hong Kong, I had three or four meetings with these contacts from Guangdong, Shanghai and Beijing. So I had to repeat myself three or four times. I guessed they came from different policy systems. They normally would give you their names, and sometimes their name cards as well. Most of these name cards only provided their names and contact phone numbers. In some rare cases, they would say they came from certain research organisations which were little known.

I accepted these contacts because I believed that it was perhaps useful to articulate the views of the pro-democracy movement so that the Chinese authorities would have a more balanced picture when they formulated their policies towards Hong Kong. These contacts typically would claim that our (the pro-democracy activists') messages would reach the very top in Beijing, and naturally we had no way to ascertain it. Since I talked to the consular community in Hong Kong, I had no reason to refuse these contacts from Mainland China. I believed that most of my activist friends shared similar views.

I realised that the information we offered might be disadvantageous for the pro-democracy movement as a whole. These contacts sometimes would explain the Chinese authorities' policy positions, emphasising their rationale and justifications. But usually there was nothing new and significant, and they were obviously more interested in collecting information. On the other hand, though our analyses were not confidential information, their meticulous meetings with the broad spectrum of the pro-democracy movement's leaders and activists would allow the united front to have a very comprehensive grasp of the different positions among the various pro-democracy groups. Such information would give them a good assessment of the solidarity within the pro-democracy movement, and facilitate its "divide and rule" strategy. These contacts also allowed the united front to identify its targets for absorption. My guess was that the top leaders of the united front would have a better understanding of the internal dynamics of the pro-democracy movement than I, because I did not have the time and resources to collect so much information. This information and understanding would be very valuable in planning the united front's strategy in elections for example.

In meeting with my contacts, my emphasis would be to correct the misunderstanding of the pro-democracy movement as reflected in the pro-Beijing media, whether they were genuine or deliberate, and to argue against any conspiracy theories that they had used in their attacks. I was always eager to propose ways to improve the movement's relations with the HKSAR government and Beijing. In sum, the kind of information that could be picked from me would not exceed the understanding and insight of a seasoned journalist or a well-grounded analyst following Hong Kong's political development.

The massive protest rally on July 1, 2003 against the legislation of Article 23 of the Hong Kong Basic Law (to prohibit acts of treason, sedition, etc., against the Chinese government) marked a turning point in the Chinese authorities' policy towards Hong Kong. In its immediate aftermath, many of the previous united front cadres and policy research agencies related to Hong Kong re-emerged. Apparently the Chinese leadership was very unhappy with the Central Policy Unit of the Hong Kong government, China's Central Liaison Office in Hong Kong and the Hong Kong and Macau Affairs Office of China's State Council, all of which almost unanimously estimated that the protest rally would only attract 30,000 to 50,000 participants. In fact, more than half a million people showed up. The Chinese authorities were dissatisfied with this overly optimistic assessment. More serious still, they wanted to better understand the dissatisfaction of the Hong Kong people as they had been given the impression that all went well in the territory.

A Central Liaison Office cadre approached me a week after the protest rally and asked if I would be willing to go to Shenzhen to meet some researchers on Hong Kong policy. This cadre had been responsible for liaison with local academics and well-known to them. I accepted the invitation and intended to return to Hong Kong on the same day. This cadre picked me up outside the Shenzhen railway station and we were driven to a nice and new two-storey villa in a suburb. We had a detailed discussion of almost two hours and I realised that I had met my two hosts before. Unlike the previous occasions where meetings were usually accompanied with meals, this was a serious and formal meeting.

My hosts acknowledged that after 1997, they had been given other assignments, but they were recently asked to return to research work on Hong Kong. In the aftermath of the 2003 protest rally, Chinese leaders realised that "the hearts of Hong Kong people had not returned". Resources in support of the united front in the territory were much expanded subsequently.

When the Civic Party was first formed in March 2006, a Hong Kong member of the National People's Congress approached the party leaders and indicated that the Chinese authorities would like to understand the party better. As the Civic Party enjoyed a good image of representing the professional elites in Hong Kong, the Chinese authorities were interested in a dialogue with the party. In the Civic Party was asked to send a representative to Shanghai and the Party decided that I should go. As a precaution, my wife should accompany me. Naturally, I insisted on paying our own expenses.

We arrived at Shanghai in mid-April 2006. I was picked up at the airport, and met two cadres who only gave me their surnames. They accompanied us for almost three whole days; the older cadre was in his fifties, had a mild but serious demeanour, of medium height and build, spoke rather softly, and did not have any distinctive facial features. The younger cadre was in his mid-twenties, did all the leg work, and he told us that he had a first degree in law and was studying his master's degree in law. An obviously more senior cadre joined us for two dinners. All meals were served in a VIP room in Chinese restaurants. The driver ate separately outside.

During our first dinner, my contact proposed that the Civic Party could choose to become a mainstream party in Hong Kong in support of the basic tenets of China's Hong Kong policy. In return the united front would assist in the party's fundraising. Since the leaders of the Civic Party did not yet have deep involvement in the traditional pro-democracy movement, it was not too surprising that the united front would make this proposal. I replied that I had to bring back the messages to the party, and that I could not give an answer at this stage. However, I indicated that the party was very committed to the democracy goal, and I sincerely hoped that the Chinese authorities would accept this demand of Hong Kong people.

Then in a following dinner with the senior cadre, I was advised that I needed not deliver a full report of this trip to the Civic Party as I had indicated. I should instead simply bear their proposal in mind, and quietly attempt to influence the party in that direction. I flatly rejected the idea. Then the senior cadre gave me the kind of look which was almost threatening, despite the presence of my wife. He revealed some of the contents and discussions in the Civic Party's very first executive committee meeting, which clearly showed that the united front had already infiltrated the party. I congratulated him on their outstanding intelligence work. He then looked at my wife in the eye and said to her, "Mrs. Cheng, it is indeed karma that we sit here and have dinner together." With a dry smile, he told her that as a good wife, she should steer me out of trouble. "But you do not have to worry, Mrs Cheng", said he, and he repeated this statement two more times. My wife remained quiet with a faint smile.

The senior cadre then mentioned a similar situation when I was with the Hong Kong Observers in 1983. I was approached by the united front, and I reported the discussions back to the group. The group's responses were divided, and my role had not facilitated my work among the members of the Hong Kong Observers. He said that "the Central [government] was not very happy about your co-ordination work on the elections, and the Civic Party's claim that it would become the ruling party." His lesson for me was that I should quietly influence the Civic Party and this would only enhance my role within the Civic Party and my efforts would be much appreciated by the united front.

I indicated that my position on the democratisation of Hong Kong was very clear and well-known, and my service as secretary general of the party was not intended to be long term, and I would step down at an appropriate time. Until then, I would do everything within my ability to further the cause of democracy in Hong Kong. Back to the hotel later, my wife asked me what she had to worry about.

During the three-day trip, my wife and I were taken to many historical and tourist sites of Shanghai, which included the museums, Wuzhen, the famous historic water town near Shanghai, the iconic Oriental Pearl Radio and TV Tower, as well as quite a few infrastructural projects. My knowledge of China impressed my host. I wanted to alter the united front's impression that the Civic Party was mainly a group of western-educated professional elites with little understanding of modern China. I guessed that I had succeeded in demonstrating that the Civic Party had a very good understanding of China and its ruling Party.

We were taken to visit a real estate project of Hong Kong's property tycoon Vincent Lo's Shui On Group at the newly developed Xintiandi area at that time. The message that my host conveyed was that Lo invested in Shanghai in a big way in the immediate aftermath of the Tiananmen incident. The Shanghai authorities were most grateful, and subsequently always supported his projects. Then he said: "The Communist Party is in fact very caring and loving, if you are their good friends. There can be many development opportunities. Your aspirations on democratic reforms might be just too simplistic and pure. The real world does not work like that... The party can be your best friend... or your worst enemy."

Grace wondered what he implied by this statement. I told her my understanding. The Communist Party of China had no friends; you were either a Party member or a target of the united front. How you were treated as a united front target depended on your value to the Party which in turn was based on the policy line of the time. The Party had no permanent friends nor permanent enemies. Sino-American relations were an excellent example.

Upon my return to Hong Kong, I sent a detailed written report to the party leader Audrey Eu and the party chairman, Kuan Hsin-chi, and I also presented an oral report to the executive committee. I suggested that executive committee members contacted by the united front should report back to the party. It was decided that while I should report to the chairman, other party members should report to me. I faithfully followed the decision. While I served in the executive committee, I always sent written reports to both the party leader and the party chairman after each meeting with my contacts. However, other executive committee members apparently neglected this decision; I had never received such reports from any executive committee member except one.

Subsequently, my host in Shanghai became my contact. He rang me and arranged meetings when he said he had arrived from Shanghai. In contrast to my other contacts, we seldom had meals together while in Hong Kong, and I often met him in his hotel room. During our sightseeing in Shanghai, Grace asked to take a photograph together with him as a courtesy, and he declined. Contacts with him stopped after the Civic Party's participation in the by-elections of the Legislative Council in all five geographical constituencies in May 2010. These by-elections were treated as a referendum on political reforms and the campaign was severely attacked by the pro-Beijing united front. Another factor was that I stepped down as secretary general in the same year (Chapter 15). At any rate, my role as the party's contact ended, and I never asked who replaced me as a contact in the Civic Party.

By the end of 2000s, the expansion in the resources deployed in China's united front work was partly reflected in the extent of infiltration of the pro-democracy groups. In 2009, a key staff member of the Civic Party reported to me that he had been contacted by the united front for a lunch meeting, and I appreciated this young man's integrity in informing me. I accompanied him to the luncheon. I explained to this contact person that, as secretary general of the party, I was given the responsibility to liaise with the united front and I had established contact already. If the united front was interested in a dialogue, they would be most welcome to contact me. The staff member told me subsequently that he had not been contacted since.

This case, however, was a rare exception. I understood that the staff members of various pro-democracy groups had been contacted by the united front. Almost without exceptions, all pro-democracy groups had been infiltrated. The Civil Human Rights Front was a good example. It was an umbrella group which involved many small civil society organisations. It was quite easy to capture one such an organisation (some of which had only a dozen members or so and perhaps three or four active ones) in order for the united front to be represented, to monitor its activities and perhaps to even influence its decisions. An alternative means was to set up a new group and seek admission to the Front which basically welcomed almost all new groups. This situation much deteriorated at the end of the 2000s, and some re-organisation work had to be performed.

When I was asked to lead Power for Democracy in 2002, there were more individual contacts. They seemed to be mainly interested in the macro political scene dominated by the controversial Article 23 legislation. They were not too focussed on Power for Democracy and its efforts to co-ordinate the District Council elections in 2015. I was glad that I had not been pressed for information on this issue.

For the following District Council elections in 2019, Richard Tsoi was in charge. Though I as convenor in 2012–14 was responsible for the 2015 District Council elections, I let Andrew Chiu handle the media and external relations. As Andrew took over as convenor in September 2014, I also introduced him to my contacts, and I asked them to contact Andrew on issues related to the co-ordination of District Council elections. Hence, I was able to avoid releasing information on District Council election campaigns to my united front contacts.

When I served as the convenor of the ATD from 2013 to 2014 (chapters 17–18), I understood that the democracy camp had been infiltrated, and we could not keep secrets even if we wanted to. Hence, we assumed that everything would go public eventually. To facilitate Legislative Councillors to attend the meetings, weekly meetings were scheduled on Wednesdays at 6:00 p.m. at the Legislative Council building. I tried to finish our meetings within one hour and no longer than one and a half hours, and I was responsible to offer a briefing to journalists after each meeting at 7:30 p.m.

Through previous experiences, local journalists knew that they could not squeeze any confidential information from me, and they turned to other targets. Very often at around 10 or 11 p.m., the press would call me to say that some of the participants in the meetings had spoken to them and asked me to confirm. It was almost impossible to stop the leaks. There were about twenty groups taking part, and they each sent a representative to attend the meetings. The representatives in turn reported back to their respective groups. Hence as convenor, I tried to maintain confidentiality, but I understood that any such attempts might be futile.

Naturally my contacts from the united front were very interested in the Alliance for True Democracy (ATD), and they often came to meet me. I could offer no more information than what could be grasped by any seasoned observer following Hong Kong politics. But they were still interested in my position on political reforms, and they suggested that the Alliance and I should maintain a certain distance from Benny Tai's Occupy Central Campaign. On my part, I explained to them that as long as Beijing offered genuine choices for the people of Hong Kong in the election of the Chief Executive, about half of the pro-democracy Legislative Councillors would accept. Such political reform legislation would be able to secure the two-thirds majority to pass in the Legislative Council. Unfortunately, there were no dialogues nor exchanges in these contacts, and they were only interested in collecting information. When I discussed the impact of the campaign for political reforms on Taiwan, they were not at all concerned. It appeared that the policy system on Hong Kong and that on Taiwan were quite compartmentalised.

There was one special contact though. A Hong Kong member of the National Committee of the Chinese

People's Political Consultative Conference maintained liaison with me and six or seven moderate pro-democracy Legislative Councillors who came from the Democratic Party, the Professional Commons group (which was established in 2007) and the Civic Party. There were no representatives from the radical political groups in the pro-democracy movement at these meetings. The contact did not seek information from us, but attempted to brief us on the Chinese authorities' position on the issue of political reforms.

My other colleagues did not seem very interested; they treated these meetings as social gatherings. I realised that it would be almost futile to try to influence the Chinese authorities' position on Hong Kong, but since I had agreed to come to these meetings, I treated them very seriously. I came prepared with arguments on behalf of the ATD, and I often had some important questions. The sole Legislative Councillor from the Civic Party apparently was the only other participant who took these meetings seriously.

Unlike my other contacts, this person posed as a rich businessman and he usually hosted expensive lunch or dinner gatherings. He frequently boasted of his close ties with senior officials in the Communist Party of China's Hong Kong policy system. He made severely critical statements against their policy positions. Meeting him was often quite entertaining. But since our first meetings in the spring of 2013, I soon learnt that Beijing was not interested in granting Hong Kong people genuine democracy. Around Christmas time in 2013, this contact already told us that the Chinese leadership would not make concessions. It was a bit theatrical that in the following March, he called a meeting and announced that this would be the last one in the series. He even took photos of the group. I understood that these photos would be evidence of his efforts to be presented to his Party leadership. I was not disappointed in the outcome; I expected it.

I did not meet this contact for some years. Then in early July 2019, he arranged to meet the Alliance members (with some changes in the membership). I went to attend the luncheon because Hong Kong by then was in a political crisis[58]. He was very critical of Carrie Lam and her team, and emphasised the significant influence of the disciplinary forces on her. Like the majority of the community leaders at that time, we could easily reach a consensus on the solutions, but the contact was not able to explain why the proposed consensual solutions were not acceptable to the Chinese authorities. As a rule, he was deferential to the top leaders in Beijing. Again, photos were taken. He informed us that he had many meetings with the society's elites in the recent weeks, including top civil servants. I was a bit confused with

---

58 The crisis was triggered by the Hong Kong government's proposed bill to amend the Fugitive Offenders Ordinance in February 2019. See chapter 22 for details.

the purpose of the meeting. I guessed that he would like to renew his network of ties in the context of a critical crisis in the territory, and he could brief us on Beijing's intentions and plans promptly should the need arise.

Chapter 20

I Became a Major Target in a Hong Kong Version of Cultural-Revolution-Style Defamation Campaign

A lie repeated many times becomes a truth. "I was made a prominent negative model in political correctness." Their "weapons": media condemnation, pressure through my employer and assistants, prolonged attacks through conspiracy theories, and humiliation tactics.

In the 2010's, especially from 2014 to 2015, there was a smearing campaign against me. The personal attacks against me were delivered at full force by the pro-Beijing media; it was unprecedented. Who could imagine that a minor administrative negligence would lead to my caricature being portrayed for a few times on the full front page of *Wen Wei Po* in July and August of 2014? Who could have thought that some unintentional omissions in academic pursuits could have been the subject of formal hearings from university investigation committees lasting for nine months? It looked to me that a modern

Hong Kong version of the Cultural Revolution style defamation machinery was in full swing. It might even have succeeded in its goals: that Hong Kong academics rarely participated actively in the pro-democracy movement nowadays.

I was not the only target. During the period before the 2014 Occupation Campaign, the Alliance for True Democracy (ATD) was working on a common pro-democracy platform to formulate a broadly acceptable proposal for democratic reforms in the elections of Hong Kong's Chief Executive and the Legislative Council. The proposal which I had worked hard for won the highest vote in June in the non-official referendum endorsed by Hong Kong people (See Chapters 17–18 Alliance for True Democracy). Around September 18, 2014, a series of attempts to implicate key pan-democrats like Alan Leong, Claudia Mo and Leung Kwok Hung for receiving money appeared in the pro-Beijing newspapers. Minutes of the ATD were leaked to the press accompanied by biased interpretations with a view to divide the pro-democracy activists including the student groups[59]. At the same time, to ensure that Beijing can retain control for the "broad stability of Hong Kong, for now and in the future", China's National People's Congress Standing Committee issued binding guidelines on who can (and

---

59 "Confidential documents revealed that '3 stooges from Occupy Central' used students as 'cannon fodder'"(in Chinese), Wen Wei Po, 2014-09-16, A14.

cannot) become candidates for the Chief Executive elections: only those who demonstrate that they "love the country, and love Hong Kong" can do so[60].

After the launch of the Occupation Campaign in late September 2014, the work of the ATD basically stopped. As before, I planned to return to quiet university life after my service at the ATD. But university life was quite different then. In the past years, I kept a very low profile at the City University of Hong Kong and did not take up responsible management positions. I avoided disturbing the university management and hoped to be left alone. I was asked to assume a role in the university's quality assurance process and to serve frequently in various recruitment panels in other faculties as an external member. Within my faculty, I often mediated in staff disputes, and my mediation efforts were well respected. I was due to retire in June 2015; in view of my political stand, I speculated that the university management would be very happy to see me go.

In the second half of 2014, numerous complaints against me arrived at the university management. They were anonymous and some even appeared in the media. I heard that this also happened to Benny Tai Yiu-ting at the University of Hong Kong and Chan Kin-man at the Chinese University of Hong Kong. But their respective

---

60   Buckley, Chris and Forsythe, Michael, "China restricts voting reforms for Hong Kong", *New York Times,* 31 August 2014. Available at https://www.nytimes.com/2014/09/01/world/asia/hong-kong-elections.html

university management teams chose to ignore them, whereas the City University of Hong Kong decided to set up two investigation committees to examine all these complaints against my alleged academic and administrative mistakes respectively. This of course meant that I had a lot of cases to answer. I was fortunate that my wife was already in retirement, and she helped me to do the necessary research in order to respond to these complaints. My daughter who is a solicitor also offered assistance.

I easily realised that I had become a major target because *Ta Kung Pao* and *Wen Wei Po* attacked me severely in the second half of 2014 during the investigation by the University. I was given full front-page treatment for several days. Obviously the Chinese authorities wanted to discredit me; as the cases against me, even if they were true, did not deserve such prominent coverage in the newspapers. Most of the "black materials" came from my two former research assistants, who had access to my emails from my university email account. The smearing tactics were not new, but the efforts made were substantial and high-handed. Basically three elements were deployed as their "weapons": media condemnation, pressure through my employer, and humiliation tactics through actions of some local pro-Beijing groups.

I could not quite understand why I had become a major target. The ATD had completed its work. I did not take part in the organisation of the on-going

Occupation Campaign in any way; I took part as an ordinary participant which went unnoticed. I served as a commentator for some international media though. Given my age, my future role in the pro-democracy movement would be very limited. There was an obvious intention to teach me a lesson. My united front contacts from China often asked me to influence the ATD to accept the political reform proposals of the Chinese authorities. I repeatedly explained that I had no intention to do so, and even if I had wanted to try, I could not have achieved this. If Beijing could offer a proposal allowing genuine democratic election of the Chief Executive, then about half of the legislators in the pro-democracy camp would endorse it and it could secure the necessary two-thirds majority support in the Legislative Council. The situation should be very clear to the Chinese officials in the Hong Kong and Macau policy system.

I suspect that I was made a prominent negative model in political correctness. There might be an attempt to generate a deterrence effect against academics taking part in the pro-democracy movement in a prominent way, and discourage anyone attempting to serve as a co-ordinator within the pro-democracy camp. Later Professor Johannes Chan Man-mun was denied the position of vice-president of the University of Hong Kong; as dean of the Faculty of Law, he handled the Benny Tai case fairly and did not give him pressure. So those who aspired to join the top-rank management positions in the local tertiary institutions knew what to do and what not to do.

When I first attended the investigation committee meeting in July 2014, I stated that I had no intention to confront the university management and I would be prepared to resign any time, as I was due to retire at the end of June 2015. I was told by Professor Lu Jian who chaired the investigation committee on my academic performance that my resignation would not be accepted, and that the University intended to pursue a very thorough investigation. Professor Lu, with an engineering/technology background, was vice-president responsible for research and he was my line manager, which meant I had to report to him.

I joined the City University of Hong Kong in 1992 as dean of the faculty of humanities and social sciences, and did not belong to any academic department. When I stepped down as dean, I then reported to the vice-president responsible for research. I had minimal contact with Lu before, and had not even had any serious discussions or contacts with him. I simply sent him my annual reports on my work. Lu originated from Mainland China, and I heard rumours that he was a Communist Party member; there were many such rumours in local universities concerning academics from Mainland China, and I never took these seriously.

Lu began to give me a hard time. Academics in Hong Kong understood very well that they might freely criticise the leaders in Beijing or the top government officials in Hong Kong, but it was wise to maintain a cordial relationship with their direct superiors or line managers. Professor Lu chaired the committee on applications for sabbatical leave. I submitted a routine application for an accumulated sabbatical leave to be taken in the second half of 2014, with a view to return to work for six months in the first half of 2015 just before my retirement due in June 2015. The university regulation was such that a staff member had to work for at least six months after his sabbatical. For an insignificant technical reason, the committee refused to approve my sabbatical leave in the second half of 2014. This meant that I could not have met the requirement for post-sabbatical duty if my sabbatical leave was delayed to the first half of 2015. I wrote to appeal to the university president directly, and was then allowed to enjoy my sabbatical leave in the first semester of 2015.

Lu adopted many small tricks to humiliate me. It was obvious that when your superiors wanted you to leave, they could always succeed. In my case, it was a bit different because I was quite prepared to resign. Lu deliberately delayed the approvals of my applications for conference leaves and reimbursements of my research expenditure from my approved research grants; the former caused me some problems in booking flights and hotels. When I returned from my leave, Lu would ask his secretary to call me around 5 p.m. on the first day of my return from leave to check if I had come back to work. This telephone call was meaningless. Even if I was not in my office, I could be in the library or elsewhere having discussions with my colleagues; there was nothing wrong if I had gone out for a cup of coffee. At one time, Lu made me sit and wait outside his office for more than an hour despite the fact that we had a prior appointment. He also refused to allow me to serve as a visiting scholar in a university in Japan during my sabbatical leave. When I indicated in my annual work report that I had completed a book manuscript on Chinese foreign policy, he asked to see it, though he obviously had no expertise in the field. These simply reflected his very mean nature which was quite unbecoming of a scholar.

One of the cases for the university investigation was the "kickbacks" I had allegedly received from a journal publisher. *Ming Pao* first published a news report against me on August 14, 2014; the primary source of the newspaper story was the emails that were illicitly stolen from my computer. (It was only a few years later that my former senior research assistant, Martin Cheung, openly admitted that he took possession of all my emails and compiled a book on them in 2018!) The University immediately set up an Investigation Committee to look into this case in September 2014.

The fact was I became the editor of a new journal, the *Journal of Comparative Asian Development,* on behalf of the Contemporary China research project at the City

University of Hong Kong. Following standard practice, the project concluded a contract with Taylor & Francis Asia Pacific to publish the academic journal. The project had to pay US$20,000 per annum to the publisher in the first three years as the new journal had a small circulation and had to rely on the publisher for printing, publicity and distribution. Taylor & Francis has been a leading publisher of academic journals; and in fact the global distribution of academic journals has been an oligopolistic enterprise very much controlled by less than five major international publishers. The publisher charged a fee for the publication and distribution of the journal, and I received US$4,500 per year for editorial expenses.

The University investigated me for taking this money as "unauthorised receipt of fees" from the publisher; in fact, the money was meant to be spent on my conference attendance to promote the journal and to solicit article contributions. This was common arrangement well known to journal editors and academics worldwide. Naturally there was no incentive for a leading international publisher to make a special deal with the editor of a new journal with an initial small circulation.

The appearance of defamatory news stories of this kind, however, would tarnish my image. Subsequent clarifications, if any, would have very limited effect. I understood later that the case was also reported to the ICAC. Some pro-Beijing groups even managed to mobilise a dozen people to wave condemning placards outside my home, and to shout their demands that the university management should take disciplinary actions against me. This was quite embarrassing for my wife and family members as we lived in university staff quarters then. It was only in November 2014 that I was cleared of such wrong doings both by the university investigation committee and the ICAC. But it was several months afterwards, and no media were interested in reporting the uneventful outcome of an investigation.

In July 2014, a former research assistant, Cheng Man-lung, who worked for me briefly from September 2002 to January 2003, openly accused me of exploiting fellow academics by assuming lead authorship in our joint publications more than a decade ago. There are of course some cases of professors exploiting their students in local and foreign universities. But my three cases were very different. Professor Zheng Peiyu of Sun Yat-sen University in Guangzhou and Professor Zhang Mujin of Tsinghua University in Beijing were very senior academics; they were both older than I and in our years of scholarly co-operation, they were in semi-retirement. So it was obvious that I had no undue influence over them and could not exploit them. Our research co-operation was simply based on common interests and friendship.

I went to Guangzhou often in the early years of the 2000s to do research work on the Pearl River Delta, and Prof. Zheng was most helpful. We attended many conferences together and jointly organised a few. We naturally had many serious discussions and we published a few articles together. In our joint publications in Chinese, she was the first author and I the second. In our joint publications in English, I was the first author and she was the second. There was a practical consideration too; as the first author, I was responsible for liaising with the journal editor for updating and revisions. It was Prof. Zheng who produced the first Chinese draft based on our discussions, and I then did the Western literature survey, the theoretical framework and the English translation. My co-operation with Prof. Zhang Mujin followed the same pattern. He was responsible for the external liaison of Tsinghua University and he often came to Hong Kong in the same period; I too visited Beijing once or twice per annum in those years.

The investigation committee contacted them, they told the truth and had no complaints. I avoided contacting them throughout the investigation, and I felt apologetic that they were involved in this way. Fortunately I was about to retire, otherwise it would be very difficult for Mainland China academics to co-operate with me in the future. Any rate, they were all aware of the Chinese authorities' attitude towards me.

The third case involved Lau Kin, a young academic at the Department of Public Policy in my university. We were friends because he was a very learned scholar in Buddhism, a subject that was not related to his teaching duties at the university. I am a Catholic, but I was interested in Buddhism out of intellectual curiosity. We often discussed and exchanged views on this subject, sometimes seriously and sometimes casually. We went to Bhutan together (my wife also went); Lau Kin organised the trip. We later visited the Dalai Lama together at Dharamsala, India on his invitation. So when I was approached to write a 500-word introductory piece on Buddhism, I asked for the help of Lau Kin who quickly produced a draft based on our discussions. He was courteous and insisted that I should be the first author. It was a brief exercise based on a mutual interest on the topic, and exploitation hardly existed. At any rate, Lau Kin wrote to the investigation committee himself to clarify the matter.

December 2006. 10,000 feet hike to Taktshang Buddhist Monastery, Bhutan, with colleague Lau Kin.

There were two more slightly complicated cases which appeared in the newspapers. The first involved my research co-operation with Professor Zhu Yapeng of the Sun Yat-sen University in Guangzhou. In a joint publication with him in the journal *Asian Public Policy*, his name was omitted when Martin Cheung, my then senior research assistant, submitted the article online on my behalf. Upon discovering the omission when the article was published, I sent an email message to Zhu to apologise, and subsequently asked the journal to report the omission in a later issue. It was an embarrassing omission, and some newspapers accused me of stealing or plagiarising Zhu's work. I was able to show the media the email exchanges between Zhu and me indicating that he had sent me the first draft in Chinese and my later apology for the omission. I was also able to show three places in the article indicating that the article was written by joint authors and not by a single author, which reflected that the omission of Zhu's name was a careless mistake.

Zhu was a Ph.D. student at the City University of Hong Kong and that was how I came to know him. We co-operated because we both worked on public policy and socio-economic developments in the Pearl River Delta. I was also able to show the media earlier email exchanges that Zhu asked me to let him be the first author in a joint publication in a prestigious academic journal because he was about to apply for promotion. I agreed. I revealed these communications to show that I had no intention at all of taking advantage of Zhu, although the process was a bit embarrassing. The piece in question was not a successful product, and it was submitted a few times, and rejected by a few journals. Hence, I had to settle for a less prestigious new journal. It was obvious that morally I did nothing wrong.

I was also accused of plagiarising Professor Jermain Lam's work in an article of mine. I was editing a book then and Jermain Lam, a colleague at the City University, was invited to contribute a chapter. I read through the manuscript of his chapter carefully and his chapter led me to two reference sources from a newspaper which I subsequently used in my article. It was obvious that Jermain Lam and I both used the same two sources of information and the wording therefore was very similar. In fact, Jermain Lam had in his article used the exact phrase from the reference source without quotations while my wording was not exactly the same. I also produced considerably more information on the two cited sources demonstrating that I had referred to these sources myself. It was sufficient for me to give the original two reference sources and not to mention Lam. The case was examined by many social scientists as it was reported in the newspapers, and the verdict was clear.

A *Ming Pao* reporter rang me at that time asking me for comments on the accusation. Apparently he felt a bit apologetic and he said his editor had asked him to write the story. I said I understood, and pointed out that I was required by standard practice to indicate the original sources only and it was legitimate not to mention Jermain Lam. I also indicated that my footnotes offered the sources in greater detail than Lam reflecting that I had gone to the original sources myself. He too agreed that it would be adequate to refer to the original sources.

The united front's attacks against me were not limited to newspaper reports. Many pro-Beijing columnists were mobilised, and staff members of local universities received anonymous email messages condemning my "crimes". My approach was to remain calm and ignore the news stories against me. Grace, my poor wife, had to go through them in detail in order to prepare my defence for the investigation committees though. My assessment was simple: my friends in the pro-democracy movement would not be affected in their opinions and they would still trust me. My true friends outside the pro-democracy movement probably would maintain their friendship with me; even if they refused to do so, I would not consider this a loss. Some colleagues at City University avoided me, and I was not bothered. Two or three colleagues from Mainland China who were scholars in Chinese politics observed that the attacks against me were quite typical of Chinese Communist practices. With the benefit of hindsight, the deterrence effect on academics was substantial. Since then, there were almost no senior academics in local universities assuming responsible positions in the pro-democracy movement.

Grace believed that she was followed in these months and at one time her "stalker" took pictures of her in the supermarket near the university residence; we could not ascertain this. But she certainly attempted to take a picture of him, and watched him run away. My most serious concern was that the attacks against me would not affect my family. It appeared that the work and social life of my son and daughter had not been much affected. Grace probably lost a few "friends". My son had to visit Mainland China often in those days because of his work, and I felt sorry for him.

My contacts with Mainland China were terminated at this stage with the exception of one link with an agent in Guangzhou that had been maintained for more than two decades. I did not know about the background of this agent. My guess was that it was a part of the national security apparatus. The contacts came to see me in the autumn of 2014; they simply came to offer their best wishes and invited me to visit Xian. Naturally I declined. After my work with the ATD, I went with my wife for a holiday at the scenic Zhangjiajie in Hunan, a group tour organised by the China Travel Service. On our return flight, I browsed some newspapers from Hong Kong and came across the first round of news attacks against me by the pro-Beijing mass media. I did not visit Mainland

China ever since. It was a bit disappointing because there were many places in China I had wanted to travel in my retirement.

I had no intention to quarrel with my Mainland China contacts. I stated that my exchanges with them had been honest and sincere. I had never lied to my contacts from Mainland China and I always stated my own views in a straightforward manner. I added that their attacks against me were against the etiquettes of their own united front work which they had developed since the early 1930s. They replied that they were not aware of the actions of other policy systems, reaffirming that their group would like to maintain contact with me.

During the period, I met some leaders of the pro-Beijing united front on a few occasions. One or two of them vaguely said that in this time of political chaos, people were attacked without obvious reasons. I smiled and did not push for further explanations because I considered that it would be futile to do so.

Towards the end of 2014 when the investigation was still in progress, I learnt from a young colleague that he had heard from his department head that the university management wanted to punish me by depriving me of my pension. I certainly wanted to secure my pension for my retirement. I approached the chairman of the university staff association who subsequently told me that the university management attempted to introduce this new measure in the University Council. The staff association strongly opposed this measure because it strongly went against the interest of the staff. The chairman of the staff association and I agreed on the following stand: if a university academic committed a serious crime, then he/she would be prosecuted by the government authorities; if the government did not take action, the misconduct could not have been criminal. Hence, the termination of employment or other disciplinary measures would be more appropriate for a genuine misconduct. A staff member might have served for thirty or forty years, and it would be unfair to deprive him/her of his/her superannuation fund, the staff member's savings over the years, for staff misconduct.

The university management finally withdrew the proposed measure. I was surprised that the university management had planned to go this far. I discussed the issue with Albert Ho, and he kindly offered to bring the university to court if I were to be deprived of my superannuation fund. I was most grateful that he offered his free legal service.

Ming Pao took a great interest in the university's investigations against me. A lady journalist often came to my office unannounced. She probed me with her questions on a few occasions and she seemed to have the latest knowledge of the ongoing investigations. On one occasion in January 2015, she asked if I was worried if I were to lose my superannuation fund as punishment imposed by the university management. I said I wanted to maintain a calm spirit, but I was surprised that she had been so well briefed and up-to-date about such a confidential case. From the extent of details, the information could only be leaked by someone within the City University's management circle who was in the know and eager to smear against me.

The united front understood that *Ta Kung Pao* and *Wen Wei Po* had extremely limited circulations, and it tended to leak information to *Ming Pao* and *Sing Tao Daily* too. It was significant that both the *Apple Daily* and the *Oriental Daily News* were not interested in this smearing campaign against me. The case with *Ming Pao* was interesting. In early 2014, when I was invited to their office for an interview, a senior journalist stated that I should influence the ATD to accept the Chinese authorities' proposal then on the Chief Executive election. "If you make a statement along that line, we would do the rest", said she. I did not pursue who were the "we", and what "do the rest" would involve. I smiled and walked away to show that I was not interested.

Later in the autumn of 2014, I met her again and she raised the subject of the pro-Beijing united front's campaign against me. I said that I was not surprised and I had been warned before by my Mainland China contacts. She asked what the warning was, and I replied that I had been warned that "I could be alienated by both sides" (my translation from the Chinese expression 兩面不是人). She said that this was exactly my present situation. I certainly did not consider that I had lost the trust of the pro-democracy camp, and I was puzzled by her comment.

On March 9, 2015, the Disciplinary Committee of City University notified me that I was found guilty of academic misconduct regarding the Zhu Yapeng case and the Jermain Lam case[61] and the committee would vary the grade of my substantive appointment from chair professor to professor. I consulted my wife and daughter; I accepted their advice not to appeal or seek a judicial review of the process. The legal procedures would be gruelling and costly; should I lose the case, the appeal might result in considerable financial loss. After all, I would be spending my own money while the university would be using public money.

There was another round of attacks against me by the united front in the second half of 2018, three years after my retirement. My former senior research assistant, Martin Cheung, released a book at the Hong Kong Book Fair in July 2018 condemning me of colluding with Western powers. Both *Ta Kung Pao* and *Wen Wei Po* had front-page headlines covering his book and his allegations against me. At this stage, Martin Cheung

---

61 The first case was an unintentional omission of the name of Zhu, a joint author, during online submission by my research assistant. The second case was not acknowledging Jermain Lam for his two references used in his manuscript chapter while citing the same two references in my article.

openly acknowledged that he had access to all my emails, and that he had painstakingly gone through them to expose my "conspiracies". This time, he used the social media as well. The united front had therefore engaged in a prolonged full frontal attack, though other media very soon lost interest.

The attacks came as a surprise to me because by then I was leading a quiet life in retirement. Why should *Ta Kung Pao* and *Wen Wei Po* attack me in their front pages? Probably these media attacks were in preparation for the trial of the nine activists for their involvement in the Occupation Campaign; the united front's propaganda machinery was trying hard to create the impression that the Occupation Campaign was funded by the U.S. and Britain. The trial was scheduled to begin on November 19, 2018. As indicated in the previous chapters, I was not actually involved in the organisation of the Occupation Campaign, and this was well known among experienced journalists.

Martin Cheung, my former senior research assistant, first used my email communications with the National Democratic Institute (NDI) to accuse the ATD of accepting money from the U.S. The NDI is a non-partisan, non-profit organisation whose mission is to work with partners in developing countries to increase the effectiveness of democratic institutions. It had an office in Hong Kong, but the operation was relatively small. In the autumn of 2013, the NDI approached me to conduct a public opinion survey jointly with the ATD in view of the community's demands for political reforms and the preparations for the Occupation Campaign. The original idea was to commission a poll agency affiliated to a local university with a budget of around HK$80,000. There were then differences on the channels of release of the survey data, and the negotiations ended. I did not report the negotiations to the ATD because the survey failed to proceed.

In reply to the media query whether the ATD had received money from the NDI, my answer was a categorical no. Member organisations of the ATD received a financial statement every one or two months during its operation, and their representatives then reported back to their respective executive committees. The accounts were very transparent, and this was well known to the journalists following the ATD then. That was why the local media soon lost interest. I also pointed out that even if the survey had gone ahead, it would have been a legitimate co-operation project.

A Television Broadcasts Limited (TVB) journalist asked me for an interview on the issue. I explained that it was not newsworthy, but she said that the television station had received requests to cover it, and I could guess where the requests came from. She then admitted that the story was not newsworthy. I did the interview and it was not released.

There was also another case involving the British consulate general. When I was serving at the ATD, I had a dialogue with a lady diplomat there on local political developments. She was kind enough to alert me that the New School for Democracy might wish to apply to a certain foundation affiliated to the British government for funding support. My research assistant serving the School put in an application for a small grant; we did not succeed because competition was as usual very keen. In submitting the application, we included the annual budget of the School which amounted to over HK$ 2 million at that time. The pro-Beijing media somehow got hold of this application, and accused the British government for financial support for the School amounting to millions of dollars. The British consulate-general had to issue a statement denying that they provided any money for the School, but the pro-Beijing newspapers refused to withdraw their news stories, and continued to accuse the British authorities for supporting Hong Kong's pro-democracy movement.

Despite the fact that the local media were not interested in these obviously groundless accusations, I still explained publicly that the ATD and Power for Democracy had never received financial support from any foreign group.

Ta Kung Pao and *Wen Wei Po* continued to release my email communications with the consular staff of the U.S. and British consulates-general in Hong Kong. It was no secret that I met the consular community occasionally to discuss political developments in the territory, and I was sure pro-democracy activists as well as pro-establishment politicians all engaged in these discussions too. In my retirement, I did not want these attacks to affect my mood and that of my wife. Since the pro-Beijing newspapers had very small circulations, I simply ignored them. There were some occasions when friends informed me that these newspapers condemned me in their front pages, I simply replied that I did not bother. I just hoped that Grace would not notice these attacks, because she would then worry for my son who frequently travelled to Mainland China on business at that time.

There was of course an alternative view. Prominent attacks from the pro-Beijing media were interpreted as indicators that the individuals and/or the organisations concerned were obviously doing important work which managed to make an impact. They alluded to the commentary on the success of the ATD which appeared in the *Hong Kong Economic Journal*[62]. Many friends offered me this view as consolation. I did not fully entertain this view, because the united front's actions normally had well-defined objectives and goals. But I was grateful for my friends' comments.

The united front's attacks against me reflected the increasing confrontation in Hong Kong society, and the

---

62 Lau K.H. "Abandon the grudge and return to the Alliance for True Democracy: a response to Albert Ho" (in Chinese), *Hong Kong Economic Journal*, July 11, 2014, A26.

lack of space for meaningful dialogues among groups with different views. Mutual respect and tolerance became impossible. The mobilisation power of the Communist Party machinery became more threatening, and the price for articulating critical views and supporting the pro-democracy movement became very high. This was bad for the pro-democracy movement and for Hong Kong.

The styles of *Ta Kung Pao* and *Wen Wei Po* gradually led to their total loss of credibility. The logic of their accusations were appallingly lacking. I was criticised as involving in Hong Kong politics while holding an Australian passport, and at the same time, condemned as a "traitor". Hong Kong people knew very well that many members of the local establishment and the elites of Mainland China as well as their family members held foreign passports or permanent residential rights in Western countries. Pro-democracy activists who were Greater-China-oriented were accused of being advocates for Hong Kong independence. Meetings with foreign politicians and diplomats were condemned as collusion activities with Western powers, when pro-establishment politicians all engaged in such activities. It was sad to see that these newspapers had fallen to such a level, although they had certainly made a contribution to the development of China's media in the early years of their long history.

Chapter 21

"Quiet" Retirement

Goodbyes to my collections of publications. Reading keeps me calm. Travelling energises. Academic pursuits continue. Political commentator on Hong Kong, China and international politics on the Net.

I left the City University of Hong Kong quietly at the end of June 2015. I did not want to retire this way, but I intended to make no complaints. The general political climate was such that as a long-time pro-democracy activist, I was not surprised by the way the university had treated me. I had been more fortunate than my counterparts in Mainland China universities.

There were the usual challenges of retirement and moving house. After working for twenty-three years at the City University of Hong Kong, I had accumulated a lot of books, journals, various types of papers, documents, etc. As chair professor, I had the privilege of having a spacious room for myself. I was rather lazy, and pretended to be too busy to occasionally tidy the room.

So books and such like simply piled up to the ceiling. Office space was extremely tight in City University, and I had to clear everything by the last day of my service without any grace period. I also enjoyed the privilege of university staff accommodation, a 1,600 square feet flat.

My wife Grace subsequently found an 800 square feet flat at Taikoo Shing renting for HK$37,500 a month. It had a beautiful harbour view, and Taikoo Shing was a very convenient privately developed residential area on Hong Kong Island with easy access to a huge variety of restaurants, public transport, and retail amenities. I could have moved to the New Territories though, but for that moment in our lives, my wife and I wanted to enjoy the conveniences of urban life without having to drive.

A small story might serve to illustrate the pro-Beijing united front's propaganda campaign against me. About two years after my retirement, the chairman of the City University Staff Association, John Tse, related the story to me. He said that he was having dinner with some colleagues at the university, and somehow my name emerged. A staunch Beijing loyalist professor observed that I was living in a luxurious house at the Peak because I had collected so much money from the American and British governments. John Tse then said that the Joseph Cheng he knew was living in a rented flat in Taikoo Shing, and he often wore the same suit for television interviews.

I then faced the problem of getting rid of things. My biggest collections are my books and journals accumulated for nearly forty years of my academic career. I had to give away all my books, keeping no more than one ordinary bookshelf of them. I witnessed the waste of some of my colleagues who had to simply throw them away. I managed to make an arrangement with the library of the Wenzao Ursuline University of Languages in Kaohsiung, Taiwan, which was ready to receive my books. It was a private Catholic university and did not have a substantial budget for its library, hence donations were welcome. Libraries of Hong Kong universities had lots of money and little space, so they normally would not accept the collections of books from retiring staff members unless they were of exceptional value.

The arrangement was made through the good office of an old friend who had taught there. So I was glad that my books had a home and potentially would be read by the students of a tertiary institution. I had to pay for the shipping charges, and there was also considerable packing work. Then I was informed that to send books to Taiwan, the sender had to produce a detailed list, providing the information on authors, book titles, places and years of publication, and the publishers. I was surprised by the requirement, as Taiwan was a very busy trading entity. The rule probably had its roots in the Cold War years. It meant extra efforts on my part.

Throughout my university academic years, I already had to give away the magazines I acquired because there was no storage space. I bought seven or eight magazines ranging from *Time, Economist,* to *Ming Pao Monthly*. They remained almost new because I was the sole reader. I usually left them near the water fountain at the corridor near my office for interested students and colleagues to pick up. Unfortunately, they were sometimes picked up by the cleaning staff to be sold as waste paper. I always envied my friends in the U.S. and Australia who had large houses and garages with ample space for old magazines. Next, I had to get rid of the many souvenirs presented me for the lectures and speeches that I had delivered in the past years, items like personalised engraved plates and cups, pens, pen holders and stands, and picture frames.

Medical insurance was obviously another important consideration for retirees. When I was at the City University, I had been asking the university management for help in devising a scheme to extend its medical insurance to cover retired staff members. This idea was to use the bargaining power of the university's group insurance scheme to negotiate for better terms for interested staff members on a voluntary basis. I understood that a lot of staff members shared my views, as individuals attempting to acquire medical insurance policies after sixty-five years of age faced difficult conditions and high costs. The university management failed to deliver.

When I retired from the university, each retired staff member was given an annual medical allowance of HK$1,500 which was just symbolic. I was fortunate because Grace had worked as the librarian of the Hong Kong Hospital Authority for many years. Her post-retirement medical care scheme also covers her spouse, hence I can enjoy free medical care at the staff clinics of public hospitals.

In my last semester at the City University, I spent part of my sabbatical leave to do field work in Nigeria and Senegal, to study China's investment and aid there. They were "hardship" trips. Nigeria is large and chaotic, a former British colony. Before the trip, I was given to understand that Lagos, the largest city of Nigeria, was a very dangerous city, with inadequate water and electricity supply, and very high crime rates. When I arrived, the hotel I stayed were fenced and protected by armed guards. I went to the concierge desk to ask how I could go visit a university. I was told then that there was little public transport I could use. I had to hire a car with a driver. They also asked if I wanted to hire a bodyguard carrying a gun at the same time. I told them that I was not rich enough to be kidnapped, and hence I did not need a gun-carrying bodyguard.

Since Nigeria had arguably the largest Chinese population in Africa, I visited Chinatown in Lagos. Housed within a red fortress with crenellated walls resembling the Great Wall of China, China Town largely contained retail outlets selling China-made clothing, footwear and toys. Apparently, business was not bad. I talked to a few Chinese traders; they revealed the difficulties they encountered, including corruption and racial discrimination. Their shops were raided before in the name of protecting local industries. They introduced me to some of their local websites so that I could learn of the situation and their feelings. Many of them came from Zhejiang and Fujian, and I was very impressed by their hard work and competence in overcoming all kinds of difficulties to survive. Some of the Chinese families they knew had already returned to China and Chinese population in Nigeria shrank substantially in those few years.

Senegal, a former French colony, was relatively small and orderly. I visited many small fishing ports in my travels, and I was shocked by the waste of fish resources. In the hot afternoons, the small fishing boats returned to the ports with their daily catch. There were many good catches favoured by Asians. However, due to the lack of refrigeration facilities (even ice), the fishes began to turn bad under the hot sun. The fishermen and their families simply rubbed salt over their catch, and sold them as salted fish later in the market. I was told that the South Korean and Chinese enterprises were interested in introducing modern fishing boats and refrigeration facilities into the country, and I hoped that the waste could be avoided soon.

In my recent retirement years, I also made some comfortable trips to Spain, Italy, Japan, India and Egypt. In my wish list, I would like to visit the Galapagos Islands in Ecuador, the Maldives, the Central Asian Republics, Saudi Arabia, and to see the Aurora lights. I realise that

I have to move fast as I am growing old, and my physical strength has been declining.

July 2011. Picture taken with a Mongolian family during the visit to Ulaanbaatar.

I had plenty of time to read in my retirement. I read plenty of novels, as I did not have the time before retirement. I went down the list of Nobel Literature Prize winners and tried to cover them. Grace suggested that I should try to write a novel. I gradually realised that I had no such talents, and was very happy to stay as a serious reader. I still read a lot of academic books in the field of political science and international relations. Reading kept me calm, and I never had to worry having nothing to do in retirement. My initial plan was to work till seventy years old, then re-assess the situation. I had started working very early as a teenager, so fully retiring at seventy would be reasonable.

I also spent time re-writing my old papers, and organised them into books. So far I published *China's Japan Policy: Adjusting to New Challenges* in 2015; *China's Foreign Policy: Challenges and Prospects* in 2016; *Multilateral Approach in China's Foreign Policy* in 2018; *The Development of Guangdong: China's Economic Powerhouse* in 2018; *Political Development in Hong Kong* in 2020; and *Evaluation of C.Y. Leung Administration* in 2020. I started writing my memoirs in 2019.

My friend, Emile Kok-kheng Yeoh, at the Department of Administrative Studies and Politics, University of Malaya, edited a journal entitled *Contemporary Chinese Political Economy and Strategic Relations: An International Journal*. He sometimes invited me to guest edit an issue. It was like editing a book, but more efficient in terms of publication, and I enjoyed the process. Upon invitation, I also wrote occasional book chapters for my academic friends. Publishers asked me to review book manuscripts; this was an anonymous task and academics working in universities nowadays were too busy to do that. Retired scholars could find more time to help. So in sum, I remained quite active in academic work during my first five years of retirement.

Andrew To Kwan-hang launched the *Hong Kong Peanut Radio* in October 2013, providing Internet video programmes with an emphasis on political commentary.

The Internet platform was mainly supported by Andrew To's League of Social Democrats colleagues and two Democratic Party elders, Albert Ho Chun-yan and Lee Wing-tat. The initial launch was supported by donations, and despite some early losses, it was soon able to secure a financial balance. Revenues mainly came from advertisements, and naturally since almost all commentators were voluntary workers (with the exception of one or two in financial difficulties), the operational expenditure mainly involved the renting of a small premise in a factory building and the wages of part-time technicians.

These Internet video programmes had become quite popular in the recent decade or so. They reflected the decline in trust for the traditional mass media and the increasing partisanship of Hong Kong people. They were not looking for objective and comprehensive news reports or balanced commentaries. They were in search of news commentaries in accord with their values. Severe criticisms of their political opponents, irrespective of the validity of the information and the logic of the arguments, were therefore most welcome. These Internet video programmes revealed the political polarisation in society and in turn reinforced it. To attract viewers and raise access rates for increased advertising revenues, these programmes often adopt very sensational titles. The joke is that they would have violated the Trade Descriptions Regulations.

With the common use of mobile phones, Internet video programmes have become easily accessible. The viewers love to see the condemnation and mocking of government officials and politicians whom they dislike, the programmes represented entertainment and comforting reinforcement of their political values and stands. Commentators found it satisfying to attract sometimes hundreds of thousands of viewers. Andrew To asked me, "How many students do you have in a lecture?" For a commentator to meet some strangers in the streets and hear them say: "I enjoyed your programmes", was undeniably rewarding.

The Hong Kong Peanut Radio was established to articulate the Greater China-oriented pro-democracy views, and to counter those of the radical pro-democracy camp which often attacked the Greater China-oriented, moderate positions of the mainstream pro-democracy movement. Hence, there was the prominent participation of Albert Ho and Lee Wing-tat. By the end of 2010s, there was a view that Internet video programmes might have to face a trend of gradual decline because technological advances would introduce new forms of Internet communication. Two or three commentators talking for three half-hour sessions was a bit boring. But the political crisis in the second half of 2019 reversed the trend, at least for a certain period of time. Supporters of the pro-democracy movement refused to accept the mainstream television stations, and the condemnation and mockery of the Carrie Lam administration, the police force and the pro-Beijing politicians had tremendous emotional appeal to them. Viewers of the pro-democracy Internet video programmes easily doubled or trebled. And the trend was maintained during the COVID-19 epidemic crisis in early 2020.

I joined the Hong Kong Peanut Radio in March 2016 at the invitation of Andrew To. We were working together at the New School for Democracy, and we were both eager to defend the Greater China-oriented, pro-democracy position. I participated in the Thursday evening programme "Humorous Observations from the Victoria Peak (my own translation of 笑看太平山)", anchored by Soro B (Ng Ming-tak). He was very skilful in identifying topics for discussions, and writing the titles and synopses for the programme sessions. They were naturally a bit sensational to attract viewing rates, and sometimes did not faithfully reflect the contents of the discussions. For a young man, he was extremely knowledgeable of Chinese politics and he had a lot of interesting information on Hong Kong's political circles. He might appear to be sceptical of all things, but he always did careful preparatory work for the programmes.

As a retired academic, I offered my usual analyses of political developments in Mainland China and Hong Kong, as well as international news. They were not very entertaining, but I hoped that they were at least informative. Suzanne Wu and Ricky Or Yiu-lam were the usual participants too; they were leaders of grassroots political groups and were both elected District Councillors in September 2019. They were able to articulate grassroots issues well, and Suzanne was also a labour activist.

Hence, I was in a very good team. Foul language frequently emerged in the programme discussions though. I avoided such use, but it did not bother me. Many of my activist friends often used foul language, and it did not hinder our discussions. Some of my academic friends considered that I should not have participated in such programmes. But on the whole, reaching out to substantial groups of viewers was meaningful to me.

The other contribution I offered to the Hong Kong Peanut Radio was a sole news commentary delivered on Mondays. They were five-to-ten-minute sessions videotaped by Anthony Tso. They were more traditional current news analyses, but its popularity was far less when compared with the "Humorous Observations from the Victoria Peak". When I was very critical of the Chinese leadership and the Carrie Lam administration, these commentaries might attract over 20,000 viewers, but when I talked about British elections or French elections, less than 2,000 people were interested.

I dropped from the news programme in January 2019 because of ill health. (I resigned from my positions at the New School for Democracy and Justice Defence Fund at the same time.) The news programme lasted from

9:30 p.m. to midnight, and when I reached home, it was about 1 a.m. My deteriorating physical strength would not allow me to continue the work. Colleagues of the programme remained good friends; Ng Ming-tak often organised most enjoyable dinner parties and I always tried to participate. I was sure that Suzanne Wu and Ricky Or would have successful political careers in the future serving their constituents well.

Soon after my participation in the "Humorous Observations from the Victoria Peak", I was also invited by Radio Free Asia to do a programme with Anthony Tso, the anchor person. It was a traditional news commentary programme, two half-hour sessions, the first on Hong Kong, and the other on China and international news. Recording took place on Friday afternoons, and it was more manageable for a retiree. I was aware that one had to explore new topics to avoid repetition. The programme started in January 2017, and the responses were not bad. Anthony Tso sent me the discussion topics the day before, and I made the preparations. I usually offered a framework of analysis, and identified the factors to examine; I made it clear that I had no access to confidential information and avoided making bold predictions. It was not my style to use these to attract large numbers of viewers.

My political participation remained quite limited in my retirement. I certainly hoped to do some serious writing and enjoyed reading. I appreciated that good eyesight would be a most valuable asset in my old age; I really did not know what to do if I could not read.

I still helped in the co-ordination of the District Council elections in September 2015 (Chapter 14: Power for Democracy, successes and failures 2006 – 2019) despite the fact that Andrew Chiu had taken over as convenor of Power for Democracy. His capacity as a District Councillor of the Democratic Party sometimes proved to be a handicap, and a small group like Power for Democracy was always short of manpower. Andrew had his own election campaign to look after. I adopted a low profile and made sure that Andrew would be seen by the media as the new "face" of Power for Democracy.

I tried to contact the activists and new groups which emerged in the wake of the Occupation Campaign. I learnt a lot about their assessments of the current political situation, their values and their preferred modes of political participation. They had very little identification with developments in Mainland China. Probably because of their age, they did not share the enthusiasm for China's economic reforms and opening to the external world which began in the late 1970s. Instead, corruption, lack of concern for environmental protection, and lack of respect for basic human rights and human dignity dominated their perceptions of Mainland China. They therefore did not have expectations regarding democratic reforms in China. Given such perceptions of China, it was natural that they did not want to be interested in developments in China and their impact on Hong Kong.

Similarly they were very disappointed with the HKSAR government. The fact that they had joined the Occupation Campaign demonstrated their dissatisfaction with the government and the establishment. In many ways, they resented the absence of opportunities in various lines of work, and they were eager to demonstrate what they could achieve. This was natural as young activists all over the world were eager to assume the lead and reluctant to accept the leadership of the older generations.

Their resentment against the establishment, however, spread to cover the mainstream, moderate pro-democracy parties as well. They said that they could not trust the Democratic Party which had engaged in secret negotiations with the Central Liaison Office in 2010. They could not work together with the Hong Kong Alliance in Support of Patriotic Democratic Movements in China because the same group of leaders had been dominating the organisation for more than two decades, and it had not engaged in meaningful activities except political posturing. They were critical of Power for Democracy for favouring the established pro-democracy political parties.

I explained to them the operational mechanisms of Power for Democracy. It mainly served the established pro-democracy political parties because it was their co-ordinating body. They planned the presentation of candidates about thirty months before the District Council elections. There were plenty of constituencies where there were still no pro-democracy candidates running, so there was no lack of opportunities for them. Challenging a pro-establishment incumbent was not an easy task.

I had no ambition of trying to convince them to accept my political position. I stated that I hoped to establish a dialogue so that we could always approach each other honestly in response to political developments in the territory. I expressed my understanding of their localism or pro-independence positions, though I could not support them. We had our differences on China's impact on Hong Kong. I realised this immense impact and therefore considered the study of China important. I hoped to see peaceful democratic changes in Mainland China, like those in Taiwan and South Korea at the end of the 1980s. I agreed with the young activists that the probability for such changes would be very low in the foreseeable future, and that the work of the New School for Democracy, the Hong Kong Alliance in Support of Patriotic Democratic Movements in China and similar groups would have very little impact on political developments in China. I appealed to them not to severely criticise the Hong Kong Alliance, but they made no promises.

The radical young activists obviously considered that the local pro-democracy movement had achieved very little in the past decades. As an elderly activist who had been participating in the movement for a long time, I certainly felt that the general political situation had been deteriorating, and my participation was based on my belief in doing the right thing. I indicated that I had full confidence that the pro-democracy movement would continue its struggle, and we, young and old, shared the same commitment.

Our differences on the issue of non-violent struggles remained prominent. I insisted on maintaining the non-violent approach because of my political values, but I also argued that Hong Kong people in general shunned violence. The movement could not attract the majority support of the community if its activities became violent, and it also had to consider securing the support of the international community. The young activists were eager to display their willingness to sacrifice and their firm commitment to their cause, and they believed that serious confrontation with the government would produce the necessary shock effect.

I found these discussions very educational for me. All the time I treated the young activists as my equals, trying hard to show my patience and my eagerness to listen. They were a minority, but a very significant minority, and they had a lot of influence on other young people. If the majority of young people failed to support the pro-democracy movement, it would have no future.

The results of the November 2015 District Council elections were very encouraging (Chapter 14: Power for Democracy, successes and failures 2006 –2019). The attention naturally turned to the Legislative Council elections in September 2016. Apparently the Legislative Yuan elections in Taiwan in January 2016 should be a lesson for Hong Kong's political parties too. The Kuomintang lost badly in the presidential election and the legislature elections; for the first time, the Democratic Progressive Party captured the presidency and a majority of seats in the Legislative Yuan. Many Kuomintang old guards like Ting Shou-chung lost their seats. Ting performed well as a legislator, he was elected the Best Ten Legislators many times by civic groups. But a record of many years of service in the legislature had become an electoral liability because a considerable segment of voters, especially the younger voters, wanted to see new faces and they thought that the old guards should make way for young people.

The pro-democracy camp did very well in the Legislative Council elections in 2016. To our surprise, four pro-democrats who were elected were disqualified for their mocking behaviours during their oath-taking. The events led to my involvement in two ways. First, a by-election would be held subsequently, and I helped the Power for Democracy in their responsibility in co-ordinating pro-democracy candidates conducted before the by-elections in 2017 and 2018 (Chapter 14: Power for Democracy, successes and failures 2006–2019).

Second, I became the trustee of the newly established Justice Defence Fund.

I offered to help Andrew the Convenor because of my long involvement in co-ordination work. It was easier for me to make contacts, including the radical groups. In the actual discussions, I could play a more active role in pushing for compromises, while Andrew could assume a strictly neutral role. My help was *ad hoc*, and I managed to obtain a donation for financing the operational costs. The negotiations demanded considerable patience. Some potential candidates took part and then dropped out at a later stage. The advantage was that activists across a broad political spectrum had been contacted. The severe challenge was that the process could antagonise some people, and could easily attract blames for the failures in elections. In many ways, it was a thankless task.

Earlier in July 2018, Frederick Fung who failed to become an electoral candidate in the co-ordination exercise (Chapter 14: Power for Democracy, successes and failures 2006–2019) released his autobiography at the Hong Kong Book Fair. He added a new chapter attacking Andrew Chiu and me; I guessed it was an attempt to discredit Power for Democracy and its work. At the same time, there was another book by Martin Cheung (my former research assistant) condemning me (Chapter 20. I Became a Major Target in a Hong Kong version of Cultural-Revolution-style defamation campaign). Apparently the pro-Beijing united front had been very unhappy with my co-ordinator role in the pro-democracy movement and Power for Democracy. I observed that Fung's autobiography was written by Liu Lanchang (劉瀾昌) and another lady. Liu was a very senior media executive with extensive ties with the pro-Beijing united front. For some years he was one of my united front contacts; he normally would not spend time writing politicians' autobiographies which would not sell many copies. At this stage, there was strong evidence that Frederick Fung was no longer a member of the pro-democracy movement.

The Justice Defence Fund was established in late 2016 to raise money to finance the court cases of Lau Siu-lai, Nathan Law, Edward Yiu and Leung Kwok-hung, the four pan-democrat legislators who were disqualified. I was invited by Albert Ho, my good friend, to serve, as I was found to be a suitable candidate by the pro-democracy movement. I agreed to serve. Rev. Chu Yiu-ming and Professor Chan Kin-man were recruited as well; they were among the three activists who initiated the Occupy Central Campaign. Albert Ho was the legal advisor, and he drafted the essential documents. The purpose of the fund was to provide financial aid to citizens to defend their rights in any criminal and civil proceedings with the benefits of legal representation and for the purpose of upholding legal justice and the rule of law.

Initially, there was the concern whether the fund should also cover the similar cases of Regine Yau and

Baggio Leung. The group decided to limit the fund for the cases of the four legislators first. We estimated that the cases would cost millions of dollars as the government would definitely appeal if they lost, and the same applied to our four defendants. The four defendants could actually seek free service from several top barristers or at much discounted prices, but there were the administrative expenditures of the law firms involved and payments for the junior barristers. Worse still, if the defendants lost, they had to pay for the legal costs of the government which employed a team of most expensive barristers.

There was no way to estimate how much the fund would collect. This was the usual problem of pro-democracy civic groups in recent years. The fund did not have fund-raising expertise; it simply relied on press conferences, communications among friends and street stations in protest rallies. Sometimes, the pro-democracy political parties gave all the funds that they collected during demonstration rallies to the Justice Defence Fund.

The initial responses exceeded expectations. Within a short period of two months or so, the fund accumulated HK$5 million. Basically it could collect more than HK$1 million in every protest rally with a participation of over 100,000 people. It was very touching to see the protest participants offering their donations, at usually a hundred dollars each. With the exception of three or four major donations exceeding HK$100,000 each, the rest were all small sum donations. We were so grateful for the overwhelming public support and felt very proud of Hong Kong people who were always ready to endorse a worthwhile cause.

The fund relied solely on voluntary assistance. Chris Lo Wai-ming spent so much time to help and he was so important in our organisational work that we subsequently offered him an honorarium of HK$20,000 per annum. Chu Yiu-ming and Chan Kin-man managed to rally a group of voluntary workers to help the fund too. Its major expenditure items were the printing of publicity materials and the setting up of street stations in protest rallies including transport, sound equipment, and so on. On the average, an established charity fund spends about 13% of its total revenues on operational costs. We spent less than 2%. Again we had no office.

Cyd Ho Sau-lan, a former Legislative Councillor from the Labour Party, eventually became the main force running the Fund. Many activists became entangled in law suits as the government and the pro-Beijing united front chose to exert pressure on the pro-democracy movement through legal means.

Cyd helped to organise the fund's stall at the Victoria Park flower market during Chinese New Year eve in early 2019 and 2020. We realised that this would not collect much donation, but would be good publicity work. Cyd was kind enough to put in the time and effort. I went to help occasionally. In early 2020, the government stopped allowing dry goods stalls in the Victoria Park flower market. The usual pro-democracy political groups that usually sell souvenirs there were discouraged as they had no experience in selling flowers, and the attendance for the flower market was expected to be low due to the political crisis then. The Justice Defence Fund continued the practice, and the two other stalls were those of the League of Social Democrats and the Hong Kong Alliance in Support of Patriotic Democratic Movements in China.

I withdrew from the Justice Defence Fund and the New School for Democracy in early 2019 because of ill health. My family wanted me to take more rest. I continued to help the two organisations on voluntary, *ad hoc* basis.

Chapter 22

The Emergence of Radical Politics and the Political Crisis in 2019-2020

The Fugitives (Amendment) Bill triggered large scale unrests and arrests of activists for months. "One country" and NOT "two systems" for national security. Unexpected decisive victory in local elections, 2019. Hong Kong's cherished values were eroded.

On June 9, 2019 (Sunday), 1.03 million Hong Kong people took part in a protest rally against the introduction of the Fugitive Offenders and Mutual Legal Assistance in Criminal Matters Legislation (Amendment) Bill 2019[63] (henceforward the "Fugitives (Amendment) Bill") by the Carrie Lam administration. Obviously Hong Kong people were angry; they knew that democracy had been denied them since the Occupation Campaign in the autumn of 2014. In the past five years, they also witnessed a gradual erosion of the rule of law in the territory.

---

63 For the full text of the bill, see https://www.legco.gov.hk/yr18-19/english/bills/b201903291.pdf

The Fugitives (Amendment) Bill would allow Hong Kong people to be extradited to Mainland China for trial for crimes that were committed inside and outside Mainland China. Hong Kong people all the time considered the right to a fair trial a basic political right, and they did not have confidence in the judicial system in China. In addition to the supporters of the pro-democracy movement, businessmen were also alarmed because they might easily be involved in corruption practices and tax evasion while doing business in China.

Immediately after the protest rally on Sunday, June 9, the Carrie Lam administration refused to make serious concessions. In a press statement released on the same Sunday night, she indicated that the legislative process would proceed on schedule, and the contents of the bill would not be altered. Although she admitted that the initiative did not come from the central government, her legislative proposal had received strong endorsement from the Party leadership. In the previous months, pro-Beijing groups went to Beijing to meet Han Zheng (Politburo Standing Committee member responsible for Hong Kong and Macau affairs) and the Chinese officials below him. A small number of business leaders, legislators and academics within the pro-establishment camp who had earlier indicated reservations soon altered their positions and returned to the fold.[64]

---

64   For example, a Beijing-friendly legal scholar no longer insisted on his counter-proposal as he noted that Beijing might view it as a challenge

Despite the massive protest rally on June 9, the president of the Legislative Council, Andrew Leung Kwan-yuen, soon announced the schedule of meetings for the deliberation of the bill, and it would be decided on a vote on June 20. It was this arrogance and total disregard for the protest rally that provoked about 40,000 young people to surround the Legislative Council in the morning of June 12, when deliberations on the amendment bill were to begin. This action led to some violent clashes with the police in the afternoon, who succeeded in dispersing the bulk of the protesters later in the evening. It was a sad scene as tear gas and rubber bullets were deployed, and at least seventy-two people were injured.

The community had much sympathy for the young people. Despite Carrie Lam's promise to shelve the bill on the following Saturday, two million people poured into the streets the next day. The Chief Executive made a public apology on June 18, indicating that the Fugitives (Amendment) Bill would likely meet a natural disappearance at the end of the present legislative session in July 2020. But she refused to resign as requested by the pro-democracy movement. She also rejected its other demands including a formal withdrawal of the bill, the retraction of labelling the previous Wednesday's confrontation as a riot, the release of those arrested

---

to its sovereignty, see https://www.scmp.com/news/hong-kong/politics/article/3011577/hong-kong-extradition-law-beijing-friendly-legal

and initiation of an independent investigation into the related police violence.

I did not take part in the protest movement in a significant way. Naturally I had been an ardent supporter of the pro-democracy movement, and I was very concerned. But due to deteriorating health, I had already withdrawn from various pro-democracy groups in early 2019. I participated in almost all related peaceful rallies and meetings to demonstrate my support. I usually went home before 6 p.m. though, and watched the later activities on television. I was invited for commentary by some international media, and I still took part in my Radio Free Asia programmes.

The developments shocked me and most Hong Kong people. It was difficult for the community to imagine the use of petrol bombs by the young protesters. Many high school students became serious concerned citizens, and their activities inside their respective schools in coalition with neighbouring schools showed superb organisational power. The experiences in their formative years probably would have a significant impact on their values and political HKSAR government and the Chinese authorities had lost a whole generation of young people.

Since the Sino-British negotiations in the early 1980s, Chinese leaders had been most concerned about investors' interests because they realised that as an international financial centre, money could leave Hong Kong very easily. This time, despite the articulation of reservations by the business community and the expatriate business community, the Carrie Lam administration only offered limited concessions in the Fugitives (Amendment) Bill and did not attempt to address the basic issue of the lack of confidence in the Chinese judicial system guided by the Communist Party. Apparently, Beijing and Hong Kong considered that the perceived political challenges from the opposition and dissidents were more significant than the protection of the territory's good business environment.

Hong Kong remains a significant source of information on China for the international media, and probably one of the most important origins of criticisms against China and its leaders. The territory's special role had been perceived more negatively with the apparently rising sense of insecurity on the part of the Xi Jinping administration. The introduction of the Fugitives (Amendment) Bill and the frequent discussions in the pro-Beijing camp on the urgency to implement Article 23 legislation probably reflected their intentions to exert stricter controls over opposition to and criticisms of the Chinese authorities through the strengthening of the deterrent instruments. But the business community's interests and the business environment of the territory would also be adversely affected.

The Chinese authorities had been tightening their Hong Kong policy, especially after the Occupation Campaign. The emergence of localism and pro-independence groups provided the Chinese authorities and the Hong Kong government a convenient excuse. In the defence of state sovereignty and national security as well as in the combat against Hong Kong independence, the Carrie Lam administration felt that it had a free hand. The then head of the Central Liaison Office, Wang Zhimin, declared in April 2018 that on issues of national security, there was only the responsibility of "one country" and not "two systems". When did ministerial officials from Beijing begin to have the power of re-defining the scope of the "one country, two systems" model?

The arrests and prosecutions of demonstrators had generated some deterrence effect. Young people sent to jail would be burdened with criminal records for life and they would suffer substantially in their career development. Given the strong, hawkish position of the government, the most serious challenge on the part of the pro-democracy movement was the lack of realisable objectives in the short-term. People no longer believed that demands for democratic reforms like the direct elections of the Chief Executive and that of all the seats in the legislature were meaningful. The disappointment and pessimism of the community meant that it was very difficult to mobilise people since the end of the Occupation Campaign. Only small numbers of people took part in various campaigns and protest rallies in the following years.

Despite the lower level of political participation among young people, their anger was definitely accumulating.

This anger needed to vent when opportunities arose, as in the second half of 2019. Hong Kong people who opposed the Fugitives (Amendment) Bill should be grateful to the radical protesters who attempted to surround the Legislative Council building in the morning of June 12, 2019 and succeeded in blocking deliberations on the Fugitives (Amendment) Bill. Their action led to the first round of violent clashes with the police. The radicals' argument for confrontation (including even the use of violence) became convincing because of the concrete result achieved.

It was obvious that even though more than one million people marched in the streets on June 9, the vast majority of the protesters did not have high expectations of the Carrie Lam administration; in her arrogance, she refused to say outright that she would withdraw the Bill, but used such semantics like "the Bill is dead". Many of them thought they would nonetheless take part in the protest rally to demonstrate their stand. It was partly for this reason that two million people again participated in the protest rally the following Sunday, despite the fact that Carrie Lam had promised to shelve the bill the previous day.

Violence soon escalated with each round of clashes between the police and the radical protesters. In the first place, the crackdown on the protesters on June 12, 2019 took place in the mid-afternoon when the situation was quiet and calm. By that time, it was clear that there would be no Legislative Council meetings on June 12 and

June 13. There was no logical rationale for the launch of a severe onslaught on the young protesters then. Furthermore, instead of giving ample advanced warning and indicating a route for retreat, the police suddenly surrounded the protesters and attacked them.

It was for these reasons that most Hong Kong people showed support and sympathy for the protesters. I always uphold the principle of non-violent political struggle, and I do not support the use of violence in protest activities even in this crisis. In this political crisis, however, many considered that the major responsibility lay with the government and the police. Initially, I did not blame the frontline police officers as in the case of the crackdown on the protesters near the Legislative Council on June 12. I believed that if the Commissioner of Police had issued a strict order to the commander and police officers concerned to exercise restraint, they would certainly have followed the order.

Unfortunately, the protesters retaliated by disturbing the police accommodation quarters, and exchanged insults with frontline police officers. In every round of clashes, the level of confrontation and mutual hostility escalated further. As could be seen on daily live television and web broadcasts, frontline officers were perceived to have lost control; even their immediate commanders could not restrain them.

Sympathisers and ordinary citizens in support of the pro-democracy movement were shocked by the level of police brutality they witnessed on the television screen and in the social media where videos and photos were shared almost real time. According to a public opinion survey in mid-November 2019, four in five respondents considered that the responsibility of the HKSAR government "substantial" or "very significant" in the escalation of violence in society. Three-quarters of the respondents felt the same way concerning the responsibility of the police, and only 41% felt the same way regarding the protesters.[65]

I was worried that the violence in the protests might adversely affect the community's support for the pro-democracy movement and that of international public opinion. In the evening of July 1, 2019, protesters occupied the Legislative Council building and caused some damages. My friends in the pro-democracy movement were very concerned about the potential damage to the image of the movement. But, as seen on live broadcasts, the mobilisation of gangsters to attack the protesters who returned home to Yuen Long (in the New Territories) in the late evening of July 21 much damaged the reputation of the police.

This was followed by the brutal crackdown on the protesters at the Prince Edward Road Mass Transit

---

[65] See the report by the Hong Kong Public Opinion Research Institute released on November 15, 2019. Available at https://static1.squarespace.com/static/5cfd1ba6a7117c00170d7aa/t/5dce635b5ad0db3a1df67fef/1573806942766/sp_rpt_rolling_survey_2019nov15_CHI_v1.1pori.pdf

Railway station in the evening of August 31. Some supporters of the pro-democracy movement believed that a few protesters had died in the crackdown, and memorial activities were often held at the site, even though there was no hard evidence in support of such rumours. By then, public opinion, local and international, crystallised. The police and the Carrie Lam administration definitely lost the public opinion war.

In September 2019 after three months of unrest, Carrie Lam announced the formal withdrawal of the controversial Fugitives (Amendment) Bill. But she refused to make further concessions. The vast majority of Hong Kong people supported the setting up of an independent commission of investigation as the first step towards reconciliation. This was one of the five major demands on the part of the pro-democracy movement.[66]

I was given a chance to give my personal view in a "Letter to Hong Kong" programme at the Radio Television Hong Kong, and the main theme I used was an appeal for an independent investigation. An independent commission of investigation would help to define the nature of the "riots", and allow perhaps considerable room of leniency in prosecuting the protesters. It needed not limit itself

---

66 The "Five demands, not one less" were: 1. the protests should not be characterised as riots; 2. there should be amnesty for those arrested during the protests; 3. an independent inquiry into the alleged police brutality should be initiated; 4. universal suffrage should be implemented; and 5. the Fugitives (Amendment) Bill should be withdrawn.

to police brutality; it should examine the political crisis as a whole, including the respective roles of the Carrie Lam administration, the pro-democracy movement and the protesters. The resignation of Carrie Lam naturally would be decided by the top Chinese leadership, and deliberations on political reforms and democratisation would be a long process.

The refusal to set up an independent commission of investigation had been generally perceived as reflecting the arrogance of Carrie Lam and her lack of interest in reconciliation. The pro-democracy movement considered that the police had a lot to hide, as both the Commissioner of Police and its trade unions rejected a commission to investigate the crisis.

This arrogance was costly in terms of the loss of people's trust. In mid-October 2019, a public opinion survey revealed that half of the respondents had zero confidence in the HKSAR government; 45% in the central government in Beijing, and 52% in the police force. In mid-May/early June in 2019 before the unrest, the average confidence score was a satisfactory 5.60 (out of 10); in mid-October after the incident, it fell sharply to 2.32. It was indeed a political crisis.[67]

---

67 The poll was conducted by the Centre for Communication and Public Opinion Survey, School of Journalism and Communication, the Chinese University of Hong Kong commissioned by Ming Pao; see https://video3.mingpao.com/inews/201910/20191015_mpsurvey.pdf

In July–August 2019, there were political gossips that the Chinese authorities might mobilise the People's Liberation Army (PLA) to quell the protests in Hong Kong. In the following two months, these rumours stopped. I did not believe in these rumours; I spoke to the international media a few times as well as in my local Internet video programmes that the probability was very low. The Chinese authorities were wise enough to understand the high political costs involved. It would severely damage Hong Kong people's confidence and the territory's functioning as an international financial centre.

To the Chinese leadership, it would mean the bankruptcy of the "one country, two systems" model and the failure of its Hong Kong policy; it would adversely affect the on-going Sino-American trade negotiations and deal a severe blow to the Kuomintang in Taiwan in the coming presidential and legislative elections in January 2020. Lastly, the People's Liberation Army was not known to be trained to deal with protesters and crowd control, while the Hong Kong police was well trained and well equipped to do so.

Just before the G20 Osaka Summit on June 28–29, 2019, the Hong Kong protesters organised a publicity campaign to articulate their position through advertisements in a number of leading international newspapers. They raised money through crowd funding on a Reddit-like forum called LIHKG; the initial target was HK$3 million, but they managed to raise HK$5.5 million in half a day.⁶⁸ The campaign was a significant success. Since the protesters had no expectations of the Carrie Lam administration and the Chinese authorities, they appealed for international public opinion support. Later they sought sanctions against officials of the HKSAR government by the Western governments, and all types of signature campaigns were launched.

This was obviously very embarrassing for the Chinese authorities and the pro-Beijing united front. They had been condemning the pro-democracy movement leaders as "traitors" for collusion with the Western governments; at this stage this collusion became popular mass action. On November 20, 2019, the U.S. House of Representatives voted 417 to 1 for the "Hong Kong Human Rights and Democracy Act" which the Senate had passed unanimously the day before.⁶⁹ President Donald Trump eventually signed it. The legislation would require the State Department to certify at least once a year that Hong Kong retains enough autonomy to qualify for special U.S. trading consideration; it also would provide for sanctions against officials responsible for human-rights violations in the territory.

---

68 Rachel Yeo, "Hong Kong protests: how the city's Reddit-like forum LIHKG has become the leading platform for organising demonstrations", August 3, 2019. https://www.scmp.com/news/hong-kong/society/article/3021224/hong-kong-protests-how-citys-reddit-forum-lihkg-has-become

69 See https://www.reuters.com/article/us-hongkong-protests-usa/us-house-passes-hong-kong-human-rights-bills-idUSKBN1XU2CJ

Exactly because the legislation involved no immediate concrete action on the part of U.S., it was able to sail through both houses of Congress almost without opposition. The protesters in Hong Kong, however, hoped that the U.S. authorities would refuse to grant visiting visas to Hong Kong's police officers, as well as cancel their permanent residential rights and reject their applications for emigration. These requests reflected their hostility towards the police force. Before the actual voting in the U.S. Congress, thousands of people marched to the U.S. Consulate-General to articulate their support for the legislation. At the same time, hundreds of people gathered in front of the British Consulate-General to request for permanent residential rights in Britain for holders of British National (Overseas) passports, which (through voluntary registration) had been granted to British Dependent Territories citizens who were Hong Kong residents before the transfer of sovereignty on July 1, 1997.

These phenomena demonstrated the disappointment and frustration of Hong Kong people. They realised that they had very limited influence on the Carrie Lam administration and the Chinese authorities in Beijing. It was hoped that potential sanctions against them by Western governments might generate a deterrence effect, at least, embarrass them.

The young protesters displayed a different type of disappointment, frustration and desperation.

Thousands of young people engaged in violent protest activities and clashes with the police, occupied the Chinese University of Hong Kong and Hong Kong Polytechnic University campuses, and to a lesser degree other campuses. The risks they took were substantial, and some of them were high school students only. If they were arrested and prosecuted, their future careers would suffer considerably. During detainment and in the arrest processes, they feared they might be beaten up, humiliated, etc. Some of them had to leave home because of differences with and sanctions from their families. Yet they expressed their willingness to sacrifice and showed tremendous dedication and commitment. I did not agree with their course of action, but I certainly had a lot of admiration for them. When I was in high school, I knew extremely little about the political and social issues in the territory. When I was in the university, I was largely occupied with my study and part-time jobs.

I was able to talk to some student union leaders; I had many occasional conversations with young protesters. I followed their press conferences, as well as their statements and exchanges on the Internet. I did not believe that they should put themselves at such risks; I hoped that they would grow up and contribute to the pro-democracy and social movements in the territory in the future. I tried to defend them in my commentaries in international media, but I felt I had done so little.

There were many sad stories of those who had not been arrested. There were cases of those who left home and could not find food and shelter, and were in substantial difficulties in continuing their education. There were also those who fled to Taiwan because of their involvement in cases of police assault. They were worried of long imprisonment and torture by the police while in detainment. I met two or three of them when I visited Taiwan during the elections in January 2020. I felt sorry for them as I could sense their alienation, loneliness and lack of purpose. Many universities in Taiwan proved to be helpful as they were willing to admit them to degree programmes whenever appropriate without charge.

The "612 Humanitarian Relief Fund" was set up on June 15, 2019, a few days after the intense confrontations on June 12, 2019 between the protesters and the Hong Kong Police Force. There were massive arrests of the protesters. Basically the Fund through the generous support of the public was able to pay to those detained or injured for the first round of the court processes, medical expenses, psychological counselling and/or emergency financial support. It could not offer unlimited support for the subsequent appeal cases because of the large number of arrests. The Fund's annual report in mid-2021 showed that a total of HK$ 236 million had been collected so far, and HK$ 232 million (AUD38.6 million) distributed. By September 2021, the Fund was being investigated by the Hong Kong Police's National Security Department for suspected breaching of Hong Kong's National Security Law. The Fund had to cease operation by the end of October 2021.

Earlier in the campaign for political reforms in 2013, I discussed with my contacts from Mainland China and the local pro-Beijing united front the potential demonstration effect of the campaign on Taiwan. I was told that the Chinese authorities would look after their policy towards Taiwan. At the end of the elections in Taiwan in January 2020, all parties concerned were aware of this significant demonstration effect, and the strong solidarity between the civil societies in Hong Kong and Taiwan. Beijing's hard-line policy towards Hong Kong had much damaged the appeal of reunification under the guise of "one country, two systems" and even the close cross-Straits co-operation in the eyes of the majority of Taiwan people.

As the Carrie Lam administration refused to make concessions, and a severe crackdown involving the People's Liberation Army would be politically too costly, the remaining options seemed to be a delay tactic and the use of the Emergency Regulations Ordinance, a law that confers on the Chief Executive in Executive Council the power to make regulations on the occasion that the Chief Executive believes to be an emergency or public danger. On October 5, 2019, the Carrie Lam administration invoked the 1922 Emergency Regulations Ordinance to implement the Prohibition on Face Covering Regulation, i.e., an anti-mask law in response to the protests in the second half of the year. The regulation came into force the very next day demonstrating what could be done by the government promptly in accordance with the Emergency Regulations Ordinance; though the regulation was largely ignored by the radical young protesters.

The delay tactic proved to be effective in the Occupation Campaign in the autumn of 2014, but this time the anger of the community was such that support for protest activities remained very strong till the onslaught of the COVID-19 epidemic in early 2020. Top Chinese leaders continued to announce their support for Carrie Lam, in view of the frequent rumours that she would soon resign or be asked to step down. The pro-Beijing united front politicians obviously had to toe the Beijing line, but apparently they too were very unhappy with her. It was reported that a lady Legislative Councillor from the Hong Kong Federation of Trade Unions insulted her face-to-face with foul language. Understandably these politicians considered that Carrie Lam's terrible performance would cost them their seats in the District Council elections in November 2019 and the Legislative Council elections in September 2020. Beijing-loyal business leaders too were unhappy with the impact of the political crisis on the economy.

While the political crisis continued, the radical protesters altered their tactics. Their clashes with the police became more dispersed, smaller in scale, and perhaps more violent. Sympathy for these clashes did not seem to have been in decline as the community became polarised. High school students organised their demonstrations and protest rallies in the early mornings. Office workers held flash demonstrations in the lunch hours in the Central District. Ordinary people gathered in shopping malls to sing "Glory to Hong Kong"; this protest song was heard everywhere and attracted over a million views on the Internet[70]. It was even treated by some in the pro-democracy movement as the territory's national anthem.

Following the success of the international advertisement campaign on the eve of the G20 Osaka Summit, the protesters repeated the same exercise on National Day, October 1, 2019, which was the seventieth anniversary of the founding of the People's Republic of China. There were many gatherings in Western cities as well as in East Asia in support of the demands of Hong Kong's protesters; I was very happy to find that such gatherings were held in the New Zealand and Australian cities where I had spent some time. Many of these gatherings and demonstrations were organised by

---

70 "Glory to Hong Kong: anthem of the Hong Kong protests", https://www.youtube.com/watch?v=6yjLlYNFKCg, and https://youtu.be/oUIDL4SB60g?t=64 (Cantonese version).

Hong Kong emigrants and students, and some of them eventually formed support groups to engage in lobbying local politicians and political parties as well as to receive Hong Kong activists who visit their cities to do lobbying work.

Chinese embassies and consulates also mobilised the Mainland China communities in these cities concerned to hold gatherings in opposition to those in support of Hong Kong. They were rude and sometimes even attacked the Hong Kong students in local university campuses. In some of these demonstrations, many Mainland Chinese students arrived in their very expensive sports cars, reminding or suggesting to observers that they came from the power elite families with excess wealth.

Apparently the prominent coverage of the political crisis in Hong Kong by the international media generated some mutual demonstration effects. On August 23, 2019, the thirtieth anniversary of the Baltic Way, the protest movement in Hong Kong appealed to the community to form a similar human chain, the Hong Kong Way, to draw people's attention to its five demands. In the early evening, supporters joined hands to create a human chain of 50 kilometres on both sides of the Victoria Harbour, along the three main Mass Transit Railway lines and on the top of Lion Rock. The demonstrators were careful to avoid any disruptions to traffic, and the organisers claimed that 210,000 people participated. Many human chain activities were organised subsequently, though on a considerably smaller scale.

In October 2019, in response to the prison sentencing of the former Catalan independence movement leaders, violence broke out in the streets of Barcelona and other Catalan cities. The protesters called for a strike and disrupted the region's transportation network, including an attempt to shut down Barcelona's airport. The airport shutdown was said to be an imitation of the occupation of Hong Kong's airport in August 2019. Apparently Tsunami Democratic, a mysterious organisation being investigated for suspected terrorism, also used language similar to the Hong Kong protest movement, and talked about its members adding up like drops of water.

In these months, I went through some literature on protest movements, like Timothy Snyder's *20 Lessons from the 20th Century on How to Survive in Trump's America* and the Serbian revolutionary Srdja Popovic's *Blueprint for Revolution*. Some of the important lessons learnt were to induce a sense of empowerment among the protesters and ensure that they would not feel lonely. I did not know whether the organisers of Hong Kong's protest movement had read these books, but they seemed to have a very good grasp of the insights offered. I subsequently wrote some book reviews to introduce this literature.

The Chinese authorities were quite successful, however, in controlling public opinion in China. They typically appealed to nationalism, accusing the protesters of advocating independence for Hong Kong and collusion with the Western powers to create trouble for China, with the intention to weaken it and contain its rise, as desired by the Western powers. This successful propaganda, however, raised tension between Hong Kong people and the Mainlanders. The overseas confrontations between supporters for Hong Kong's pro-democracy movement and the Mainland Chinese communities mobilised by the Chinese diplomats obviously did not help. These schisms were expected to last.

Resentment against the Chinese authorities naturally escalated. Hong Kong people believed that the Carrie Lam administration merely implemented the Chinese leadership's hard-line Hong Kong policy, and that she was only too eager to please her masters in Beijing; the ultimate decisions including the tenure of Carrie Lam were made by Xi Jinping. Rumours had it that Chinese agents had joined the local anti-riot police force, and they were most brutal in making arrests. Further, there were stories of arrested protesters being sent across the border for detainment. These rumours were widely believed by the participants in the pro-democracy movement, though admittedly there was no hard evidence in their support. Hong Kong visitors entering China however were sometimes searched, harassed and detained if their mobile phones contained materials revealing their support for the protest movement.

In the wake of the protests against Article 23 legislation in 2003, Chinese officials responsible for Hong Kong affairs realised that while Hong Kong had returned to the Motherland, the hearts of Hong Kong people had not. At this stage, as expected, their identification with China fell to a new low. According to a poll conducted on December 4–10, 2019, by the Hong Kong Public Opinion Research Institute, 55% of the respondents identified themselves as Hongkongers; 11% identified themselves as Chinese; 22% as Hongkongers of China; and 10% as Chinese of Hong Kong.[71] All four indicators set new records.

The local District Council elections in November 2019, viewed as a referendum on the occupation campaign and subsequent street unrests, proved that the government's delay tactic failed. The pro-democracy camp won an unexpected decisive victory in gaining 389 of 452 directed elected seats. A record high voter turnout rate (71%) and a majority of the voters intending to teach the Carrie Lam administration a lesson were the key factors. When I was invited by a few international media to comment on the coming District Council elections, I said that a 60% turnout rate would be most satisfactory since previous turnout rates had never exceeded 50%.

---

71 "The latest public opinion results, 17 December 2019" (in Chinese). Available at https://static1.squarespace.com/static/5cfd1ba6a7117c00170d7aa/t/5e0aca9a014e1a25d2a91fca/1577765538579/PORI_PC_20191217_v1.5.pdf

No one however optimistic dared to predict a turnout rate of over 70%. Hong Kong delivered a small miracle, and their message was clear. As Carrie Lam herself admitted, the nature of the protest movement had been transformed, it was no longer about the Fugitives (Amendment) Bill. The protesters' slogan had changed to "Resist!".

Shortly before the Lunar New Year in late January 2020, the COVID-19 epidemic had spread to the territory. Protest activities could no longer be organised. This could have been an opportunity for the Carrie Lam administration. The combat of the epidemic was non-political, and people expected the government to act. There was a period of political calm. It was a matter of good governance. If she had performed as well as Ho Iat-seng, the newly elected Macau Chief Executive, Hong Kong people would have been satisfied; and Ho remained politically correct all the time from Beijing's point of view.

At the Backchat radio programme of Radio Television Hong Kong during the Lunar New Year in early 2020, I openly appealed to Carrie Lam to turn the difficult epidemic situation into an opportunity. I did not have high expectations of her, but as a concerned citizen, I wanted to offer my advice for the good of Hong Kong. Basically the advice was to launch a process of reconciliation to combat the epidemic in solidarity with the entire community. She should meet all the pro-democracy Legislative Councillors as she had not done so at least since June 2019. She should meet all the "newly-elected" District Councillors as she had not done so even by early March 2020. She should resume her programme of meeting the public; she did it once only and then dropped the idea. Above all else, she should ensure the supply of masks, etc., for Hong Kong people, especially those in financial difficulties and the elderly.

She failed to do all these, and she maintained contacts only with the pro-Beijing camp. When the newly elected pro-democracy District Councillors met, they sometimes could not secure the support service of the Home Affairs Department staff concerned; there were occasions when they were even denied the use of the conference rooms. I had suggested that the Carrie Lam administration should enlist the help of the District Councillors to help the needy at the grassroots level so as to create a win-win situation. Instead she seemed to treat the pro-democracy District Councillors as political enemies.

The shortage of face masks in Hong Kong at the start of the COVID-19 pandemic (in late January till mid-February 2020) resulted in an uproar in the community. People had to queue up for hours and still ended up disappointed. Comparisons were made between Hong Kong and Macau as well as Taiwan, and Hong Kong people were shocked to find that the Macau government had done much better. Why did the performance of the Carrie

Lam administration and the civil service deteriorate? The controversy over the Fugitives (Amendment) Bill generated a political crisis, and the incompetence in the combat of the epidemic was perceived to be a governance crisis.

In February 2020, thousands of medical staff working for the Hong Kong Hospital Authority called for a strike through their newly established trade union. The objective of the strike was to call upon the government to implement a complete quarantine of visitors from Mainland China; this complete quarantine was demanded by a majority of Hong Kong people and the pro-democracy movement, but was rejected by the Carrie Lam administration. There were suggestions that the refusal to enforce a complete quarantine was to ensure a channel for the power elite in China to depart for foreign countries through Hong Kong. Subsequently the Carrie Lam administration much tightened the entry into Hong Kong from Mainland China, but some channels such as the Shenzhen Bay Port (just 50 km. from the Hong Kong International Airport) still remained open. The controversy reflected Hong Kong people's lack of trust for the Chinese authorities and people from Mainland China, as well as strong suspicions against the Carrie Lam administration which was seen to always place Beijing's interests above those of Hong Kong people.

The disappointing performance of the Carrie Lam administration generated considerable discussions on its causes. In earlier chapters, I highlighted some of the weaknesses of the administrative service system. However, Hong Kong civil servants were still considered clean, efficient, intelligent and well-educated. There appeared to be a consensus on two factors. In the first place, Carrie Lam's arrogant style had alienated the senior civil servants; they were reluctant to offer their advice, especially views in contradiction to those of the Chief Executive. Further, for a considerable period of time since before the Carrie Lam administration, the civil service had been frustrated with the leadership of the HKSAR government; it was aware that the community's respect and trust for it had been in decline and felt that it could not do a good job.

A majority of Hong Kong people supported the strike by health workers, and were sympathetic to their shortage of masks and various essential protective gears for health care. This sympathy was partly transformed into dissatisfaction with the incompetence of the Carrie Lam administration. Carrie Lam refused to meet the medical staff on strike, while the pro-Beijing united front severely condemned them.

The pro-Beijing united front's other major target was Radio Television Hong Kong (RTHK). For many years, it could not accept the adoption of the BBC model by RTHK, and it argued that as a government agency funded by the government budget, it should defend the government. Instead RTHK produced a number of current affairs programmes which were very critical of the government. It could not be denied, however, that these programmes, especially the satirical ones, proved to be very popular. In early March 2020, both the pro-Beijing united front and members of the pro-democracy movement initiated signature campaigns condemning and supporting the RTHK respectively.

In the past decades, as an academic and a current affairs commentator, I had been invited to take part in a number of RTHK talk show programmes. I was always impressed by the dedication and professionalism of its staff. In the past years, the HKSAR government had been exerting pressure on the RTHK staff; the most obvious being budget cuts. I could clearly witness its impact as seen in the outdated equipment, the old furniture, etc. According to the annual reports of Reporters Without Borders and the Hong Kong Journalists Association, Hong Kong's freedom of the media had been steadily deteriorating since 1997, and according to the former's World Press Freedom Index, the territory ranked 70th in 2018 and fell to 148th in 2022.

The HKSAR administration had certainly failed to protect Hong Kong people's cherished values. They should feel shameful that they were not elected by universal suffrage and they could not even honestly face criticisms from the media. As an academic who had been engaged in media commentary in my entire career, I was very concerned about the plight of RTHK. The pro-

Beijing "patriotic" groups during the political crisis in the second half of 2019 organised demonstrations outside the RTHK office to intimidate its staff. The backbone of RTHK had been the dedicated senior staff with civil servants' permanent status who used to feel safe about their jobs; I was worried about its future when these staff members were to retire.

In its annual budget released in late February 2020, the Carrie Lam administration reversed its position and agreed to give direct financial subsidies of HK$10,000 each to all permanent citizens who had suffered from the adverse economic impact of the COVID-19 epidemic. This was welcome by the community, though it was largely perceived as an attempt to win back the support of Hong Kong people in preparation for the Legislative Council elections in the coming September. The pro-Beijing political parties were eager to claim credit for the measure. I was in full support too; obviously it would help to relieve a little of the financial burden of the people, especially those at the grassroots level. Naturally I would like to see the Carrie Lam administration to do more in the building of hospitals and provision of public housing, but I did not have much expectation. Support for the budget diminished as people soon understood that the budget also offered substantial additional funding for the police including the expansion of the Police Tactical Unit.

On January 4, 2020, it was announced that Wang Zhimin, director of the Central Liaison Office in Hong

Kong, was transferred to serve as the vice-president of the Central Institute for Party History and Literature Research. It was generally perceived that he had to assume responsibility for the political crisis in Hong Kong and the disastrous defeat of the pro-Beijing united front in the November 2019 District Council elections. China's official media indicated that Wang would retain his ministerial rank though. His replacement, Luo Huining, came from outside the Hong Kong and Macau policy system, and had served as Party secretary of Qinghai and Shanxi provinces. He maintained a low profile in the early months of his tenure in Hong Kong, and it was expected that he would initiate some personnel changes in the Central Liaison Office and the pro-Beijing united front.

On February 13, 2020, it was announced that Zhang Xiaoming would step down as director of the State Council's Hong Kong and Macau Affairs Office, though he would now serve as its standing deputy director while maintaining ministerial rank. His successor Xia Baolong also came from outside the Hong Kong and Macau policy system, and served as vice-chairman and secretary-general of the Chinese People's Political Consultative Conference before his new appointment. While Xia was Party secretary of Zhejiang, he attracted international attention for being a hardliner removing crosses from Christian churches in eastern China.

It seemed that Xi Jinping wanted to assume tighter control of Hong Kong policy through the appointments of his trusted cadres to the above positions, and the replacement of those groomed by Liao Hui who, together with his father Liao Chengzhi before him, had controlled the Hong Kong and Macau policy system for decades. It did not appear that the personnel reshuffles represented a change of Xi Jinping's hard-line policy towards Hong Kong.

The above personnel changes generated speculation about Carrie Lam's tenure, and there were many rumours that she would step down. In late February 2020, *Apple Daily* released her recent report to the Chinese leadership, which was not denied by her office. In the alleged report, she was very critical of her political allies, including members of the Executive Council; it thus exposed her isolated position. Without doubt, she became the most detested politician in the history of the territory, and probably no one could forecast this when she was elected Chief Executive in 2017. It is sad to see the competence of a former administrative officer decline to this state. Actually most Hong Kong people realised that her departure would not imply much change of the *status quo*, but they would like to see political justice done.

During the epidemic, I stayed at home most of the time like the vast majority of Hong Kong people. As in the SARS crisis in 2003, it was perhaps a blessing in disguise that families could eat together much more often. In my retirement, I did not have many social activities and I ate at home with my wife all the time. The small blessing to me was that I was able to read more. I felt sorry for my grandchildren and all the children who could not go to school; given the very crowded housing conditions for Hong Kong people, it was a bit depressing to have to stay indoors all the time. My wife reminded me frequently that victims of the epidemic were largely old people like us.

As the epidemic was a crisis; and in crises, one can see man's true nature more vividly. Many Hong Kong people tried to help by acquiring masks and disinfectants and distributing them among the elderly people and the less well to do. There were also people who stocked up rice, clamoured for toilet rolls in supermarkets, and let others press buttons in elevators so as to minimise their own risks. I tried to maintain my peace of mind and continue my role as an observer.

Epilogue

"Hong Kong is not what it used to be." I didn't and still don't believe that the Chinese Communist would grant us genuine democracy. Non-violent struggle for democracy and justice remains my preferred approach, and a worthwhile pursuit.

When Sir David Akers-Jones retired from the civil service in 1987, I asked him whether he would write his memoirs; I said that would be most interesting reading for people interested in Hong Kong's political development. Sir David stated that he would not do this. He explained that if he did not mention any friend, he or she would think that he/she was neglected; and if he criticised someone, he might attract resentment. In sum, it was not a worthwhile exercise. I still remember clearly what Sir David said, although later in 2004, he did publish a book of reminiscences called *"Feeling the Stones".*

Why should I write my autobiography then? I was born in November 1949, and my life experiences represent the first generation of residents who consider themselves Hongkongers and possess a sense of identity and pride regarding the territory. It is worthwhile to record these experiences so that the readers would have a better understanding of Hong Kong. I chose to write it in English because I hope the international community would have a better understanding of Hong Kong too. I focussed on my observations of Hong Kong's development, and I do not intend to concentrate on my personal ties with various pro-democracy leaders and politicians of the pro-establishment camp.

There is a danger that it might read like one of my academic books on Hong Kong's political development, and my wife Grace encourages me to offer more personal perspectives. At the same time, my family does not welcome talking about them in detail in my book. Hence, it is difficult to maintain a balance. But I did talk about my observations of Hong Kong as a school student, a university student, an academic and, above all, a pro-democracy activist. I hope my perspectives prove to be informative and interesting, and this is why I wrote this book.

Looking back, I do not have many complaints about my life. I had a poor childhood since I was seven, but my academic results made me proud in my student years, and I never felt inferior to anyone. I was respected by my teachers and classmates. There were moments when I would like to go camping as a Boy Scout, but I realised that my family would not have the money for me to do so. When I was in Form 4 and Form 5 (Years 10 and 11 in Australia), some of my rich classmates went to attend prestigious public schools in Britain and then to the top universities there or in the U.S.; I wished I had a chance to do that. But those were no causes for complaints or regrets.

From Form 4 onwards, I began to take up part-time jobs and at the same time had to work hard for the public examinations to come. I therefore had to restrain myself from taking part in extra-curricular activities. The same situation applied in my university years. I regretted a little that I could have taken a much more active role in the student movement then; I could learn a lot and the experiences would be rewarding. My best friend then, Terence Yau, was more active as he did not have financial burden. In his final year at university, he applied to live in a student dormitory just to enjoy "dormitory life". I could not afford to do that and was a bit envious.

My parents were old fashioned and conservative. They never took me (or my brother and sisters) for a picnic in the New Territories nor for a swim. Hence, I could not swim nor ride a bicycle; I felt a little bit ashamed. They did not think that extra-curricular activities were of any importance, and refused to allow me to play with other children in the neighbourhood.

I am very fortunate in that my mother was a good cook and my wife is a good cook too. My mother cooked the family meals for us until she was in her sixties; by then she felt she could not cope and few would be willing to do the dishes afterwards. So we started eating out in family gatherings. Grace did the cooking when I was a postgraduate student overseas; I performed the unskilful tasks of boiling soup and cooking rice in an electric rice-cooker. Through reading a lot of Chinese novels, I had a good grasp of Chinese cooking theories, but I never managed to acquire the practical skills.

I enjoy good food; I ate a lot when I was young. In my thirties, I still had three bowls of rice per meal. But good food to me does not have to be expensive food; wonton noodles, freshly fried dough, stirred fried beef rice noodles are my favourites when they are cooked nicely. I like to have one or two good meals a week. Due to my upbringing, I can accept very simple food for my daily meals. I do not want to waste food, and I often finish the leftovers in the following meal. When my children were small, I always made sure that we all had a fair share of the leftovers. Certainly I did not want to leave them to the Filipino helper that we had then.

I enjoy moderate drinking with good friends. I am not particular about expensive wines, etc. I enjoy beer, wine, whisky and cognac, and I have never been drunk. I am rather Confucian regarding drinking. I believe that one should respect the limits. The companionship is most important; in recent years, I quite enjoy the drinking parties organised by my young activist friends. I am eager to listen to their political views in free and unconstrained exchanges.

I am a reserved person. Even when I was most involved in the pro-democracy movement, I did not organise dinner parties to gather friends together and to build and strengthen ties. When I was invited, I often went if I expected good discussions. I have had the opportunity to join the prestigious Hong Kong Jockey Club and the Hong Kong Club, but I declined. This probably revealed that I did not want a political career. There were periods in my career during which I often participated in dinner parties organised by top government officials and pro-Beijing united front leaders for political discussions. I went prepared, though I never made an attempt to cultivate good relations with them.

I enjoyed social activities with students though. I started with drinking parties in Fiji when I briefly taught at the University of South Pacific in Suva. In my tenure at the Chinese University of Hong Kong, I served as dean of students of the United College for two years, and one of my responsibilities was to attend almost all major student activities of the college. My department (Department of Government and Public Administration) had always upheld a good tradition of close staff-student relations, and there were many lunch and afternoon tea sessions with small groups of students. Occasionally there were staff-student soccer matches and basketball matches. I was elected "Best Teacher of the Department" in the only election held when I was there.

I had less time for students when I joined the City University of Hong Kong as faculty dean. The class size and tutorial group size became considerably larger later and I concentrated more on teaching. There were less social interactions, but many students came to see me about their postgraduate study plans, as well as their intentions to join local political parties. I always emphasised the importance of their genuine interests in further studies, and that hard work would always be rewarded. I often tried to persuade them not to be discouraged if they failed to secure admissions to the very top universities in the U.S. and Britain, and I used my personal experiences as an example. I reminded them that they should also consider their emotional relationships and attachments with girlfriends/boyfriends, etc. I attempted to be objective on students' choice of political parties; if they desired government appointments later, I suggested that they should opt for the Democratic Alliance for the Betterment and Progress of Hong Kong and New People's Party.

In Hong Kong, university academics are paid very good salaries, so again I had no complaints. I realised that as a political science professor and my wife a librarian, I might have to take up second jobs if we were working in South America. My academic friends there had to do this if they had children attending expensive private schools and private universities. My counterparts in Europe also had to save up for a family holiday. In Hong Kong, university professors easily enjoy upper middle-class living standards, although successful doctors and lawyers earn much more.

When I retired from the City University of Hong Kong in June 2015, I received about HK$14 million from my superannuation fund after working there for twenty-three years. It appeared to be a substantial sum in the eyes of retiring academics in Asia, but the 800-square-feet rented flat in Taikoo Shing that I moved in upon retirement costed more than HK$16 million if we were to purchase it then. The cost of living would be much lower if I choose to move to Taiwan, and considerably less expensive if I choose to emigrate to Australia or New Zealand.

Grace and I believe that if we have money in our retirement for dining out and for overseas holidays whenever and wherever we like, that would be adequate. Fortunately we do not have to worry about that. I have never thought about acquiring expensive watches, clothing, and the like; I am happy with a simple life. I love travelling, and I still have a short bucket list of where I would like to visit before I become too old. My job as a university professor offered a holiday allowance for me and my family (including children under nineteen years old), and I often combined my travel plans with my attendance of academic conferences. Hence, I did not have to spend too much. I travelled on low budgets: economy airfares and tourist class hotels were just fine.

I have been most fortunate as far as family life goes. Grace has been almost perfect, and my two children treat their parents well. We have a family meal every week, and my mother used to join us until two years ago when she suffered from a fall. I visited her every week, often with the whole family. Occasionally we went for a short holiday together. My first and only grandson arrived in July 2014 when I had much pressure from my university; we were also blessed with a granddaughter some 2 years later. My wife and I have a weakness for them.

I follow my son to become a Manchester United fan. Watching soccer matches has been an entertainment for me, and it is good for father-son relationship if we support the same team. It is more fun watching soccer matches when you have a team to support. I always wanted to attend World Cup soccer matches in person, but did not make a serious effort to achieve the goal.

Looking back, I consider myself a serious academic, and have produced considerable publications in the fields of Chinese foreign policy, Chinese politics and political development in Hong Kong. I probably could have done a bit better academically if I had not been heavily involved in the pro-democracy movement. It is always very difficult to maintain a balance.

I have not taken part in elections for public office, although I had assumed some important positions in the local pro-democracy movement. These factors led me to assume a co-ordinator role a number of times within the movement. Despite the thankless nature of the tasks, I believe that my work has won the trust of various parties concerned in the movement. I am proud of my contributions.

I am a serious dedicated person. When I gather a team of academics to write a book, I always deliver. When a pro-democracy organisation asks me to organise a conference and produce a compendium of papers, I always complete the task. I arrive at all meetings punctually; Emily Lau, Audrey Eu and I share a good reputation for being punctual within the pro-democracy circle. When I attend a meeting, I come prepared and make sure I have a contribution to offer. When colleagues come up with a proposal, I always try to help, to improve it, and make it work.

This meant maintaining an interest and enthusiasm in one's work. I have seen some academic friends who had gradually lost interest in research and sometimes in teaching too. This is understandable. One might be very interested and enthusiastic at the very beginning of one's career. But when one has reached his late forties and fifties, one might realise that he could no longer secure breakthroughs, and he might gradually lose interest. At this stage, it would be very difficult to change career.

The same applies to politicians. A few Legislative Councillors I know gradually lose the initial dedication and enthusiasm. When cases and issues reach him, he no longer has the drive to challenge the injustice involved. He just "manages", so that it would look good in the media. He would not like to lose the position and status as Legislative Councillor though.

For politicians, especially grassroots politicians, there is always the temptation of a good life. A politician in his contacts with the rich and the powerful easily knows what good life involves. He believes that he has worked hard, has done so many good things, and therefore deserves a taste of luxury. He goes to dinner, is offered very expensive wine; on the next day, his rich host sends him two more bottles of wine. Corruption often begins this way. In Mainland China, expensive cigarettes and liquor are often the first test. A cadre who accepts them would be perceived as willing to take something more expensive.

University academics do not have many opportunities of receiving bribes. But if one enjoys invitations by tycoons and top government officials, this may be a dangerous signal. If one receives many appointments to government advisory bodies, one may be reluctant to criticise the government publicly. When a senior professor proudly tells me that he has been invited to attend the National Day banquet or military parade in Beijing, it then hit me that he has never criticised the Chinese authorities publicly, and has never participated in June 4 memorial activities.

I always remind myself to minimise my personal desires if I intend to preserve my dignity. My greatest pleasures in life are a happy meal with my family, a dinner party with good friends for political discussions, and an overseas holiday with my wife. This is especially so when I grow old. We all seek satisfaction and meaning in life; I know what I want.

As a university academic and a pro-democracy activist, I have observed many "power struggles" which involved very little power. For example, two or three senior academics in a university department might not be able to stand each other for some reasons; their ill feelings poisoned the atmosphere of the entire department of less than twenty people and made life a bit difficult for everyone. I came across "memo wars" between colleagues in the university, and I always wondered why they had so much time to write these long memos. Apparently they did not have more meaningful things to do. Similar scenarios might emerge in a political party or a non-governmental organisation, and it could be quite destructive. I made it a habit to avoid spending time on these mutual attacks, as I believed that my time could be spent in a more constructive way. It was simpler to forget and forgive.

I worked very long hours since I was a teenager. I sleep seven or eight hours every day, and I envy my friends who need only five hours of sleep per day. I am quite an efficient person, but I probably have the tendency to over commit myself. When my colleagues asked me to contribute a book chapter, I always said yes. When friends in the pro-democracy movement ask me to take up a task, I cannot refuse. In the end, I have to forego reading a novel I like, or watching a soccer match I would enjoy. In my last five years working at the City University of Hong Kong, I did not read one single novel. I made up for that in my retirement years. I always tried to have time for my family; I probably did not do too well, although Grace got used to it and is very forgiving.

When I attended the University of Hong Kong, I was conscious of the elitist values of my peers. Later when I participated in the activities of the Hong Kong Observers, all meetings were held in English. We met in a small restaurant in Central owned by the family of a member. I once overheard the resentful conversations of the waiters who could not accept that we were all Chinese and our discussions were in English. When I was active in the Civic Party, I realised that some members had the perception that the party leadership favoured those who had legal qualifications and who spoke good English. I attempted to address this misperception.

Throughout my life, I always remind myself to treat all people equally. How could you convince others of your commitment to fight social injustice if you always put yourself above others? When I was a university academic, I always showed respect to the cleaning staff and other junior staff members. When I met senior government officials, I always treated their junior colleagues with courtesy. I too treat the staff members of the pro-democracy groups with respect too. I always help even with the menial tasks. When we organised street stations, I was always among the first to arrive and the last to leave, especially when I was responsible for the activity. I always helped in arranging furniture, carrying things, serving tea, etc. I never shun physical labour. Many politicians would arrive late for a fundraising function in the streets, stay for fifteen minutes for the journalists, and then slip away. I never do that.

Punctuality has been an issue among pro-democracy activists. On the basis of my excellent record throughout the decades, I am in a better position to enforce discipline. I said to my young activist friends: civil servants are usually very punctual; if you cannot perform better than they do in this aspect, how can you be critical of their performance? If you work in a bank, would you be late for your meetings? If not, why should you think that you can be late for meetings of pro-democracy groups?

I always come prepared for meetings and discussions, and I try to make a contribution. I prepared myself thoroughly when I served as chairman. I hoped that my preparations would ensure results and avoid wasting time. Very often, leaders and senior politicians come to meetings without preparations; they would try to say something to remind people of their presence and participation. Such behaviour, if repeated often, would lead to a loss of respect. Of course, politicians can always claim that they are very, very busy, and often their presence in meetings is mainly intended as a gesture of support. Yet people notice.

I have been rather pessimistic about the prospects of democracy in Hong Kong, and I sometimes avoid discussions of the reasons behind my pessimism. When I was at the Civic Party in its early years, I was once criticised by Margaret Ng for being too pessimistic as she was concerned that I might dampen the enthusiasm of our party members. I stated that I had been working for electoral reforms in Hong Kong for decades because I believe in democracy, not because I think it would come soon. I then hastened to add that for a political forecast beyond five years, the reliability tended to be low, and I respected alternative views.

The Falun Gong group had been saying since the late 1990s that the Chinese Communist regime would fall in six months. More than twenty years had passed, and they still deliver similar messages in early 2020. In the wake of the Tiananmen incident, famous activists like Liu Binyan were telling the world that the Chinese Communist regime would fall in three months. There was no lack of treatises like Gordon Chang's *The Coming Collapse of China* with a similar view.

I have maintained my position not to underestimate the regime's staying power, especially in the era of economic reforms and opening to the external world. The vast majority of people in China have enjoyed a substantial improvement in living standards, and they still expect improvements in the years ahead. Like ordinary people all over the world, Chinese people continue to engage in a pragmatic cost-benefit analysis, and they easily realise that the cost of opposing the regime would be very high. There is of course the option of exit. Nowhere in the world would you find such a high proportion of a country's elites who are sending their families and wealth abroad. Even average middle-class families are quite ready to send their only child to study abroad with the hope that they can develop promising careers outside of China. If they own decent flats in large cities, they are often ready to sell their properties in order to finance their children's studies in Western countries. This is ironically one of the factors contributing to political stability under the authoritarian regime.

Chinese leaders have been responsive to the acceptable demands of the people and ready to remove the serious sources for discontent and instability. The Hu Jintao administration (2002–2012) realised the dangers of the rapid marketisation of basic social services including medical care and housing. It reversed the trend and attempted to provide a basic social security net covering the entire population including pension, medical care, unemployment benefits, compensation for work injuries and subsidy for pregnancy. The Chinese authorities carefully monitor the prices of housing and food to ensure the avoidance of rising social discontent. Similarly the employment of fresh graduates from tertiary institutions (8.74 million in 2020) is accorded a priority.

The Chinese leadership's principal objective has been the regime's survival. It therefore attempts to remove any potential challenges and has been most reluctant to give up its monopoly of political power. In the 1980s, before the Tiananmen incident, there was considerable expectation of serious political reforms, but the optimism has long vanished. In the beginning of the Hu Jintao and Xi Jinping administrations, there were suggestions that they were reform-minded leaders. These speculations were soon proven wrong. Increasingly, Chinese leaders are worried that political reforms would be destabilising and therefore dangerous; such reforms would certainly generate higher and higher expectations. Their formula for political stability has been respectable economic growth, a basic social security net and a responsive and efficient administration.

All these elements would probably help to maintain the regime in the coming five to ten years. The challenges, however, are becoming severer. For a mature economy, economic growth rates would most likely be on the decline. The basic social security net is perceived to be inadequate. In the absence of effective checks and balances mechanisms, corruption remains a problem. At the beginning of the 2020s, speculations on the fall of the regime again arose because of domestic and external problems ranging from slower economic growth rates, the COVID-19 epidemic, to the Sino-American confrontation.

Xi Jinping's concentration of power in his own hands and his aggressive foreign policy do not help. The erosion of collective leadership means that he alone has to absorb the blame for any policy failures. His generosity in offering foreign aid is perceived to be at the expense of the Chinese people's own welfare. These problems have triggered further suppression and political tightening targeted especially at the underground churches, autonomous labour groups, human rights lawyers and the national minorities. Hong Kong felt the impact of this suppression too. This suppression has led to the international community, especially the Western countries, to re-assess the true nature of the Chinese Communist regime.

At the government level, foreign political leaders are still cautious in maintaining cordial relations with China because of its impressive economic impact. At the community level, however, more and more people are concerned about China's behaviour patterns, ranging from the violations of religious freedom and the suppression of the Uighurs and Tibetans, to the peddling of influence in Western societies as symbolised by political lobbying in Australia and the insistence on political correctness on the part of the Confucius Institutes. Even authoritarian countries in the Middle East oppose the suppression of their fellow Muslims in Xinjiang.

Many Hong Kong people, especially the pro-democracy commentators in their Internet video programmes, share these speculations of the fall of the Chinese Communist regime. They may be exaggerating, but the legitimacy of the regime has been on the decline as the intelligentsia can clearly perceive the trends of the erosion of their already limited freedoms, and ordinary people feel the widening gap between the rich and poor in China. At the same time, Chinese people may be more emboldened to engage in protest activities to fight for their rights, especially those related to labour issues and environmental protection. In view of the high debt level of private sector enterprises and their dependence on the underground banking sector in China, the danger of financial crises is on the rise.

In sum, the situation in China is similar to that in Eastern Europe in the beginning of the 1980s: civil society is expanding but it is in no position to challenge the regime yet. The regime in turn has still been able to satisfy the demands for economic growth and service delivery. It is my conviction that a regime which does not respect its people's dignity and basic rights cannot maintain its legitimacy. But it is possible that a sophisticated authoritarian regime can suffer a long atrophy.

The recent problems of the Xi Jinping administration probably means that it will maintain its hard-line policy towards Hong Kong. This, together with the political suppression in Mainland China, have exacerbated the decline of the trust in the Chinese authorities and in the community's identification with the Chinese nation especially among the young people. At the end of 2019, according to public opinion surveys in Hong Kong, slightly over 40% of the respondents had zero confidence in the Carrie Lam administration and the central government in Beijing.

China's hard-line policy implies that in the foreseeable future, there would be no negotiations or consultations on political reforms and democratisation, and the pro-democracy movement would be more inclined to engage in political confrontation. The casualties in the political crisis in the second half of 2019 naturally mean that concessions on the part of the pro-democracy movement would be difficult. Hence, in the foreseeable future, violent confrontations with the police might re-emerge when the COVID-19 epidemic subsides. This was the observation of a group of mass communications scholars who has scientifically surveyed the Internet platforms, the communication channels of the radical wing of the pro-democracy movement.

Xi Jinping's hard-line policy towards Hong Kong has been faithfully implemented by the Carrie Lam administration, which has contributed to its extremely low popularity ratings. Massive arrests of protesters and the pressures on Cathay Pacific employees and medical staff members ready to strike in support of their demand for a complete quarantine of visitors from Mainland China, teachers and social workers sympathetic towards the radical protesters, etc., are intended to generate a deterrence effect. While the severe crackdown managed to suppress protest activities since the second half of 2020, the hard-line policy has prevented reconciliation in the community.

This hard-line policy has other important elements besides deterrence. The Chinese authorities would like to reduce the significance of Hong Kong as an international financial centre first by cultivating Shanghai, and in recent years, Shenzhen as well. The idea is to teach Hong Kong a lesson, and to acquire an insurance policy through the reduction of China's dependence on Hong Kong. The integration of Hong Kong into the Greater Bay Area (Pearl River Delta) has been stepped up in the recent decade too. This is in line with China's regional development strategies, but as a part of the Greater Bay Area, Hong Kong's autonomy would be compromised. The Chinese authorities expected that more people from Hong Kong would move to the Greater Bay Area to live and work; at the same time, more major enterprises from Mainland China would move to Hong Kong as well.

The Carrie Lam administration and its successors would strongly support these policy programmes which are not welcome by most Hong Kong people. These developments plus the frequent, strong interferences from Beijing will continue to sap the legitimacy of the HKSAR government, and Hong Kong people will increasingly feel that the territory has changed to such an extent that their way of life can no longer be maintained. Some will emigrate, and it is estimated that 1.2 to 1.5 million people have already acquired foreign passports and the rights of permanent residence in foreign countries. Since the second half of 2019, emigration agencies have been advertising the easier and cheaper emigration options of Taiwan, Malaysia, Malta, Portugal, etc.; and Britain and other countries have offered various schemes to help Hong Kong people depart.

As reconciliation and meaningful dialogues as well as deliberations on political reforms were nowhere in sight, the political confrontation since the second half of 2019 led to the eclipse of many previous taboos. The slogan "Recover Hong Kong - Revolution of the Epoch" appeared in protest marches and the social media, and it was accused of bearing pro-independence overtones by the pro-Beijing united front. The old British colonial flags as well as U.S. flags often appeared in protest rallies and seemed to be a standard phenomenon. Slogans like "Chase Away the Communist Party" also emerged.

The Carrie Lam administration obviously had the strong backing of Xi Jinping. Beijing decided to introduce the National Security Law at the Party Central Committee plenum held in October 2019. Under such circumstances, a crackdown of the pro-democracy movement became the logical conclusion. In the final months of 2019, the protest activities became more dispersed, smaller in scale but more violent. In this period, the clashes between the protesters and the police escalated and shut down traffic in many instances. The unprecedented use of Molotov cocktails became rather frequent in the later clashes. At the end of 2019, over 8,000 protesters were arrested. The arrival of the COVID-19 pandemic brought all protest activities to an abrupt halt.

At the end of May 2020, the National People's Congress passed a resolution to introduce a Hong Kong version of the National Security Law. Mainstream official media in China defended this as an essential move for China's security to close a gap that might be exploited by hostile countries to introduce a "colour revolution" to China. The earlier street violence provided a convenient excuse for Beijing to assume much more direct control of Hong Kong's political processes and suppress the activism of the pro-democracy movement.

The move was regarded as the end of the "one country, two systems" model. The National Security Law was imposed on Hong Kong people without consultation and totally bypassed the local legislature. The Law prohibits connections of the pro-democracy movement with foreign countries. Under the Law, lobbying in Western countries, maintaining formal ties with civic groups, and receiving financial and other means of support from them are prohibited. Advocacy activities, including articulation of slogans in protest rallies and spreading messages over the Internet may be construed as violating China's sovereignty and calling for Hong Kong's independence and prosecuted as such.

Cases against the National Security Law will be adjudicated by judges designated by the Hong Kong Chief Executive. The accused may also be extradited to Mainland China to be tried in courts and imprisoned there if so sentenced. To say that the Law has no retrospective effect (as promised by the Chief Executive) is not entirely accurate; past behaviour patterns of the accused had been used for disqualifying legislators and pursuing prosecutions.

Facing the challenges of deteriorating domestic and international environments, Xi Jinping maintained a hawkish line and appealed to nationalism and patriotism. People in China supported their leaders on the Hong Kong issue, even though Hong Kong's struggle won the sympathy of the international community. It was the general belief that the Chinese leadership anticipated a strong response from the Western world to the arrest of the pro-democracy leaders and the release and implementation of the National Security Law in Hong Kong. But it was willing to pay the price.

China's political control over Hong Kong did not end with the National Security Law. On February 22, 2021, the director of the Hong Kong and Macau Affairs Office, Xia Baolong, indicated that the Chinese authorities would implement the "patriots govern Hong Kong" policy. To do that, Beijing would have to "perfect the electoral systems concerned".

The Chinese authorities considered that the existing electoral systems would still allow the pro-democracy movement considerable room of manoeuvre. The overwhelming victory at the last District Board elections in November 2019 by the pro-democracy candidates shocked those in power and reinforced the general belief that the electorate intended to punish the HKSAR government for toeing the unpopular pro-Beijing line. Changing the rules of the game would enable the Chinese authorities to exert complete control. Not only would it deny opportunities for the pro-democracy movement to serve as checks and balances, but also considerably reduce the lobbying influence of the local pro-Beijing united front groups.

At this stage, Hong Kong people's responses were muted. They realised that there was not much they could do when the Chinese leadership was willing to pay the price to secure complete control. They were in despair and had a strong sense of impotence. With the exception of *Apple Daily* before its forced closure, the mainstream mass media were heavily influenced by self-censorship. Self-censorship could also be discernible in social media such as WhatsApp group discussions, as those arrested usually have their mobile phones searched and used as evidence. There are cases when statements made on the Internet are used as evidence of advocating for the independence of Hong Kong.

The massive arrests and prosecutions in 2019 to 2020 (estimated to be over 10,000) had generated a substantial deterrence effect. Young people sent to jail with criminal records suffer substantially in their career development. Atypically, higher education student unions, which were believed to be leading the student protests earlier, went silent. Six out of eight publicly funded university administrations announced that they would stop collecting union fees on their union's behalf from September 2021, thus severing official ties with them. Only two (out of eight) universities had full teams running for the elections of student unions in early 2021. One of them, the Chinese University of Hong Kong team, under the pressure from the university management, was forced to resign soon after its inauguration, and finally disbanded in October 2021. The University of Hong Kong Students Union announced that they were closed in August 2021.

"Hong Kong is not what it used to be" is a frequent expression by Hong Kong people nowadays. By 2021, a lot of them feel that the "one country, two systems" model has gone. When the Chinese authorities can unilaterally change the institutions and systems including the electoral systems, so can the "one country, two systems" model be abandoned at will by Beijing. Such pledge in the past has not been kept, and the local community has no control. When the Index of Economic Freedom was released in early March 2021, Hong Kong disappeared from the list because the Heritage Foundation and *The Wall Street Journal* considered that Hong Kong had become a part of Mainland China and therefore it no longer deserved a separate, independent assessment and ranking. In other words, the "one country, two systems" had gone.[72]

Most Hong Kong people cannot understand why the territory has been perceived by the Chinese Communist regime as a threat to its monopoly of political power. It was my educated guess that probably Chinese leaders cannot tolerate Hong Kong's demonstration effect, hence their decision to treat the local pro-democracy movement as an enemy. Their relationship with it is deemed a contradiction between enemies. It therefore has to be wiped out and there should be no room for manoeuvre. To achieve this purpose, Chinese leaders are ready to compromise the freedoms and the rule of law that ordinary Hong Kong people used to enjoy and cherish even in the absence of genuine democracy in the past.

I left Hong Kong in July 2020, soon after the implementation of the National Security Law. I feel threatened, but above all else, I believe that I can no longer do anything meaningful. My departure was not

---

72 Edwin J. Feulner, Hong Kong Is No Longer What It Was," *Wall Street Journal*, March 3, 2021, https://www.wsj.com/articles/hong-kong-is-no-longer-what-it-was-11614804021?mod=article_inline.

a secret. There were a few farewell dinners with close relatives and friends. In view of my age and state of health, I understand very well that my very limited contribution would be writing an autobiography and a history of Hong Kong's pro-democracy movement.

From July 2020 to July 2021, the territory's population dropped 1.2% due to emigration (89,000 out of 7.5 million people). More emigration is expected. In the year or so after my departure, many of my pro-democracy activist friends were detained, prosecuted, and imprisoned. More than 10,000 arrests were made during the 2019–20 unrests, and 150 arrests were made by the Police Force's new National Security Department since June 2020. According to an analysis by Bloomberg, a vast majority of charges relate to what have been "said, written, published or waved on a banner". Of those arrested, including prominent activists, academics, lawyers and journalists, about 65% of them were being pursued, and the rest were released. Fourteen were accused for financing activities such as crowd funding, and 14 others for plotting attacks.[73]

The short-term future is bleak. In the year up to November 2021, over 50 civil society organisations, like the Alliance for True Democracy (2013 – August 2021), Amnesty International's Hong Kong Chapter

---

73 Kari Soo Lindberg and others, "How Hong Kong's national security law is changing everything", October 5, 2021. https://www.bloomberg.com/graphics/2021-hong-kong-national-security-law-arrests/.

(1980 – 2021), Civil Human Rights Front (2002 – August 2021), Hong Kong Confederation of Trade Unions (1990 – September 2021), Power for Democracy (2002 – February 2021), and the Professional Teachers' Union (1973 – September 2021), had to close down.[74]

The independence and survival of the news media in Hong Kong were threatened. Quite a few prominent commentators declared that they would no longer offer their analyses as they would be useless and dangerous under Hong Kong's national security law. At the end of December 2021, owners and executives (including previous board members) of two pro-democracy online news media, Apple Daily and Stand News, were prosecuted. With their assets frozen and documents and computers confiscated, they had to close down. A third online news website founded by ten veteran journalists in Hong Kong through crowd funding, the Citizen News, announced that they would cease operation voluntarily in January 2022 due to "deteriorating environment for the media's survival".

---

74 The largest and oldest teachers' union with 95,000 members representing 90% of Hong Kong teachers was disbanded under enormous pressure. See Mimi Leung, "University Student union disbands amid civil society meltdown" *University World News*, October 7, 2021. https://www.universityworldnews.com/post.php?story=20211007140203859, and Rhoda Kwan, "Explainer: over 50 groups gone in 11 months: how Hong Kong's pro-democracy forces crumbled", *Hong Kong Free Press*, November 28, 2021. https://hongkongfp.com/2021/11/28/explainer-over-50-groups-gone-in-11-months-how-hong-kongs-pro-democracy-forces-crumbled/.

The price at the individual level is high. Blood and tears had indeed been shed in terms of imprisonments, injuries, exiles, and collateral damages such as loss of jobs, businesses or relationships. Would pan-democrats in Hong Kong be able to uphold their values and dignity by continuing with their struggles for democracy? Will they succeed in the long run? Only time will tell! But then, I don't think that I can vouch for a happy ending with my Hong Kong story.

Joseph Yu-shek Cheng
1 January 2022

Appendix I: District Council Election Results, 1999–2019

	1999	2003	2007	2011	2015	2019
Number of voters turnout	810,000	1,066,000	1,148,000	1,202,000	1,467,000	2,943,842
Voter turnout rate	36%	44%	39%	41%	47%	71.23%
Major parties:			*Seats won (Success rate: % Elected / standing)*			
Pan-democrats						388 (75%)
Democratic Party	86 (50%)	95 (79%)	55 (55%)	47 (35.6%)	43 (45%)	91 (92%)
Civic Party	--	(new party)	8 (19.5%)	7 (17%)	10 (40%)	32 (89%)
Association for Democracy and People's Livelihood	19 (59%)	25 (67%)	17 (45%)	15 (57.7%)	18 (69%)	19 (90%)

675

	1999	2003	2007	2011	2015	2019
League of Social Democrats	--	(new party)	6 (20%)	0 (100%)	0 (0%)	2 (67%)
The Frontier	4 (44%)	6 (43%)	3 (20%)	0[75]	1 (100%)	0
Pro-Beijing / pro-establishment						62 *(12.4%)*
DAB	83 (47%)	62 (30%)	115 (66%)	136 (75%)	119 (69.5%)	32 (11.6%)
Hong Kong Federation of Trade Unions	1 (100%)	0	32 (53%)	11 (55%)	27 (56%)	5 (11.6%)
New People's Party	--	--	(new party, 2011)	4 (33%)	26 (62%)	0
Liberal Party	15 (44%)	14 (52%)	14 (25%)	9 (37.5%)	9 (45%)	5 (45%)
Civil Force	11 (79%)	17 (77%)	18 (90%)	15 (75%)	0[76]	0

75 Merged into Democratic Party. Not all parties are represented in this table.
76 Alliance with New People's Party

www.ingramcontent.com/pod-product-compliance
Lightning Source LLC
Chambersburg PA
CBHW030236170426
43202CB00007B/23